CHRISTINE DE PIZAN

ROUTLEDGE MEDIEVAL CASEBOOKS
Christopher Kleinhenz and Marcia Colish, *Series Editors*

The Chester Mystery Cycle
A Casebook
edited by Kevin J. Harty

Medieval Numerology
A Book of Essays
edited by Robert L. Surles

Manuscript Sources of Medieval Medicine
A Book of Essays
edited by Margaret R. Schleissner

Saint Augustine the Bishop
A Book of Essays
edited by Fannie LeMoine and
 Christopher Kleinhenz

Medieval Christian Perceptions of Islam
A Book of Essays
edited by John Victor Tolan

Sovereign Lady
*Essays on Women in Middle English
 Literature*
edited by Muriel Whitaker

Food in the Middle Ages
A Book of Essays
edited by Melitta Weiss Adamson

Animals in the Middle Ages
A Book of Essays
edited by Nona C. Flores

Sanctity and Motherhood
*Essays on Holy Mothers in the
 Middle Ages*
edited by Annecke B. Mulder-Bakker

Medieval Family Roles
A Book of Essays
edited by Cathy Jorgensen Itnyre

The Mabinogi
A Book of Essays
edited by C.W. Sullivan III

The Pilgrimmage to Compostela in the
 Middle Ages
A Book of Essays
edited by Maryjane Dunn and
 Linda Kay Davidson

Medieval Liturgy
A Book of Essays
edited by Lizette Larson-Miller

Medieval Purity and Piety
*Essays on Medieval Clerical Celibacy
 and Religious Reform*
edited by Michael Frassetto

Hildegard of Bingen
A Book of Essays
edited by Maud Burnett McInerney

Julian of Norwich
A Book of Essays
edited by Sandra J. McEntire

The Mark of the Beast
*The Medieval Bestiary in Art, Life, and
 Literature*
edited by Debra Hassig

The Book and the Magic of Reading in
 the Middle Ages
edited by Albert Classen

Conflicted Identities and Multiple
 Masculinities
Men in the Medieval West
edited by Jacqueline Murray

Imagining Heaven in the Middle Ages
A Book of Essays
edited by Jan Swango Emerson and
 Hugh Feiss, O.S.B.

Anna Komnene and Her Times
edited by Thalia Gouma-Peterson

William Langland's *Piers Plowman*
A Book of Essays
edited by Kathleen M. Hewett-Smith

The Poetic Edda
Essays on Old Norse Mythology
edited by Paul Acker and
 Carolyne Larrington

Regional Cuisines of Medieval Europe
A Book of Essays
edited by Melitta Weiss Adamson

The Italian Novella
edited by Gloria Allaire

Christine de Pizan
A Casebook
edited by Barbara K. Altmann and
 Deborah L. McGrady

"Christine de Pisan présente son livre à un riche admirateur." Illustration by Colette Deblé. Courtesy of Margarete Zimmermann.

CHRISTINE DE PIZAN
A CASEBOOK

EDITED BY
BARBARA K. ALTMANN
AND
DEBORAH L. MCGRADY

LONDON AND NEW YORK

Published in 2003 by
Routledge
2 Park Square, Milton Park
Abingdon, Oxfordshire OX14 4RN

Published in Great Britain by
Routledge
711 Third Avenue
New York, NY 10017

First issued in paperback 2014

Routledge is an imprint of the Taylor & Francis Group, an informa business

Copyright © 2003 by Barbara K. Altmann and Deborah L. McGrady

All rights reserved. No part of this book may be reprinted or reproduced or utilized in any form or by any electronic, mechanical, or other means, now known or hereafter invented, including photocopying and recording, or in any information storage or retrieval system, without permission in writing from the publishers.

Library of Congress Cataloging-in-Publication Data

Christine de Pizan : a casebook / edited by Barbara K. Altmann and Deborah L. McGrady.
    p. cm. — (Routledge medieval casebooks, v. 34)
    Includes bibliographical references and index.

ISBN 978-0-415-93909-6 (hbk)

ISBN 978-1-138-79904-2 (pbk)

    1. Christine, de Pisan, ca. 1364-ca. 1431 I. Altmann, Barbara K., 1957- II. McGrady, Deborah L., 1967- III. Medieval casebooks.
PQ1575.Z5 C464 2002
841'.2—dc21

2002068028

BKA: To my mother and in memory of my father
DLM: To Terry and my beloved parents

Contents

Foreword

    Charity Cannon Willard   xi

1. Introduction

    Barbara K. Altmann and Deborah L. McGrady   1

Part I   Christine in Context

2. Christine de Pizan and the Political Life in Late Medieval France

    Renate Blumenfeld-Kosinski   9

3. Christine de Pizan as Translator and Voice of the Body Politic

    Lori J. Walters   25

4. Somewhere between Destructive Glosses and Chaos: Christine de Pizan and Medieval Theology

    Earl Jeffrey Richards   43

5. Christine de Pizan: Memory's Architect

    Margarete Zimmermann   57

Part II   Building a Female Community

6. Christine de Pizan as a Defender of Women

    Rosalind Brown-Grant   81

7. Christine's Treasure: Women's Honor and Household Economies in the *Livre des trois vertus*
   Roberta L. Krueger — 101

8. Who's a Heroine? The Example of Christine de Pizan
   Thelma Fenster — 115

9. *Le Livre de la cité des dames*: Reconfiguring Knowledge and Reimagining Gendered Space
   Judith L. Kellogg — 129

Part III Christine's Writings

10. Love as Metaphor in Christine de Pizan's Ballade Cycles
    Tracy Adams — 149

11. The *Querelle de la Rose* and the Ethics of Reading
    Marilynn Desmond — 167

12. The Lessons of Experience and the *Chemin de long estude*
    Andrea Tarnowski — 181

13. The *Livre de l'advision Cristine*
    Liliane Dulac and Christine Reno — 199

14. "Nous deffens de feu, . . . de pestilence, de guerres": Christine de Pizan's Religious Works
    Maureen Boulton — 215

Part IV Christine's Books

15. Christine and the Manuscript Tradition
    James Laidlaw — 231

16. Modern Editions: Makers of the Christinian Corpus
    Nadia Margolis — 251

Bibliography — 271

Contributors — 287

Index — 291

Foreword

Charity Cannon Willard

It was in the spring of 1935, while preparing for the final examination of my first course in Old French, that I discovered Christine de Pizan. I was reading Bédier and Hazard's *Histoire de la littérature française illustrée*. Although there are only two pages of discussion of her writings, they are accompanied by two interesting illustrations from her manuscripts. In looking for more information, I came across the observation that this author would be better appreciated if more of her works had been published in modern editions. For some reason I immediately developed a desire to publish one of these works.

This was not considered a suitable undertaking for completing an M.A. in French at Smith College, but it was suggested that I might give some attention to the poem inspired by Jeanne d'Arc. So it was that I prepared a thesis entitled "Jeanne d'Arc comme source d'inspiration littéraire au quinzième siècle," of which the first chapter was devoted to the "Ditié de Jehanne d'Arc." It was not until I was selecting a subject for a Ph.D. thesis at Radcliffe (Harvard) that an edition of one of Christine de Pizan's unpublished works became a possibility. I selected her *Livre de la paix* because there were only two known manuscripts, making it seem a reasonable undertaking for an initial effort.

It was primarily during the unhappy summer of 1939 that I transcribed the text of the *Livre de la paix*. It often sounded like a commentary on the current troubles in Paris as the country worked its way toward war with civil dissension in addition to growing threats from Germany. My thesis, the edition of this text, was defended on May 28, 1940, the day Belgium fell to the German invader, and the Ph.D. was conferred the week in June that marked the fall of France. I was indeed an intellectual refugee.

With war in full swing during most of the 1940s, there was little progress in medieval scholarship. Obviously one could not go to Europe and books from Europe did not cross the Atlantic. Furthermore, teachers were needed to replace those called to military service and there were other more immediate demands, so there was little opportunity for research.

At the end of the decade, shortly after peace had been restored in Europe, the Boston Public Library acquired a manuscript of the *Livre des trois vertus*. As few people there knew anything about Christine de Pizan, I was invited to write an article about it for the *Boston Public Library Quarterly*. At that time I was a visiting professor at St. Lawrence University in Canton, New York. I learned by chance that P. G.-C. Campbell, whose studies of the *Epistre Othea* I of course knew, was living in retirement near London, Ontario. I wrote asking him if we might call on him. He and his wife very graciously invited us to tea. He was by then quite old and really more interested in his stamp collection than in Christine de Pizan, but we had a conversation about his work on the sources of the *Epistre Othea*. In the meantime his wife quietly observed to my husband that she had really resented all the time her husband had "devoted to that woman."

Soon after that we moved back to the New York region and I began working from time to time at the Pierpont Morgan Library, with its admirable resources. There I met Curt Bühler. He was friendly as well as helpful and when I saw him he would greet me cordially and say: "You know, Mrs. Willard, I think we are the only people in the United States interested in Christine de Pizan."

It was not long, however, before we both met Millard Meiss, who was working on his monumental study of medieval manuscripts. I had a number of discussions with him over a period of time, for he was particularly interested in discussing the details of Christine de Pizan's life and her associations. Through our conversations, I learned the importance of looking at the illustrations of manuscript as well as text.

Fortunately, I was also able to get to Paris in the fall of 1951 and my pursuit of manuscripts began. In Paris, at the Bibliothèque Nationale, I met Suzanne Solente, who was then working on her monumental (four volume) edition of Christine de Pizan's *Mutacion de Fortune*. Later, at the Bibliothèque Royale in Brussels, I met for the first time the important codicologist L. M. J. Delaissé. He, very kindly, took an interest in what I was doing, and encouraged me to examine the writing and marginal notations in manuscripts. Through him I came to know Gilbert Ouy, whose seminar on manuscript study at the Ecole des Hautes Etudes was most influential for a number of people. I was fortunate to be able to participate in the seminar one year, and through this group came to know Franco Simone and Gianni Mombello from the University of Turin, both of whom have made significant contributions to Christine de Pizan studies, notably Mombello's extensive study of the *Epistre Othea* manuscripts.

Foreword　　　　　　　　　　　　　　　　　　　　　　　　　　　　　　　　*xiii*

It was in 1982 that a notable contribution was made to a larger audience for Christine de Pizan. This was an English translation of the *Cité des dames* by Earl Jeffrey Richards, published by the Persea Press of New York, which also commissioned my biography of her. These two books introduced Christine to a large number of readers, notably to scholars in areas other than medieval French, and opened a completely new chapter in studies of this author. Several translations of this text into other languages followed: it was translated into Dutch by Tine Penfoort, into German by Margarete Zimmermann, and into modern French by Thérèse Moreau and Eric Hicks. Curiously, the original French text did not become available in print until 1997, when it was published in Italy, edited by the original translator, Earl Jeffrey Richards.

Modern editions of other works also began to appear in impressive numbers: Jacqueline Cerquiglini's *Cent balades d'amant et de dame*, Barbara Altmann's *The Love Debate Poems of Christine de Pizan*, Angus Kennedy's edition of *Le Livre du corps de policie*, and Andrea Tarnowski's *Le Livre du chemin de longue étude* among others. The most recent item on this list is the new edition of *Advision Cristine* by Christine Reno and Liliane Dulac. New translations are appearing at a steady pace as well, and a further development that has greatly expanded interest in Christine de Pizan's writings has been a series of international meetings devoted to them, four to date.

At the end of Book II of *Advision Cristine*, Christine de Pizan expressed her belief that her writings would be more appreciated after her death than during her lifetime. At the end of Part II, one of the shadows that make up Dame Opinion reassures her:

> Et le temps a venir plus en sera parlé qu'a ton vivant. Car tant te dis je encore que tu es venue en mauvais temps. Car les sciences ne sont pas a present en leur reputacion, ains sont comme choses hors saison . . . Maiz, aprés ta mort, venra le prince plain de valeur et sagesce qui par la relacion de tes volumes desirera tes jours avoir esté de son temps et par grant desir souhaitera t'avoir veue. (Christine Reno and Liliane Dulac, eds., *L'Advision Christine* [Paris: Honoré Champion, 2001], 89–90)

(In times to come, more will be said of it than in your lifetime. For this much I tell you again: you have come at a bad time. The sciences are not highly esteemed at present but are like things out of season. . . . But after your death, there will come a prince, full of wisdom and valor, who—because of your books—will wish you had lived in his time and will long to have known you [Glenda K. McLeod, *Christine's Vision* (New York and London: Garland, 1993), 88].)

Surely not even Christine herself, however, could ever have imagined such an expansion of her literary reputation.

1
Introduction

Barbara K. Altmann and Deborah L. McGrady

How dramatically a field can change over the course of a career! The observations of Charity Cannon Willard, a pioneer in Christine de Pizan research, provide a standard of measure. In her foreword to this volume, she traces the development of Christine studies from a personal perspective, charting her own entry into the profession, her early encounters with other "Pizanistes" on both sides of the Atlantic, and the increasing appeal of this author, witnessed by the number of publications that grew steadily from a trickle into the current outpouring of scholarship, editions, and translations.

Mrs. Willard reminds us in her narrative that the revival of interest in Christine in this century took place against a backdrop of war and strife just as Christine's career did. Like the author they were studying, Willard and other major figures of medieval studies persevered, undaunted by practical and institutional obstacles. During the postwar years, they laid the foundation for subsequent generations of scholars. The work of preparing reliable modern editions and translations continues. But by now, the basic information is readily available and a critical corpus is in place. We have access to Christine's biography, increasingly comprehensive descriptions of her manuscripts, and an array of well-informed and thought-provoking analyses of the texts. As a result of the explosion, we now have the luxury of engaging with a whole community of scholars and its received ideas.

An adjective often used to describe Christine is "unique." Early critics expended a good deal of effort to prove the merit of this woman writer, an anomaly of her time. The result was the shift from the perception of Christine as "bluestocking," in Gustave Lanson's infamous phrase, to the current common designation of her as the first French woman of letters. The challenge now is to nuance our understanding of her uniqueness. The following chapters exemplify this new shift in Christine studies. Each contributor analyzes Christine's work in relation to her milieu and inherited traditions, all the while accenting how her goals and achievements distinguish her from her contemporaries.

Certainly Christine has proved to be one of the pivotal authors of late medieval Europe; her body of work is broad and copious enough to reflect in some measure all the major facets of late medieval society. As a result, she makes the ideal subject for a Casebook. The purpose of this volume is two-fold: it is intended both as an overview of the state of Christine de Pizan studies at this moment in their evolution and as a collection of new research in the field. We began by defining four research areas representative of prevailing trends of our day and essential to an understanding of Christine's significance: the historical context of her writing; her abiding interest in the status and nature of women; the major texts she authored and the different genres in which she worked; and the production of her works in manuscript and their reception in the ensuing centuries. We then commissioned articles from experts to address those topics. Each of the 15 chapters is thus new work; unlike other collections, this one contains no reprinted articles. Every contribution frames original, groundbreaking scholarship of interest to specialists with a discussion of the established literary and cultural traditions necessary for a reader new to the field. Each chapter is self-contained, with substantial notes and full bibliographic references. We have added a bibliography of selected works that functions as a resource list. The collection as a whole provides an initiation to Christine studies as the field currently stands.

The section divisions in this Casebook are organized into the research areas mentioned above, corresponding roughly to four categories: historical approaches; feminist readings; close literary readings; and issues of codicology and reception history. It goes without saying that there is a good deal of overlap among these concerns and methodologies.

The first section, "Christine in Context," establishes Christine and her writings in the larger framework of the sociopolitical and intellectual history of her day. Renate Blumenfeld-Kosinski explores the impact on Christine of the turbulent political situation of France in the early fifteenth century and how Christine engages it in her writing. Blumenfeld-Kosinski shows that it is not a topic Christine restricts to her overtly political texts, but one that filters into her entire corpus, from her lyrical poetry to her allegories. Lori J. Walters analyzes Christine's place in the tradition of translation as literary practice and metaphor. Going beyond the obvious definition of translation as the rendering of a work in a different language, Walters reveals that Christine used the multivalent term both to affiliate herself with a long line of illustrious translators associated with Charles V and to create her own unique authorial identity as a writer. Christine's use of theology is taken up by Earl Jeffrey Richards, who challenges the view that Christine's knowledge of the subject was superficial. Through a study ranging from discrete terminology to her developed arguments regarding the status of women, Richards contends that Christine was directly engaged with the writings of Thomas Aquinas, albeit as a reader who systematically questions and reworks the arguments of the great thinker. In the final chapter Margarete Zimmermann investigates the author's strategies for ensuring her future legacy. Intertwining her own *memoria* with that of her father and her noble patrons, Christine implements a series of strategies that depend on text, image, and reader reception to ensure her survival as a woman writer.

The second section, "Building a Female Community," explicates Christine's profeminine agenda from several different perspectives. Rosalind Brown-Grant counters anachronistic disappointment that Christine failed as a feminist, arguing that only when placed in the context of Aristotelian and theological arguments can we appreciate the extent to which Christine challenged accepted views of women's nature and role in medieval society. With regard to Christine's pragmatic conduct book for women of all classes, Roberta L. Krueger's chapter on the *Livre des trois vertus* demonstrates that Christine understands women's management of financial resources as a key to their well-being. Christine's advice makes it clear that women's moral standing, their honor, and their spiritual welfare are all tied to proper conduct in their economic lives. Her portrayal of women stresses the interdependence of women's economic activities across social strata and recognizes women's significant contribution to medieval economic life. Focusing on Christine's fictional portrayals of women, Thelma Fenster notes the absence of the typical romance heroine. Instead, Christine adapts and develops the complex figure of the sibyl who stands both as exemplar and purveyor of advice, overlapping to some degree with her own authorial identity. On the topic of Christine's most elaborate realization of the female community, Judith L. Kellogg explores the innovative configurations of space in Christine's *Cité des dames*. Kellogg argues that the allegorical city regenders the notion of the body politic, based on a redefined body of knowledge and resulting in a reformulation of power structures that allows women to participate.

The section entitled "Christine's Writings" includes fresh readings of some of Christine's best known works as well as an assessment of her achievements in lesser known genres. Tracy Adams reassesses Christine's lyric poetry in the context of her writings as a whole, explaining her use of the courtly love topos and her bereft narratorial figure as metaphors for the political situation in France and the vulnerability of the disempowered, including women and writers. Marilynn Desmond revisits the debate on the *Roman de la Rose*, examining Christine's participation in the *querelle des femmes* in terms of her remarks on the ethics of reading. Whereas scholars have identified Christine's attacks on the *Rose* as based on her belief that it is a misogynistic text that verbally abuses women, Desmond argues that Christine defines the moral *utilitas* of a work through the concrete impact it can have on an individual. Desmond concludes that the *Rose* serves as a manual of erotic violence and is, therefore, unworthy. Andrea Tarnowski writes on the *Chemin de long estude*. She argues that it marks an intermediate phase in Christine's oeuvre, one in which she assigns herself the dual function of fictional character and producer of texts, claiming, although still somewhat tentatively, the authority to write as an apprentice in the realm of learning. On the question of social progress that lies at the heart of the *Chemin*, Christine shows her preference for human solutions based on knowledge and experience. In her combination of allegory and social commentary, literary erudition and pragmatism, she forges for herself a legitimate role in the large debates of her day. The focus of Liliane Dulac and Christine Reno's chapter is the *Advision Cristine*. They survey the struggle in current scholarship to define that text: although scholars tend to classify it as either autobiography or political writing, Dulac and Reno contend that the autobiographical and political are inextricably intertwined, concluding that any appreciation of the text must begin with a recognition of its hybrid nature. Finally, Maureen Boulton reads Christine de Pizan's religious works within the larger context of late medieval devotional practices. Boulton argues that when Christine's devotional writings are compared with medieval religious material (including books of hours, Catholic doctrine, Psalms, etc.), it is clear that the dominant concerns of her secular writing, especially the plight of women, are not only manifest in these works, but represent Christine's unique contribution to religious writing.

The fourth and last section, "Christine's Books," deals with the material artifacts and scholarly processes that make Christine's work available. Taken together, James Laidlaw and Nadia Margolis's articles give a diachronic view of how and in what state Christine's works have reached her readers. Laidlaw details the production of Christine's writings during her lifetime through a discussion of the fifty manuscripts identified as autograph copies, explaining the significance of this unusually rich body of textual witnesses to our understanding of the many facets of Christine's career. He also describes two projects currently underway that will promote scholarly access to Christine's manuscripts: the "Album Christine de Pizan" and the plan to digitize British Library manuscript Harley 4431, one of the best known compilations of Christine's work. Margolis shifts our focus to the fate of that work long after the author's lifetime, providing a detailed study of Christine's posterity in the form of critical editions published from the eighteenth to the twentieth centuries. Margolis makes clear that the story of the editing of Christine's corpus is inevitably tied to political and intellectual histories and rivalries, and to trends in disciplinary concerns and institutional policies, all of which shaped the way Christine's texts were transmitted by a long line of scholars, including several compelling personalities.

This Casebook does not claim in any way to be the final word. It is meant much more modestly as a contribution to what might be considered the third wave

Introduction 5

of Christine studies. We are long past disdaining Christine's erudition, but we are also past the surprise of discovering in Christine a late medieval author who speaks to modern and postmodern concerns. Her place in the evolving canon of medieval literature would seem to be secure, and such a wealth of secondary material is available that keeping up with the field has become a daunting prospect. Without making too grand a claim, the regular appearance of Christine on the list of conference topics and in books and articles of all kinds suggests that her corpus is bountiful and rich enough to sustain close and extended scrutiny for a long time, in the manner of the inexhaustible sources best exemplified in medieval and early modern studies by Dante or Chaucer. The wealth of approaches used of late to elucidate her work has not only enhanced our appreciation of the complexity and depth of her *oeuvre*, but has also reshaped the boundaries of various disciplines. This volume represents how we understand Christine de Pizan at the outset of the twenty-first century. It is not intended to fix Christine in time, but to stimulate further discussion and discovery.

Finally, we would like to thank Paul Szarmach for first suggesting that we undertake this project and Angus J. Kennedy for his true generosity in sharing editorial materials that made our job much easier.

I
Christine in Context

2

Christine de Pizan and the Political Life in Late Medieval France

Renate Blumenfeld-Kosinski

Christine de Pizan came to France as a small child in 1368, four years after the accession to the throne of Charles V the Wise. In her *Livre des fais d'armes et de chevalerie*, written in 1410, she refers to herself as a "femme ytalienne"—just like Minerva, goddess of arms and chivalry.[1] But there is no doubt that her allegiance always lay with France. The fate of her adopted country affected her deeply and informed many of her works. In this chapter we will explore the evolution of her political thought and the many literary genres Christine used to express her ideas. In particular, we will see how the worsening situation in France conditioned her own literary output, which ranged from lyrical works to allegories and finally straightforward political and polemic treatises. Indeed, Christine's trajectory from being an observer and chronicler of the events surrounding her to attempting to intervene in these events is reflected in the forms she chose for her works and the voice she adopted in them.

The three major crises addressed in her works are the Hundred Years War (1337–1453), the Great Schism of the Western Church (1378–1417), and the French civil war.[2] The Hundred Years War, in reality a long series of military campaigns interrupted by many truces, began in 1337, when the English King Edward III, as a grandson of Philippe IV le Bel, laid claim to the French throne as a response to Philippe VI's occupation of the English fief, the duchy of Guyenne. It was punctuated by several major battles, almost all ending in defeat for the French. After the battle of Agincourt (1415) France became an occupied country. It was not until Joan of Arc (d. 1431) that, in a major drive, the French began to chase the English from their territory, but it would take more than another twenty years before the war can be said to have ended.

The Great Schism of the Western Church had its origins in a double papal election in 1378. Pope Gregory XI had returned to Rome from Avignon, where the papacy (almost exclusively French) had spent most of the fourteenth century, and promptly died. The cardinals elected the archbishop of Bari as Urban VI, but—or so they later claimed—they did so in fear and under duress, threatened by the Roman populace clamoring for a Roman pope. Urban VI was an austere and intransigent person, lacking any diplomatic skills. He had no intention of letting the cardinals enjoy the sumptuous life and relative independence they had enjoyed before. In response, the cardinals soon left Rome and proceeded to elect another pope, Robert of Geneva, as Clement VII, thus in effect creating two papal obediences that split Europe into two parts, with France and England on opposite sides. Charles V quickly came to support Clement VII, located in Avignon, whereas Richard II adhered to Urban's Roman papacy. The French monarchy played an important role in trying to end the Schism, in 1398 even going so far as to withdraw obedience from the Avignon pope Benedict XIII in order to pressure him,[3] and, they hoped, the Roman pope as well, to abdicate. But both popes were tenacious and hung on to their office even after the Council of Pisa (1409) had elected another pope who was to replace both of them. Only the Council of Constance (1414–1417) succeeded in electing a new pope, Martin V, to whom most of Europe was willing to adhere.

The French civil war, long in the making through the rivalry of Charles V's uncles and cousins during the regency and finally the madness of Charles VI, started in earnest around 1407 with the assassination of Louis of Orléans, the brother of King Charles VI, on the orders of his cousin, the Duke of Burgundy. In 1410 Louis's son, Charles d'Orléans, formed the league of Gien with the dukes of Berry, Bourbon, and Bretagne and several counts to oppose the duke of Burgundy. This internal conflict was inseparable from the continuing hostilities of the Hundred Years War. It is difficult to keep track of the shifting allegiances of the great families with respect to the English, but in the end the Burgundian faction allied itself most strongly with France's enemy, whereas the Armagnacs supported the king and then the dauphin.[4] The factious warfare within France had, of course, contributed to making the country ever more vulnerable to an English invasion.[5]

At the end of Christine's life the Great Schism had ended, but the wars were continuing. It was at this moment that Joan of Arc appeared like the answer to Christine's prayers: a consideration of her poem in praise of Joan will thus be a fitting end to this chapter.

Christine worked the historical events and political life of her time into her texts in a variety of ways. In her early lyric poetry (1390s) Christine alluded to and celebrated specific occasions or persons, such as the birth of a royal prince or the courage of a particular knight. The *Epistre Othea* of 1399 marks her first explicit foray into the "mirror of princes" genre and thus into a type of politically engaged textual production.[6] From fragments of mythological tales Christine (or Othéa) extracts lessons for the good knight and the care of the soul. The political message is more implicit here than in later texts, and it is especially in the frontispieces of the various presentation copies that her differentiated views of the noble recipients become apparent.[7] Christine's political savvy is also in evidence here: she cultivated patrons from the different ducal families, refusing to take sides in the frequent conflicts between them. Her principal concern was to find paying patrons and, more and more, to try and prevent the fragmentation of France caused by internal hostilities. The combination of these two goals—disparate as they may seem—in fact allowed her to preserve her neutrality and, within her literary works, play the role of a mediator.

In the *Epistre Othea* it was Christine's invention, the goddess of wisdom, who drew out the lessons for the noble reader. Two years later, Christine herself felt called upon to try and intervene in the events of her time. In the verse *Chemin de long estude* (1402) Christine as author figure goes on a heavenly journey, accompanied by the Cumaean Sibyl, to find a solution to the earth's woes. The two women eventually end up in heaven where they witness a debate between four allegorical ladies, Wealth, Nobility, Chivalry, and Wisdom, as to whose fault the terrible state of the world is, and who should be chosen as a savior. Christine is supposed to return to earth to report back to the French princes from whose ranks this savior will be recruited. For the *Chemin* Christine chose the traditional form of the allegorical dream journey with herself as protagonist. Her voice is still hidden behind those of the allegorical ladies—she is nothing but the conveyor of their wise decision—but the message is nevertheless clear: France must take on a leadership role in the resolution of the world's multiple crises, from wars and the Great Schism to more general injustices inflicted upon people.

In the *Mutacion de Fortune*, written in verse in 1403, we find a universal history, "read" from the wall paintings in Fortune's castle and transmitted by Christine, prefaced by an allegorical version of Christine's own life and a moral evaluation of the different parts of society.[8] The gender transformation she describes here, that is, her being changed into a man through Fortune's manipulations, allows her to become a historian, a role until then reserved for males in medieval culture. This is the first time in her *œuvre* that she linked her own personal fate to history at large. But she did not yet establish explicit links between developments of world history and her own life: Part II goes on to describe Fortune's castle, without Christine suggesting specific connections between the allegorical/autobiographical first part and what follows. Fortune's power in governing history and humans' individual fates is the overarching theme that ties the different sections of the *Mutacion* together. The description of the inhabitants of Fortune's castle allows Christine to severely criticize the current state of society. All classes are taken to task for their failure to maintain a just and unified society.

She also indicts both popes as perpetuators of the Great Schism. Women however, Christine emphasizes, will not be treated in this text. She admits that some readers may be surprised at this omission, but in an argument that would find no place in the *Cité des dames*, we learn that not all women are virtuous (though most are). But even if they are evil, their influence on world affairs is negligible, and they do little harm "car peu s'empechent des affaires/En gouvernemens neccessaires" (vv. 6629–30, II:81) (for they occupy themselves little with the things necessary for governing). Christine also addresses the great problems of her time, such as revolts and civil wars, and toward the end of the book, she turns to the fates of Richard II, Johanna of Naples, Pedro the Cruel of Aragon, and other rulers.

In the *Mutacion*, then, Christine lays out in verse form and in a straightforward allegory her own story and the history of the world up to her own time. As in the *Chemin de long estude*, Christine indicts the nobility, whose lack of virtue and prudence opens up France to disasters. But here her criticism encompasses all strata of society, thus articulating for the first time the idea that will become prominent in the *Livre du corps de policie* (1406–1407): all parts of society must be virtuous and collaborate for the sake of the health of the body politic. The same themes will appear in her later, overtly polemic, texts. For Christine an evaluation of history and politics can take place only in a moral framework. Her historian's voice becomes linked to that of a moralist, already familiar from the *Chemin*, who will offer her own suggestions for the improvement of society.

Not until the opening section of the *Advision Cristine* of 1405 do we find Christine's first serious treatment of French history in prose.[9] The text features an intricate structure of multiple allegorical layers wrapped around a veiled account of history. But unlike the chroniclers of the time, such as Jean Froissart or Michel Pintoin, also known as the *religieux de Saint-Denys*,[10] Christine positions her French history as the first part of a very elaborate three-part allegory, where the second and third parts deal with the intellectual life of her times and her own life story. Her own story is thus no longer the preface to history, as in the *Mutacion*, but rather the culmination. In the preface to the *Advision* she makes the connection between her own fate and that of France explicit:

> Nous avons ja dit comment la fiction de cestui livre se puet alegorisier triblement, c'est assavoir assimiler au monde general, qui est la terre, aussi a homme singulier et puis au royaume de France.

(We have already stated that the fiction of this book can be allegorized in a triple fashion, that is to say, applied to the world as a whole, which is the earth, and also to the individual man, and then to the kingdom of France.)[11]

This "homme singulier" is she herself, as the autobiographical Part III shows. Thus French history is inseparable from her own and her family's fate.

In Part I of the *Advision* Christine pinpoints the beginning of France's downfall as the beginning of the Hundred Years War, a downfall that parallels that of her own family after the death of Charles V in 1380:

> Car pour moy ravir et embler s'assembloient diverses provinces et gens estranges, qui a grant ost deffoulerent ma terre et bruslerent mes villes et mes manoirs, faisoient de mes gens grant exart et toute me pilloient en tres grant quantité de fois. Pareillement ai esté en peril d'estre perdue, ravie, prise a force et du tout deshonnoree...[12]

(For in order to plunder and rob me, there assembled many provinces and foreigners who desolated my land with a great army and burned my towns and manors. They brought great destruction to my people and robbed me of everything. Often I have been similarly imperiled by loss, abduction, rape, and complete dishonor.)[13]

"Or fu la porte ouverte de noz infortunes" (the door to our misfortunes then opened; 152, 110)—this is how Christine describes the beginning of her family's decline. And in a parallel to France's fate, after her husband's death she is plundered and robbed by her creditors, saddened by the losses of her husband and father, and brought close to dishonor by the shabby treatment she receives in the law courts: a far cry indeed from the initial good fortune the de Pizan family experienced at the court of Charles V.

After the honors of the early phases of the Hundred Years Wars, punctuated by the defeats of Crécy (1346) and Poitiers (1356), and the imprisonment of Charles's father Jean le Bon, the reign of Charles V (1364–1380) had begun on a more promising note. When Charles was still regent for his father, the English king Edward III had demanded four million gold écus as ransom for Jean le Bon, as well as all the territories in Aquitaine that had belonged to Henry II in the twelfth century. The treaty of Brétigny-Calais (1360) increased the English possessions in Aquitaine (though not as dramatically as Edward had hoped) but also reduced the ransom. In addition, it stipulated that the English king should renounce his claims to the French throne, and that the French king should abandon his idea of sovereignty in Aquitaine. But Jean le Bon died in English captivity and the treaty was never fully ratified. Nonetheless, there was a lull in open hostilities that lasted well into the reign of Charles V.

When the duke of Burgundy, Philippe le Hardi, asked Christine in 1404 (over twenty years after the death of Charles V) to write his late brother's biography, she had nothing but good things to say about Charles. His relatively peaceful and prosperous reign had, of course, coincided with the good fortunes of Christine's own family, and though Charles V was also portrayed positively by other chroniclers, Christine's almost saintly image of the king stands out.[14] In a work commissioned by the late king's own brother, criticism of Charles's reign was obviously not called for. But the period between 1364 and 1380 was truly one of considerable recuperation of French territories and cultural revival,[15] as well as of peace overtures that endured into the reign of Charles VI. It was not until the end of the century that Charles VI's madness as well as the deposition and death of Richard II put an end to any hopes for a resolution of this long-standing conflict. Thus Christine, writing in 1403–1404, was certainly justified in looking back on the reign of Charles V as a golden period in French history.

The *Livre des fais et bonnes meurs du sage roi Charles V* is not a biography in the modern sense but rather an appreciation of the king's qualities and political prudence,[16] a mirror for princes (drawing on the wisdom of the ancients), and also, here and there, a memoir of Christine and her family's life at the court. She recalls, for example, that the duke of Burgundy had helped her in the troubled financial situation caused by her widowhood (II.1), that her father was present at Charles V's death (III.70), and that she herself saw Charles ride by in all his splendor (III.31). In terms of political analysis, her remarks on certain events of the Hundred Years War and the Great Schism are particularly interesting.

Christine treats the Hundred Years War in Part II of the *Charles V* in the context of Charles's feats of chivalry. Part I had established the king's superior moral character. In a striking contrast to France's tearful lament on this war in the *Advision*, Christine presents it here as a string of glorious victories, examples of Charles's unsurpassed military skill. This skill was largely strategic, since Charles himself rarely ventured out on the battle field, as Christine explains in Part II, Chapter 10. The humiliation of the English is a recurring theme. Chapters 26 and 27 of Part II, for example, tell about the failed campaign of the Duke of Lancaster and how he was chased from French territory; Chapters 34 and 35 describe in glowing terms Charles's reconquest of the duchies of Guyenne and Bretagne. What is especially important here is that Christine never loses sight of the purpose of the *Charles V*: the celebration of Charles's virtues; that is, factual history is always in the service of moral teaching. Thus, she interlaces very skillfully exciting accounts of Charles's military achievements with general remarks on the origins of chivalry and quotations from the venerable authors, often adduced in the mirrors for princes, and reused by Christine herself in the *Corps de policie*, begun around the same time. For a variety of reasons, then, the Hundred Years War is not depicted here as the unmitigated disaster of the *Advision*. One reason is, of course, that the phase from 1364–1380 was indeed a period of recovery for the French. But this different vision of the war is also linked to the book's purpose: to teach perfect chivalry through Charles's example and to celebrate the late king.

The English represent the enemy for Christine; the question of partiality has therefore a clear-cut answer. The problem of the Great Schism was somewhat murkier, since both popes had been elected by the same College of Cardinals. The *Charles V* was not the first text in which Christine tackled this thorny question.[17] She had lamented the Great Schism already in the *Chemin de long estude* and had done so in very emotional terms: "L'Eglise de Dieu desolee/Est plus qu'oncques adoulee;/ Or en sont ferus les pastours,/ Et les brebis vont par destours/Esperses et esperdües" (vv. 371–75) (God's Church is desolated and more afflicted than ever before. The pastors have been stricken and the lambs wander around, scattered and distraught). She considers the problem of the Schism within the context of human destructiveness but does not assign blame to any particular party, nor propose any specific solutions. In the *Mutacion* she offers us the memorable image of the "plus hault siege" (the highest seat) onto which the two papal contenders attempt to squeeze themselves. She does allude to the attempts at intervention by some princes and condemns "Berthelemi," i.e., Urban VI, for the murder of several cardinals, but the specifics remain rather vague and no solution is proposed.[18] Instead, Christine goes on to a rather conventional indictment of a corrupt clergy. This lack of precise political references is rather surprising, since 1403 marked the moment when the French monarchy reestablished its obedience to the Avignon Pope Benedict XIII. Its withdrawal in 1398 was an issue that divided the ducal houses, with Louis d'Orléans staunchly supporting Benedict. The purpose of the withdrawal was to force Benedict XIII to abdicate and, in what was hoped would be a bilateral renunciation of both popes, to bring about a new unified papal election. From 1403 to 1406 France again adhered to Benedict—with all the financial obligations this entailed.[19] When the obedience was again withdrawn in 1406, Louis's continued approval of Benedict helped set the stage for his assassination. Of all these intricate and eventually fateful diplomatic activities there is no direct trace in the *Mutacion*. In the context of this allegorical universal history, then, Christine presents the Schism merely as one of the countless disasters caused by Fortune and humans' moral failings. By contrast, in the *Charles V* Christine shows great insight into Charles V's attitude early in the Schism and the political wrangling that ensued.

Ten chapters of Part III of the *Charles V* are devoted to the Schism. Christine begins by describing the death of Pope Gregory XI in Rome in March 1378. The cardinals assembled in April to elect the new pope, and the lodgings meant for them were hit by thunder and lightning, presaging the disasters to come: "laquel chose fait moult à noter par ce qu'il s'en est ensuivi" (III.51; 2:136) (a remarkable fact in view of what was to come), remarks Christine. Around the conclave, pandemonium reigned. Rome's populace, armed and enraged, threatened the cardinals within by shouting "We want a Roman"—or else! The new pope, Urban VI, was not a Roman, but at least an Italian, Bartolomeo Prignano, the archbishop of Bari.[20] It was not until May that the French king learned of Urban's election, and initially he adopted a wait-and-see attitude, wishing to ascertain the facts of this contentious election (III.51). Shortly after Urban's appointment the cardinals realized that they had made a huge mistake. The new pope instantly showed himself to be autocratic, not deferring in the least to the cardinals, who saw their role as becoming more and more important in the governance of the Church, reflecting in fact a general trend in Europe for more political control by councils and "parlaments."[21]

Christine then reports on the missives from the cardinals in which they described the circumstances of the election: they had voted in fear and under duress, and therefore the election was invalid. In September the cardinals, by now outside of Rome in the more pleasant surroundings of Fondi, proceeded "à l'election de vray pape" (*Charles V.* III.56; 2:146) in the person of Robert of Geneva, a powerful Frenchman, as Clement VII. In November 1378 Charles called a council in Paris and after hearing reports of a number of witnesses, concluded that Clement VII was the true pope. Hoping to sway other European rulers in Clement's favor, Charles sent out various teams of ambassadors but did not succeed in persuading the king of Hungary nor the Flemish of Clement's legitimacy (III.57). This is where Christine leaves things, except to add a violent lament that reflects the state of affairs in 1404:

> [ce] doloreux sisme, et envenimée plante contagieuse, fichée par instigacion de l'Anemi ou giron sainte Eglise. O quel flayel! O quant douloureux meschief, qui encore dure et a duré l'espace .xxvi.ans, ne taillée n'est ceste pestillence de cesser, se Dieux, de sa sainte misericorde n'y remedie, car ja est celle detestable playe comme apostumée et tournée en acoustumance ...; si est grant peril que mort soubdaine s'en ensuive quelque jour en la religion crestienne, c'est assavoir une si mortel de Dieu vengence que à celle heure faille tous crier: "Miserere mei, Deus!" (III.61; 2:155–56)

(this painful schism, poisonous, contagious plant that was thrust into the bosom of Holy Church at the instigation of the devil. Oh, what a scourge! What a painful calamity, which now has lasted twenty-six years; this pestilence is not close to being extinguished unless God in His holy compassion brings a remedy, for this wound has become purulent and one has become accustomed to it ...; there is a danger that sudden death will result from this one day in the Christian faith, such a deadly divine vengeance that at the moment we will all have to cry: "Miserere mei, Deus!")

The period between 1378 and 1404 brought to light the grievous consequences of the Schism. Christine's metaphors of the contagious plant, the purulent wound,[22] and the idea that the Schism represented God's vengeance on Christianity can all be found in other writers of the time, but this passage is nonetheless extremely powerful, especially in its contrast to her sober and approving tone when describing Charles's policies regarding the Schism. In the *Charles V* Christine stressed the careful judgment of Charles's decision to support Clement, a decision that in hindsight could be seen as one of the major factors in creating the Schism and dividing Europe. As historian/biographer looking back at the year 1378 Christine approves of Charles's policies, but as the writer living in 1404, she cannot but bemoan the heavy price paid for Charles's course of action.

Finally, in the *Sept psaumes allégorisés* of 1409–1410 we find a prayer for "sainte Eglise catholique, de laquelle par lonc temps il a semblé que tu eusses retrait ta sainte main" (Holy Catholic Church, from whom it seems that You have withdrawn Your holy hand for a long time now; Rains ed., 127) and for Pope Alexander V, elected in June 1409 at the Council of Pisa. But this prayer was in vain, for the other two popes refused to step down and Europe remained divided.

The split of Europe was not the only cost of the Schism. As alluded to above, it also contributed to the internecine warfare of the French nobility, exacerbating the conflicts caused by the power struggle that began with Charles V's death in 1380 and was perpetuated through Charles VI's madness, starting in 1392.[23] Just four years earlier Louis d'Orléans had persuaded his brother Charles VI to sideline the powerful uncles (the dukes of Berry and Burgundy, in particular) in favor of the *Marmousets*, his father's old councilors. But with the king's madness—which started dramatically on 5 August 1392 in a forest shimmering with heat[24]—the uncles resumed their powerful roles. When Philippe le Hardi of Burgundy died in 1404, just before Christine finished her biography of Charles V,[25] his son Jean sans Peur became one of the most powerful men in the realm and the archrival of Louis d'Orléans. This rivalry culminated in the treacherous murder of Louis by Jean's henchmen on a dark Paris street on 23 November 1407. An inquiry quickly discovered who the culprits were, but instead of undermining Jean sans Peur's power, the incident enhanced it. Heaping insults and accusations on the victim, Jean painted himself as a reformer who had extirpated a tyrant. The university scholar Jean Petit proceeded to write a famous treatise on tyrannicide, refuted by Jean Gerson, chancellor of the University of Paris.[26] This debate on whether it is lawful to kill a tyrant[27] helped to polarize France. In 1410 the chronicler of Saint-Denys, Michel Pintoin, describes the astonishment and dismay of the French populace when they realize that the preparations for war are not meant for a campaign against the English but for a "civil war, almost a domestic war, between relatives, both sides of French origin."[28] This is the moment when the League of Gien prepares for hostilities and starts moving on Paris in order to curb the influence of the power-hungry Jean sans Peur on the king. The monk of Saint-Denys does not often become very emotional in his vast chronicle, but this is one instance where he does. Tragedy, rather than history, is the correct genre for what he now has to tell. If he had not sworn to transmit both good and bad events to posterity he would now put down his pen, rather than tell of the blindness of French chivalry that, moved by implacable hatred, begins to turn arms against the very viscera of France. And he quotes Christ's words: "every kingdom divided against itself is brought to desolation" (Matthew 12:25), words Christine had also used in her letter to Queen Isabeau in 1405,[29] and that will also appear as the motto of Chapter 3 of Christine's *Livre de la paix* (1412–1413).

Christine was moved to despair by the events in France. In her *Lamentacion sur les maux de la France* of 1410 we find the same themes as in the *Chronique du religieux de Saint-Denys*, but presented even more dramatically. The *Lamentacion* is Christine's *cri de cœur* directed at the French nobility.[30] Where Pintoin is ready to put down his pen, Christine cannot write anymore because tears stream down her face and wet the parchment (84). She stands "seulette a part" (84) as a witness to the blindness and self-destructiveness of the French nobility. In an appeal to the Duke of Berry she evokes the natural bonds that should tie the families together and the shame of seeing cousins and uncles tear into each other's flesh (90). As she had done in the *Epistre a la reine* of 1405,[31] she addresses herself to Queen Isabeau, this time with a wake-up call. Five years earlier Christine had implored the queen to prevent further conflict, citing her role as mother of France and her feminine qualities that naturally qualify her to be peacemaker. Now, in 1410, Christine's exasperation comes to the fore: "Hé! Royne couronnee de France dors-tu adés?" (Oh, crowned Queen of France, are you still asleep?; 88). The *Lamentacion* ends with a moving appeal to the Duke of Berry and to God to let Christine see peace returned to France and "a moy, povre voix criant en ce royaume, desireuse de paix et du bien de vous touz . . ." (to me, a poor voice crying in this kingdom, desiring peace and welfare for all of you; 94). This eloquent polemic is framed by multiple inscriptions of Christine's self. The "subversive" *seulette* as her "authorial signature" and the tears that "dramatize the conflict between Christine's gender and her profession"[32] open the text; her voice crying in the wilderness, or rather in the desolated kingdom of France, closes it.[33] But the despair of the *Lamentacion* gives way once more to hope in Christine's *Livre de la paix*, where the emotional female voice clamoring for peace is replaced by the already familiar voice of the moralist, fighting, however, for the same goal.

With the *Livre de la paix* Christine inscribes herself in a tradition of late medieval peace theory, just wars, and similar topics.[34] It also is another mirror of princes, addressed to the dauphin Louis de Guienne, since for Christine the proper education of the prince is a precondition for the well-governed state, the only state capable of maintaining a lasting peace. But, as Liliane Dulac observes, the mode of composition of the *Paix* is quite different from that of previous mirrors, "parce que l'urgence de l'actualité s'y [fait] sentir à chaque instant."[35]

This long and complex work represents a culmination as well as an intensification of many of Christine's political ideas. For example, the people or third estate who were seen as a flock of sheep in need of a just protector in the *Corps de policie* are here called "le diabolique menu gent" (*Paix*, 136) (the diabolical simple people), who should not be given arms and be kept away from any form of governance. The fable of the sick body that needs all its members' cooperation to get well used by Christine in the *Policie* is replaced here by that of the autophageous madman, who stands for a nation that devours itself.[36]

Christine uses the occasional fable and plenty of *exempla*,[37] put forth in a forceful and eloquent exhortatory voice. But nothing reflects the political upheavals of the years 1412–1413 as much as the text's very redaction: begun 1 September 1412, the work was interrupted on 30 November because of the broken truce between the Burgundians and Armagnacs. In the wake of another peace treaty, Christine then took up her pen in September 1413 and finished the work on 1 January 1414. Christine's work here goes beyond peace theory to the political *actualité*: with her own writing activity she tracks the ups and downs of truces and resumed hostilities. She writes herself and her reactions into the text. Her breaking off in mid-text dramatizes in the strongest terms the destruction wrought on French culture and its productions through the continuing civil war.

The *Livre de la paix* was Christine's last appeal to the French nobles. After the disaster of Agincourt she turned away from any attempt at political intervention. She also abandoned the didactic and polemic genres in favor of the *consolatio*, a letter of consolation on the death of loved ones that has a venerable tradition dating back to antiquity. Her moving *Epistre de la prison de vie humaine*, finished in January 1418 and addressed to Marie de Berry, the daughter of the Duke of Berry who had lost many family members at Agincourt, offers hope for the afterlife, not for life on earth.[38] Its message is one of hope for Paradise but mostly one of resignation. The *Epistre* ends on a personal note: Christine apologizes for delaying this letter because of "plusieurs grans ennuis et troubles de courage" (many great worries and a troubled heart). Later that year the Burgundians would take Paris and the dauphin Charles (Louis of Guienne had died in 1415) would begin his erring around France. Christine herself would leave Paris and take refuge with her daughter at the abbey of Poissy. Thus, in the *Livre de la paix* Christine again links her textual production to the disasters surrounding her: her own life and intellectual activity are bound up with the fate of France.

At that point no one could know that a ray of hope would appear about ten years later in the shape of Joan of Arc. Written on 31 July 1429, only two weeks after Joan's crowning of the dauphin in Reims, the *Ditié de Jehanne d'Arc* celebrates Joan's victories and portrays her as a divinely inspired savior.[39] Where the *Lamentacion* began with Christine submerged in tears, the *Ditié* opens with "je, Christine," authenticating herself as a witness and expressing her joy and relief. As Kevin Brownlee observes, "eleven years of political disappointment and literary silence" have come to an end and "the cause of her deeply personal joy is a political event: the approach of the newly crowned Charles VII" (374). The prophecies and sibylline pronouncements she adduces as proof of Joan's legitimacy give authority to her own voice. The heroines she had celebrated in the *Cité des dames* now seem to be reincarnated in the maid of Orléans. All the hopes she had expressed in previous works—that women should be recognized for their true worth, that France should come together under its legitimate king, that the Church should be reunited,[40] that peace should be at hand—now seem to have come true. As for her own life, its *raison d'être*, that is, her literary activity in the service of her poetic and political ideals, has also been restored. The *Ditié* thus represents the ultimate confluence of the personal and the political, evident in so many permutations in the works studied in this chapter.

"Is there a feminine style of writing history?"[41] Probably not, but there certainly is a Christinian style. The most striking feature of her historical and political writing is that it is not confined to any one genre.[42] From allegory to political treatise, polemic text, and religious epistle, she manages to give a variety of shapes and expressions to her political thought and historical analysis. She also writes herself into her texts in multiple ways: as witness or emotional participant; as sufferer or political advisor; as a lamenting tearful voice or a joyful celebrant. Unlike the principal chroniclers of her time, such as Froissart or Pintoin, she sees her own fate as inextricably linked to that of France, indeed, she even seems to become France—the weeping widow abandoned by her loved ones—at certain moments. Thus this "femme ytalienne" turned out to be France's voice, alternating between despair and hope, but strong and forceful to the end.

NOTES

1. "O Minerve, deesse d'armes et de chevalerie . . . je suis comme toy femme ytalienne" (BNF 603, fol. 2v). See the translation by Sumner Willard and Charity Cannon Willard, *Book of Deeds of Arms and of Chivalry* (University Park, PA: Pennsylvania State University Press, 1999), 13.
2. Generally on these crises, see Edouard Perroy, *La Guerre de Cent Ans* (Paris: Gallimard, 1945. Rpt. 1971); Desmond Seward, *The Hundred Years War* (New York: Atheneum, 1978); Walter Ullman, *Origins of the Great Schism* (1948. Reprinted London: Archon, 1967); Noël Valois, *La France et le Grand Schisme d'Occident*, 4 vols. (Paris: Picard, 1896–1902); Bernard Guenée, *Un meurtre, une société. L'assassinat du duc d'Orléans 23 novembre 1407* (Paris: Gallimard, 1992).
3. See Howard Kaminsky, "The Politics of France's Subtraction of Obedience from Pope Benedict XIII, July 27, 1398," *Proceedings of the American Philosophical Society* 115 (1971): 366–96.
4. The Armagnac faction got its name from Charles d'Orléans's father-in-law, the Count of Armagnac.
5. On Christine's different conceptions of who the true enemy of France was see R. Blumenfeld-Kosinski, "'Enemies Within/Enemies Without: Threats to the Body Politic in Christine de Pizan," *Medievalia et Humanistica* n.s. 26 (1999): 1–15.
6. The genre of the "mirror of princes," a didactic handbook focusing on the education of the ruler and the qualities necessary for good government, was already well established at this time. On Christine's "conversion" to more serious subject matter and the beginning of her political engagement see Joël Blanchard, "L'entrée du poète dans le champ politique au XVe siècle," *Annales E.S.C.* 41 (1986): 43–61; and "Christine de Pizan: les raisons de l'histoire," *Le Moyen Age* 92 (1986): 417–36.
7. See Sandra Hindman, *Christine de Pizan's 'Epistre d'Othéa': Painting and Politics at the Court of Charles VI* (Toronto: Pontifical Institute of Mediaeval Studies, 1986).

8. On the Dantean echoes of the mimesis of history and the involvement of the self, see Kevin Brownlee, "The Image of History in Christine de Pizan's *Livre de la Mutacion de Fortune*," in *Contexts: Style and Values in Medieval Art and Literature*, ed. Daniel Poirion and Nancy Freeman Regalado, a special issue of *Yale French Studies* (New Haven: Yale University Press, 1991), 44–56. Universal histories started to be written in French in the early thirteenth century. They usually begin with the creation of the world and often reach into the author's own time, as does the *Mutacion*. But the biting critique of all social strata we find in the *Mutacion* is more characteristic of moral treatises than universal histories.

9. For an excellent analysis of the voice Christine uses in her prose texts see Liliane Dulac, "Authority in the Prose Treaties of Christine de Pizan: The Writer's Discourse and the Prince's Word," in *Politics, Gender, and Genre: The Political Thought of Christine de Pizan*, ed. Margaret Brabant (Boulder: Westview, 1992), 129–40.

10. The author of the *Chronique du Religieux de Saint-Denys* (covering the years 1350–1421) has now been identified as Michel Pintoin. See the preface in the reprinted edition by Bernard Guenée, *Chronique du Religieux de Saint-Denys*, 6 vols., ed. and trans. M.-L. Bellaguet, new ed. (Paris: Editions du Comité des travaux historiques et scientifiques, 1994).

11. Christine Reno, "The Preface to the *Avision-Christine* in ex-Philipps 128," in *Reinterpreting Christine de Pizan,* ed. Earl Jeffrey Richards (Athens: University of Georgia Press, 1990), 207–27, at 212–13.

12. Text quoted from Christine Reno and Liliane Dulac, ed., *Le livre de l'advision Cristine* (Paris: Champion, 2001), 20–21.

13. English translation by Glenda K. McLeod, *Christine's Vision* (New York and London: Garland, 1993), 18.

14. It is interesting that Edouard Perroy in his classic work on the Hundred Years War begins this chapter on Charles V with a reference to Christine's flattering portrayal of the king: "entre autres thuriféraires, il eut la chance de trouver une aimable Italienne, fille d'un de ses médecins, Christine de Pise ou de Pisan, dont la plume louangeuse ne contribua pas peu à auréoler de légende le souvenir de son règne réparateur. Les historiens modernes n'ont pas su se dégager pleinement des touchantes anecdotes, de l'admiration de commande, des pieuses louanges...." See *La Guerre de Cent Ans* (Paris: Gallimard, 1945; reprinted 1971), 119.

15. From 1369 to 1377 (the year of Edward III's death) Charles's armies reconquered all of Aquitaine, except the areas around Bordeaux and Bayonne. On Charles's cultural activities, especially in the area of translation and patronage of literary and political texts, see Chapter 3 by Lori J. Walters in this volume.

16. See Jeannine Quillet, "Sagesse et pouvoir selon *Le Livre des Fais et Bonnes Meurs du sage roi Charles V* de Christine de Pizan," in Quillet, *D'une cité à l'autre: Problèmes de philosophie politique médiévale* (Paris: Champion, 2001); 305–12. Generally on the ideal prince at this time see Jacques Krynen, *Idéal du prince et pouvoir royal en France à la fin du moyen âge (1380–1440)* (Paris: Picard, 1981), and his chapter on "Le métier du roi" in *L'empire du roi: Idées et croyances politiques en France XIIIe-XVe siècle* (Paris: Gallimard, 1993), 167–239. Christine presented her ideas on the education and conduct of

the perfect prince more systematically in the *Livre du corps de policie.* See Kate Langdon Forhan, *The Political Theory of Christine de Pizan* (Burlington, VT: Ashgate, 2001).

17. For a quick overview of Christine's writings on the Schism see Giani Mombello, "Quelques aspects de la pensée politique de Christine de Pisan d'après ses oeuvres publiées," in *Culture et politique en France à l'époque de l'Humanisme et de la Renaissance,* ed. Franco Simone (Turin: Academia delle Scienze, 1974), 43–153, at 74–85.

18. Barbara Wagner makes the interesting argument that the miniatures of the presentation copies, probably produced under Christine's supervision, to a certain extent contradict the text: the popes are shown in a discussion rather than fighting, which seems to suggest that they are meeting in a council. Christine sees her role as that of a mediator, according to Wagner. See "Tradition or Innovation? Research on the Pictorial Tradition of the Miniatures of the *Livre de la Mutacion de Fortune* de Christine de Pizan: The Miniature 'Le Plus Hault Siège,' " in *Contexts and Continuities: Proceedings of the IVth International Colloquium on Christine de Pizan (Glasgow 21–27 July 2000),* 3 vols., ed. Angus J. Kennedy in collaboration with Rosalind Brown-Grant, James C. Laidlaw, and Catherine Müller (Glasgow: Glasgow University Press, 2002), vol. 3, 855–72.

19. On the ups and downs in France's relationship with the Avignonese papacy see Howard Kaminsky, *Simon de Cramaud and the Great Schism* (New Brunswick, NJ: Rutgers University Press, 1983).

20. According to witnesses, the Romans screamed: "Romano, romano! Romano lo volemo o italiano!" (Valois, *La France et le Grand Schisme d'Occident,* 1:39). Christine's account corresponds in most details to what Valois has gleaned from a variety of chronicles. See Valois 1: Chapters 1 and 2. For a dramatic account of the events surrounding the conclave see also Ullmann, *Origins of the Great Schism,* Chapter 1.

21. See Ulmann, *Origins,* 7 and Robert-Henri Bautier, "Aspects politiques du Grand Schisme," in *Genèse et débuts du Grand Schisme d'Occident,* ed. Michel Hayez (Paris: Editions du Centre National de la Recherche Scientique, 1980), 457–81, at 459.

22. See Jean-Louis G. Picherit, *La Métaphore pathologique et thérapeutique à la fin du Moyen Age,* Beihefte zur Zeitschrift für Romanische Philologie 260 (Tübingen: Niemeyer, 1994).

23. On the state of French society at this time and for a fascinating account of Louis d'Orléans's assassination and its aftermath see Guenée, *Un meurtre, une société.*

24. See Perroy, *La Guerre de Cent Ans,* 165–66.

25. See her emotional farewell to the duke, her patron and benefactor, in *Charles V,* Part II, Chapter 1.

26. Gerson (1363–1429) had been Christine's ally in the "Débat sur le *Roman de la Rose.*" Many of his later sermons contain strong warnings about the French civil war. In many ways, Christine's and Gerson's political ideas resemble each other.

27. This debate has been brilliantly studied by Bernard Guenée. See *Un meurtre, une société,* Chapter 10. Of course the question of whether Louis d'Orléans was a tyrant depended on the faction consulted.

28. The original reads "civili et intestino prope simillimum bello, inter parentes natosque, gallicam utramque prolem . . ." (4:324).
29. On this letter see below. The letter can be found in Josette A. Wisman, ed. and trans., *Christine de Pizan. The Epistle of the Prison of Human Life, with an Epistle to the Queen of France and Lament on the Evils of the Civil War* (Garland Library of Medieval Literature, 21A. New York and London: Garland, 1984) 70–83. The quotation is on p. 2.
30. On this text see Margarete Zimmermann, "Vox Femina, Vox Politica: The *Lamentacion sur les maux de La France*," 113–27; Linda Leppig, "The Political Rhetoric of Christine de Pizan: *Lamentacion sur les maux de la guerre civile*"; and Mary McKinley, "The Subversive 'Seulette.' " All three articles appear in *Politics, Gender, and Genre*, ed. Brabant, 113–27, 141–56, and 157–69, respectively.
31. On Isabeau's role during the civil war see Rachel Gibbons, "Les conciliatrices au bas moyen âge: Isabeau de Bavière et la guerre civile," in *La guerre, la violence et les gens au moyen âge*, 2 vols, ed. Philippe Contamine and Olivier Guyotjeannin (Paris: Comité des travaux historiques et scientifiques, 1996): 2:23–33; and on the letter and its imagery Rosalind Brown-Grant, "Les exilées du pouvoir? Christine de Pizan et la femme devant la crise du Moyen Age finissant," in *Apogée et déclin en Europe, 1200–1500*, ed. Claude Thomasset and Michel Zink (Paris: Université de Paris-Sorbonne, 1993), 211–23, especially 218–20.
32. McKinley, "The Subversive 'Seulette,' " 158–59.
33. On Christine's prophetic voice see Andrea Tarnowski, "Le geste prophétique chez Christine de Pizan," in *Apogée et déclin*, 225–36.
34. For context see Berenice A. Carroll, "Christine de Pizan and the Origins of Peace Theory," in *Women Writers and the Early Modern British Political Tradition*, ed. Hilda L. Smith (Cambridge: Cambridge University Press, 1998), 22–39.
35. "In this [text] the pressure of current events is palpable at every instant." Liliane Dulac, "Poétique de l'exemple dans le *Corps de policie*," in *Christine de Pizan 2000*, ed. John Campbell and Nadia Margolis (Amsterdam-Atlanta: Rodopi, 2000), 91–104, at 102.
36. *Le Livre de la paix*, 135–36. For a closer reading of these passages and for a comparison with Gerson's ideas see Blumenfeld-Kosinski, " 'Enemies,' " especially 4–7.
37. Dulac's point that the *exempla* in the *Corps de policie* present a kind of "reflet d'un espoir et une promesse de résurrection" ("Poétique," 103) also seems applicable to the *Livre de la paix*, where, more than in the *Policie*, the ancient past represents a stark contrast to the disastrous present.
38. For a reading of this text and a comparison with Alain Chartier's *Livre des quatre dames*, also written as a response to Agincourt, see R. Blumenfeld-Kosinski, "Two Responses to Agincourt: Alain Chartier's *Livre des quatre dames* and Christine de Pizan's *Epistre de la prison de vie humaine*," in *Contexts and Continuities*, 2002, 75–85.
39. For a close reading of the *Ditié* see Kevin Brownlee, "Structures of Authority in Christine de Pizan's *Ditié de Jehanne d'Arc*," in *The Selected Writings of Christine de Pizan*, ed. R. Blumenfeld-Kosinski (New York: W. W. Norton, 1997), 44–56. Unlike the *Lamentacion*, where the enemy to peace had been the French

themselves, Christine now returns to the idea of the English as the enemy, in part by using identical terms to accuse the two groups. See R. Blumenfeld-Kosinski, " 'Enemies,' " 1–2.

40. In the *Ditié* Christine (in the tradition of Catherine of Siena and Philippe de Mézières) also advocated a crusade that would heal the aftereffects of the Schism and bring all Christians together in one common purpose.

41. Margolis, "Christine de Pizan: The Poetess as Historian," *Journal of the History of Ideas* 47 (1986): 361–75, at 373. On this page Margolis makes an extremely interesting comparison between Christine's and Froissart's accounts of the death of Charles V. She concludes "Froissart concerns himself with surface and sequence, while the poetess of imposed allegory is ever on the lookout for the hidden meaning of a real event."

42. Froissart also wrote verse poems but their subject matter was love and myth, not history. His chronicles are extremely interesting and entertaining, and he himself appears in them, but he does not establish actual parallels between his own fate and that of France.

3

Christine de Pizan as Translator and Voice of the Body Politic

Lori J. Walters

Critics have pointed out that the medieval concept of translation had political and cultural implications. This is an understatement. The term implied a world view, an ideology that was reformulated throughout the Middle Ages.[1] "Translation" and its cognates appear in two main contexts in Christine's works, both related to Charles V, king of France from 1364 to 1380. Charles was responsible for Christine's translation from Italy to Paris and for commissioning the translation of some thirty works from Latin into the French vernacular. Over the course of her career Christine moves from a conception of herself as passive self translated by Charles to that of an active translator by molding herself on the image of the king as translator and on those of the translators he had formed. Christine refines official ideology in order to make a place for herself as female advisor within the system, as well as to redirect the troubled monarchy under Charles's son, nicknamed "le Fol" (the Crazy). In this chapter I will study how Christine establishes her authority as translator and voice of the body politic within a developing ideology that sought to legitimize the royal family, the "nation françoise," and its language, which as early as the mid-twelfth century Chrétien de Troyes had referred to as the "lengue françoise."[2]

A related goal is to show how Christine represents herself as a translator who makes her voice known through the material operations of translation, which are carried out by organs of the human body. The translator first conceives of texts, whether written or oral, in the mind, out of memory, either personal or collective. The mind was equated with the spirit or the heart as the seat of consciousness in the Middle Ages. The translator speaks by means of the lips, mouth, and tongue, and copies words down by hand.[3] In the Middle Ages the concept of voice was tied to sacred models of the Word of God, most particularly to John's Verbum

(1:1), which as substantive and verb, encompassed both the living, oral voice and voice translated into written text.[4] Translation for Christine was an ethical practice based upon the adaptation of scriptural models for use in secular society.

TRANSLATION AND *TRANSLATIO STUDII ET IMPERII*

The semantic field of the term "translation" has narrowed considerably over time. Today it is commonly understood to mean word-for-word translation from one language to the next. That, however, was only one of its original definitions.[5] For our subject, Christine de Pizan, the Latin terms *translatio*, its medieval French equivalent *translacion*, together with its cognate *translater*, had a rich nexus of meaning. Cassel's Latin Dictionary[6] defines *translatio* as a feminine noun signifying a transferring, a handing over, and grafting, when applied to plants.[7] Synonymous with transformation, it came to mean paraphrase, commentary, or even interpretation.[8] In a metaphorical sense, *translatio* could mean translation, trope or figure, or metaphor itself,[9] which Christine, as several later examples will show, ingeniously employs in order to generate images of herself in her reader's inner eye. *Translatio* designated both physical and symbolic transferals, and those transferals more often than not entailed appropriation of one sort or another.[10] Uniting our modern categories of politics, religion, and ethics, the medieval senses of these terms circumscribed a conceptual and ideological grid for viewing existence and human actions.

That grid was best expressed by the theme of *translatio studii et imperii*, the movement of the preferred locus of political power and culture from one country to another. This theme was reformulated many times in Latin and the vernacular throughout the Middle Ages by writers such as Hugh of St. Victor, Otton de Freising, and Chrétien de Troyes in the twelfth century, and Helinant de Froidmont, Vincent de Beauvais, Jean de Meun, and Primat in the thirteenth century.[11] To cite an early statement of the theme in the French vernacular, Chrétien de Troyes, writing in the prologue to his verse romance *Cligés* (ca. 1176), proclaimed that the seat of knowledge (*savoir*, *clergie*) and power (*pouvoir*, *chevalerie*) had moved from Greece to Rome to settle definitively in "France," so long as that country remained worthy of the honor. *Translatio* in time and space was followed by translation of works from one language to another, as Chrétien illustrates by presenting himself, in the same prologue, as the translator of Ovid. Extending far beyond the establishment of word-for-word equivalencies, translation was understood in the Middle Ages as a thorough adaptation, a wholesale rewriting of texts endowed with authority.

The subsequent evolution of the theme of *translatio studii et imperii* would increasingly take its momentum from royal patronage. In the second half of the thirteenth century Jean de Meun developed the concept of the writer-as-translator. In restating the *translatio* in *Le Roman de la Rose*, he posits himself and Guillaume de Lorris as continuators of the tradition of classical love poetry exemplified by Gallus, Catullus, and Ovid. In his adaptation of Boethius's *Consolation of Philosophy*, known as *Li Livres de Confort de Philosophie*, Jean establishes his authority to undertake the present work by citing his prior works in a list headed by the *Rose* and followed by several texts he refers to as translations. Rita Copeland, in her groundbreaking look at the role of translation in the emergence of vernacular literary culture in the Middle Ages, shows how Jean situates himself "within a political culture that defines itself through vernacularity."[12] In dedicating his translation of Boethius to Philip IV the Fair, the descendant of Philip Augustus and Saint Louis, Jean transfers "possession of the wisdom of the ancients from the center of intellectual power, the university, to the center of French political power, the court of Philippe IV, 'roy des François.'"

Charles V was a dominant player in the evolution of the *translatio*. During his reign, in Copeland's words "the emergent power of the French language as a medium of *translatio studii*" authorized itself "through a material identification with royal power." The *translatio* statement in the prologue to *Les Grandes Chroniques de France* (*GCF*) had special pertinence for Charles V.[13] This work was a vernacular prose history kept by the monks of the royal abbey of Saint-Denis beginning in the 1270s. Louis IX (reigned 1226–1270) had initiated the composition of the *GCF* by having a monk named Primat adapt existing Latin chronicles into the vernacular. Primat presented the first copy to Louis's pious son and successor, King Philip III the Bold, in 1274.[14] The monks of Saint-Denis continued composing these royal chronicles well into the early fourteenth century. Charles V had his own copy of the *GCF* updated at court to legitimize his image as monarch in the new Valois dynasty.

In his prologue, Primat explains that God had given France an advantage over all other countries because it was the most faithful defender of the Christian faith.[15] The first reason he gives is that the faith was guaranteed by Saint Denis, the glorious martyr and apostle who had first converted France to Christianity. The second is that the *fountain of clergie* (learning, culture), by which Holy Church is maintained, flourishes in Paris. Although his statement of the displacement of culture and political power from Greece to Rome and then to France closely resembles Chrétien's, Primat introduces a significant change by recasting it in prose, increasingly identified with truth beginning in the mid-thirteenth century. Unlike Chrétien, he clearly associates the concept of *translatio* with the French monarchy as God's representative on earth whose legitimacy is guaranteed by association with Saint Denis, the inspired proselytizer and patron saint of France.

The medieval *translatio studii et imperii* had ethical underpinnings, since loss of favored country status was seen to come about as punishment for sin.[16] Aristotle's *Politics* and *Ethics*, known in the translations undertaken by Nicole Oresme at the request of Charles V, tied good governance to the virtues of the ruler.

Another translation undertaken at Charles's bidding, the Franciscan Denis Foulechat's adaptation of John of Salisbury's *Policraticus*,[17] insists upon the ethical basis of *translatio*. By quoting Ecclesiastes in IV. xii to say that kingdoms lose their right to rule because of deceit and other misuses of their power, John and his Middle French translator ground the *translatio* in scriptural authority. Christine allies herself with that same authority when in the *Chemin de long estude* of 1403 she cites the *Policraticus* to say that the Persians destroyed themselves "pour de luxure le peché" (because of sexual sin, v. 4382). In terms of the medieval "master" narrative, *translatio* was the result of Original Sin, since God the Father expulsed Adam and Eve from the garden because they had ignored his injunction not to eat of the forbidden fruit. *Translatio* (diaspora, dispersal, migration) was a direct consequence of the Fall. Christians yearned to return to the unity of language before the breakup and dispersal signified by Babel. The impetus to "translate" expressed the desire to return to the point of intersection between the human and the divine, as well as the realization that in the here and now humans are condemned to translate and to adapt themselves to new contexts.

It is in Christine's prose biography of the king, *Le Livre des fais et bonnes meurs du sage roi Charles V* (hereafter *Charles V*)[18] that she herself most clearly enunciates the theme of the *translatio studii et imperii*. In III.xiii Christine exposes the basis for Charles's *translatio studii* in Charlemagne's relationship with Alcuin, who "fist translater les estudes des sciences de Romme à Paris" (had the study of sciences translated from Rome to Paris) for Charles's ninth-century forerunner and namesake. In *Charles V*, I.v Christine approaches the theme in a more general way. When she prefaces her remarks by saying she is supporting the noble lineage of the kings of France, she echoes Primat's stated purpose of establishing once and for all the genealogy of those same kings. She draws many of her details of the *translatio* from the *GCF*. Invoking memory of the Romans who "se translaterent en la terre de Gaule, que ilz appellerent France" (transported themselves into the land of Gaulle, which they called France), Christine places herself and her country at a crucial point in the moving spiral of generations:

> Ainsi fu le commencement de *celle noble nacion françoise* couronné d'ancienne noblece, laquelle [Dieux mercis!], d'oir en hoir, est continuée, maulgré les flots de la descorable Fortune jusques cy en amendent en bien.

(Thus was the beginning of *this noble French nation* crowned with ancient nobility, which—thanks be to God!—from one inheritor to the next, has continued, despite the contrary movements of inconstant Fortune, to grow in goodness [my emphasis], *Charles V*, I.v.)

Christine here calls upon her readers to grasp God's transcendent purpose for France behind the workings of inconstant Fortune, the divine logic behind the mutations of persons, countries, and language. Sublunary shape-shifting reflects "as through a glass darkly" (I Corinthians 13) the perfect forms of the Incarnation and the ritualistic imitation of this mystery in the miracle of transubstantiation celebrated in the Mass. Christine connects the monarchy with these higher truths when, at the conclusion of her biography (III.lxxi), she has the dying Charles contrast the royal crown with the more glorious crown of thorns that Saint Louis had brought to France. By evoking the image of the crown of thorns worn by Christ at the Crucifixion, King Charles and Christine, his loyal subject and spokesperson, enlist the mystery of the Incarnation to affirm their belief in the ultimate success of the monarchy despite reversals, however dire these might appear (and it would be difficult to find setbacks more serious than the Crucifixion and Saint Louis's death on his failed second Crusade).

FROM TRANSLATED SELF TO TRANSLATOR

Before turning to Christine's use of the body politic metaphor, let us examine her evolution from passive self transported to Paris by Charles to active translator like Charles, who like all other Christian kings represents the image of Christ on earth. In many of her early verse works, written upon command from court patrons, Christine inscribes her name in anagrams marked by recurrent statements of fear. She signs herself "Creintis" (fearful) in *Epistre au dieu d'Amours*, dated May 1, 1399, and in *Dit de Poissy*, dated April 1400. In *Dit de la Rose* of 1402 her play on the letters "cri" in her name is a cry of desperation, the cry of someone whose voice is being stifled.[19] Christine frees her voice from its symbolic imprisonment by learning to translate her name. This entails understanding its true significance for the role that she wishes to assume as spokesperson for the monarchy instead of the role of writer of light verse that the court wishes to impose upon her.[20] In *Mutacion de Fortune* of 1403 Christine realizes the sacred potential latent in her use of the first-person: the relationship between herself and Christ inherent in her name,[21] which she glosses as the name of the most perfect man, Christ, with "INE" added (ll. 371–78). The French suffix indicates that she was "derived from" Christ.[22] In *Mutacion* Christine comes to the realization that the unhappy facts of her life, ostensibly the effects of ever-mutable Fortune, were actually the manifestation of God's will working itself out in human affairs.

When Christine learns to translate her name, or when she abbreviates her name in her manuscripts as the Greek cross + ine, she draws parallels between her destiny as a figure of Christ and Christ's own destiny as a fact of language.[23] This theme recurs with great frequency in the gospels ascribed to John: God is the divine Verbum, at once noun and verb, being and activity; the universe is a language game in which God codes and humans decode, a hermeneutical conundrum of concealing and revealing (John 1:1); the events of Christ's life and passion were but a working out of the already scripted (John 19:28); God is the Alpha and the Omega, the beginning and the end (repeated three times, in

Revelation 1:8, 21:5, 22:13). Christine's Christian name, given to her by her parents, confirmed by baptism, and guaranteed by the name of her patron saint (significantly *sainte patronne* or holy exemplar) provided her with the means to her own personal salvation, as well as her country's. It is as if the divine will had written itself out on the text of her lowly physical self, as if God had subjected her to undeserved trials so that she could interpret them as a recasting of Christ's own undeserved sufferings. Through her divinely ordained mission on earth, revealed to through misfortunes that forced her, as we would say, to "man" the ship of fate by interpreting her life story, Christine was to become her country's official spokesperson and intercessor among God, the monarch, and the French people.

Between 1403 and 1405 Christine progressively changed her outlook from that of a passive self who had been worked upon by exterior forces into an active translator of herself, of books, and of ideologies.[24] During that short period Christine produced an astonishing number of long and complex works in which "autobiography" serves ends beyond itself.[25] Christine does not yet name herself in the *Chemin* of 1403, but she begins to describe Charles V's translation campaign to her readers by stressing the moral and educational function of translation, which exists "Pour les cuers des François attraire/A nobles meurs par bon exemple" (to attract the hearts of the French/To noble conduct through good example, ll. 5024–25). Like Charles who governs through example, Christine will increasingly become a living example to her readers in works with a political import. The function of "autobiography" for Christine can be summed up as follows: applying Charles's precepts for translating authoritative Latin works to her own life, Christine treats her unhappy past as a letter to be glossed, corresponding to the literal level of events in the Bible, which are to be mined for their many levels of meaning. Her name, given to her at baptism, becomes a sign and a prophecy of her destiny, which is to be a translator. She raises a fortuitous happening, her naming in the Christian faith, to the level of Christian predestination, an event that she reads as typology. She becames, as it were, a living letter, an image of John's Verbum as voice-in-action.[26]

The force of Christine's demonstration that she had understood the enduring lessons behind the transitory events of history—both hers and her country's—was not lost on her noble addressees. Christine received the commission from Philip the Bold to compose the biography of his brother Charles V, deceased twenty-four years previously, largely because she had proven her value as a political advisor in *Mutacion*.[27] In *Charles V* Christine establishes the king as the ideal spiritual and intellectual leader for France. In writing her biography, Christine was attempting to circumvent the instability of Charles VI's reign by focusing on and even embellishing his father's more successful reign; she hoped that her work would inspire leaders to follow the father's example rather than his son's. To be successful at this, she aligned herself and Charles V with the "ideology of France," as set forth in the *GCF* and in the works that Charles had translated. In her biography, Christine takes care to project an image of Charles that complemented those perpetuated by the chroniclers of Saint Denis and by Charles's translators.

Christine represents the king as the consummate human translator, who mirrors God the Father's function as divine translator. Charles initiated physical and symbolic transferals and fostered literary translation. In *Charles V*, Christine tells how the king had her father summoned to Paris because of Tommaso's reputation in speculative sciences and as astronomer "par lequel commandement et volenté fu puis ma mere, avec ses enfens, et moy, sa fille, translatez en ce reaume, si comme encore est sceu par mains vivans" (by whose command and wish was my mother, with her children, and myself, her daughter, transported in this kingdom, as it is still known by many people still living, I.xv). Charles's verbal summons of Tommaso was by that same act responsible for Christine's displacement from Italy to Paris.

Charles was not only the agent who had translated Christine and her family from Italy to Paris by his verbal command, he was also the one who carried out an extensive translation campaign in order to strengthen the monarchy. According to Kate Forhan, Charles V originated the idea of "mediated monarchy"[28] by solliciting the advice of a hand-picked board of counselors whom he kept well versed in political theory through the knowledge imparted through the translations he commissioned. In *Charles V* ("Cy dit comment le roy Charles amoit livres, et des belles translacions, qu'il fist faire," Here it is said how king Charles loved books, and about the beautiful translations that he had made, III. xii), Christine lists the ten "plus notables livres" (most noteworthy books) that the king had adapted into the vernacular. Of these works, two are by Saint Augustine, and his *Cité de Dieu* heads the list (in the translation by the unnamed Raoul de Presles, whose identity is nonetheless suggested by the French title). The three other works in the top five are by Aristotle, and all three were translated by Nicole Oresme, who supervised the production of the manuscripts of these translations down to their minute physical details.[29] Serge Lusignan views Oresme as the major theoretician of Charles V's revamping of the *translatio studii* as a philosophy of culture whose underlying principles had political implications. In Lusignan's words, "l'union de *clergie* et de *chevalerie* se hisse au niveau d'une politique pensée et réfléchie."[30] Lusignan believes moreover that Oresme played a capital role in the rethinking of the *translatio* by recognizing that for the Romans Latin had originally been a living vernacular, rather than an ossified language of erudition. This realization exploded the entrenched opposition between Latin, learned by rule, and French, learned without rules and by imitation of others' speech.[31]

Even as she constructs an idealized image of Charles that complements the ones that he perpetuated in the *GCF* and in the translations made at his request, Christine patterns her role as translator on the example set by her patron, the "*patron*" (model, in the French sense) of the body politic.[32] Although she must have originally been called "Cristina da Pizzano," she never refers to herself by that name.[33] As she tells us in *Advision Cristine* of 1405, at the height of her financial difficulties she turned down a chance to reassume her original Italian identity by refusing a lucrative offer to go into the service of the Duke of Milan, Giangaleazzo Visconti (III.xii). Instead of returning to her native land, Christine constructs an alternate adoptive French lineage for herself, in which she is the French child of an Italian father transplanted to France by the voice of the French sovereign, Charles V.

The ways in which Christine casts herself into the role of translator on Charles's example can become quite complicated, as the following case illustrates. Among the twenty of Charles's translations that Christine does not name but lumps together with the phrase "un tres grant foison d'aultres" (a great abundance of others) is Petrarch's *De remediis utriusque fortunae*, completed in 1377 by Jean Daudin. In her *Cité* II.7.1 Christine does a paraphrase, complete with mention of Petrarch's name, of a passage from this work greatly indebted to Daudin's Middle French adaptation. In so doing, Christine appropriates Petrarch, an Italian writing in Latin, for her very own, and very French purposes.[34] Claire Richter Sherman speculates that Charles V commissioned the translation of the *De remediis* to compensate for Petrarch's failure to deliver a scheduled talk on Fortune to the French court in 1361. She also believes that Petrarch's devotion to Saint Augustine's *Civitas Dei* may have incited Charles to order Raoul's adaptation of the text.[35] If Christine in her *Cité des dames*, her feminized reformulation of the *Civitas Dei*,[36] projects herself in a limited fashion as Petrarch's literary daughter who preferred to be adopted by the French rather than to return to her native Italy, she does it by following the lead of her "*patron*," her French spiritual and intellectual stepfather, Charles V. The *Mutacion de Fortune* can be seen as Christine's response to Charles's wish to have Italian humanist wisdom concerning Fortune disseminated in Paris.

Christine also casts herself into the role of translator by imitating many of the techniques of Charles's translators. This becomes most evident when she adapts Biblical materials. Christine perpetuates the tradition, begun by Charles, of having Latin texts translated into the vernacular on the pattern of the three levels of Biblical exegesis: text, text and gloss, and allegorized commentary ("*alegorisée*," *Charles V*, III.xii). Rather than theological controversy, these translations encouraged preaching, prayer, and lay piety—the constitutive elements of what has been called the "royal religion." The Biblical books most often translated or adapted as poetry were the Psalms of David, which Marc Fumaroli calls "the great spiritual text of the royal religion," which had more to do with the "devotion of the heart than with religious doctrine."[37]

Christine creates her own glossed version of the Psalms in her *Sept psaumes allegorisés* of 1409, whose title, which includes the term "*allegorisés*,"[38] indicates that she is patterning her own work as translator on Charles's prescriptions for producing vernacular translations. In her allegorized version of the seven penitential psalms, Christine in effect ventriloquizes the Old Testament patriarch David, the purported author of the psalms, to have him speak French to influence her patron, Charles III the Noble, King of Navarre from 1385 to 1425, to remain neutral in the disputes between Armagnac and Burgundian factions. (Although Charles the Noble appears to have heeded her advice, civil conflict nonetheless broke out soon afterward.) One of her last writings, *Heures de contemplacion sur la Passion de Nostre Seigneur* (ca. 1420–1424), sole among her works to be presented as a translation from Latin,[39] borrows the form of a devotional Book of Hours. In this meditation on Christ's passion addressed to women for all that they have suffered over the course of history, Christine turns her women readers, along with herself, into figures of the suffering Christ and his grieving mother.[40]

CHRISTINE AS EMBODIED VERNACULAR VOICE

Christine's interpretative reading of her name and of her life story in *Mutacion* is accompanied by a change in her voice. Christine's gender change from woman to man, her own personal *translatio*, involves a mutation of her voice into a male one.[41] Her voice is "forment engrossie" (v. 1350), "much stronger" or "lowered," like a man's. The term "engrossie" nonetheless has decidedly female connotations, implying that her voice is pregnant with new strength and meaning. When we see Christine again at the beginning of *Cité des dames*, she has been restored to her female form. Because of her symbolic two-way metamorphosis from woman to man and back again, she has been born anew, with a voice that has acquired the authority of the male tradition *and* that lives in a female body that speaks with the authority of her own lived experience.

Christine uses male and female sacred models to raise the status of her embodied voice. Mary, the mother of Christ, is a favorite. Christine introduces her biography of the Wise King Charles by repeating the first words of the Hours of the Virgin:

> Sire Dieux, euvre mes *levres*, enlumines ma pensée, et mon entendement esclaires à celle fin que m'ignorance n'encombre mes sens à expliquer *les choses conceues en ma memoire*, et soit *mon commencement, moyen et fin* à la louenge de toy, souveraine poissance et digneté incirconscriptible, à sens humain non comprenable!

(Lord God, open my *lips*, enlighten my thought, and clear up my understanding so that my ignorance does not prevent my senses from explaining *the things conceived in my memory*, and let *my beginning, middle and end* be for the praise of you, sovereign power and uncircumscribable dignity, incomprehensible to the human mind! [my emphasis].)[42] So saying, Christine becomes a second Mary who invokes God to open her lips and illuminate her understanding. She represents the work to come as a body that will be born from "things conceived" in her memory, her imagery evoking a womb. Christine's metaphoric "child born of memory" conflates herself and her written text. While constructing an exemplary image of Charles to guide present and future rulers, she correspondingly generates a second version of herself, based upon her real person but separate from it, that legitimizes her role as counselor for the monarchy.

Whereas in *Charles V* she represents herself as a new Mary whose prayers help her to construct ideals of wisdom and eloquence for rulers and their royal advisors, Christine in other works likens herself to a voice that is called upon to substitute for the royal tongue of Charles VI, Charles's ineffectual son. The official function of the king's voice was to dictate the will of God on earth. The king traditionally stands for the head of the body politic and more specifically its tongue. Fumaroli describes the language of Ile-de-France as the king's tongue, "the Living Word from which the kingdom sprang":

> The French of Ile-de-France was numbered among the sacred attributes of the crown, along with the abbey-cemetery of Saint-Denis, the relics of the Sainte-Chapelle, the lilies of the French coat of arms, and the scepter and holy ampulla of the anointing ritual at Reims. A Nation-Church, France was built around a King-Word, a King-Christ, whose tongue sang praises, issued ordinance and edicts, and assembled his loyal subjects.[43]

The royal tongue of Christine's time was more often than not ailing and inarticulate. The reign of Charles VI, which extended from 1380 to 1422, was destabilized by the king's intermittent bouts of madness beginning in 1392, which culminated in his complete mental breakdown in 1415. Christine frequently depicts herself as a voice and a tongue (Latin *glossa*) who feels constrained to give or ask for help because the king's own voice is not functioning properly.[44]

In the third and final part of the *Cité des dames* Christine represents herself as a sacred tongue authorized to complement or substitute for the king's tongue. In III.10 she recounts the story of Saint Christine,[45] her patron saint on whom she patterns her own rise to the semisacred function of interpreter of God's will to the monarchy. Even when her persecutors cut the saint's tongue out by the root, it continued to reproach them. The tongue that continues to speak even when severed from the body is known as the "lingua palpitans" (palpitating tongue).[46] This disembodied tongue is another form of the Pentecostal tongue of the evangelists, who could go out and proselytize all nations, speaking to each in their own language. Christine bases her version of her patron saint's story upon the *Miroir historial*, the vernacular adaptation of Vincent de Beauvais's *Speculum historial* by Jean de Vignay, one of Charles's translators.[47] The holy-tongued saint and her fifteenth-century avatar, Christine, symbolically anchor the French monarchy's concerted program of translation of Latin texts into the vernacular.

By personifying herself as a female tongue, Christine couples it with Saint Denis's male tongue, thereby associating herself and her message with its symbolic resonances. She glorifies the tongue of her patron saint in order to establish herself as a female counterpart to Saint Denis. One of the two miraculous events associated with the saint's legend was that his severed head and its "lingua palpitans" continued to sing the Lord's praises.[48] Saint Denis was patron saint and proselytizer of France, and his relics sanctified the royal abbey and necropolis.[49] Christine's tongue becomes a living relic which, along with the other symbols mentioned by Fumaroli, reinforces the positive evolution of the *noble nacion françoise* despite momentary reversals by Fortune.

If, as synecdoche for the body, Christine's tongue is sacred, so also is her entire body. Christine develops the notion of the king's two bodies, the ideological principle that the king had two bodies, a natural one and a political one. The latter, called the body politic, was identified with the king's semisacred office and invested with great symbolic meaning.[50] By interpreting her name in the *Mutacion* as that of Christ with -ine added, Christine posits for herself a second symbolic identity. When in *Charles V* Christine constructs an ideal image of the king from the facts of Charles's life, turning even the king's royal weaknesses into strengths, she also leaves behind an image of herself as a wise and eloquent advisor worthy of her mentor. By redefining herself as femininized version of Christ, Christine creates a place for herself as the feminine counterpart of the king who is the representative of Christ on earth. Christine gives herself, the king's advisor, two bodies, as a fitting complement to the king's twin self in legitimacy and power.

Christine identifies her second, official body with the body politic. This is evident from the opening lines of her *Corps de policie* of 1406–1407:

> Se il est possible que *de vice puist naistre vertu*, bien me plaist en ceste partie estre *passionnee comme femme*. Ainsi que plusieurs hommes au sexe femenin imposent non savoir taire ne tenir soubz silence l'abondance de leur *courage*, or viengne donc hors hardiement et se demonstre par plusieurs clers ruisseaux la source et fontaine interissable de mon *couraige* qui ne peut estanchier de getter hors les desirs de vertu. O vertu, chose digne et deifiee, comment m'ose-je vanter de parler de toy, quant je congnois que mon entendement ne te sauroit bien au vif comprendre ne exprimer?

(If it is possible *for vice to give birth to virtue*, it pleases me in this part to be *as passionate as a woman*. Since many men assume that members of the female sex do not know how to silence the abundance of their *courage*, let it [the abundance] come forth boldly, then, and show by several clear streams the source and inexhausible fountain of my *courage*, which cannot be stanched when it expresses the desire for virtue. Oh, Virtue, noble and godly, how can I dare boast of speaking about you, when I know that my understanding can neither comprehend nor express you well [my emphasis]?)[51]

We would usually expect to encounter the male body that typically represents the body politic, and to hear a male voice addressing us; just as John of Salisbury appears in the prologue to his *Policraticus*, the founding text in the medieval body politic tradition, to tell us about his role as philosopher-advisor to Henry II, king of England from 1154 to 1189. Instead, we discover a female voice who speaks of the work she will produce using female bodily metaphors. Christine evokes the image of her passionate heart spouting streams of blood that cannot be stanched[52] by her repetition of the Middle French term "courage," whose root signifies the heart, the organ identified as the seat of consciousness. Because the heart was a synecdoche for the entire body,[53] Christine metaphorically offers her own passionate body, the body that produced the voice we hear and that will be embodied in the collection of virtuous advice to come, as evidence that woman's body is not the source of vice it is commonly claimed to be. The concrete proof of her virtue is palpably present to readers, whether male or female, in the book they see or hold in their hands, or in the voice that reads the text to them in a public reading. Christine creates a second and eminently virtuous body through the experience of reading her text. If her birth imagery makes us think of a maternal body bloodied by childbearing, Christine's second body with its bleeding heart also recalls mystical devotion of the heart associated with Jesus. Through a clever turn of metaphor, Christine suggests that her body, labeled as evil by antifeminists, more rightly has similarities with the bodies of Mary and of Christ, who sacrificed himself for humanity's salvation and instruction. Christine's bountifully bleeding heart attains some of the force of the image of Christ's crucified body with blood streaming forth from his wounds. This was one of the most common images reproduced in visual media throughout medieval Europe.

Through adroit manipulation of the first-person and of metaphor, Christine establishes her authority on two different, but complementary, levels. As a historical person having a real body, she is able to testify to the truth of her first-person, female experience in the world. As a symbolic person having a semimystical body combining male and female characteristics, she can speak for the commonweal as the king's advisor. Her tongue acquires the status of a living relic capable of perpetuating the idea of France as do other enduring symbols of royalty like the fleur-de-lis and the crown. So closely does Christine associate her second self with the corporate civic body that she seems to become the very voice of the body politic, both during her lifetime and afterward. In a famous passage at the conclusion of Part II of *Advision*, Christine expresses the hope that future princes will benefit from the advice she leaves behind in her volumes.[54]

Symbolically incarnate in her manuscripts, Christine's voice is able to survive the demise of her physical body. Because of her books, many of which were produced under her supervision, some of which she executed in whole or in part herself, her vernacular voice will continue to speak and to shape the French "*nacion*" in the manner of the *GCF* and the relics of Saint Denis. Christine's writerly service to the nascent nation-state resembles Primat's because it deals with all the mundane details of administration (which she treats in detail in *Charles V*) that for practical reasons are conducted in the vernacular. Christine, like Primat, is proud to exercise her functions as civil servant, a position honored with particular reverence in the French establishment to the present day. Like his, her use of the vernacular goes beyond the practical to join the mystical, whereby human translators are transformed into the traces left by their voices and hands on the pages of their manuscripts. These eucharistic "text relics,"[55] rendered in the lowly bread of the vernacular, invested the royal religion of the time with a broadly based legitimacy. The manuscripts that survive the physical death of their human authors—Primat's *GCF* and Christine's entire textual corpus—remain as articulate witnesses to,[56] and powerful shapers of, a developing national entity whose definition and very lifeblood was, and continues to be, "translated" through its language.

NOTES

1. To quote Ernst Robert Curtius, *European Literature and the Latin Middle Ages*, trans. Willard R. Trask (Princeton: Princeton University Press, 1973), 29: "the concept of *translatio* . . . is basic for medieval historical theory."
2. *Le Chevalier de la Charrette (The Knight of the Cart)*, ed. Mario Roques (Paris: Champion, 1981), 1.40. On ideology, see Colette Beaune, *The Birth of an Ideology: Myths and Symbols of Nation in Late Medieval France*, ed. E. Fredric L. Cheyette, trans. Susan Ross Huston (Berkeley: University of California Press, 1991). On the role of language in defining French cultural identity, see Marc Fumaroli, "The Genius of the French Language," in *Realms of Memory: The Construction of the French Past*, ed. Lawrence D. Kritzman, trans. Arthur Goldhammer (New York: Columbia University Press, 1996), Vol. 3: *Symbols*, 555–606.
3. The image of the translator as Divine Scribe is implicit in *Charles V*, III.xii, where Christine develops the analogy between Charles and Ptolémée Philadelphe, the Egyptian king who had "la loi de Dieu escripte de son doy" (the law that God had written with his finger) translated from Hebrew to Greek by a team of seventy-two wise men (who, if Saint Augustine is to be believed, all arrived at the exact same translation!).
4. See Paul Zumthor, *La Lettre et La Voix de la Littérature Médiévale* (Paris: Seuil, 1987): "L'idée, profondément ancrée dans les mentalités d'alors, de la puissance réelle de la parole engendre une vue morale de l'univers," 83. See also A. J. Minnis, *Medieval Theory of Authorship: Scholastic Literary Attitudes in the Later Middle Ages* (Aldershot: Wildwood House, 1988), for scriptural models employed by secular authors.
5. See Lori J. Walters, "*Translatio Studii*: Christine de Pizan's Self-Portrayal in Two Lyric Poems and in the *Livre de la mutacion de Fortune*," in *Christine de Pizan and Medieval French Lyric*, ed. Earl Jeffrey Richards (Gainesville: University Press of Florida, 1998), 155–65, with accompanying bibliography, 165–67.
6. New York: Macmillan, 1959, 612.

7. For a discussion of how Christine uses the plant-and-graft metaphor, see Lori J. Walters, "The Royal Vernacular: Poet and Patron in *Charles V* and *Les Sept Psaumes allégorisés*," in *The Vernacular Spirit*, ed. Renate Blumenfeld-Kosinski, Duncan Robertson, and Nancy Warren (NY: Palgrave, 2002), 145–182 (150–153).
8. Rita Copeland, *Rhetoric, Hermeneutics, and Translation in the Middle Ages: Academic Traditions and Vernacular Texts* (Cambridge: Cambridge University Press, 1991), 22, 88–92.
9. See Douglas Kelly, *The Conspiracy of Allusion: Description, Rewriting, and Authorship from Macrobius to Medieval Romance* (Leiden: Brill, 1999), for a discussion of cognates of the term *mutation*. *Mutatio* included the principal operations involved in rewriting, i.e., invention, disposition, addition, substitution (*immutatio*), and transposition (*transmutatio*). *Mutatio* was the lifting of source material (either actual subject matter or a theme or motif that will serve as a model for rewriting) that would be used in the new work.
10. Serge Lusignan, "Nicole Oresme traducteur et la pensée de la langue française savante," in *Tradition et innovation chez un intellectuel du XIVème siècle*, ed. P. Souffrin and A. Ph. Segonds (Paris: Les Belles Lettres, 1988), 93–104 (97). See the articles on translation in *The Idea of the Vernacular: An Anthology of Middle English Literary Theory, 1280–1520*, ed. Jocelyn Wogan-Browne et al. (University Park: Pennsylvania State University Press, 1999).
11. See A. G. Jonkees, "*Translatio Studii*: les avatars d'un thème médiéval," in *Miscellanea Mediaevalia in memoriam Jan Frederik Niermeyer* (Groningen, The Netherlands: J. B. Walters, 1967), 41–52. Jonkees emphasizes Chrétien's key part in expressing the theme.
12. All quotations are from Copeland, *Rhetoric*, 135. Copeland gives the text and an English translation of Jean's prologue, 133–34.
13. The *GCF* are a major source for both *Charles V* and the *Advision*. *Le Livre des fais et bonnes meurs du sage roy Charles V*, ed. Suzanne Solente, 2 vols. (Paris: honoré Champion, 1936, 1940), I. xli; *Le Livre de l'Advision-Cristine*, ed. Christine Reno and Liliane Dulac (Paris: Champion, 2000), xxxvii–xxxviii. Christine in fact acknowledges that the *GCF* furnished background information for two of the episodes of *Charles V* (I.xxxii; III.lii). Echoes of the *GCF* in her work can be discerned as early as the *Cent Ballades* and the *Autres Ballades*. See Anne D. Hedeman, *The Royal Image. Illustrations of the 'Grandes Chroniques de France', 1274–1422* (Berkeley: University of California Press, 1991), for background information on the *GCF*.
14. See Lori J. Walters, "Constructing Reputations: *Fama* and Memory in Christine de Pizan's *Charles V* and *L'Advision-Cristine*," in *FAMA: The Politics of Talk and Reputation in Medieval Europe*, ed. Daniel L. Smail and Thelma Fenster (Ithaca, NY: Cornell University Press, forthcoming), and "The Royal Vernacular," for further discussion of Christine and the *GCF*.
15. Jules Viard, ed., *Les Grandes Chroniques de France*, 10 vols. (Paris: Honoré Champion, 1920–53), I:5.
16. Curtius, *European Literature*, 29.
17. See Eric Hicks, "A Mirror for Misogynists: John of Salisbury's *Policraticus* (8.11) in the Translation of Denis Foulechat (1372)," in *Reinterpreting Christine*

de Pizan, ed. Earl Jeffrey Richards, with Joan Williamson, Nadia Margolis, and Christine Reno (Athens: University of Georgia Press, 1992), 77–107.

18. I justify this abbreviated title because, for Christine, the biography represented Charles's textual and symbolic body. All translations from this text and other primary sources are my own unless otherwise indicated.

19. See Claire Nouvet, "Writing in Fear," *Gender and Text in the Later Middle Ages*, ed. Jane Chance (Gainesville: University Press of Florida, 1996), 279–305, and Andrea Tarnowski, introduction to her edition/translation of *Le Chemin de longue étude* (Paris: Livre de Poche, 2000), 25.

20. See Lori J. Walters, "Chivalry and the (En)Gendered Poetic Self: Petrarchan Models in the *Cent Balades*," in *The City of Scholars: New Approaches to Christine de Pizan*, ed. Margarete Zimmermann and Dina De Rentiis (Berlin and New York: Walter de Gruyter, 1994), 43–66.

21. This was suggested in the riddle with which she signs the *Débat de deux amans* of 1400: "Quel est mon nom, sans le querir planté, / S'il le cercher, trouver le peut enté / En tous les lieux ou est Cristïenté" (ll. 2021–23). Christine here develops the arboreal metaphor implicit in one of the definitions of *translatio*.

22. For Christine's relationship to Christ and the saints, see Lori J. Walters, "Metamorphoses of the Self: Christine de Pizan, the Saint's Life, and Perpetua," in *Sur le chemin de longue étude: Actes du colloque d'Orléans, juillet 1995*, ed. Bernard Ribémont (Paris: Champion, 1998), 159–82. The list of works cited, unintentionally deleted from this article by the publisher, can be reconstructed from the notes in Lori J. Walters, "Fortune's Double Face: Gender and the Transformations of Christine de Pizan, Augustine, and Perpetua," *Fifteenth-Century Studies* 25 (2000): 97–114.

23. The name "Christ" is derived from the tenth-century Latin ecclesiastical name "Christos," itself derived from the Greek "Kristos," the annointed one, a term related to the Hebrew word for "messiah." In Middle French the word "Christ" designated a crucifix as well as the savior's name.

24. See Lori J. Walters, "Constructing Reputations," forthcoming; Mary McKinley, "The Subversive 'Seulette,'" in *Politics, Gender and Genre: The Political Thought of Christine de Pizan*, ed. Margaret Brabant (Boulder: Westview Press, 1992), 157–71; Kate Forhan, *The Political Theory of Christine de Pizan* (Aldershot: Ashgate, 2001), 115.

25. See the reservations about the use of the term "autobiography" expressed by Reno and Dulac: "L'autobiographie n'est donc pas une fin en soi; elle fournit l'occasion et le moyen d'un dépassement exemplaire" (*L'Advision-Cristine*, xvii) and Rosalind Brown-Grant, *Christine de Pizan and The Moral Defence of Women: Reading Beyond Gender* (Cambridge: Cambridge University Press, 1999): "Christine's use of autobiography in this way to inculcate more universal truths is in line with other medieval autobiographical texts" (92); "Christine put her autobiography squarely at the service of her political aims" (93), as well as her remarks, 113–26.

26. See Laura Kendrick, *Animating the Letter: The Figurative Embodiment of Writing from Late Antiquity to the Renaissance* (Columbus: Ohio State University Press, 1999), for representations of Charles V within historiated letters of royal charters, Figs. 84 and 85, 187–88, and her discussion of Charles's translation campaign,

202–5, where she speaks of the translator displacing the original author in illustrations of manuscripts of the translations.
27. *Charles V* was her first large-scale work in prose and the first work in which she signed herself as "Christine de Pizan" since she had assembled and presented the documents in the *Rose* debate to Queen Isabeau de Bavière.
28. Forhan, *The Political Theory*, 95.
29. Claire Richter Sherman, *The Imaging of Aristotle: Visual and Verbal Representation in Fourteenth-Century France* (Berkeley: University of California Press, 1995), 23–33, gives the best summary to date of Charles's translation campaign.
30. "Nicole Oresme traducteur," 93–104, at 103.
31. "La logique de la *translatio studii* et les traductions françaises des textes savants au XIVe siècle," in *Traduction et traducteurs au Moyen Age*, ed. Geneviève Contamine (Paris: Editions du CNRS, 1989), 303–15, (312).
32. Christine may have borrowed the idea from Jean Golein, who along with Raoul de Presles and Nicole Oresme was one of Charles's three most favored translators. In his preface to the *Rational des divins offices* (*Rationale of Divine Offices*) Golein refers to Charlemagne as the "droit patron" of the kings of France. Sherman, *The Imaging*, 8–10.
33. Christine was not the first in her family to undergo a significant transformation at the French court: her father, originally Tommaso di Benvenuto da Pizzano, achieved a new identity there as "Thomas de Pizan." See Lori J. Walters, "Constructing Reputations," forthcoming.
34. Lori J. Walters, "'Translating' Petrarch: *Cité des dames* II.7.1, Jean Daudin, and Vernacular Authority," in *Christine de Pizan 2000: Studies on Christine de Pizan in Honour of Angus J. Kennedy*, ed. John Campbell and Nadia Margolis (Amsterdam: Rodopi, 2000), 283–97.
35. Sherman, *The Imaging*, 8–11.
36. Lori J. Walters, "La réécriture de saint Augustin par Christine de Pizan: De la *Cité de Dieu* à la *Cité des Dames*," *Au Champ des escriptures: Third International Colloquium on Christine de Pizan*, ed. Eric Hicks, with Diego Gonzalez and Philippe Simon (Paris: Champion: 2000), 197–218.
37. "The Genius," Vol. 3: *Symbols*, 562.
38. There is a discrepancy in the way Solente and Rains write this term in their editions of the two works.
39. "Translatee de latin en françois et mis en forme de service de Heures" (translated from Latin into French and presented as a Book of Hours). I thank Liliane Dulac for giving me access to a prepublication version of her forthcoming edition of this text.
40. See Nadia Margolis, "La Progression polémique, spirituelle et personnelle dans les écrits religieux de Christine de Pizan," in *Une Femme de Lettres au Moyen Age*, ed. Liliane Dulac and Bernard Ribémont (Orléans: Paradigme, 1995), 297–316.
41. See Nouvet, "Writing in Fear," 279–305.
42. Solente, *Charles V.* Christine here develops Psalm 50.xvi, the traditional opening of the Hours of the Virgin. See Roger Wieck, *Painted Prayers: The Book of Hours*

Christine de Pizan as Translator and Voice of the Body Politic 41

       in Medieval and Renaissance Art (New York: George Braziller, in association with the Pierpont Morgan Library, 1997), 52.
43. "The Genius," Vol. III: *Symbols*, 560.
44. In her *Lamentacion sur les maux de la France* of 1410, in which she asks Jean de Berry to intervene to stop the warring factions, Christine signs herself as a poor voice crying out in the realm, desirous of peace and of good for the entire country. Christine, like a female John the Baptist, cries out for Jean to intervene in the troubled political events that would soon tear France apart.
45. Kevin Brownlee, "Martyrdom and the Female Voice: Saint Christine in the *Cité des dames*," in *Images of Sainthood*, ed. Renate Blumenfeld-Kosinski and Timia Szell (Ithaca, NY: Cornell University Press, 1991), 115–35.
46. David Williams, *Deformed Discourse: The Function of the Monster in Mediaeval Thought and Literature* (Montreal and Kingston: McGill-Queen's University Press, 1996), 298.
47. He translated Vegetius, one of the authors that Christine lists in *Charles V*, III.xii.
48. Williams, *Deformed Discourse*, 298.
49. Regarding the legend of Saint Denis, see R. Loernetz, "La légende parisienne de Saint Denis l'Aréopagite, sa genèse et son premier témoin," *Analecta Bollandiana* 69 (1951): 217–37.
50. Ernst Kantorowicz, *The King's Two Bodies: A Study in Mediaeval Political Theology* (Princeton: Princeton University Press, 1957), 46–7.
51. The edition is by Angus J. Kennedy (Paris: Champion, 1998); quotation, 1.
52. My study of Christine's use of imagery in this passage does not claim to be exhaustive. Christine's "clear streams," for instance, also evoke tears. Blood and tears come together in the Crucifixion scene when Christ's blood runs clear, announcing his death and the official period of mourning, represented most graphically by the tears of the three Marys.
53. See Eric Jager, *The Book of the Heart* (Chicago: University of Chicago Press, 2000). My study is greatly indebted to Jager's analysis of the analogies among the heart, the self, the relic, and the manuscript book.
54. Opinion says: "Et le temps a venir plus en sera parlé qu'a ton vivant [. . .] aprés ta mort, venra le prince plain de valeur et sagesce qui la relacion de *tes volumes* desirera tes jours avoir esté de son temps et par grant desir souhaidera t'avoir veue" (And in times to come there will be more spoken about it [this work] than during your lifetime [. . .] after your death, a worthy and wise prince will come who will wish that you and what you relate in *your volumes* had been of his time, and he will have a great desire to have seen you, II.xxii, 89–90 [my emphasis].)
55. Hagiographic transmission narratives often describe the text as a relic. Wogan-Browne, ed., *The Idea of the Vernacular*, 7.
56. When in her last extant work, the *Ditié de Jehanne d'Arc*, Christine seemingly raises her hand to say "Je, Christine," she adds her female witness, speaking in the vernacular, to the male vernacular witness of Primat and subsequent Dionysian chroniclers in celebrating the acts of Jeanne d'Arc, a political leader who would soon be recognized as a saint.

4

Somewhere between Destructive Glosses and Chaos

Christine de Pizan and Medieval Theology

Earl Jeffrey Richards

Hitherto scholars have largely tended to qualify Christine de Pizan's knowledge of theology and jurisprudence, areas barred to women, as sketchy and derivative. This consensus is premature and overlooks important evidence to the contrary. For example, Christine's aside during the *Querelle de la Rose* concerning "the common proverb about the glosses of Orléans that destroy the text" paraphrases the opening remarks on the nature of justice in the leading late medieval commentary on Roman law by Bartolo da Sassoferrato found nowhere else in juristic literature. Because Gontier Col did not rush to respond, "which common proverb?," it is fair to assume he knew what Christine meant. If Christine possessed more than a superficial knowledge of medieval jurisprudence,[1] then how much did she know about the restricted field of medieval theology?

Any answer to this question can only be provisional. The first step is to list the kinds of theological materials found in Christine's works. These range from popular hagiographic legends to saints' lives recounted by Vincent de Beauvais, popular Mariology to patristic reflections on the Virgin, including skillful citations from Church Fathers on a variety of topics (many, but by far not all, found in the *Manipulus florum*), mature observations on allegoresis, and skillful treatments of Thomist arguments on gender differences. On first view, the initial evidence consists of the occurrence of a few catchwords (destructive glosses, chaos, living stones, perfect man and true man) that, taken together, are the fragments of a much more extensive and profoundly coherent theological reflection. These catchwords reveal as well a firm grasp of a substantial body of theological—primarily Thomist—thought, and show that her visionary work springs from an intensely intellectual preoccupation with the situation of women. Although she often relied on patristic compilations such as the *Manipulus Florum* of Thomasius Hibernicus, her deployment of arguments from the Fathers shows extensive familiarity and sophistication.[2] Her treatment of mythological materials is indebted to a long tradition of scriptural exegesis. By understanding the original context of Christine's use of theological sources as concretely as possible, we can evaluate more objectively her treatment of many otherwise slippery theological topics, including the concept of being, and understand that the practical goal of enhancing women's position within the Church lies behind what at first glance seems like just so much Scholastic verbiage.[3]

The occurrence of a single but rare word, such as "chaos," points to Christine's familiarity with specific Thomist texts. At the beginning of Christine's *Advision*, a hitherto unknown allegorical figure arises out of the deep with the name "Chaos" written on its forehead. One might assume that Chaos was as well established an allegory as one of the deadly vices. Quite the contrary. As an inspection of the entries in the *Patrologia Latina*, and in the standard medieval Latin lexica (Forcellini, Du Cange, Lehman/Stroux) shows, patristic and medieval Latin writers generally use chaos to mean "chasm" (as in the gulf or *chaos magnum* separating Dives and Lazarus in Luke 16.24). Thomas Aquinas revived the original sense of chaos as primordial confusion (e.g., Ovid, *Metamorphosis*, I.7, *chaos, rudis indigestaque moles*, frequently cited by medieval Latin authors) in connection with the concept of the *poeta theologus*, a term that occurs six times in his works, three times in the *Commentary on the Metaphysics of Aristotle*, a work whose influence on Christine in the *Advision Cristine* has been demonstrated by Liliane Dulac and Christine Reno.[4] Although "chaos" as "confusion" is found in Dante and the *Ovide moralisé*,[5] works that Christine knew, Thomas Aquinas appears to be her source. When she writes in the *Advision*, "les premiers en Grece renommez de science fussent appellez poetes theologisans—ainsi dis poetes, car de ce qu'ilz disoient ilz formoient dictiez et parloient saintement, theologisans aussi, qu'ilz parloient des dieux et des choses divines" (the first in Greece famed in learning were called poet-theologians: poets because they made poems from what they said and spoke in a holy way, and theologians because they spoke of the gods and divine subjects), she is citing Thomas's commentary on Aristotle's *Metaphysics* (*In Metaphysicorum Aristotelis Expositio*, I,4,83): *fuerunt quidam poëtae theologi, sic dicti, quia de divinis carmina faciebant* (there were certain poet-theologians so called because they composed poems about divine matters). This linking of poet-theologians and chaos is more explicit in Thomas's commentary on a passage treating the transformations of physical bodies (*mutationes physicorum corporum*) in Aristotle's *Physics*. Thomas speaks of the opinion of Hesiod as "one of the ancient poet-theologians, who claimed chaos was first created" (*unus de antiquis poetis theologis, qui posuit primo factum esse chaos*, 4.1.nr.9.4). Christine's original allegory of Chaos at the beginning of *Advision* demonstrates that she had defined herself as a poet-theologian following Thomas's explanation.

Christine provides stunning documentation of her extraordinary self-consciousness as a poet-theologian in both the *Epistre Othea* and the prologue to the *Advision*. As Rosemund Tuve noted, Christine is invaluable for understanding late medieval Christian allegory, not only because she "tells us outright how she expects to be read,"[6] but also because her allegorical explanations are tied to illuminations whose execution Christine herself supervised. Christine clearly took her cue from the *Ovide moralisé*, as Gabriella Parussa has forcefully demonstrated.[7] Research on Christine's sophistication as an allegorical writer has barely scratched the surface,[8] and will require detailed comparison of allegory in her work with allegoresis in the *Roman de la Rose*, Dante, and the *Ovide moralisé*, to mention only the most obvious vernacular texts. Such research will demonstrate that Christine's critique of Jean de Meun's use of a non-Christian allegory in the *Rose* is consistent with her own rigorous allegorical practice in the *Epistre Othea*. Any reading of the prologue to Christine's *Advision* must remove any doubts about the rigor of Christine's understanding of allegory. There she gives an extended explanation of the allegory of Chaos, textbook in its presentation and all the more remarkable as it lacks patristic precedent.

The best historical evidence for Christine as a theological thinker comes from Jean Gerson. Writing in the *Montaigne de Contemplation* (April/May 1400), he speaks of an unspecified *femelete* who, forced by illness to retire to her *chambrete*, made good time of her imposed solitude to think about God and herself: "I'ai sceu d'une femelete qui a cause de maladie estoit constrainte per long temps se tenir en une chambre; et une fois en parlant a moy: ie ne scai, dist elle, que ie ferai quant ie perdray ceste chambrete car il n'est aultre lieu ou ie puisse si bien penser en Dieu et en moy[9] (I knew of a little woman who because of illness was constrained for a long time to retire to a room, and once said to me, "I do not know what I will do when I lose this little room for there is no other place where I can think so well about God and myself.") Here *femelete* must refer to Christine because she popularized the term to describe herself, as Nadia Margolis has shown.[10] The *femelette*'s love of the contemplative life matches Christine's celebration of solitude and contemplation at the end of the *Mutacion de Fortune*.[11] In the crucial role of the Virgin in the *Cité des dames*, Christine innovatively connects Gerson's oratorical appeals to the Virgin with a carefully selected compilation of hagiographic materials. Future scholars will need to examine Christine's treatment of hagiographic materials in light of her theological expertise.

Traditionally the saints were the living stones of the Heavenly Jerusalem, and Christine adapts this time-honored metaphor for her virtuous women as living stones of the City of Ladies. Christine's depiction of herself and Reason laying the first stones of the City, well known from the opening illustration of the Queen's Manuscript, seems to borrow from standard illuminations of Psalm 126. Such a readily identifiable allusion reinforces the association of the living women of the City with the living stones of the Heavenly Jerusalem, as described in 1

Peter 2.4–5, "So come to him, our living Stone—the stone rejected by men but choice and precious in the sight of God, and let yourselves be built, as living stones, into a spiritual temple." At least four patristic writers commented on the living stones of the Heavenly Jerusalem, including Hilary of Poitiers, Honoré d'Autun, Bernard of Clairvaux, and Hildegard of Bingen,[12] so Christine was certainly employing a commonplace, but in a profoundly innovative manner. An eighth-century Latin hymn traditionally sung at the vespers of the dedication of a new church expands this concept of living stones. Because Christine recounts the construction of several new convent churches in Paris under Charles V (e.g., St. Anthoine and the Royal Convent of the Célestins, both in the Marais, and St. Pol near the Louvre), she must have heard this hymn frequently. It salutes "the blessed city of Jerusalem called the vision of peace that is built in heaven from living stones" (*Urbs beata Ierusalem dicta pacis visio / quae construitur in caelis vivis ex lapidibus*).[13] The residents of the Heavenly Jerusalem gain entrance to the City *virtute meritorum*, by virtue of their merits, a conventional remark that Christine also adapts as the admission criterion for the women in her City. Christine situates women's virtues in their actions, and recounts their virtues in her recuperation of their concrete history.

Her concern with women's real experiences stems directly from her stance as poet-theologian: in effect she follows the example of Hesiod, always cited in explaining the term *poeta theologus*, in that she proposes what amounts to a female theodicy, a new female-centered universal history of humanity where women's experiences afford the literal sense of the creation itself. The issue here is how Christine interpreted historical experience through a filter of Christian allegoresis. Being a poet-theologian no more restricted Christine from being a political commentator than it had limited Dante, the first vernacular poet to whom the term had actually been applied. The influence of medieval political theology (to use the term most readily associated with the scholarship of Ernst Kantorowicz, Oliver Donovan, and Francis Oakley) is perhaps most evident when Christine describes the death of the French King Charles V, when the monarch ordered that the relic of Christ's Crown of Thorns, used in coronation rites of the French kings, be brought to his death bed or when she celebrates Joan of Arc's historical mission squarely within the greater plan of salvation history.[14] Above all, as Kate Forhan has shown, Christine's extensive political writings are heavily indebted to John of Salisbury and Giles of Rome, especially the tradition of a mirror for princes.[15] Christine's self-conscious cultivation of the position of a poet-theologian, however, helps us explain in part why she ultimately shied away from the question of universal empire in favor of the allegory of her City of Ladies. In other words, the practical and theoretical shortcomings of contemporary schemes of universal empire—certainly obvious to Christine from explicit remarks she makes about the civil unrest in Italian city-states, and from other less overt remarks about the political situation in France and England—seem to have prompted Christine to propose her allegorical City of Ladies as a highly sublimated alternative to a universal empire that could not be realized in human history.

In this light, her decision to select Semiramis as the first stone in the foundation of her City was a highly charged political and theological reaction to the commentary tradition surrounding Semiramis, epitomized by Dante's phrase *libito fé licito* (*Inf.* v.56, roughly, "her lust she made law"), which also went so far as the association of Semiramis with universal empire (found in *De Monarchia*, II.viii.3). Semiramis functions in Christine's City as the cornerstone originally rejected by the builders (Psalms 118.22, Matthew 21.42, Mark 12.10). This first stone of the City had been repudiated by male authors for committing incest with her son, an incest Christine excuses by explaining that it occurred before *written law* forbade it, where the term written law refers to Roman law and to the classic Pauline definition of natural law (Romans 2.14). Thus Christine sees the incestuous Semiramis as a keystone in her foundation, an *angularis fundamentum lapis*, as a type of Christ, rehabilitated in the name of *ius naturale*, to found her allegory of universal empire in the City of Ladies.[16] As an allegorical type of Christ, Semiramis represents in Christine's political theological vision a new christologically sanctioned tradition of queenship.

By presenting herself as a *poeta theologus*, Christine directly answers the question raised in the late thirteenth century by Henry of Ghent whether a woman could be "a doctor or 'doctress' of theology" (*doctor seu doctrix theologie*). Henry of Ghent's query goes back to the Pauline prohibitions on women speaking in church (I Corinthians 14.34–35 and I Timothy 2.11–12), which prompted the claim in canonic law (Decretum C.33 q.8 c.19) that women must cover their heads in church because they were not created in the image of God *(non est imago Dei)*. In the *Mutacion* Christine presents her own transformation into a man as an answer to this decretalist claim.

By showing that she was both woman and man, Christine calls into question the Thomist principle of individuation, to wit, the claim that it was impossible for a single being to possess several substantial forms *(impossible est unius rei esse plures formas substantiales)*.[17] Aquinas's discussion of the body of women, the *corpus mulierum*, especially his classic treatment in the *Summa theologiae*, I. i. 91. iv. 4. of the proposition that the form of the human body is the soul itself *(forma humani corporis est ipsa anima)* (*Deutsche Thomas-Ausgabe*, 31), continues Aquinas's linkage between ontology and epistemology, between who one is and what one knows, that is elaborated extensively somewhat earlier in the *Summa* (I. i., *Deutsche Thomas-Ausgabe*, 76). This chapter discusses several questions (all of which relate in contemporary terms to the question of "writing the body"), for example, whether understanding is united or linked to the body, *utrum intellectivum principium uniatur corpori ut forma*, or what kind of body it is whose form constitutes its basis of understanding, or whether the intellectual soul is united to the body by means of accidental dispositions, or "whether the soul is united to the animal body by means of some body" (*utrum anima uniatur corpori animali mediante aliquo corpore*). Aquinas judges the tie between soul and body as essential, "the intellectual soul is united to body as the form of its being" (*anima intellectiva unitur corpori ut forma per suum esse*) (Deutsche Thomas-Ausgabe, 76).[18] Significantly, Christine parts company with this Thomist concept of corporeally based knowledge. This tie between knowledge and biology implied the fitness of men for science and learning and the corresponding unfitness of women, those biologically defective men, and Christine was not prepared to accept this conclusion.

Her disagreement with the Thomist theory of woman's creation in the *Summa* could not have been more profound, and therefore in the *Mutacion* she gives a clear counterexample. By underscoring her mother's stronger will (rather than her father's defective seed), Christine lends weight to the Scholastic theory of an intrauterine struggle between male and female seed and undermines the Aristotelian claim that a male seed produces a female child because of adverse weather. Christine's specific theological purpose in the *Mutacion* is to show how the creation of woman corresponds to the image of God. St. Paul had written in I Corinthians 11:7–8 that the man should not cover his head because he is the image and glory of God, but that the woman is the glory of the man, for man was not created from woman, but woman from man. Christine in the *Mutacion* perhaps plays a little joke on Paul, for there she is created as a man from a woman, or in the more precise theological terms, Christine here combines the imitation of Christ with patristic commentary on the virago or virile woman. Just as the single word chaos in the *Advision* reveals the richness of Christine's theological culture, two catchwords in the *Mutacion—homme naturel* and *vray homme*—are instantly recognizable as allusions to medieval theological discussions of the nature of Christ himself.

The "perfect, natural man" (*homme naturel parfaict*) that Christine has become in this work continues to bear her name, which includes the name of the most perfect man (*le nom du plus parfait homme*). The phrase *perfectus homo* or "perfect man" is a common patristic characterization of Christ, just as the phrase *vray homme* (*Mutacion*, v.1361 and v.1390) alludes to the stock patristic expression *versus homo* used to explain the nature of the Trinity. The phrase "perfect man" is found in Venantius Fortunatus (PL 55:585), Hugh of St. Victor (PL 176:70), and Abelard (PL 192:762).

Christine's phrase *homme naturel* requires more commentary. This use of *naturel* does not conform to what might be called "standard" medieval French usage as illustrated by the examples in Godefroy ("de naissance, par sa naissance; pur, sans alliage, franc au propre et au figuré; humain, affable") or in Tobler-Lommatzsch, which adds the sense of "noble." None of these meanings fits the context of *homme naturel parfait* because Christine has not been *born* a man but has *become* a man. Medieval French usage diverges somewhat from the patristic use of the term *naturalis*: the phrase *homo naturalis* occurs only three times in the *Patrologia*, and thus cannot be considered a stock theological phrase. Nor is *naturalis* biblical. The term does, however, have an important meaning for Aquinas in his commentary on Aristotle's *De anima*, as a synonym of *homo realis*, in opposition to *homo abstractus*. Thus, when Christine says in the *Mutacion* that she has become a *homme naturel parfait* she means that she has become incarnated like Christ and has become a man in this world, in the here and now. Significantly, however, this *homme naturel* is linked with the *femme naturelle*, which Christine presents herself as being in the *Cité des dames*.[19] A phrase such as *mulier* or *femina naturalis* occurs neither in the *Patrologia* nor in the works of Aquinas; thus Christine's crucial phrase *femme naturelle* in her observation *je pris a examiner moy mesmes et mes meurs comme femme naturelle* ("I began to examine myself and my behavior as a natural woman") *(Cité des dames*, I.1, 42) is all the more provocative. The term *naturel(le)* implies that Christine wants to recuperate the real, historical experiences of women, presented by a woman called to a position entirely consistent with her orthodox understanding that in the Incarnation, God intervenes directly into history, into the here and now.

Two more profound theological intentions underlie Christine's description of her birth: first, she shows her similarity to her father; and second, she stresses how her name, retained regardless of gender, includes the name of the most perfect man, Christ. Her physical conception reveals the competition between her father's desire for a son and her mother's power. She explains that her mother was more potent than her father ("pouoir/trop plus que luy") to dispense with the Thomist and Aristotelian claims that a woman was a defective male (*mas occasionatus*) produced by a weakness in the sperm. By claiming that her mother was more potent than her father, Christine refutes indirectly the Thomist assertion of paternal superiority over the mother in generation (*De generatione animalium*, II-II,26,10c). For Christine, the enhanced potency of the mother's will, not the father's defective sperm, produces a female child: "M'engendrerent en celle attente/Mais il failli a son entente,/Car ma mere, qui ot pouoir/Trop plus que lui, si voult avoir/Femelle a elle ressemblable,/Si fus nee fille" (They engendered me in this expectation [of having a son], but his intention was lacking, for my mother who had much greater power than he, so much wanted to have a female like her that I was born a girl) (*Mutacion*, ll.386–91).

Yet before she tells how she became a man, she again links her name and her sex change: "Or est il temps que je raconte/l'estrange cas, le divers compte,/Si comme au premier je promis/De cestui livre, ou mon nom mis/Comment de femme homme devins" (Now it is time for me to relate the strange case, the different account, just as I promised at the start of this book where I set my name, how I became a man from a woman) (*Mutacion*, ll.1025–29). She mentions in passing the transformations of Tiresias and Iphys, consciously departing from the allegorical interpretation of these tales given in the *Ovide moralisé*. Instead she recounts the superficial allegory of her marriage as a sea voyage, with her husband as the ship's captain. A violent storm blows up and washes her husband overboard. Her grief knows no limits and she nearly jumps out of the boat to join him. Fortune suddenly intervenes before the ships sinks and changes the sleeping Christine into a man. The change is effected by Fortune massaging her limbs (ll.1327–28). The ship strikes a rock and she wakes up, and senses that she has been completely transformed and that her limbs are stronger than before: "Transmuee me senti toute/Mes membres senti trop plus fors/Qu'ainçois" (I felt myself completely changed, I felt my limbs much stronger than before) *(Mutacion,* ll.1336–8).

She makes no mention of genitalia or reproduction. The portrayal of her metamorphosis shows how Christine shifts her focus from the nature of *woman* to the conditions of *women* (her own terms). Christine stresses that Fortune is primarily responsible for her sex change, so that gender, even understood anatomically, is not eternal but subject to the whims of Fortune. The only loss Christine notes is that of her wedding ring, not of her female body. She feels lightened and sets out to repair the ship. Now she declares herself to be a "true man," capable of steering ships. Although physical strength is the mark of gender, Christine, whether gendered as woman or man, remains the same Christine. Yet she is not an hermaphrodite with physical characteristics of both sexes, a figure that she calls in the *Epistre Othea*, Chapter 82, "laide chose est et villanie" (It is an ugly thing and villainy). Instead, in the *Mutacion,* Christine claims that she really does change from female to male, that all traces of her physical identity as woman have vanished.

To reject any link between knowledge and biology—traditionally a masculinist centering of knowledge—Christine uses the female as an allegory for the universal. Christine makes the "truth" of her *mutacion* an allegory for divine truth: the truth of one woman's contingent experience in becoming a "true man" recalls the mystery of the Incarnation itself. Christine brings a new twist to the notion of Incarnation, for she uses this universalizing tradition to redefine the meaning of women's history as an allegory of human history. In all her writings, she seeks to recuperate the immediacy and particularity of women's experiences, or in medieval terminology, the *hic et nunc*, the here and now of women's history, and to recast it as an allegory of the universal. In her lyrics she substitutes the real, historical experiences of women for courtly conventions of the silent but desired beloved. In her prose writings, she takes the real, historical experiences of women as recounted in pagan, Christian, and contemporary French sources as the first, literal level of her allegory. This allegorical practice means that Christine does not denigrate local reality in the name of a higher principle. The contrary is the case, for Christine's allegorical use of the female to represent the Incarnation, as in the *Mutacion de Fortune*, takes the very localness, the here and now, of her transformation from woman to man to forge a universal symbol of human identity, and following Christian allegory, she must insist that the literal events portrayed are real and historical. All the while substituting her transformed female body for the traditional male body of Christian doctrine, she presents herself as a "true man," and as such a type of Christ.

Christine's dovetailing reflections on the woman as an allegory of Christ and her rejection of essentialist claims regarding the nature of woman become even more refined in the *Advision*. In Part II, Lady Opinion explains the first principles in philosophy. Nothing, says Lady Opinion, can be changed from imperfect to perfect or from potential to actual except through the action of some perfect being: "nulle chose n'est ramenee d'imperfait a perfait ou de puissance en fait, se non par aucun ens parfait, c'est a dire par aucune chose estant de fait perfaicte," (*Advision*, 73) (For nothing is changed from imperfect to perfect or from potential into fact except through the intervention of some perfect being, that is, by some thing being perfect in fact). Lady Opinion invokes this Thomist position as part of a larger discussion of God's perfection and role in creation in order to differentiate between divine actions and those of Fortune in the course of history. Here Christine first translates *aliquod perfectum ens* with the technical term "ens parfait" (perfect being) and then glosses it as "aucune chose estant de fait perfaicte" or "something being in fact perfect."

Christine in fact then gives a much more extensive commentary on this phrase. Aquinas's text ends by saying "Nihil enim reducitur de imperfecto ad perfectum, vel de potentia in actum, nisi per aliquod perfectum ens actu" (*In Metaphysicorum Aristotelis Expositio*, I,12,188) (For nothing can be changed from imperfect to perfect, or from potential into act, except by some perfect being in action). Christine translates, glosses, and then comments:

> Car nulle chose n'est ramenee d'imparfait a parfait ou de puissance en fait, se non par aucuns ens parfait, c'est a dire par aucune chose estant de fait perfaicte. *Et est cy assavoir que j'appelle puissance, en tant que je la distingue contre fait, la puissance de quelconque effait, lequel n'est, c'est a dire de quelconques chose produisible et menable en aucune nature, soit bonne ou mauvaise, ycelle nature non estre ore maiz pouoir estre. Et pour ce la nomme l'en puissance de pouoir estre ou non. Mais quant elle est, elle est nommee fait, a difference de pouoir estre. Et par ce il appert que fait est le plus noble.* (*Advision*, 73)

(For nothing is changed from imperfect to perfect or from potential into fact except through the intervention of some perfect being, that is, by some thing being perfect in fact. *And so it is that I call potential, in as much as I distinguish it from fact, the potential of some effect, which does not exist, that is, of some thing which can be produced and changed into some nature, either good or bad, this nature not existing at the present but capable of existing. And for this reason one speaks of the potential of being able to be or not. But when something exists, it is called fact, to distinguish it from being able to exist. And for this reason it appears that fact is the most noble.*)

The extensive commentary on *aliquod perfectum ens actu* supplies an implicit answer to the theological claim that the female is a defective male based on a difference in potential between female and male essence, and it functions as a perfect gloss on Christine's own claim that at the moment of her own conception her mother had more power or potency, *pouoir*, than her father. Although the argument is abstract, it also pertains directly to the perfection of virtue that confers nobility and that transcends gender differences. If one interprets the linkage in the *Cité des dames* between *vertu* and *perfeccion* in light of this gloss in *Advision*, the perfection of virtue is linked to the perfection of being, which is not dependent on gender at all: "cellui ou celle en qui plus a vertus est le plus hault, ne la haulteur ou abbaissement des gens ne gist mie es corps selon le sexe mais en la perfeccion des meurs et des vertus" (*Cité*, 81) (he or she in whom there is more virtue is the higher, nor does the height or depth of people lie in the body according to sex but in the perfection of deeds and virtues).

Christine's theological reflections have direct practical implications for her ideals of community. Whereas her City of Ladies is provocatively intended as a rigorous allegory of the Heavenly Jerusalem, extending the possibilities of identification with the joys and sorrows of women, Christine dresses this allegory with what appears to be contemporary political reflections on the rights and privileges of Italian city-states, for she chooses the city as an autonomous corporation rather than the convent as a model of her female community.[20] Part of her repudiation of an essentialist theology of gender differences as found in Thomas leads her to show that women and men can follow identical monastic rules. The story, told in Part Three of the *Cité des dames*, of St. Marina, who pretended to be a monk in order to remain with her father in the abbey, speaks directly to the contemporary controversy over different monastic rules for women and men. In their famous correspondence, Heloise asks Abelard whether monks and nuns should follow the same monastic rule. In arguing for identical rules, Abelard notes that some women, zealous in embracing the chastity of the religious life, have broken the law forbidding women to wear men's clothes in Deuteronomy, but nevertheless deserve to become abbots through the preeminence of their virtue.[21] Christine takes a similar tack, arguing implicitly for identical rules, for example, when she recounts the life of St. Marina. After her father's death, Marina retains her monk's disguise and performs exactly the same tasks as the men in the abbey, including buying provisions in a nearby town. When nightfall forces Marina to stay the night at an inn during one of these excursions, the innkeeper's daughter sees a chance to blame the disguised Marina for impregnating her. Marina accepts responsibility rather than reveal herself to be a woman, prompting the abbot to throw her out of the abbey, but she still raises the child whom she had been accused of fathering. Eventually the abbot relents and allows Marina back into the abbey. She dies shortly thereafter, and only as her body was being prepared for burial is her secret revealed. Christine recounts this tale not only, as she explicitly says, as proof of the constancy of women, but also as implicit testimony that women were men's equals in the monastic life and did not require a different rule than men. She does not comment in theological terms on the implications of her story, assuming that the meaning would have been clear enough to her medieval audience.

This all too brief survey of Christine's theological thought redefines the context in which her work needs to be read. As fitting and as provocative as her decision was in 1405 to have the Virgin rule over her City of Ladies, we might miss in our own secular world the profound ramifications of this selection. Christine was a serious and profound thinker, and she chose her ground carefully when she resolved to plead *la cause des femmes*. But her works are solidly grounded in scholastic theology, even if they often challenge its implicit fundamental masculine assumptions. That she knew Thomas's works and commented upon them should be beyond doubt, despite generations of scholars who could not conceive that a woman like Christine not only could read the Angelic Doctor, but also disagree with him. When one recalls again Jean Gerson's description of a *femelette* who wondered how she would continue her meditation about herself and God when she had to leave her sickroom and return to the world, we now know. Christine did leave her *chambrete* and went on to articulate and deepen her meditations about God in all of her subsequent works. In so doing, she advanced the limits of theological speculation about women in order to advance the cause of women, not only before the throne of the Most High, but before the thrones and principalities of men here below.

NOTES

1. See my article "Christine and Medieval Jurisprudence," in *Contexts and Continuities: Proceedings of the IV International Colloquium on Christine de Pizan (Glasgow 21–27 July 2000)*, 3 vols., ed. Angus J. Kennedy in collaboration with Rosalind Brown-Grant, James C. Laidlaw, and Catherine Müller (Glasgow: University Press, 2002), vol. 3, 747–66.
2. On Christine's use of patristic material in general, see my article, "In Search of a Feminist Patrology: Christine de Pizan and the *glorieux dotteurs* of the Church," in *Une femme de lettres au Moyen Age. Études autour de Christine de Pizan*, ed. Liliane Dulac and Bernard Ribémont (Orléans: Paradigme, 1995), 281–95.
3. The most important synthesis of the Scholastic theology of women is Antonio Placanica, "La concezione della donna nella dottrina di alcuni teologi scolastici," *Seminari sassaresi* 4 (1989): 105–27. I have dealt with some of the topics in this essay elsewhere, including "Christine de Pizan and Dante: A Reexamination," *Archiv für das Studium der neueren Sprachen und Literaturen*, Bd. 222, Jhrg. 137 (1985): 100–11; "Rejecting Essentialism and Gendered Writing: The Case of

Christine de Pizan," in *Gender and Text in the Later Middle Ages*, ed. Jane Chance (Gainesville: University Press of Florida, 1996), 96–131; "Where Are the Men in Christine de Pizan's City of Ladies? Architectural and Allegorical Structures in Christine de Pizan's *Livre de la Cité des Dames*," in *Translatio Studii: Essays in Honor of Karl D. Uitti*, ed. R. Blumenfeld-Kosinski et al. (Amsterdam: Rodopi, 1999), 221–44; and "Christine de Pizan and Jean Gerson, An Intellectual Friendship," *"Rien ne m'est seur que la chose incertaine. Etudes sur l'art d'écrire au Moyen Age offertes à Eric Hicks par ses anciens élèves et ses amis*, edited by Jean-Claude Mühlethaler and Denis Billotte (Geneva: Slatkine, 2001).

4. Liliane Dulac and Christine Reno, "L'humanisme vers 1400, essai d'exploration à partir d'un cas marginal: Christine de Pizan traductrice de Thomas d'Aquin," in *Actes du Colloque "Pratiques de la culture écrite en France au XVe siècle*," ed. Monique Ornato and Nicole Pons (Louvain-la-Neuve: Féderation Internationale des Instituts d'Études Médiévales, 1994), 161–78.

5. Dante speaks only once, in *Inferno* 12.43, of chaos when he has Virgil allude to Aristotle's repudiation of the theory that periodic destruction in the world stemmed from the alternation of strife and love, *più volte il mondo in caòs converso*. The *Ovide moralisé*, another one of Christine's favorite sources, seems to provide the first French-language example of chaos in the sense of confusion: Chaos' avoit non li monciaux,/Dont traist la terre et les ciaux. *Ovide moralisé, Poème du commencement du quatorzième siècle*, ed. C. de Boer, Verhandelingen der Koninklijke Adademie van Wetenschappen te Amsterdam, Afdeeling Letterkkunde, nieuwe reeks, deel XV (Amsterdam: Noordhollandsche Uitgevers-Maatschapij, 1915–36), Vol. 1, ll. 153–54.

6. Rosemund Tuve, *Allegorical Imagery, Some Medieval Books and Their Posterity* (Princeton: Princeton University Press, 1966), 34.

7. Christine de Pizan, *Epistre Othea*, ed. Gabriella Parussa (Paris: Droz, 1999), 32–6.

8. Two important beginnings are Charity Cannon Willard, "Christine de Pizan's Allegorized Psalms," and Armand Strubel, "Le style allégorique de Christine," in *Une femme de lettres au Moyen Age*, ed. Dulac and Ribémont, 317–24 and 357–72.

9. Jean Gerson, *Oeuvres*, ed. Palémon Glorieux (Paris: Desclée, 1960–73), v. 7, 33. The dating of the *Montaigne de Contemplation* to April/May 1400 is supplied by Brian McGuire in the notes to his translation of Jean Gerson, *Early Works* (New York: Paulist Press, 1998), 399.

10. Margolis, "Elegant Closures: The Use of the Diminutive in Christine de Pizan and Jean de Meun," in *Reinterpreting Christine de Pizan*, ed. Earl Jeffrey Richards et al. (Athens, GA: University of Georgia Press, 1992), 111–23, especially 116–7.

11. *Le Livre de la Mutacion de Fortune*, ed. Suzanne Solente, 4 vols, SATF (Paris: A. & J. Picard, 1959–1966), 4: 80, ll. 23635–36: "Paix, solitude volumtaire/ Et vie astracte et solitaire" (Peace, voluntary solitude, and a life apart and solitary).

12. The phrase *vivis ex lapidibus* is subsequently used by Patristic writers in connection with the *civitas Dei*: Hilarius Pictaviensis, *Tractatus super psalmos*, PL 9, col. 868, commentary on Psalm CXXV, 7, "Quae Sion sedes regni Dei, vivis ex lapidibus." Honorius Augustodunensis, *Expositio in Psalmos*, PL 172, col. 284 B, "Significat autem quod Sion, id est Ecclesia, hic a paganis et haereticis destruatur,

sed per Iesum summum sacerdotem et regem Christum in coelestem Jerusalem vivis ex lapidibus reaedificatur." Bernardus Claraevallensis, *In dedicatione ecclesiae*, PL 183, col. 521, "Ipsa est quae construitur vivis ex lapidibus, angelis scilicet et hominibus." Hildegard of Bingen, *Liber divinorum operum simplicis hominis*, PL 197, col. 911, "justitiae inter protectionem Dei civitas vivis es lapidibus constructa, ad judicium Dei aspectum."

13. F. J. E. Raby, *Medieval Latin Verse* (Oxford: Clarendon, 1959), 82, no. 63.
14. Ernst Kantorowicz, *The King's Two Bodies, A Study in Mediaeval Political Theology* (Princeton: Princeton University Press, 1957); Oliver Donovan, *The Desire of the Nations, Rediscovering the Roots of Political Theology* (Cambridge: Cambridge University Press, 1996); and Francis Oakley, *Politics and Eternity, Studies in the History of Medieval and Early Modern Political Thought* (Leiden: Brill, 1999). For the text of Christine's *Charles V*, see Suzanne Solente, ed., *Le Livre des fais et bonnes meurs du sage roy Charles V*, 2 vols. (Paris: Honoré Champion, 1936–1940), III.71, vol. 2, 186.
15. Kate Langdon Forhan, *The Political Theory of Christine de Pizan* (Aldershot: Ashgate, 2002). My thanks to Professor Forhan for being able to read the proofs of her book.
16. For a different interpretation of Semiramis, see Maureen Quilligan, *The Allegory of Female Authority, Christine de Pizan's Cité des dames* (Ithaca: Cornell University Press, 1991), 69–87.
17. Klaus Bernath, *Anima forma corporis, Eine Untersuchung über die ontologischen Grundlagen der Anthropologie des Thomas von Aquin* (Bonn: Bouvier, 1969), 46. The claim is also found in *In Metaphysicorum Aristotelis Expositio* (I,4,74): "Materia autem, quam dicebant esse substantiam rei, manet in omni transmutatione; sed passiones mutantur, ut forma, et omnia quae adveniunt supra substantiam materiae," and translated in *Advision*, II.6.
18. See also Joan Cadden, *Meanings of Sex Difference in the Middle Ages: Medicine, Science and Culture* (Cambridge: Cambridge University Press, 1993), especially 133–34. For the current discussion of women's bodies in feminist thought, see Elizabeth Grosz, *Volatile Bodies: Toward a Corporeal Feminism* (Bloomington: Indiana University Press, 1994) and Vicki Kirby, *Telling Flesh, The Substance of the Corporeal* (New York: Routledge, 1997).
19. Other examples of *naturel[le]* in Christine correspond more to patristic and Thomist practice than to medieval French usage, and of the twenty-six examples of *naturel[le]* in the *Cité des dames*, there are seven examples of the patristic notion of *sens naturel*.
20. See my discussion of late medieval political theories of the city in "Where Are the Men in the City of Ladies?"
21. *La Vie et les Epistres Pierres Abaelart et Heloys sa fame, traduction du XIIIe siècle attribuée à Jean de Meun, avec une nouvelle édition des textes latins d'après le ms. Troyes Bibl. mun. 802*, ed. Eric Hicks (Paris: Champion, 1991), 147: "Quarum etiam plereque tanto ad castimoniam zelo sunt accense, ut non solum contra Legis decretum pro custodienda castitate virilem presumerent virtutibus ut abbates fieri mererentur."

5

Christine de Pizan

Memory's Architect

Margarete Zimmermann*

INTRODUCTION

No other author has inscribed herself so successfully and so enduringly into cultural memory as Christine de Pizan has done, and no one has been continuously present from the early modern period up to the debates in the twentieth and twenty-first centuries in the way that she has been.[1] And which other woman writer commands such a *longue durée* in the memory of succeeding generations of readers, such a presence in two of the most important storage media, namely texts and images? Evocations of Christine de Pizan abound in early texts from the *Querelle des femmes* and in artwork owned by female rulers such as Margaret of Austria. The works of different women writers of the sixteenth century—e.g., Anne de Beaujeu, Gabrielle de Bourbon, Marguerite de Navarre, or Georgette de Montenay—acknowledge their familiarity with the great late medieval *écrivaine* and express their claim to power by referring to the *Cité des dames*.[2] The humanist librarian Gabriel Naudé planned to edit the *Livre de la paix*. In their reference works *encyclopédistes* such as Denis Diderot,[3] Louis Moréri,[4] or Prosper Marchand[5] dedicated long entries to her, and bibliophiles such as the Comte d'Argenson were passionate collectors of manuscripts and printed editions of her writings. Christine is also accorded a prominent place in the early archives and storage media of feminine culture, for example, in Louise-Félicité Guinement de Kéralio's *Collection des meilleurs ouvrages françois, composés par des femmes* (1786–89).[6] With an increasing emphasis on patriotism this strong presence continues in the positivist collections of the nineteenth century. For the twentieth century a single example will suffice: in the context of early twentieth-century feminism a reference to Christine is almost obligatory, be it in a socialist-intellectual context (Lily

Braun[7] or Léon Abensour[8]), where Christine is seen as a precursor of the contemporary feminist movement, or in a conservative context (Théodore Joran[9] or Henry Roujon[10]), where Christine is hailed as a representative of an "honorable feminism" and her writings are used as a rhetorical bulwark against the rebellious English suffragettes.[11] It is also remarkable that Christine appears to have been convinced during her own lifetime that she would live on in the memory of later generations, as can be gathered from the following famous passage from the *Advision Cristine* in which "Dame Opinion" addresses the fictitious author persona Christine with these words: "In time to come, even more will be spoken of you than during your lifetime, for . . . you have lived in a bad time, when sciences are not held in great esteem. . . ."[12]

Christine's exceptional position is particularly striking when compared to all those losses of texts and images that characterize the way in which works by women writers are usually handed down to posterity. In spite of this, women writers seem to have been particularly conscious of the fragile nature of memory and tradition with regard to their writings—the best known example of such an awareness being Marie de France who discusses this problem again and again in her prologues. But male gynophilous authors are equally aware of this danger: only a few years after Christine's death, around 1440, Martin Le Franc points out in his *Champion des Dames* that the memory of important women intellectuals and artists is in bad hands with the contemporary custodians of memory, the *clercs*.[13] Martin Le Franc remedies this—and later many other authors of gynophilous works follow suit within the context of the *Querelle des femmes*[14]—by keeping alive and handing down to future generations the memory of Christine de Pizan and other *clergesses* with the help of memorial portraits. But as an intellectual taking an active interest in the future Christine herself ensured that her *memoria* would be kept even during her own lifetime. Already in her first collection of poems, the *Cent balades* (1399), she undertakes the careful modeling of her own textual persona and a "construction d'un personnage soigneusement délimité"[15] (construction of a carefully delimited character), a development that intensifies in the succeeding works and at whose end stands the self-confident inscription of a female author-subject in her texts. No other woman writer developed such effective strategies against the danger of falling into oblivion as she did and no other worked so intensely on her own inscription onto the memory of her contemporaries and of succeeding generations. It is therefore well worth investigating the strategies Christine used to achieve this aim.

MEMORIA

But first some terminological remarks concerning *memoria* are necessary. *Memoria* can be considered as an element of rhetoric or as a memorial art (*ars memoriae*) as studied by Frances Yates.[16] Christine used this concept, for example, in a much-quoted passage from the *Advision Christine*. Here, in accordance with a tradition common from the ancient period onward that equates *liberi* (children) and *liberi* (books),[17] "Dame Nature" likens the act of giving birth to the act of publishing a book: "Or vueil que de toy naissent nouveaulx volumes, lesquelz le temps a venir et perpetuelment au monde presenteront *ta memoire* devant les princes et par l'univers en toutes places, lesquelz en joie et delit tu enfanteras *de ta memoire, non obstant le labour et traveil.* . . ."[18] (my emphasis) (Now I want new books brought forth from you which will present your memory before the worldly princes in the future and keep it always and everywhere bright; these you will deliver from your memory in joy and pleasure notwithstanding the pain and labor).[19]

Here, the book is simultaneously seen as a product of memory, of the author's (historical) knowledge, and as a medium for her continuing presence in the memory of future generations. In the following and in contrast to the rhetorical definition of memory, however, I will adopt a concept of *memoria* as a *fait social total*, as an all-encompassing cultural phenomenon. Not only was this concept of *memoria* particularly important for the Middle Ages,[20] it has also recently become a central interest and almost a new paradigm in cultural studies and avant-garde art.[21] With Otto Gerhard Oexle and recent sociohistorical studies *memoria* can therefore be defined as "a form of social action . . . [which] refers to the relations between the living and the dead, . . . and to social action that the living direct towards the dead."[22] *Memoria*, following the phrasing of the French sociologist Marcel Mauss, is "a total social phenomenon . . . which concerns all areas of life: religion and the economy, law and politics, everyday life and art." Such a concept of *memoria* simultaneously gives access to period-specific collective mentalities as well as to individual ways of forming memory, since creating and maintaining *memoria* are a social phenomena insofar as they require the context of a group to keep the memory alive. At the same time creating memory is a highly individual act, indelibly linked to the naming of an individual.[23]

In the following, Christine is presented as a woman writer who is concerned about her *memoria* and who even consciously and intently works on her own *memoria*, traits she shares with other medieval authors. One might consider it an interest of all literature and art to create memory and to be remembered by posterity. The concern for one's own *memoria* is therefore also a highly productive phenomenon in cultural terms.[24]

But still Christine occupies a special position because she creates *memoria* in an encompassing sense and on different levels, as she not only works on her own *memoria* but also on the *memoria* of her father and her noble patrons. In her writings she thus combines individual *memoria* with that pertaining to groups. At this point it is impossible to overlook the importance of Augustine to her thinking, as the first extended reflection of time and memory following the ancient period can be found in the tenth book of Augustine's *Confessiones*, in his remarks on the "vast palaces of memory, those places where the treasure of innumerable images, created by manifold sensory perceptions, is kept."[25] In his *Confessions*, Augustine defines *memoria* as *praesens de praeteritis*, that is as the presence of the past, and for the first time *memoria* thus becomes a general, all-encompassing historical and cultural phenomenon. A first and more than obvious trace of Augustine can be found in the phrase "le ventre de la mémoire" (the stomach of memory) in Christine's biography of Charles V in which she uses it to justify that as a woman she sets down in writing her knowledge of armoury: this, she writes, serves to inform the ignorant; she then continues: "comme aussi il soit impossible que le ventre de la mémoire puist retenir et avoir recort continuelment de toutes les choses ydoines et expedientes à faire es offices de quoy l'ome se veult entremettre. . . ."[26] (for it is impossible for the stomach of memory to retain and have continual recourse to all things suitable and appropriate to the offices that man wants to assume).[27] It is precisely this phrase about the "uenter memoriae" that we find several times in the tenth book of the *Confessions*.[28] One can assume that Christine was familiar with Augustine's concept of time as a three-dimensional phenomenon. Memory and the future constitute the present; the force of Augustinian thinking, in this context, lies in the fact "of having linked the analysis of memory with that of time."[29]

Finally, the concept of cultural memory, developed by the Egyptologist Jan Assmann, refers to the fact that only a certain part of the past is stored in the memory of groups or individuals, recalled with the help of symbolic figures or ritual acts and thus recorded and canonized. In this sense memory is an instrument of symbolic power in the hands of specialists whose names vary according to culture and period and who may be priests, shamans, intellectuals, wise men, artists, professors, etc.[30] Women, by contrast, only rarely participate in these procedures. The principal instruments of such a memorial evocation are music, sacred texts, and rites of commemoration; within literary history the canon is an important means for the construction of cultural memory. To put it more precisely, in the words of Aleida Assmann: "Cultural memory has its anthropological origin in the memory of the dead. This consisted in the obligation of friends and family to remember the names of their dead and to hand them down to posterity. Remembering the dead has a religious dimension and a worldly dimension which one can summarise by opposing 'pietas' and 'fama'. . . . 'Fama' is a secular form of making oneself eternal which in many ways resembles a theatrical *mise en scène*."[31]

We have now set the scene for a more precise view of Christine de Pizan's role and meaning as an architect of memory. I would contend that her survival as a woman writer is closely connected to her concern for her own and others' *memoria* and that her whole *œuvre* can be reread in this light.

CHRISTINE DE PIZAN: ARCHITECT OF MEMORY
Epistre Othea

While with her mythological and didactic poem *Epistre Othea* (1399) Christine remains within the boundaries of ancient memorial art, one can already detect the first signs of a broader concept of memory. The focus of this "poetic picture book"[32] lies on the education of a young man—Hector—at the hands of the goddess Othea who addresses the young, male reader with the following words:

> Or mets dont bien en ta memoire
> Les dis que je te vueil escripre
> Et se tu m'os compter ou dire
> Chose qui soit a avenir
> Et je te dis que souvenir
> T'en doit, com s'ilz fussent passees,
> Saches qu'ilz sont en mes pensees
> En esperit de prophecie.[33]

(Place therefore in your memory the tales that I want to write for you and if you hear me recount or say things that regard the future, and I tell you that you should remember them, as if they had already occurred, understand that they are, to my mind, said in the spirit of a prophecy.)

She imparts her lessons with the help of a close connection between images and text: each of the hundred mostly mythological exempla is illustrated by a miniature. The young reader constantly moves between these two media and is virtually unable to resist being led in his perception by them. The miniature at the beginning of each chapter depicts a moment of crisis and a climax. The image is followed by a mnemonic rhyme naming the central character of the story and summarizing the lesson to be drawn from it, often with the added injunction "Souviengne toy" or "Bien te souvienge." Then with the gloss a short summary and practical interpretation follow, often heightened further by an ancient philosophical phrase. An allegory with a theological interpretation closes the chapter. It ends with a mnemonic phrase in Latin that, in most cases, is taken from the Bible or the writings of the Church Fathers. Overall, Christine does not only develop a hitherto unknown textual model but also a new pedagogical concept that relies on the miniatures to support the act of memorizing. Moreover, the author integrates the ancient and the Christian tradition in a manner hitherto unknown. The *Epistre Othea* shows that Christine was familiar with the primarily rhetorical memorial tradition but by using the miniatures as mnemotechnical storage media she drew on this tradition in an innovative fashion.[34]

Livre de la mutacion de Fortune

In her *Livre de la mutacion de Fortune* Christine describes herself as possessing a "nobel chappel de grant pris"[35] (a crown of great worth) decorated with precious stones; and the last and most valuable of these stones "est Memoire appelee" (*Mutacion*, 1.629) (is called Memory). This important work on the philosophy of history can be read as a description of the battle between two antagonistic forces, the force of continuous change and uncertainty—Fortuna—and the force that maintains and remembers—Memoria. Further textual traces allowing us to characterize Christine de Pizan as a writer who is concerned about her own *memoria* can be found in paratexts of her works, in particular in introductory and concluding passages, and in connection with the references to her noble patrons. First, it is liturgical *memoria* she requests, which can be defined as the "memory of the defunct ensured by prayer, the sacrifice of Mass and charity. It is thus an active memory which notably goes beyond the simple emotional and cognitive level, an active memory that is an instrument of grace and which can simultaneously have an effect on the living and on the dead, the former finally joining the latter."[36]

At the end of the *Livre du corps de policie* and with the intention of ensuring such a liturgical memory for herself, Christine, strictly observing the social order, addresses her noble patrons and then her readers from all other walks of life: they should, as a form of payment for the pleasure that Christine's texts have afforded them, remember her and pray for her:

> Encore depri en remuneracion eulx vivans et leur nobles successeurs roys et autres princes françois qui par memoire de mes dittiez le temps a venir oront ramentevoir mon nom, quant l'ame sera hors du corps, que par prieres et devotes oroisons, par eulx ou de par eulx offertes, vuellent pour moy vers Dieu requerir indulgence et remission de mes deffaux. Et pareillement requier chevaliers et nobles françois, et tous generaument de quelconque part qu'ilz soient, lesquelz par aucun plaisir de mes petites choses lire ou oir aront memoire de moy, qu'ilz dient en guerdon Pater noster.[37]

(Again in recompense I pray those living and their noble successors, kings and other French princes who by remembering my poems in times to come will recall my name, after the soul has left my body, that by their prayers and orisons, offered by them or on their behalf, they request in my name and before God indulgence and remission for my faults. And, similarly, I request of knights and noble Frenchmen, and everyone in general wherever they are from, those who will remember me because of the pleasure they took in reading or listening to my little things, that they say as recompense a Pater Noster.)

Although this request to be remembered can be found in the works of many other medieval authors it is unusual that Christine combines it with what today would be called the publisher's concern for the distribution of her works. An even more impressive proof of this can be found toward the end of the *Livre des trois vertus*, which first provides us with an insight into the author's specific publishing strategies. Again, she lets her work end with the request for liturgical memory, asking that worthy ladies and women of influence keep her "in their grace and memory." She further requests, "Et aprés ce que l'ame du corps sera partie, en merite et guerdon de son service leur plaise offrir a Dieu pour elle paternostres, oblacions et devocions. . . ."[38] (after my soul has left my body, may these good women recognizing and rewarding me for my services offer to God on my behalf Pater Nosters, oblations, and other devotions).[39]

In the *Epistre Othea* Christine uses a different strategy yet again. Here she skilfully combines paying homage to Louis d'Orléans with the memory of his royal father, Charles V—"vous, tres noble prince excellant,/D'Orlïens duc Loÿs de grant renom,/Filz de Charles roy quint de cellui nom"[40] (you, very worthy and most excellent prince, Louis, duke of Orléans of great reputation, son of King Charles, fifth of that name). In a parallel move she associates her own *mise en scène* as an author with the memory of her own father: "moy, povre creature,/Femme ignorant de petite estature,/Fille jadis philosophe et docteur/Qui conseiller et humble serviteur/Vostre pere fu, que Dieu face grace,/Et jadis vint de Boulongne la grace" (*Epistre Othea*, 195). (I, but a poor creature, ignorant woman of little stature, the daughter of a philosopher and doctor who was an advisor and humble servant of your father, may God give him grace, and who had previously come from the gracious Boulogna.) From this double procedure—inscribing two living persons onto the memory of future generations, in addition to their association with "two great deceased" fathers—grows a seminal form of memory highly typical for Christine.

Livre des fais et bonnes meurs du sage roy Charles V

But Christine de Pizan's construction of her own individual *memoria* and that pertaining to other people can best be observed in two substantial prose works: her biography of Charles V and the *Livre de la Cité des dames*. These two important prose treatises, written virtually at the same time between 1404 and 1405, are linked to one another by a comprehensive reflection on *memoria* with express recourse to Augustine. A further link is created by the fact that in these texts Christine employs two forms of "sapiental writing" allowing her to explore and strengthen the possibilities of a public female voice.[41] These elements make the *Livre des fais et bonnes meurs du sage roy Charles V* and the *Cité des dames* a textual pair, lending themselves especially well to an explanation of how Christine constructed two kinds of memorial texts.

Conspicuous traces of a close relation between the two works can also be found in the passages of her biography of Charles V in which the author takes to task those critics who deny her the right to express in writing her views about the art of armoury. At the end of her deliberations and in order to close with a strong final point she confers authority upon herself by drawing on history, ancient mythology, and the goddess Minerva:

> et quant ad ce que femme suis oser parler d'armes, il est escript que es anciens aages, comme autrefois ay dit, une sage femme de Grece nommée Minerve trouva l'art et science de faire armeures de fer et d'acier, et tous les harnois, que on seult porter en bataille, fu par lui premierement trouvé; si n'y a nulle force qui que donne la dottrine, mais que bonne et salutaire soit.[42]

(And that as a woman, I dare to speak of arms, it is written that in ancient times, as I have said before, a wise Greek woman named Minerva created the art and the science of making arms out of iron and steel, and all the armour that is usually worn in battle was first discovered by her; it matters not from whom comes the knowledge, as long as it is good and salutary.)

She develops similar strategies of self-authorization in the *Cité de dames*. But let us remain for a moment with her *Charles V*. At its beginning Christine emphasizes its significance for the works she has so far produced and characterizes it as a "nouvelle compilacion menée en stille prosal et hors le commun ordre de mes autres choses passées...." (Solente, I.5) (new compilation undertaken in prose and out of the ordinary when compared with my previous writings). She presents herself as an author who undertakes, at the request of her patron Philip the Bold, the creation of the deceased king's memory by drawing on her own memory and by traveling through the *lata praetoria memoriae*. It is impossible to ignore the references to Augustine in this context; indeed, one might read the whole treatise as an illustration of Augustine's dictum "Magna ista uis est memoria" (X, 15).

The attraction of this royal biography also lies in the fact that Christine does not simply present her readers with a final product. She lets them participate in the slow creation of the book and in the act of remembering, in the process of recalling someone to memory and in the memorial labor for the deceased king. Thus in the introductory remarks we find, with reference to Philip the Bold:

> Ainsi plaist au tres redoubté susdit que le petit entendement de mon engin s'applique à *ramener à memoire* les vertus et fais du tres sereins prince, le sage roy Charles ... ; des quelles choses, pour emplir le dit commandement, me suis informée, tant par croniques, comme par pluseurs gens notables encore vivans jadis ses serviteurs, de sa vie, condicions, meurs et ordre de vivre, et de ses fais particuliers .... (my emphasis; Solente, IX.9)

(Thus it pleases [Philip the Bold] that the little understanding of my mind apply itself *to bring back to memory* the virtues and deeds of the serene prince, the wise king Charles ... ; so as to fulfil this duty, I informed myself about his life, conditions, beliefs, habits, and of his particular accomplishments, as much from chronicles as from several notable individuals who are still alive and were in the past his servants.)

The overlapping levels of description culminate in ever new approaches and approximations to Charles V as a Christian, ruler, intellectual, and patron but also to his physical appearance (in her famous portrait of the king in Chapter 17 of Book I), thus creating by degrees that multifaceted memorial portrait that the author had announced:

> Ainsi sera mon dit volume contenu en .III. parties, qui toutes assembleront à une seule chose, c'est assavoir: en la singuliere personne du tres illustre, hault et tres loué prince, feu le sage roy Charles, Quint d'ycellui nom, en laquelle reverence ceste presente œuvre est emprise, ramentevant sa vie et louables vertus et meurs dignes de perpetuelle memoire. (Solente, I.6)

(Thus my volume will contain three parts which are unified by a single thing, that is the singular person who is the very illustrious, high and much praised prince, the late wise King Charles, the fifth of this name, out of reverence for whom the present work is undertaken, recalling to perpetual memory his life and his praiseworthy virtues and worthy habits.)

Christine fills the palaces of *memoria* with different material taken from other sources such as *Les Grandes Chroniques de France* (*GCF*), her own memories, and statements from witnesses. She assumes the role of the collector who orders and forms this material as well as the role of the writer who gives it its final written shape. She justifies her approach by claiming an emotional tie with the deceased king: "en ma jeunesse et enfance, avec mes parens, je fusse nourrie de son pain" (Solente, II.193) (in my youth and my childhood, along with my parents, I was nourished by his bread). Among the many witnesses she interrogates in the context of her reconstruction of a past era and the personality of the deceased ruler, her father therefore holds a special position. On the one hand, he was a learned man from the king's entourage and thus a privileged *témoin*; on the other hand, he was a deceased person whose memory she thus keeps alive and consolidates. This again reminds one of Augustine's *Confessions*, which also function as a memorial book for the author's mother.[43]

But with this book Christine also creates a panorama of the whole period of Charles V's life and regency, which at the time of writing had already become history. Her work is therefore situated on the threshold between memory and history, which Pierre Nora distinguishes in the following manner:

> Memory is life, always borne by living groups and as such it constantly evolves and is open to the dialectic of remembering and forgetting, unconscious of its successive

deformations, vulnerable to all uses and manipulations, susceptible to long periods of latency and to sudden revitalisation. History is the always problematic and incomplete construction of that which no longer exists. Memory is an always topical phenomenon, a true tie with the eternal present; history is a representation of the past.[44]

By shaping the collective memory of a historical period Christine breaks new ground, a terrain on which women would establish themselves permanently only in the twentieth century. That she was most successful in her endeavor can be observed from the fact that even to this day no historical study of Charles V is written without drawing on Christine de Pizan's work. At the same time she has managed to secure for herself and her own writings a permanent place within cultural memory: since the seventeenth century and far into the nineteenth century interest focused mostly on Christine as the biographer of this important late medieval ruler.[45]

Livre de la cité des dames

When reading *Charles V* from a gender historical point of view, it is apparent that it is a "male memory" that is constructed in the text, leaving little room for female identification; rather, it is the memory of three deceased fathers—the ideal ruler-father Charles V, the patron Philip of Burgundy, and her natural father Tommaso—as whose architect Christine de Pizan legitimizes herself by her "sapiential writing" and her emotional connection with all three father figures. Perhaps this memorial labor for her fathers is the prerequisite for the building of the gender-specific memorial space that she undertakes in the *Livre de la cité des dames*. Both works incidentally are similar in that they react to a crisis: the book about the deceased King Charles V has to be read against the backdrop of the political crisis in France, whereas the starting point for the *Cité des dames* and before that for the *Epistre au dieu d'Amours* and the quarrel over the *Roman de la Rose* is a crisis in gender relations.

In the *Cité des dames* the author shapes the memory of a group defined by the two characteristics of (female) sex/gender and *vertu*. With this work she creates an archive of cultural history, a utopia grounded in history. That this text, even if in a different sense than her biography of the king, is also a significant political project becomes obvious when one accepts that any form of subject formation has to be situated historically. In the words of Jacques Le Goff: "Memory is an essential element of what one calls [. . .] individual or collective identity whose search is one of the fundamental activities of individuals and societies and [. . .] collective memory is not only a conquest but also an instrument and an object of power."[46] Stated differently: when individuals or groups lack historical foundation, this causes fragile or insufficient embeddedness in the present. The naive search for female models is not the point here but the simple conclusion that a historical dimension is necessary for any form of being. If this is absent a vital element of individual and collective identity is lacking.

With this premise in mind, let us take a look at the beginning of the *Cité des dames*.[47] Here, Christine presents her textual persona in a melancholy pose, suffering from and nearly collapsing under a conflict of images—that of her own image and the image that is projected of the female sex as a whole. She is unable to defend herself against the defamatory images projected by others because in this instance she is capable of seeing herself only against the backdrop of the present. Christine illustrates this by letting her textual persona take refuge in conversations with women of the present, without, however, letting her find a way out of her self-destructive attitude.[48]

This attempt to heal herself is unsuccessful because a perspective based entirely on the present dominates and a group- and gender-specific memory is lacking. This is provided in the subsequent dialogues in the *Cité des dames*, by the introduction of a historical level developed more and more strongly in the conversations between the textual persona Christine and her allegorical female interlocutors. Without exception it is the historical examples that provide the "building blocks" for the city of ladies and with which the foundations and reinforcements of the utopian city are constructed; it is the women's contributions to the well-being of all humankind over the centuries that form the substance of Christine's book. In this fashion the author combines femininity and historicity and constructs a feminocentric canon in which exemplary representatives of different feminine characteristics and activities find their place. In the animated conversations with Dame Raison, Rectitude, and Justice, the names, achievements, and fates of these exemplary women are evoked in almost ritualistic fashion and their importance for the history of human culture and civilization is remembered. The permanence and indestructible character of the imaginary city of ladies, which in this respect are even superior to the Amazons,[49] result in the whole construct becoming part of the *longue durée*, and the success of this strategy is amply borne out by the fact that to this day the book remains topical and popular.

But Christine does not limit herself to such a historicizing of femininity and to the construction of a vast and imposing feminocentric archive. She also lends it a singular literary form that reaches far beyond Boccaccio's model in *De claris mulieribus*. The significance of the *Cité des dames* becomes clear only when one takes into account its originality as a text belonging to the *Querelle des femmes*. This originality is based first on the clever selection of the extensive material and its ordering according to thematic foci and second on the literary form used to convey them to the readers. Christine does not rely only on the quantity of her exempla, and unlike the majority of her successors she does not content herself with a hasty and excessive compilation of material or with a loose sequence of arguments. After cleverly choosing exempla and ingeniously arranging her material in order to increase its rhetorical effect, the author then presents it in brilliantly constructed instructive dialogues between the "naively" questioning Christine and the allegorical characters instructing her, drawing on all the tricks of the rhetorical and stylistic trade. The elegance and the sparkling wit of these dialogues afford the readers of the *Cité des dames* a subtle pleasure and a subversive experience of reading that endures to this day.

Furthermore, these characteristics make the *Cité des dames* a *texte de jouissance* in Barthes's sense, defined as "celui qui met en état de perte, celui qui déconforte (peut-être jusqu'à un certain ennui), fait vaciller les assises historiques, culturelles, psychologiques, du lecteur, la consistance de ses goûts, de ses valeurs et de ses souvenirs, met en crise son rapport au langage"[50] (the text that imposes a state of loss, the text that discomfits [perhaps to the point of a certain boredom], unsettles the reader's historical, cultural, psychological assumptions, the consistency of his tastes, values, memories, brings to a crisis his relation with language).[51]

From this aesthetic shape and the pleasure of reading following from it, from the many ways of reading this work, and from its continuous updates the *Cité des dames* derives its unique position with regard to a genre—the genre of a *Querelle des Femmes* text—that usually impresses neither by its literary form nor by its elegance.

It is the conceptual and formal originality of Christine's construction of a historically based memorial space that constantly inspires new versions of a similar kind. In France during the sixteenth century and when the *Querelle des femmes* climaxed, many apologies for women were written based on similar spatial constructs, for instance the numerous metaphorical ships, galleries, and castles that serve as frames for gynophilous arguments in the early modern period.[52] But the power of such a virtual city of ladies and its realization in a medium other than literature did not even wane in the twentieth century. Judy Chicago's *Dinner Party* (1979), the construction of a great memorial table in the form of an isosceles triangle with thirty-nine famous women as place settings and a further 999 names of women engraved in the marble floor beneath the table, is based on a principle similar to Christine's City of Ladies: a gender-specific cultural memory is given a spatial shape. It is surely not accidental that in Judy Chicago's memorial monument Christine de Pizan is accorded a prominent place.

A PERMANENT VISUAL MEMORY

A final aspect concerns the role of the image as a storage medium and Christine's most successful creation of a permanent visual memory. Apart from the iconographic presence of aristocrats such as Marguerite de Navarre or Margaret of Valois, no other author has inscribed herself so markedly as an intellectual and as an *écrivaine* onto visual memory, and is therefore still visually as present as Christine de Pizan.[53] This can be illustrated by numerous examples. Particularly interesting in this respect is the order of miniatures in the London manuscript Harley 4431, where the dedicatory image is directly followed by a representation of the author. Immediately after the representation of her patron, which shows Christine presenting her works to queen Isabeau de Bavière and which (like the following dedicatory poem) shows her as the queen's dependent, the next miniature presents the author in a different attitude. Here she has intentionally and confidently represented herself as an intellectual in the solitude of her writing chamber, her *studiolo*, where she is seated at her desk, busy writing in a large book that lies open before her. She is almost entirely turned toward the observer. Like the dedicatory image this page is richly decorated with lush vine leaves and gold leaf, but it is also more sombre and austere in style than the dedicatory image. With this miniature Christine consciously opposes the image of the patron surrounded by her ladies-in-waiting with her own self-portrait as an intellectual and, precisely because of this form of self-(re)presentation, she obtains a permanent place in contemporary (visual) memory as well as in the memory of later generations of readers.[54] The success of this strategy can be illustrated not least by the fact that it is this visual representation by which she is most often remembered today.

But with this author portrait created during her lifetime and supervised by herself, Christine also owns an effective means of opposition against the *topoi* of humility and belittlement that we encounter again and again in her prologues. At the iconographic level of her self-presentation, no traces of such belittlement or signs of modesty remain. Rather one can observe the *mise en scène* of a self-confident late medieval intellectual presenting herself in repeated images of herself as a reader or writer, conversing with or instructing others and thus ensuring that she is regarded in her true light. One example among many may illustrate this consciously created discrepancy between text and image: the author portrait at the beginning of the *Corps de policie* from manuscript 2681 at the Bibliothèque de l'Arsenal, a copy made during the author's lifetime that carries traces of her own handwriting.[55]

The miniature on the initial page, decorated with vine leaves, shows Christine de Pizan at her desk, in front of an oversize open book in which she is writing; the expression of her face, her eyes directed at the book, reveals a tense concentration (Figure 1). On the table lies a closed blue book, an indication that she is incorporating other works into her own writings and that, like all respected writers of her period, she draws on the authority of other authors to give more weight to her own ideas. The author portrait clearly conveys Christine's claim to belong to the rank of the *clercs*.

But Christine is aware that her contemporaries may have found provocative a woman who writes a political reform treatise, and she counters such objections with a self-confident, at times slightly ironic and provocative, form of visual or textual self-presentation. In the short prologue that immediately follows the

Fig. 1: Christine de Pisan. *Livre du corps de policie*. MS2681, folio 4 recto. Courtesy of Bibliothèque de l'Arsenal.

Christine de Pizan 71

image she seems to take back the presentation as an intellectual and as a writer as it is depicted in the miniature, since the text begins with these words:

> Se il est possible que de vice puist naistre vertu, bien me plaist en ceste partie estre passionnee comme femme. Ainsi que plusieurs hommes au sexe femenin imposent non savoir taire ne tenir soubz sillence l'abondance de leur courage, or viengne donc hors hardiement et se demonstre par plusieurs clers ruisseaux la source et fontaine interissable de mon couraige qui ne peut estancher de getter hors les desirs de vertu. O vertu, chose digne et deifiee, comment m'ose-je vanter de parler de toy, quant je congnois que mon entendement ne te sauroit bien au vif comprendre ne exprimer?[56]

(If it is possible that virtue be born from vice, then it pleases me in this case to be passionate like a woman. Since many men impose on the feminine sex the notion that they do not know how to keep quiet or keep silent the abundance of their courage, let the source and the bottomless fountain of my courage, which cannot stop emitting the desire for virtue, flow forth bravely and show itself in the form of many clear streams. O virtue, such a deified and worthy thing, how can I dare to speak of you, when I know that my understanding will never know you well enough to understand or describe you?)

In this passage Christine de Pizan plays with gender stereotypes and with misogynous commonplaces by presenting herself as an emotional creature who is incapable of any kind of linguistic reserve. The combination of this paratext with the author portrait just described nevertheless produces a suggestive tension and a subversive effect that we can still perceive today. At the same time the image overlaps with and eclipses the text, creating a permanent support for the memory of the author and her work.

CONCLUSION

The textual examples amply document Christine's manifold activities as an architect of memory and illustrate that at first the author moves, as is to be expected, within the contemporary conceptualizations of memory. At the same time it is obvious that within the context circumscribed by the period's *outillage mental* she still manages to set new trends. Although she uses the mnemotechnical concept of memory in her *Epistre Othea*, the unusual combination of text and images also creates new possibilities for didactic instruction. Similar developments can be observed within the field of *"memoria* as culture," to use Oexle's term. Christine follows Augustine here, which raises the question whether it is accidental that her great literary models from the time following the ancient period—Augustine, Dante, Petrarca, Boccaccio—are also authors and thinkers who made memory the central topic of their works. The manner in which Christine creates her own liturgical memory and that of her patrons shows how cleverly she combines her own *memoria* with that pertaining to her patrons or to social groups. In particular the construction of her own visual memory was decisive for her permanent place in the different storage media of posterity's cultural memory. And it even stimulated modern artists such as the French painter Colette Deblé to create a postmodern *City of Ladies* in which the references to Christine de Pizan's iconography occupy a central position (Figures 2 and 3). What remains largely unresolved but deserves further investigation are questions concerning the biographical and historical background to the conspicuous emphasis Christine places on *memoria*. A connection between her origins and her manner of creating different types of memory may be assumed: recent sociohistorical studies have shown that in late medieval Italy in particular there was a strong interest in the construction of *memoria* of social groups, be it in the *Ricordanze* of the Florentine merchants[57] or in the monuments of learned men and the "subtle visual *mise en scène*"[58] of the lawyers Giovanni d'Andrea and Giovanni da Legnano from Bologna. It is quite possible that Christine knew these examples of secular memorial art, since the astrologers, to whose ranks her father belonged, also used such strategies of "pictorial self-presentation and of professional and social categorisation" (von Hülsen-Esch, 206).

Fig. 2: "Christine de Pisan présente son livre à un riche admirateur." Illustration by Colette Deblé. Courtesy of Margarete Zimmermann.

Fig. 3: "Christine de Pisan à sa table de travail." Illustration by Colette Deblé. Courtesy of Margarete Zimmermann.

Perhaps Christine's partial deracination, her experience of living at the intersection of different cultures, increased her desire to inscribe herself onto the memory of future generations. Undoubtedly, her intense experience of death, one she shared with her contemporaries, but which in her case radically changed her familial and social situation, making her a writer and forcing her to take up a new gender role, played an important part. Christine's awareness of herself as a female intellectual must have increased her consciousness of the power of a written *memoria* and the importance of a feminine identity grounded on history.

NOTES

* Translated by Gesa Stedman
1. See Glenda K. McLeod, ed., *The Reception of Christine de Pizan from the Fifteenth Through the Nineteenth Centuries. Visitors to the City* (Lewiston/Queenston/Lampeter: Mellen, 1991); Angus J. Kennedy and James Steel, "L'esprit et l'épée ou la résistance au féminin: Christine de Pizan, Jeanne d'Arc et Edith Thomas," in *Une femme de lettres au Moyen Age. Études autour de Christine de Pizan*, ed. L. Dulac and B. Ribémont (Orléans: Paradigme, 1995), 469–81; Angus Kennedy, "Gustave

Cohen and Christine de Pizan: A Re-Reading of the *Ditié de Jehanne d'Arc* for Occupied France" and Margarete Zimmermann, "Christine de Pizan et les féminismes autour de 1900," in *Sur le chemin de longue estude* . . . , ed. B. Ribémont (Paris: Champion, 1998), 101–11 and 183–204; Barbara K. Altmann, "Christine de Pizan: First Lady of the Middle Ages," in *Contexts and Continuities. Proceedings of the IVth International Colloquium on Christine de Pizan (Glasgow 21–27 July, 2000)*, 3 vols., ed. A. J. Kennedy in collaboration with R. Brown-Grant, James C. Laidlaw and C. Müller, published in honor of Liliane Dulac (Glasgow: University Press, 2002), vol. 1, 17-30.

2. Cf. Susan Groag Bell, "A Lost Tapestry: Margaret of Austria's *Cité des Dames*," *Une femme de lettres au Moyen Age* . . . , 449–69 and "A New Approach to the Influence of Christine de Pizan: The Lost Tapestries of the *City of Ladies*," *Sur le chemin* . . . , 7–13.

3. Denis Diderot, *Encyclopédie ou Dictionnaire raisonné des sciences, des arts et des métiers*, 35 vols., vol. 18 (Paris: Briasson, 1765), 9.

4. Louis Moréri, *Le Grand Dictionnaire Historique ou Le Mélange curieux de l'histoire sacrée et profane*, vol. 8 (Paris: Libraires Associés, 1759; reprinted Geneva: Slatkine, 1995), 377–8.

5. Prosper Marchand, *Dictionnaire Historique ou mémoires critiques et littéraires concernant la vie et les ouvrages de divers personnages distingués, particulièrement dans la République des Lettres*, 2 vols. (The Hague: P. de Hondt, 1758–59), vol. 2, 150.

6. See Margarete Zimmermann, "Gedächtnis-Korrekturen. Das literaturgeschichtliche Archiv der Louise-Félicité Guinement de Kéralio," in *Das Schöne im Wirklichen—Das Wirkliche im Schönen. Festschrift für Dietmar Rieger zum 60. Geburtstag*, ed. Klaudia Knabel (Heidelberg: C. Winter, 2002).

7. Lily Braun, *Die Frauenfrage. Ihre geschichtliche Entstehung und wirtschaftliche Seite* (Leipzig: Hirzel, 1901).

8. Léon Abensour, *Histoire générale du féminisme. Des origines à nos jours* (Delagrave: Paris 1921) and *La femme et le féminisme avant la Révolution* (Paris: E. Leroux, 1923).

9. Combative polygraph and among other things the author of *Au cœur du féminisme* (1908) and *Les féministes avant le féminisme* (1910).

10. Roujon was a member of the Académie française and in March 1912 gave a lecture entitled "Christine de Pisan," published in *Journal de l'Université des Annales* II (21) (1912): 479–93.

11. Margarete Zimmermann, "Christine de Pizan et les féminismes autour de 1900."

12. Quoted from Charity Cannon Willard: *Christine de Pizan. Her Life and Works* (New York: Persea, 1984), 223.

13. Martin Le Franc, *Le Champion des Dames*, ed. R. Deschaux, vol. 4 (Paris: H. Champion, 1999), 177:

    Mais les nostres lasches et vains/Ont par courage trop faly/Le nom des bons et des haultains/Avecq les corps ensevely./Si me complains de leur paresse,/Car se de France plusieurs dames/Je ne te nomme, par Eulx esse./Doubter ne fault que sous les lames/Maintes reposent dont les ames/Furent apertes et habiles,/Et firent vergongnes et blasmes/Aux homes en champs et en villes.//Mais au fort, des choses passees/Jugons par ce que veons or,/Et que les dames trespassees/Eurent de clergie tresor/Plus precieux que ne soit or. . . .

14. See Gisela Bock and Margarete Zimmermann, "Die *Querelle des Femmes* in Europa. Eine begriffs- und forschungsgeschichtliche Einführung," in *Die europäische "Querelle des Femmes." Geschlechterdebatten seit dem 15. Jahrhundert*, ed. G. Bock and M. Zimmermann [*"Querelles." Jahrbuch für Frauenforschung*, vol. 2] (Stuttgart: J. B. Metzler, 1997), 9–38; and Margarete Zimmermann, "The Querelle des Femmes as a Cultural Studies Paradigm," in *Time, Space, and Women's Lives in Early Modern Europe*, ed. A. Jacobson Schutte and Th. Kuehn (Kirksville, Missouri: Truman State University Press, 2001), 17–28.
15. Barbara K. Altmann, "L'art de l'autoportrait littéraire dans les *Cent Ballades* de Christine de Pizan," in *Une femme de lettres au Moyen Age*, ed. L. Dulac and B. Ribémont (Orléans: Paradigme, 1995), 227–336 (328).
16. Frances A. Yates, *The Art of Memory* (London: Routledge & Kegan Paul, 1966).
17. See Ernst Robert Curtius, *Lateinische Kultur und europäisches Mittelalter* (Bern: Francke, 1949), 143, 552.
18. *Le livre de l'advision Cristine*, ed. C. Reno and L. Dulac (Paris: Champion 2001), 110.
19. Translation from Glenda K. McLeod, *Christine's Vision* (New York: Garland, 1993), 119.
20. Patrick Geary, "Mémoire," in *Dictionnaire raisonné de l'Occident médiéval*, ed. J. Le Goff and J.-Cl. Schmitt (Paris: Fayard, 1999), 684.
21. It is sufficient to mention contemporary artists such as Rebecca Horn, Christian Boltanski, and Jochen Geerz and the film director Jean-Luc Godard in this context, whose latest work *Éloge de l'amour* (2001) is conceived as a complex filmic variation on the topic of individual and collective memory (cf. the article "Le dessin dans le tapis magique de Jean-Luc Godard," *Le Monde*, 17 May 2001, 29).
22. Otto Gerhard Oexle, "*Memoria* as a Form of Social Action," forthcoming.
23. Oexle, "Memoria als Kultur," *Memoria als Kultur* (Göttingen: Vandenhoeck and Ruprect, 1995), 9–78 (50).
24. Friedrich Ohly argues along these lines in his groundbreaking article "Bemerkungen eines Philologen zur Memoria," in *Memoria. Der geschichtliche Zeugniswert des liturgischen Gedenkens im Mittelalter*, ed. K. Schmidt and J. Wollasch (Munich: W. Fink, 1984), 9–68.
25. Cf. Saint Augustine, *Confessions*, Books IX–XIII (Paris: Les Belles Lettres, 1989), 248: "lata praetoria memoriae, ubi sunt thesauri innumerabilium imaginum de cuiuscemodi rebus sensis inuectarum."
26. Christine de Pizan, *Le livre des fais et bonnes meurs du sage roy Charles V*, ed. S. Solente (Paris: Champion, 1936–40; reprinted Geneva: Slatkine, 1977), vol. 1, 190.
27. All translations of primary texts are by Deborah McGrady and Barbara K. Altmann unless otherwise indicated.
28. Cf. Augustine, *Confessiones*, Liber decimus, Chapter 14: Nimirum ergo memoria quasi uenter est animi, laetitia uero atque tristitia quasi cibus dulcis et amarus:

cum memoriae commendantur, quasi traiecta in unetrem recondi illic possunt, sapere non possunt" (255). Here we also find the food metaphor "ruminando": "Forte ergo sicut de uentre cibus ruminando sic, ista de memoria recordando proferentur" (256). (In the same manner that, by rumination, nourishment returns from the stomach to the mouth, perhaps by a similar act these impressions return from the depths of memory.)

29. Paul Ricœur, *La mémoire, l'histoire, l'oubli* (Paris: Seuil, 2000), 117.
30. Jan Assmann, *Das kulturelle Gedächtnis. Schrift, Erinnerung und politische Identität in frühen Hochkulturen* (Munich: C. H. Beck, 1994), 52, 54.
31. Aleida Assmann, *Erinnerungsräume. Formen und Wandlungen des kulturellen Gedächtnisses* (Munich: C. H. Beck, 1999), 33.
32. Christoph Martin Wieland, "Verzeichniß und Nachrichten von französischen Schriftstellerinnen," in *Werke. 35. Theil. Kleinere Schriften zur Culturgeschichte* (Berlin: Gustav Hempel, n.d.), 72.
33. Christine de Pizan, *Epistre Othea*, ed. G. Parussa (Droz: Geneva, 1999), 199.
34. Preliminary ideas concerning Christine as an author actively concerned with her own *memoria* and that of social groups can be found in Margarete Zimmermann, "Christine de Pizan ou la *memoria* au féminin," in *Contexts and Continuities. Proceedings of the IVth International Colloquium on Christine de Pizan* (Glasgow 21–27 July, 2000), 3 vols., eds. A. J. Kennedy in collaboration with R. Brown-Grant, James C. Laidlaw, and C. Müller (Glasgow: University Press 2002), vol. 3, 919–30.
35. Christine de Pizan, *Le Livre de la mutacion de Fortune*, ed. S. Solente (Paris: Picard, 1959–66), 4 vols.; vol. 1, l. 537.
36. Henri Platelle, "L'épouse, 'gardienne aimante de la vie et de l'âme de son mari.' Quelques exemples du haut Moyen Age," in *La femme au Moyen Age*, ed. M. Rouche and J. Heuclin (Maubeuge: Publications de la Ville de Maubeuge, 1990), 171–184 (173).
37. Christine de Pizan, *Le Livre du Corps de Policie*, ed. A. J. Kennedy (Paris: Champion, 1998), 110–11.
38. *Le Livre des Trois Vertus*, ed. Ch. Cannon Willard and E. Hicks (Paris: Champion, 1989), 224.
39. Charity Canon Willard, *A Medieval Woman's Mirror of Honor* (New York: Persea, 1989), 224–5.
40. Christine de Pizan, *Epistre Othea*, ed. G. Parussa (Geneva: Droz, 1999), 195.
41. See Helen Solterer, *The Master and Minerva. Disputing Women in French Medieval Culture* (Berkeley: University of California Press, 1995), 171: "Her sapiential writing [...] explores the conflicted position of 'wise women' in the polis. To what degree can their actions constitute a critical part of a community's deliberations? .... Indeed, her sapiential writing projects a determining ethical/political role for women."
42. Christine de Pizan, *Le Livre des fais et bonnes meurs du sage roy Charles V*, ed. Susanne Solente (Paris: Champion, 1936–40, reprinted Geneva: Slatkine, 1977), vol. 1, 192.
43. Oexle, *Memoria als kultur*, 37.
44. Pierre Nora, "Entre Mémorie et Histoire. La problématique des lieux," in *Les lieux de la Mémoire*, ed. Susan Solente and Pierre Nora (Paris: Gallimard, 1984), vol. 1, xix.

45. For a more detailed analysis cf. Margarete Zimmermann, "Mémoire—tradition—historiographie. Christine de Pizan et son *Livre des fais et bonnes meurs du sage Roy Charles V*," in *The City of Scholars. New Approaches to Christine de Pizan*, ed. M. Zimmermann and D. De Rentiis (Berlin: W. de Gruyter, 1994), 158–74.
46. Jacques Le Goff, *Histoire et mémoire* (Paris: Folio, 1988), 174.
47. For an interpretation of this sequence see Jacqueline Cerquiglini, "Fondements et fondations de l'écriture chez Christine de Pizan. Scènes de lecture et Scènes d'incarnation," in *The City of Scholars*, 79–97.
48. Christine de Pizan, *La città delle dame*, ed. E. J. Richards, trans. Patrizia Caraffi (Rome: Luni Editrice, 1998), 42.
49. See Margarete Zimmermann, "Utopie et lieu de la mémoire féminine: la *Cité des dames*," in *Au champ des escriptures. IIIe Colloque International sur Christine de Pizan*, ed. E. Hicks (Paris: Champion, 2000), 561–78.
50. Roland Barthes, *Le plaisir du texte* (Paris: Seuil, 1973), 25–6. Although Barthes uses this category only for modern texts, it is legitimate to employ it for a more precise explanation of the aesthetic pleasure that the *Cité des Dames* affords its readers as it is this pleasure that makes this work a classic text of world literature and is the key to its continuing success.
51. *Roland Barthes: The Pleasure of the Text*, trans. Richard Miller (New York: Hill and Wang, 1975), 14.
52. A small selection of titles, all from the sixteenth and seventeenth centuries, will suffice here: François de Billon, *Le Fort inexpugnable de l'honneur femenin*, Symphorion Champier, *La Nef des Dames Vertueuses*, Jean Dupré, *Le Palais des nobles dames*, François de Grenaille, *La Galerie des dames illustres*.
53. In this respect only the twentieth-century writer Colette can compete with Christine. However, Colette's iconography is considerably more heterogeneous than Christine's.
54. On the role that iconography plays in constructing Christine's authority, see Deborah McGrady, "What Is a Patron? Benefactors and Authorship in Harley 4431, Christine de Pizan's Collected Works," in *Christine de Pizan and the Categories of Difference*, ed. Marilyn Desmond (Minneapolis: University of Minnesota Press, 1998), 195–214, and "Authorship and Audience in the Prologues to Christine de Pizan's Commissioned Poetry," in *Au champ des escriptures*, 25–40.
55. The author portrait can be found on fol. 4r.
56. Christine de Pizan, *Le Livre du corps de policie*, ed. A. J. Kennedy (Paris: Champion, 1998), 1.
57. Cf. Christiane Klapisch-Zuber, "L'invention du passé familial à Florence (XIVe–XVe siècle)," in *Temps, mémoire, tradition au Moyen-Âge* (Aix: Publications de l'Université de Provence, 1983), 95–119.
58. Andrea von Hülsen-Esch, "Zur Konstitutierung des Juristenstands durch Memoria," in *Memoria als Kultur*, ed. Oexle, 185–206 (206).

II
Building a Female Community

6

Christine de Pizan as a Defender of Women

Rosalind Brown-Grant

Just as modern readers are often shocked by the misogynist views that circulated within medieval culture, so they can often be disappointed by the seemingly timid response to such views from those writers of the period who sought to defend women. Christine de Pizan is one such author who, although praised by some scholars as a forerunner of twentieth-century feminist thought, has been criticized by others for a lack of radicalism when judged by modern standards.[1] It is certainly true to say that Christine did not change the ground on which the medieval debate about women was conducted in that, unlike modern feminists, she did not move from defending the moral and intellectual equality of the sexes to demanding equality for women in terms of their legal rights, political representation, and access to education. However, although Christine's defense of women may appear conservative when seen from a modern perspective, a rather different picture emerges if her views are compared with those of other profeminine authors of the Middle Ages.[2] What then were the accusations leveled against women that Christine had to refute in order to champion her sex? On what earlier arguments in favor of womankind was she able to draw? To what extent did her own defense of women advance beyond the existing terms of the profeminine response?

MEDIEVAL MISOGYNY

Judaeo-Christian theology had bequeathed to the Middle Ages the view that women were inferior to men in all respects: morally, physiologically, and intellectually. The Church Fathers, particularly St. Paul and St. Augustine, interpreted key verses from Genesis (1:26–7 and 2:21–3) and I Corinthians (11:7) to propound the idea that although woman was made in God's image to the extent that she, like man, possessed a rational soul, she was nevertheless subordinate to him, being created for the specific purpose of helping him to perpetuate the human species.[3] This subordination of woman to man in the order of creation and the limited purpose of her existence meant that she was endowed with not only a body different from his but also an inferior rationality. Moreover, because of her lesser reason, which supposedly had made her an easier target for the Devil than Adam, Eve was often held to be more responsible than he for the Fall, her punishment reflecting this in that it entailed both suffering the pains of childbirth and subjection to her husband.[4] As the daughters of Eve, all women were held to be guilty by association of the same moral failings of disobedience, garrulity, and pride that Eve had displayed in seducing her husband into eating the forbidden fruit. These vices were thus cited by misogamous clerics such as St. Jerome in their attempts to dissuade men against marriage as the reason why wives chafe against their subjection to their husbands and make men's lives miserable.[5] Even the undoubtedly worthy example of the Virgin Mary was not enough to counteract this negative view of women, as her virtue did not erase women's guilt for their part in the Fall. In constant remembrance of Eve's transgression, all women were therefore ordered to keep silent in church and to cover their heads in shame when praying (I Corinthians 11:5–13).

These theological views were buttressed within medieval culture by arguments about women's inferiority drawn from the medical and scientific works of classical antiquity. According to Aristotle's *Generation of Animals*, the female was a defective male in both physical and intellectual terms as she was made from weaker sperm than that used to produce the male child.[6] However, he stopped short of claiming that men and women were different species altogether as, in his *Metaphysics*, he presented gender as being an "accidental" (i.e., material) difference between the sexes, like skin color, rather than an essential one that served to differentiate between species.[7] This conception of women's defective physiology was further bolstered by the application to gender of the theory of the four elements that make up all things in creation: earth, fire, water, and air, each with its related quality of coldness, heat, moisture, or dryness.[8] Because medieval thinkers believed that heat was the primary instrument of nature, they concluded that man was superior to woman, as he was allegedly the warmer and the dryer of the two sexes, whereas woman's coldness and moistness were seen as making her more unstable, changeable, and irrational.

Literary texts of the Middle Ages were heavily influenced by many of these theological and scientific ideas. A key tendency in such works was to discuss individual women as if they were representative of their entire sex whereas men were more often treated as individuals. For instance, short moralizing texts, which formed a distinctive subset of the genre of the *dit*,[9] ascribed stereotypically pejorative traits to women as an entire group, citing the familiar arguments about Eve's responsibility for the Fall, the faithlessness and instability of the female sex, and its lesser degree of godlikeness.

THE MEDIEVAL CASE FOR WOMEN

Despite the mass of antifeminist sentiment to be found in all branches of medieval culture and learning, a considerable body of counterargument began to emerge from the twelfth century onward, although it was not to be as influential as the misogyny that it was designed to refute. Because many of the misogynists derived their views by quoting selectively from biblical and patristic authorities, profeminine writers also tended to employ this "citational" method, extracting arguments in favor of women from exactly the same sources.[10] Certainly, biblical and classical sources provided many virtuous examples of the female sex, such as Judith or Esther, Penthesilea, or Andromache. In theology, a series of stock arguments known as the "privileges of women" were invoked to defend women's honor.[11] These privileges claimed that the female was superior to the male in the sense that Eve was made in a nobler place than Adam (inside rather than outside Eden), from a nobler material (bone rather than earth), and was the culmination of God's work (being created after rather than before him). Even in scientific thought, women's supposed physical and mental inferiority might have been seen as disqualifying them from public office but it also meant that they were deemed to be more affectionate than men, particularly toward children. It was this caring quality that was used by theologians from St. Augustine onward to counter the misogamous tradition and put a more positive slant on marriage. Some medieval clerics in their marriage sermons even encouraged wives to act as "preachers to their husbands" in bringing them back to reasonable forms of behavior.[12]

As Alcuin Blamires has shown, this case for women as rational, constant, and loving beings was taken up by a number of male writers such as Marbod of Rennes, Peter Abelard, Albertano of Brescia, Jean le Fèvre, and Eustache Deschamps.[13] Yet it was not always clear what the intention was behind such writings. For example, although Abelard, in his correspondence with Heloise, seems to be genuinely attempting to raise the prestige of women who took the veil, others such as Deschamps in his *Miroir de mariage* appear to be merely playing an ironic, scholastics' game in juxtaposing statements that were for and against women and wedlock.[14] As Christine herself once suggested in her *Epistre au dieu d'Amours* (1399), it was perhaps only when a female writer took up her pen that a truly unequivocal case for women would be put forward.[15] However, in conducting a systematic defense of her sex, Christine did not restrict herself simply to rehearsing traditional arguments about women's moral capacities. Rather, she transformed them into a broader social ethic that would legitimate the place of women at the very center of the body politic.

A WOMAN'S RESPONSE TO ANTIFEMINISM

For Christine, the fundamental error made by misogynists was in presenting women as if they were a race of less than human beings, inferior to men in terms of rationality, moral judgment, and intelligence. Her response was to emphasize not only the essential sameness of men and women but also their possession of identical moral and intellectual faculties. In putting forward this positive view of womankind, she stressed its implications for the way in which the relations between men and women were understood. As she pointed out in her reply to Jean de Montreuil, which forms part of the documents in the famous "Querelle de la *Rose*" (1401–1402),[16] once women are regarded as members of the same species as men, they can no longer be seen simply as objects to be desired or feared. On the contrary, they should be accorded the respect due to them for their central role within human society as partners with men in every facet of the latter's existence as husbands, lovers, sons, and brothers (ed. Hicks, 139, ll.775–83, ed. and trans. Baird and Kane, 136). As Christine saw it, the debate about women thus centered on two key issues: sameness versus difference and complementarity versus incompatibility. Let us examine how she discussed each of these issues.

Sameness versus Difference

To argue that men and women shared a common humanity and possessed an equal rationality, Christine's strategy was to show that the sexes were distinguished from each other purely by external bodily differences. Her trump card here was her adoption of Aristotle's theory that the differences between men and women were "accidental" rather than essential.[17] Thus, in the *Livre de l'advision Cristine* (1405),[18] in her allegorical account of her own birth, Christine describes how Nature began by pouring her spiritual essence into a mold, mixed it with matter to give her a human form, and only then, at the end of the process, endowed it with a specifically female gender:

> Lors, comme elle ja eust mis le mole atout la matiere en la fournaise, mon esperit prent, si le fiche ens, et tout en la maniere que aux corps humains donner fourme acoustumé avoit, tout mesla ensemble et ainsi cuire me laissa par quantité de temps tant que ung petit corps humain me fut parfaict. Mais comme le voulsist ainsi celle qui la destrempe avoit faicte, a laquel cause se tient et non au mole, j'aportay sexe femmenin. (ed. Reno and Dulac, 14, ll.4–10)[19]

(When she had put the mold with all the material into the oven, she took my soul and placed it in, and just as she usually did to give form to human bodies, she mixed it all together and let me bake for a certain time until a little human body was ready for me. But, according to the wishes of she who had made the mixture, I was given the female sex, since this was up to her to decide rather than being due to the shape of the mold.) Similarly, in the *Livre de la cité des dames* (1405),[20] on the question of woman's godlikeness, Christine offers her own interpretation of the account of human creation in Genesis by arguing that Adam and

Eve differed only on the level of the body, not of their rationality, as humankind was spiritually but not *physically* created in God's image.[21] As Dame Raison explains to Christine:

> Mais aucuns sont si folz que ilz cuident quant ilz oyent parler que Dieu fist homme a son ymage que ce soit a dire du corps materiel. Mais non est, car Dieu n'avoit pas lors pris corps humain, ains est a entendre de l'ame qui est esperit intellectuel et qui durera sanz fin a la semblance de la deité, *laquelle ame Dieu crea et mist aussi bonne, aussi noble en toute pareille en corps femenin comme ou masculin*. (ed. Richards, 78, emphasis added)

(There are, however, some who are foolish enough to maintain that when God made man in His image this means His physical body. Yet this is not the case, for at that time God had not yet adopted a human form, so it has to be understood to mean the soul, which is immaterial intellect and which will resemble God until the end of time. *He endowed both male and female with this soul, which He made equally noble and virtuous in the two sexes* [emphasis added].[22])

For Christine then, what divided the sexes in biological terms was far less important than what united them in spiritual terms: their common rationality and capacity for virtue. Proof of this was provided by her selection of the women whose illustrious deeds and virtuous acts as warriors and artists, inventors and prophets, teachers and saints, are commemorated in the *Cité des dames*. Likewise, in her courtesy books she treats her audience, whether male or female, as having an equal ability to make reasoned moral choices. Hence, in the *Livre des trois vertus* (1405),[23] in addressing women of each estate in society, she appeals to the rationality of all her readers—be they princesses, peasants, or prostitutes, baronesses, nuns, or bourgeoises—in order to persuade them to pursue virtue and so, effectively, "write" themselves into the City of Ladies.[24]

Having argued that the difference between men and women was limited to the level of the body, Christine nevertheless refused to conceptualize even this bodily difference in terms of inferiority and superiority. In the *Cité des dames* (I.1) she rejects Aristotle's argument that woman is a defective male (which she probably knew from reading St. Thomas Aquinas's Commentary on the *Metaphysics*),[25] quoting the theological "proof" that women, as God's creation, were not misbegotten (Genesis 1:31) and that it is heterodox to claim otherwise. Although she concedes, like many other medieval defenders of women, that the female sex is generally less physically strong than the male—with the exception of women like the Amazons—Christine does not interpret this as a sign of innate deficiency on the female's part.[26] Indeed, whereas other profeminine writers simply made such physiological frailty into a "strength in weakness" topos by citing it as evidence of women's greater compassion and affection,[27] she used it as the basis of an even more positive argument. On the grounds that what Nature has taken away with one hand she compensates for with the other, Christine claims that women's physical weakness in fact gives them both a lesser tendency toward aggression and violence and a greater inclination for study (ed. Richards, 104, 152; and trans. Brown-Grant, 34, 57, respectively).

Yet this moral defense of women in terms of the rationality and propensity for virtue that they shared with men was only one aspect of Christine's contribution to the debate on sameness versus difference. Equally important, to her mind, was the need to convince her audience, particularly male clerics, of the need to read beyond the biological differences of the sexes so as to be able to see women as exemplars of the human in moral discourses. Paradoxically, given that it was a commonplace of misogynist thought that women were capable of reading only literally and failed to grasp the higher allegorical levels of meaning,[28] Christine sought to show that it was, in fact, the misogynists themselves who were the literal readers in their refusal to interpret women as signifiers of a higher import than just their bodily gender.

Thus, as Jeff Richards has argued, Christine uses the female to exemplify the human when she constructs her City of Ladies as an allegorical representation of St. Augustine's City of God such that, in her universal history of women, all forms of social and cultural division have been transcended.[29] This strategy is even more in evidence in Christine's other works such as the *Epistre Othea*,[30] her mythographic "mirror for princes,"[31] in which she teaches her male audience to adopt modes of reading that deliteralize and desexualize female signifiers. Here, instead of simply recounting women's literal deeds—whether praiseworthy or reprehensible—in her tales from classical antiquity, she exhorts her readers to interpret stories of female figures such as Echo, Hero, Criseyde, and Pasiphae as lessons in moral and spiritual behavior.[32] Hence, in the different levels of interpretation contained in the "glose" (gloss) and "allegorie" (allegory) that accompany each of the hundred, four-line "textes" (texts) that make up this work, Christine allegorizes such female figures as vices, virtues, or the human soul. In so doing, she replaces all literal references to these actual women with more sex-neutral references to "les personnes" (people) who are prone to a specific vice or "le bon esperit" (the good soul) who must adopt a particular moral conduct, thereby ensuring that her audience grasps the universal meaning of these *exempla* rather than drawing any hasty judgments about the female sex. For instance, in her version of the story of Echo, which might easily be understood as a tale of female lust, Christine glosses this figure first as a sex-indefinite "personne qui par grant necessité requiert autrui" (Parussa, 323, ll.25–6) (person in great need of another's help) and then as the virtue of "misericorde" (mercy) that the male reader must cultivate in his own heart (Parussa, 1.43).

We can see a similar process at work in the *Advision*, although the moral exemplar presented to the princely reader here is now Christine herself. In this text, which has a more pressing political agenda than that of the *Epistre Othea*—

having been written at a time when civil war was brewing in France—Christine uses her autobiographical account of how she was metaphorically consoled by the figure of Philosophie to deliver an important message to the prince.[33] Prompting the type of polysemous interpretation that she requires from the reader of this text, Christine explains in her prologue: "la fiction de cestui livre se puet alegorisier triblement, c'est assavoir assimiller au monde general, qui est la terre, aussi a homme simgulier et puis au royaume de France" (ed. Reno and Dulac, 6, ll.111–13) (the fiction of this book can be allegorized in triple fashion, that is to say, applied to the world as a whole, which is the earth, and also to the individual man, and then to the kingdom of France).[34] Interpreting this work as both a political and a moral allegory gives a coherence to its seemingly disparate elements and clearly sets out the link Christine wishes to make for her reader between the realms of politics and individual responsibility. Whereas the first two parts of the book are devoted to identifying the ills of the country, and more generally of human society, as being the result of the ruthless pursuit of self-interest on the part of its rulers, in the third part Christine offers herself up as an example of how the virtuous soul must learn to humble itself and put aside the search for worldly gain.[35] Dame Philosophie thus encourages Christine to ignore the "accidental" aspect of her existence, her frail female form and state of relative powerlessness in society, and to see herself instead in terms of her essential human condition, namely as a soul in relation to God. Rather than wishing to change her "corps foible et femmenin en homme pour estre transmuee de condicion" (ed. Reno and Dulac, 129, ll.27–8) (weak female body for that of a man in order to change condition), she must realize that in suffering tribulation, she is in fact one of "les plus beneurez en tant comme plus s'aprochent de la vie Jhesucrist" (Reno and Dulac, 119, ll.20–1) (the most blessed as their lives come closest to imitating that of Christ). This lesson is then extended to the prince himself who must set aside the "accidental" advantages of his gender, status, and wealth and see himself anew, as Christine had done, as a soul accountable to God for his actions on this earth:

> Se tu veulz . . . avoir la vraye extimacion de l'omme et savoir quel ou quan grant il est, regarde le tout nu. Ostes son patrimoine, ostes ses honneurs et les autres mençonges de Fortune, et le regarde, se tu peus, non pas ou corps mais ou couraige. (Reno and Dulac, 135, ll.29–33)

(If you wish to have the true measure of a man, and find out who he is and how great he is, look at him in all his nakedness. Strip him of his worldly goods, strip him of his honors and all the other illusions of Fortune, and look at him, if you can, not on the level of the body but of the heart.)

The claim that it is only through ethical self-government by the ruler (rather than through reform of the institutions of power themselves) that the ills of a state can be remedied was a highly traditional one within medieval political theory.[36] What distinguishes the *Advision* from other political texts of the time is that it delivers this message by using a female exemplar to signify the human, a far less common feature of political writing but one that formed a vital part of Christine's works in defense of women.

Complementarity versus Incompatibility

If Christine was concerned to assert the shared humanity of men and women, she was no less energetic in combating the view of misogynists and misogamists that the sexes were fundamentally incompatible and that the relations between them were necessarily antagonistic.[37] For her, such opinions were particularly evident in works such as Jean de Meun's *Roman de la Rose* whose representation of love and marriage she criticized as being both harmful and self-contradictory.[38] To Christine's mind, Jean's text offered an impossible choice between marriage, which he depicts as a hellish institution in which men and women destroy each other, and passionate love outside marriage (synonymous with courtly love), which he shows as leading not only to the physical and moral degradation of women but also to the spiritual perdition of both sexes.

Christine proposed to challenge this pessimistic conclusion about the incompatibility of the sexes by launching a concerted attack on the conception of love that underpins it. She thus counsels women against passionate love on the grounds that it leads them to losing their self-control and makes them vulnerable to trickery at the hands of men. For example, in the *Cité des dames* she includes a number of cautionary tales of women whose love brought them tragedy. Recounting the stories of Hero, Medea, Dido, and others, Dame Droiture attempts to dissuade Christine's readers from throwing themselves into

> celle mer tres perilleuse et dampnable de fole amour, car tousjours en est la fin a leur grant prejudice et grief en corps, en biens et en honneur et a l'ame. Qui plus est, si feront que sages celles qui par bon sens la saront eschever et non donner audience a ceulx qui sanz cesser se traveillent d'elles decepvoir en tel cas. (ed. Richards, 404)

(the perilous and treacherous sea of passionate love. This is because such liaisons always have a tragic ending and the woman invariably loses out in terms of her health, status, reputation and, most important of all, her soul. Those women who are sensible and wise would do well to avoid embarking on affairs like this and not to waste any time on listening to men who are always looking for ways of leading them into such traps [trans. Brown-Grant, 186].)

Despite their otherwise laudable qualities, such as their great learning (Medea) or their steadfastness (Dido), these women serve as *exempla in malo* for

Christine de Pizan as a Defender of Women 89

having allowed their passions to blind them to the male deceit or faithlessness that would ultimately lead to their tragic end.

This lesson to women about the danger of losing one's autonomy through accepting male advances is equally present in Christine's lyric poetry.[39] Although at the end of both the *Livre du duc des vrais amans* (1403–1405)[40] and the *Cent balades d'amant et de dame* (1409–1410)[41] both the male and female protagonists have suffered the various pains of love, it is only the lady whose reputation or life has been lost. By contrast, the male lover in each of these texts carries on much as before: he may be brokenhearted but his respected position in society is left intact. Christine underlines this fundamental asymmetry in the fates of the sexes within courtly love by giving the female voice the last word in each of these lyric sequences.[42] In the *Cent balades d'amant et de dame* in particular, the despair expressed by the lady in the final verse is reinforced in a lyric coda, the aptly named "Lay mortel"[43] (Mortal lai), in which she breathes her last and condemns Love for the suffering it has brought her at the hands of an unworthy lover.[44]

Yet it is perhaps in her courtesy book for women, the *Trois vertus*, that Christine demythifies this form of loving most completely when she reprises the letter of advice sent to the princess in the *Duc des vrais amans* by her governess Sebille, Dame de la Tour.[45] The chief lesson of Christine's courtesy book is that it is in the rational self-interest of all women, but particularly high-born ladies such as princesses, to adopt virtuous conduct both to refute misogynist opinion and to ensure a lasting reputation for themselves.[46] Passionate love is shown to be a disaster because it disempowers those who need to hold on to whatever power they possess, and undermines ladies' mastery of those codes of behavior (dress, speech, and bearing) they need to manipulate in order to fashion a virtuous name for themselves.[47] As the governess states in her letter to the princess, the physical signs of love will give the lady away because they subvert these codes on which her chastity and reputation crucially depend:

> Et comme ces dictes condicions et toutes manieres convenables a haulte princepce fussent en vous le temps passé, estes a present toute changee, si come on dit, car vous estes devenue trop plus esgaiee, plus enparlee, et plus jolie que ne soliez estre, et c'est ce qui fait communement jugier les cuers changiéz quant les contenances se changent. (ed. Willard and Hicks, 112, ll.68–73)

(Although this conduct and all other behavior appropriate to a great princess were yours formerly, you are at present, it is said, quite changed, for you have become very much more abandoned, more talkative and merrier than you used to be, and that is the kind of thing that usually causes people to have a shrewd idea. Hearts change when the manner changes [trans. Lawson, 180].[48])

In a society where even a rumor of adultery or misplaced passion could discredit a woman forever,[49] Christine presents courtly love as a game that no woman can win and so is best not played.

Having rejected passionate love as a desirable form of relationship between men and women on moral and pragmatic grounds, Christine put forward an alternative that stressed the fundamental complementarity of the sexes.[50] She thus valorized the bond between male and female as one between mutually affectionate helpmeets, a conventional argument in the profeminine armory that she derived from one of the "privileges of women" topoi and a theological gloss popularized by Hugh of St. Victor and Peter Lombard.[51] Although the *e materia* topos stated that the bone from which woman was made was superior to the earth from which man had been fashioned, the gloss argued that the creation of woman from man's side meant that she was intended to be his cherished companion and partner in life, not his despised slave as it would be if she had been made from his foot (*Cité des dames*, I.9). In the *Epistre au dieu d'Amours* these arguments serve as the basis for an alternative view of love, one that, for both sexes, is ennobling rather than corrupting, and is harmonious rather than acrimonious, because it is based on mutual respect and profound compatibility. Here the God of Love spells out to men that it is their duty to love and honor women because "C'est son droit per qui a lui est semblable,/La riens qui plus lui peut estre agreable" (For she's his kindred soul, so much like him,/The being most compatible with him) (ed. and trans. Fenster and Erler, 68–9, ll.731–2). In the *Cité des dames*, Christine celebrates marriage as the fitting institution in which this ideal of reciprocal affection can be realized. Thus, in Book I she cites Solomon's encomium from Proverbs 31:10–31 on the benefits to men who have worthy wives (I.43) and devotes a key section of Book II to the praise of wives such as Queen Hypsicratea (II.14) who, far from bringing trouble and strife to their husbands, gave them great happiness and solace. Given these and many other examples of wifely affection, Christine argues that it is up to husbands to prove themselves deserving of their wives' devotion by accepting their good counsel, valuing their constancy, and returning their love.

Although this emphasis on complementarity was a commonplace in the medieval case for women, Christine was to develop it significantly further than any of her male predecessors had. Rather than simply defending love and marriage, she uses the notion of complementarity as the basis of a broader social ethic that enabled her to legitimate women as an estate that, like the three traditional estates of men as *oratores*, *bellatores*, and *laboratores* (those who pray, those who fight, and those who labor), has a crucial role to play in ensuring social cohesion.[52] Thus, although the misogynist and misogamous clerics espoused a separatist view of the social relations between male and female,[53] Christine countered their arguments with a highly inclusive conception of society that stressed the indispensability of women to men's well-being. This did not mean that Christine

Christine de Pizan as a Defender of Women

thought that women should play the same roles within society as men did. On the contrary, she made it clear that the unity of the sexes could be achieved only by a complementary division of labor (*Cité des dames*, I.11). Her task then was to valorize the role in which women could make their most visible contribution to society, that of the *mulier economica*,[54] as it was this role that, although reviled by misogynists and misogamists as one in which women abusively exercise their power in the household, had traditionally always been theirs.

Whereas Boccaccio's *De Claris Mulieribus* (Christine's main source for the *Cité des dames*) had found virtue in those women who, as viragoes displaying "manly" qualities, succeeded in transcending their sex,[55] Christine devoted over half of her text to women who, as wives, had virtuously performed the role that was specific to their sex. More importantly, Christine presents these good wives as not only benefitting their own husbands but also serving to maintain or restore social cohesion in general. For instance, she praises Tertia Emilia for hiding her husband's adultery so as not to damage his exalted status as military leader of Rome (II.20), the wife of Alexander the Great for persuading her husband to make plans for his succession to avoid plunging the country into chaos (II.29), and Queen Clotilde for converting her husband King Clovis and so bringing the Christian faith to the people of France (II.35).

Thus, even if Christine's own female contemporaries could not perform exactly the same deeds as these classical and historical women, they could, nonetheless, still seek to emulate the qualities of discretion, peacemaking, and persuasion displayed by each of them. More explicit instruction as to how this could be done is provided in the *Trois vertus* in which, once again, Christine stresses the importance of women's contribution to men's lives as their partners and complementary helpmeets.[56] Here, she outlines how the women in each specific social class can bring comfort and support to their husbands and so ensure both solidarity between the sexes and cohesion within society. She encourages the princess to maintain a respectable court, love her children and husband, and display largesse toward the deserving and compassion toward the needy (Book I); counsels baronesses and other ladies of noble rank to run their husbands' estates in their absence with justice, firmness, and sobriety (Book II); and advises women of the artisanal and merchant classes to share their husbands' workloads, maintain a respectable household, and refrain from social climbing through their mode of dress (Book III). For Christine then, harmony in the home and stability in society go hand in hand, and women have a crucial role to play in creating both, one that should be properly acknowledged by those who in the past have so consistently attacked them.

Yet perhaps the clearest instance of Christine's development of traditional profeminine ideas about the complementarity of the sexes into a broader social ethic is that she does not simply outline what women have done for men but also turns to the question of men's own responsibility toward women. Adopting her male predecessors' standard argument that men's failure to give women credit for all they do for them constitutes personal ingratitude toward the female sex, she goes on to transform this point into a wider issue of moral and social injustice. In her view, it was not just that men should honor women because of the Virgin Mary's role as mother of the Redeemer and be grateful to them for their capacity to give birth, their talent for making garments that dignify the male sex, and their diligence in looking after their menfolk.[57] Although she clearly thought these points were important and dealt with each of them in the *Epistre au dieu d'amours* and the *Cité des dames*,[58] Christine also saw her defense of women as an attempt to call misogynists to account for the damage they had caused to the body politic in slandering one of its most hard-working estates. As numerous scholars have noted, this emphasis on justice can be seen in the fact that Christine conducts her defense within a strongly legalistic framework: a court of love in the *Epistre au dieu d'Amours* and a case for the defendant in the *Cité des dames*.[59] However, what has not previously been commented on is that Christine conceives of justice in the terms set by contemporary social theory. As a result, she was able to condemn misogyny as a destabilizing and injurious force within society precisely because it encouraged men to abrogate their responsibility toward women as an estate.

Social cohesion in the Middle Ages was theorized not in terms of equality but of complementarity and reciprocity, with each estate being naturally or providentially fitted to play its particular role.[60] Subscribing to this theory in her political works such as the *Livre du corps de policie* (1406–1407),[61] Christine declares that all the estates are interdependent and so should be mutually supportive:

> Car tout ainsi comme le corps humain n'est mie entier . . . quant il lui fault aucun de ses membres, semblablement ne peut le corps de policie estre parfait . . . se tous les estas dont nous traictons ne sont en bonne conjonction et union ensemble, si qu'ilz puissent secourir et aidier l'un a l'autre, *chascun excercitant l'office de quoy il doit servir, lesquelz divers offices ne sont a tout considerer establis et ne doivent servir ne mes pour la conservacion de tout ensemble.* (ed. Kennedy, 91, ll.16–23, emphasis added)[62]

(For just as the human body is not whole, . . . when it lacks any of its members, so the body politic cannot be perfect . . . if all the estates of which we speak are not well joined and united together. Thus, they can help and aid each other, *each exercising the office which it has to, which diverse offices ought to serve only for the conservation of the whole community* [ed. and trans. Forhan, 90, emphasis added].[63])

Using many of the same terms but applying them to gender relations, Christine in the *Cité des dames* explains through her mouthpiece Dame Raison that this is also how male and female roles in society should be conceived:

Christine de Pizan as a Defender of Women

> *Dieux a establi homme et femme pour le servir en divers offices et pour aussi aydier, conforter et compaigner l'un l'autre*, chacun en ce qui lui est establi a faire et a chacun sexe a donné tele nature et inclinacion, comme a faire son office lui appartient et compette. (ed. Richards, 92, emphasis added)

(*God created man and woman to serve him in different ways and to help and comfort one another*, according to a similar division of labor. To this end, He endowed each sex with the qualities and attributes which they need to perform the tasks for which they are cut out [trans. Brown-Grant, 29, emphasis added].)

Given this division of labor, medieval social theorists argued that reason and natural justice demanded that each member of the body politic, whether a member of the prestigious preaching or fighting classes or the more lowly laboring classes, should show gratitude for the contribution of the others by rendering unto each his due.[64] Thus, in the *Corps de policie*, Christine herself upbraids the nobles for acting irrationally in denigrating the important role played by the common people in contemporary society:

> Et vraiement ceulx qui tant de mal leur font ne prennent pas garde a ce de quoy il servent, car qui bien y viseroit, *toute creature raisonnable se tendroit obligee a eulx. Si est pechié d'estre ingrat de tant de services comme ilz nous font*. Et vraiement ceulx icy sont bien les piez qui soustiennent le corps de la policie, car ilz soustiennent par leur labour le corps de toute personne. (ed. Kennedy, 108, ll.21–6, emphasis added)

(And really those who do them so many evils do not take heed of what they do, *for anyone who considers himself a rational creature will hold himself obligated to them. It is a sin to be ungrateful for as many services as they give us*! And really it is very much the feet which support the body politic, for they support the body of every person with their labor [trans. Forhan, 107, emphasis added].)

In her texts in defence of women, Christine criticizes the behavior of misogynists on exactly the same grounds. For instance, in the *Cité des dames*, she inveighs against them for having gone against reason and divine providence in denying the huge debt rightfully owed by men to women:

> a tout homme qui voulentiers mesdit de femme vient de tres grant vilté de courage, *car il fait contre raison et contre nature*: contre raison en tant que il est tres ingrat et mal congnoissant des grans biens que femme lui a fais . . . ; contre nature en ce que il n'est beste vive quelconques, ne oysel, qui naturellement n'aime cherement son per, c'est la femmelle. (ed. Richards, 72, emphasis added)

(*any man who willfully slanders the female sex does so because he has an evil mind, since he's going against both reason and nature*. Against reason, because he is lacking in gratitude and failing to acknowledge all the good and indispensable things that woman has done for him.... Against nature, in that even the birds and the beasts naturally love their mate, the female of the species [trans. Brown-Grant, 19–20, emphasis added].)

That Christine clearly conceived of gender relations in "estate" terms can be seen most strikingly in the fact that she singles out the two most powerful estates of men—clerks and knights—for particular criticism. This is because, as she explains in the *Cité des dames*, it is precisely these two sections of the body politic that have benefitted most from the contribution made by women to human society and yet have been the least grateful to them. Because it was the female sex that brought the alphabet and arms into the world, along with so many other inventions such as weaving, spinning, and agriculture (I.33–I.40), it is all the more unreasonable and unjust that clerks and knights have persisted in their attacks on women when in fact they owe their very livelihood to them:

> or apperçoy ... la tres grant ingratitude et descongnoissance d'iceulx hommes qui tant mesdient des femmes ... or se taisent d'orenavant les clercs mesdisans de femmes ... voyant ceste noble dame Carmentis, laquelle par la haultece de son entendement les a appris ... les nobles letres du latin. Mais que diront les nobles et les chevaliers ... refraignent leur bouche d'orenavant, avisant que le usage des armes porter, faire batailles et combatre en ordenance ... leur est venu et donné d'une femme. (ed. Richards, 182–4)

(I've now realized the full extent to which those men who attack women have failed to express their gratitude and acknowledgement.... Those clerks who slander women ... really should shut their mouths once and for all ... they owe a huge debt of thanks to this noble lady Carmentis, for having used her fine mind to ... endow them with ... the noble Latin alphabet.... But what about all the many noblemen and knights who ... should hold their tongues, given that all their skills in bearing arms and fighting in organized ranks ... have come down to them from a woman [trans. Brown-Grant, 72].)

Thus, for Christine, the concept of complementarity did not serve simply to value women in their roles as the affectionate, constant, and morally dependable spouses of men, as her male predecessors in the medieval debate had argued. It was also the means by which she could require men themselves to face up to their responsibilities, reminding them of their social and moral duty to love, protect, and show gratitude to women for their contribution to society. In so doing, Christine was able to adapt the traditional premises of medieval social theory to new ends, using them to strengthen her case for women and to argue that it was in the interests of both social cohesion and natural justice that the estate of women be allotted its rightful, acknowledged, and honored place in the body politic alongside that of men.

CONCLUSION

As a defender of women, Christine de Pizan cannot help but disappoint modern feminists for omitting to make a connection between the moral equality of the sexes and the need for their social, legal, and political parity. Yet it should be borne in mind that the society in which she lived reserved education only for a tiny fraction of even the male population and similarly denied any right of political representation to the vast majority of men. Seen in this context, the failure by profeminine writers such as Christine to demand a political voice for women or equal educational opportunities becomes more understandable. Furthermore, although it was a commonplace of medieval culture that in the next life, differences between men and women—like those between lord and peasant—would become immaterial (Galatians 3:28), in this life inequality between both the sexes and the classes was a necessary and inevitable part of human existence. All members of the body politic had a valuable role to play in maintaining the cohesion of society, but each could play this part only within his or her designated estate. Given that most social theorists of the Middle Ages largely excluded women from their vision of human organization, or at best thought them deserving of only a brief mention,[65] perhaps Christine's most important contribution to the medieval debate on women was that she claimed for the female sex a vital place in the body politic. Whereas marriage sermons and courtesy books declared that women's chief role in society consisted of preserving their chastity and acting with sobriety,[66] Christine argued that because women shared the same rationality and potential for making moral choices as men, their worth was not limited to these qualities alone. Thus, rather than being reviled as the greatest threat to men's well-being and peace of mind, as the misogynist and misogamous traditions would have it, women, as the necessary complement to men, should be valued as their greatest asset in every aspect of their lives.[67]

NOTES

1. See, for example, Rose Rigaud, *Les Idées féministes de Christine de Pizan* (Neuchâtel: Attinger, 1911; Geneva: Slatkine Reprints, 1973); Blanche Hinman Dow, *The Varying Attitude toward Women in French Literature of the Fifteenth Century: The Opening Years* (New York: Publications of the Institute of French Studies, 1936); Beatrice Gottlieb, "The Problem of Feminism in the Fifteenth Century," in *Women of the Medieval World*, ed. Julius Kirschner and Suzanne Wemple (Oxford: Blackwell, 1985), 337–64; Sheila Delany, *Medieval Literary Politics: Shapes of Ideology* (Manchester: Manchester University Press, 1990), 74–87 and 88–103; and Maureen Quilligan, *The Allegory of Female Authority: Christine de Pizan's Cité des dames* (Ithaca: Cornell University Press, 1991).
2. See Alcuin Blamires, *The Case for Women in Medieval Culture* (Oxford: Clarendon Press, 1997). See also Alcuin Blamires et al., eds., *Woman Defamed and*

Woman Defended: An Anthology of Medieval Texts (Oxford: Clarendon Press, 1992).
3. Marie-Thérèse d'Alverny, "Comment les théologiens et les philosophes voient la femme," *Cahiers de Civilisation Médiévale* 20 (1977): 105–29; and Kari Elisabeth Børresen, *Subordination and Equivalence: The Nature and Rôle of Woman in Augustine and Thomas Aquinas* (Washington, DC: University Press of America, 1981).
4. Ian Maclean, *The Renaissance Notion of Woman: A Study in the Fortunes of Scholasticism and Medical Science in European Intellectual Life* (Cambridge: Cambridge University Press, 1980), 8–27.
5. Katharina M. Wilson and Elizabeth M. Makowski, *Wykked Wyves and the Woes of Marriage: Misogamous Literature from Juvenal to Chaucer* (Albany: State University of New York Press, 1990).
6. Cited in Blamires, *Woman Defamed*, 39–41.
7. *Aristotle's Metaphysics*, ed. and trans. John Warrington (London: Dent, 1956), 325. See also Vern L. Bullough, "Medieval Medical and Scientific Views of Women," *Viator* 4 (1973): 485–501; and Joan Cadden, *Meanings of Sex Difference in the Middle Ages: Medicine, Science, and Culture* (Cambridge: Cambridge University Press, 1993).
8. Cited in Blamires, *Woman Defamed*, 41–2.
9. For examples of works in this genre, see *Three Medieval Views of Women: La Contenance des Fames, Le Bien des Fames, Le Blasme des Fames*, trans. and ed. Gloria K. Fiero, Wendy Pfeffer, and Mathé Allain (New Haven: Yale University Press, 1989).
10. R. Howard Bloch, "Medieval Misogyny: Woman as Riot," *Representations* 20 (1987): 1–24.
11. Paul Meyer, "Mélanges de poésie française, IV: Plaidoyer en faveur des femmes," *Romania* 6 (1877): 499–503; and "Les Manuscrits français de Cambridge, ii: Bibliothèque de l'Université," *Romania* 15 (1886): 236–357.
12. Sharon Farmer, "Persuasive Voices: Clerical Images of Medieval Wives," *Speculum* 61.3 (1986): 517–43. See also S. H. Rigby, *Chaucer in Context* (Manchester: Manchester University Press, 1996), 155–60.
13. Blamires, *The Case for Women*.
14. Blamires, especially Chapter 8 on Abelard and pp. 33–6 on Deschamps.
15. *Poems of Cupid, God of Love: Christine de Pizan's "Epistre au dieu d'Amours" and "Dit de la Rose," Thomas Hoccleve's "The Letter of Cupid," with George Sewell's "The Proclamation of Cupid,"* ed. and trans. Thelma S. Fenster and Mary Carpenter Erler (Leiden: E. J. Brill, 1990), 54–55, ll.417–18. Text hereafter referred to as the *Epistre au dieu d'Amours*.
16. See Christine de Pisan, Jean Gerson, Jean de Montreuil, Gontier et Pierre Col, *Le Débat sur le Roman de la Rose*, ed. Eric Hicks, Bibliothèque du XVᵉ Siècle, 43 (Paris: Champion, 1977). Text hereafter referred to as the "Querelle." See also *La Querelle de la Rose: Letters and Documents*, ed. and trans. Joseph L. Baird and John R. Kane, University of North Carolina Studies in the Romance Languages and Literatures, 199 (Chapel Hill: University of North Carolina, Department of Romance Languages, 1978).

17. Earl Jeffrey Richards, "In Search of a Feminist Patrology: Christine de Pizan and 'les Glorieux Dotteurs,' " in *Une femme de lettres au Moyen Age: Etudes autour de Christine de Pizan*, ed. Liliane Dulac and Bernard Ribémont, Etudes christiniennes (Orléans: Paradigme: 1995), 281–95; and "Rejecting Essentialism and Gendered Writing: The Case of Christine de Pizan," in *Gender and Text in the Later Middle Ages*, ed. Jane Chance (Gainesville: University Press of Florida, 1996), 96–131.
18. *Le livre de l'advision Cristine*, ed. Christine Reno and Liliane Dulac, Etudes christiniennes, 4 (Paris: Champion, 2001), hereafter referred to as the *Advision*. All translations of this work are mine, unless otherwise stated.
19. For a fuller discussion of this issue of accident versus essence, see Rosalind Brown-Grant, *Christine de Pizan and the Moral Defence of Women: Reading beyond Gender* (Cambridge: Cambridge University Press, 1999), 120–22.
20. *La Città delle Dame*, ed. Earl Jeffrey Richards and trans. Patrizia Caraffi (Milan, Trento: Luni Editrice, 1998), 2nd ed.; text hereafter referred to as the *Cité des dames*.
21. Lori J. Walters, "La ré-écriture de Saint Augustin par Christine de Pizan: de *La Cité de Dieu* à la *Cité des dames*," in *Au champ des escriptures: IIIe Colloque international sur Christine de Pizan, Lausanne, 18–22 juillet 1998*, ed. Eric Hicks, Diego Gonzalez, and Philippe Simon, Etudes christiniennes, 6 (Paris: Champion, 2000), 197–215; and Thelma S. Fenster, "Possible Odds: Christine de Pizan and the Paradox of Woman," in *Contexts and Continuities: Proceedings of the Fourth International Colloquium on Christine de Pizan (Glasgow 21–27 July 2000)*, 3 vols., ed. Angus J. Kennedy in collaboration with Rosalind Brown-Grant, James C. Laidlaw, and Catherine Müller (Glasgow: University Press, 2002), 355–66.
22. *The Book of the City of Ladies*, trans. Rosalind Brown-Grant (Harmondsworth: Penguin, 1999), 22–3.
23. *Le Livre des trois vertus*, ed. Charity Cannon Willard and Eric Hicks, Bibliothèque du XVe siècle, 50 (Paris: Champion, 1989); hereafter referred to as the *Trois Vertus*.
24. Marie-Thérèse Lorcin, "Le *Livre des Trois Vertus* et le *sermo ad status*," in Dulac and Ribémont, *Une femme de Lettres*, 139–49; and Brown-Grant, *Christine de Pizan*, 182–92.
25. Richards, "Rejecting essentialism."
26. Renate Blumenfeld-Kosinski, " 'Femme de corps et femme par le sens': Christine de Pizan's Saintly Women," *Romanic Review* 87 (1996): 157–75.
27. Blamires, *The Case for Women*, especially 132–7.
28. See, for example, the interpretation of the Wife of Bath as a literal reader in D. W. Robertson, Jr., *A Preface to Chaucer: Studies in Medieval Perspectives* (Princeton: Princeton University Press, 1962), 321–2.
29. Earl Jeffrey Richards, "Christine de Pizan and Sacred History," in *The City of Scholars: New Approaches to Christine de Pizan*, ed. Margarete Zimmermann and Dina De Rentiis, European Cultures, Studies in Literature and the Arts, 2 (Berlin: W. de Gruyter, 1994), 15–30. See also Glenda McLeod, *Virtue and Venom: Catalogs of Women from Antiquity to the Renaissance* (Ann Arbor: University of Michigan Press, 1991), 133–7.

30. *Epistre Othea*, ed. Gabriella Parussa (Geneva: Droz, 1999); hereafter referred to as the *Epistre Othea*. All translations of this text are my own.
31. For studies of this text as a political work, see Sandra Hindman, *Christine de Pizan's "Epistre Othéa": Painting and Politics at the Court of Charles VI* (Toronto: Pontifical Institute of Medieval Studies, 1986); Gabriella Parussa, "Instruire les chevaliers et conseiller les princes: *L'Epistre Othéa* de Christine de Pizan," in *Studi di storia della civiltà letteraria francese, Mélanges offerts à Lionello Sozzi par le Centre d'études franco-italiennes, Universités de Savoie et de Turin*, vol. 1, Bibliothèque Franco Simone, XXV (Paris: Champion, 1996), 129–55; and Rosalind Brown-Grant, "Miroir du prince, miroir d'amour: *L'Epistre Othéa* and John Gower's *Confessio Amantis*," in *Sur le chemin de longue étude... Actes du colloque d'Orléans Juillet 1995*, ed. Bernard Ribémont, Etudes christiniennes, 3 (Paris: Champion, 1998), 25–44.
32. Brown-Grant, *Christine de Pizan*. 78–87.
33. Ibid., 89–127. See also Roberta Krueger, "Christine's Anxious Lessons: Gender, Morality and the Social Order from the *Enseignemens* to the *Avision*," in *Christine de Pizan and the Categories of Difference*, ed. Marilynn Desmond, Medieval Cultures, vol. 14 (Minneapolis: University of Minnesota Press, 1998), 16–40.
34. Christine M. Reno, "The Preface to the *Avision-Christine* in ex-Phillipps 128," in *Reinterpreting Christine de Pizan*, ed. Earl Jeffrey Richards et al. (Athens: University of Georgia Press, 1992), 207–27, 213.
35. Brown-Grant, *Christine de Pizan*, 89–127.
36. Jacques Krynen, *Idéal du prince et pouvoir royal en France à la fin du Moyen Age* (Paris: Picard, 1981), 118.
37. See Glenda McLeod and Katharina Wilson, "A Clerk in Name Only—a Clerk in All But Name: The Misogamous Tradition and *La Cité des dames*," in Zimmermann and De Rentiis, *The City of Scholars*, 67–76.
38. Kevin Brownlee, "Discourses of the Self: Christine de Pizan and the *Rose*," *Romanic Review* 59 (1988): 199–221.
39. See many of the articles in Earl Jeffrey Richards, ed., *Christine de Pizan and Medieval French Lyric* (Gainesville: University of Florida Press, 1998).
40. *Le livre du duc des vrais amans*, ed. Thelma S. Fenster (Binghamton, NY: Medieval and Renaissance Texts and Studies, 1995); hereafter referred to as the *Duc des vrais amans*.
41. *Cent ballades d'amant et de dame*, ed. Jacqueline Cerquiglini (Paris: Union Générale d'Edition, 1982).
42. Charity Cannon Willard, "Lovers' Dialogues in Christine de Pizan's Lyric Poetry from the *Cent ballades* to the *Cent ballades d'amant et de dame*," *Fifteenth Century Studies* 4 (1981): 167–80; and Liliane Dulac, "Dissymétrie et échec de la communication dans les *Cent ballades d'amant et de dame* de Christine de Pizan," *Lengas* 22 (1987): 133–46.
43. Barbara K. Altmann, "Last Words: Reflections on a 'Lay Mortel' and the Poetics of Lyric Sequences," in Richards, *Christine de Pizan and Medieval French Lyric*, 83–102.
44. Charity Cannon Willard, "Christine de Pizan's *Cent ballades d'amant et de dame*: Criticism of Courtly Love," in *Court and Poet. Selected Proceedings of the Third*

Congress on the International Courtly Literature Society, Liverpool, 1980, ed. Glyn S. Burgess (Liverpool: Francis Cairns, 1981), 357–64.
45. Allison Kelly, "Christine de Pizan and Antoine de la Sale: The Dangers of Love in Theory and Fiction," in Richards et al., *Reinterpreting Christine de Pizan*, 173–86. See also Roberta L. Krueger, "A Woman's Response: Christine de Pizan's *Le Livre du Duc des vrais amans* and the Limits of Romance," in her *Women Readers and the Ideology of Gender* (Cambridge: Cambridge University Press, 1993), 217–46.
46. Brown-Grant, *Christine de Pizan*, 193–206; and M. Bella Mirabella, "Feminist Self-fashioning: Christine de Pizan and *The Treasure of the City of Ladies*," *European Journal of Women's Studies* 6.1 (1999): 9–20.
47. Eric Hicks, "Discours de la toilette, toilette du discours: de l'idéologie du vêtement dans quelques écrits didactiques de Christine de Pizan," *Revue des Langues Romanes* 92.2 (1988): 327–42; and Roberta L. Krueger, "*Chascune selon son estat*: Women's Education and Social Class in the Conduct Books of Christine de Pizan and Anne de France," *Papers on French Seventeenth Century Literature* 24 (1997): 19–34.
48. *The Treasure of the City of Ladies*, trans. Sarah Lawson (Harmondsworth: Penguin, 1985).
49. Thelma Fenster, "La fama, la femme, et la Dame de la Tour: Christine de Pizan et la médisance," in Hicks et al., *Au champ des escriptures*, 461–77.
50. June Hall McCash, "Mutual Love as a Medieval Ideal," in *Courtly Literature: Culture and Context. Selected Papers from the Fifth Triennial Congress of the International Courtly Literature Society, Dalfsen, The Netherlands, 9–16 August, 1986*, ed. Keith Busby and Erik Kooper (Amsterdam: Rodopi, 1990), 429–38.
51. Blamires, *The Case for Women*, 101.
52. S. H. Rigby, "Literature and social ideology," in *A Companion to Britain in the Later Middle Ages*, ed. S. H. Rigby (Oxford: Blackwell, 2003), 497–520.
53. Dyan Elliott, *Spiritual Marriage: Sexual Abstinence in Medieval Wedlock* (Princeton: Princeton University Press, 1993).
54. This concept is derived from Aristotle's *Economics*: see Aristotle, *Oeconomica*, trans. E. S. Forster, in *The Works of Aristotle Translated into English*, ed. W. D. Ross (Oxford: Clarendon Press, 1966), revised edition, Book I, 3.
55. Constance Jordan, "Boccaccio's In-famous Women: Gender and Civic Virtue in the *De Claris Mulieribus*," in *Ambiguous Realities: Women in the Middle Ages and the Renaissance*, ed. Carole Levin and Jeanie Watson (Detroit: Wayne State University Press, 1987), 25–47; and McLeod, *Virtue and Venom*, 59–80.
56. Charity Cannon Willard, "Women and Marriage around 1400: Three Views," *Fifteenth Century Studies* 17 (1990): 475–84.
57. For these traditional arguments used in women's defense, see Blamires, *The Case for Women*, Ch. 3.
58. On Mary, see *Epistre au dieu d'Amours*, ll.571–90, and *Cité des dames*, II.30; and on women in general, see *Cité des dames*, I.39.
59. For studies of legalistic aspects of Christine's work, see Charity Cannon Willard, "A New Look at Christine de Pizan's *Epistre au dieu d'Amours*," in *Seconda Miscellanea di studi e ricerche sul Quattrocento francese*, ed. Jonathan Beck and

Gianni Mombello (Chambéry: Centre d'études franco-italien, 1981), 71–92; Maureen Cheney Curnow, " 'La pioche d'inquisicion': Legal-Judicial Content and Style in Christine de Pizan's *Livre de la Cité des Dames*," in Richards, *Reinterpreting Christine de Pizan*, 157–72; and Helen Solterer, *The Master and Minerva: Disputing Women in French Medieval Culture* (Berkeley: University of California Press, 1995), 151–75.

60. Cary J. Nederman, "The Expanding Body Politic: Christine de Pizan and the Medieval Roots of Political Economy," in Hicks et al., *Au champ des escriptures*, 383–97.
61. *Le Livre du corps de policie*, ed. Angus J. Kennedy, Etudes christiniennes, 1 (Paris: Champion, 1998).
62. On Christine's social and political theory, see Gianni Mombello, "Quelques aspects de la pensée politique de Christine de Pizan d'après ses oeuvres publiées," in *Culture et politique en France à l'époque de l'humanisme et de la Renaissance*, Atti del Convegno Internazionale promosso dall'Accademia delle Scienze di Torino in collaborazione con la Fondazione Giorgio Cini di Venezia, 29 Marzo–3 Aprile, 1971 (Turin: Accademia delle Scienze, 1974), 43–153; and Kate Langdon Forhan, "Polycracy, Obligation, and Revolt: The Body Politic in John of Salisbury and Christine de Pizan," in *Politics, Gender, and Genre: The Political Theory of Christine de Pizan*, ed. Margaret Brabant (Boulder, CO: Westview Press, 1992), 33–52.
63. Kate Langdon Forhan, ed. and trans., *The Book of the Body Politic*, Cambridge Texts in the History of Political Thought (Cambridge: Cambridge University Press, 1994).
64. Andrew Galloway, "The Making of a Social Ethic in Late-Medieval England: From *gratitudo* to 'Kyndenesse,' " *Journal of the History of Ideas* 55.3 (1994): 365–83.
65. See, for example, Jacques Legrand: *Archiloge Sophie, Livre des Bonnes Meurs*, ed. Evencio Beltran, Bibliothèque du XVe siècle, 49 (Paris: Champion, 1986).
66. See D. L. d'Avray and M. Tausche, "Marriage Sermons in *ad status* Collections of the Central Middle Ages," *Archives d'Histoire Doctrinale et Littéraire du Moyen Age* 47 (1980): 71–119; Alice A. Henstch, *De la littérature didactique du moyen âge s'adressant spécialement aux femmes* (Cahors: A. Coueslant, 1903; Geneva: Slatkine Reprints, 1975); Ruth Kelso, *Doctrine for the Lady of the Renaissance* (Urbana: University of Illinois Press, 1975); and Diane Bornstein, *The Lady in the Tower: Medieval Courtesy Literature for Women* (Hamden, CT: Archon Books, 1983).
67. I would like to thank Thelma Fenster and S. H. Rigby for kindly making their work available to me prior to publication and to express once again my gratitude to S. H. Rigby for his invaluable comments on earlier drafts of this chapter. I am also grateful to the Arts and Humanities Research Board for funding the period of study leave in which this chapter was prepared.

7

Christine's Treasure

Women's Honor and Household Economies in the *Livre des trois vertus*

Roberta L. Krueger

Critics have long acknowledged that the *Livre des trois vertus* occupies a distinct place both within Christine de Pizan's corpus and within late medieval didactic literature.[1] A companion volume to the *Cité des dames*, the book of advice that Christine dedicated in 1405 to the young Margaret of Burgundy is more practical and more direct than the *Cité des dames*. As she advises contemporary women on how to maintain virtue and honor in their own communities, Christine addresses matters of "real" life in compelling detail and uses historical exempla sparingly. Unique among Christine's works and among late medieval conduct books, the *Trois vertus* is addressed specifically to women of all ranks. It is one of the rare female-authored books of conduct from the Middle Ages, the only medieval female-authored treatise for women in French.[2] Filtering her voice through various allegorical figures or speaking directly, Christine tailors her voice, tone, and precepts for each class, as in *ad status* sermons.[3] The book's intricate layering of embedded voices highlights the skillful use of female speech, which is one of the overarching concerns of the book.[4] Compared to near-contemporary male-authored didactic texts for women such as the *Livre du Chevalier de la Tour Landry pour l'enseignement de ses filles* or the *Menagier de Paris*,[5] Christine spends less time extolling chastity or obedience to one's husband, and her interactive approach is less threatening; it appeals to women's reasoning and eschews frightening punitive exempla. Christine pays far more attention to women's proactive roles in enhancing their social reputations through moral behavior and good works and fosters what Rosalind Brown-Grant has called a "politics of visibility."[6] The book's varied narrative voices, its often personal tone, the diversity of its advice—on piety, social and marital relations, dress, children's education, household management, domestic and civic duties—and its broad audience—

101

from the princess, to lady on manor, to merchant's wife, to prostitute—guaranteed the book's popularity among noble and bourgeois circles. It was translated into Portuguese, and disseminated in paper manuscripts and early printed editions through the mid-sixteenth century.[7]

The *Trois vertus* also stands out in the way it portrays women's economic lives.[8] My analysis will demonstrate that Christine's portrayal of women's management of financial resources is key to the moral vision of *Trois vertus* and that Christine does far more than depict sociohistorical realities. Christine goes much further than her predecessors or contemporaries in discussing women's roles as managers of household finances. As she offers practical counsel on luxury goods, revenues, and expenses, Christine shows that women's economic lives are closely tied to moral standing and spiritual well-being and that female honor depends not only on chastity and reputation but also on proper economic activity. Furthermore, Christine not only advocates prudent financial management and social responsibility within a particular class, she also stresses the *interdependence* of women's economic activities throughout society.

In a recent article on political economics in Christine's works, Cary J. Nederman suggests that Christine is one of the first medieval European thinkers to reflect in a comprehensive way about the social effects of economic activity;[9] her treatment of economic issues reflects an awareness "of the new social and economic realities that were altering the landscape of late medieval institutions and practices" (388) and is particularly remarkable for its "economic conception of community and governance" (390). Just as Christine explicitly articulates an "organic" theory of the male-ruled polis in the *Livre du corps de policie*, where the metaphor of the "body politic" is pointedly invoked,[10] so in the earlier *Trois vertus*, she carefully outlines an interdependent model of women's social organization, showing how the financial activities and welfare of women of different ranks, in courts, in households, on manors, and in cities, are intertwined.

As Nederman observes, the effects of Christine's "organic" socioeconomic approach are complex: on the one hand, the organic model tends to uphold the status quo, "to justify hierarchy, inequality, exclusions, and subordination"; on the other hand, the sense of mutual participation of members can also be forward-reaching, suggesting "an inclusive, reciprocal, and interdependent conception of community," one that is more sensitive to social change (388). Even as *Trois vertus* exhorts women to uphold the values of traditional medieval society, respecting separation of privileges and function by rank, it promotes an ethos of social and material improvement that appeals to the rising merchant and bourgeois classes. Through her deployment of economic metaphors and her precise attention to financial details throughout the book, Christine attacks privilege and luxury among elite women and advances an ethos of self-enhancement and financial prosperity in a way that prefigures social changes that will occur.

The complexity of Christine's social and economic thought is nowhere more apparent than in her portrayal of women's "treasure," whose material, moral, and spiritual meanings resonate throughout the *Trois vertus*, which was alternately entitled the *Tresor de la cité des dames*. Christine's deployment of the word "treasure" exploits the term's many meanings in medieval culture. The "tresor" is, first, a treasury, a collection of gold, silver, jewels, and other precious objects that were stored or hidden away; it could also refer to the storage place or the receptacle in which the goods were kept and to the accumulation of revenues of a state.[11] By extension, the word "tresor" was used metaphorically to refer to any object or quality that was highly valued, most preciously guarded, most highly esteemed. In this sense, "treasury" can entitle a literary work that encloses a wealth of texts or an abundance of important knowledge, as in the thirteenth-century encyclopedic *Livre dou tresor* of Brunetto Latini, which Christine would have known, and in Christine's own *Tresor*. In literature, "tresor" was often used as a metaphor for female chastity, either premarital virginity or conjugal fidelity. This meaning is apparent in the *Menagier de Paris*, when the Menagier glosses Matthew's parable of the man who sells all he has to acquire a field containing a precious stone: a chaste woman is just such a "tresor" or a "pierre precieuse," and there is none finer: "ne peut avoir meilleur tresor que de preude femme et saige.... car en quelque estat qu'elle soit, pucelle, mariee, ou vesve, elle peut estre comparee au tresor et a la pierre precieuse; car elle est si bonne, si pure, si necte, qu'elle plaist a Dieu."[12] (There can be no finer treasure than the honest and wise woman ... for no matter what her estate, be she maiden, wife or widow, she can be compared to the treasure and the precious stone; for she is so good, pure and honorable that she is pleasing to God.) More broadly, woman's "tresor" was the accumulation of her good qualities, her moral probity, her social reputation, her perceived virtue and honor. The material connotation of "tresor" often evokes a desire for its stability and inviolability.

Christine de Pizan's *Trois vertus* expands upon the vocabulary of her predecessors and redefines the scope of female virtue. She recasts the aristocratic notion of "honor" and the material sense of "tresor" within a complex framework that portrays women within each social class who actively construct their social identities through economic activity. Yet even as she attempts to attach a stable value to female virtue, Christine portrays the volatility of female honor, whose meanings and value vary according to rank and according to the desires of the female subject. Ultimately, Christine's book reveals that women's economic activity may lead to social changes that will ultimately transform the hierarchy upon which honorable distinctions are based.

In her dedication to twelve-year-old Margaret of Burgundy, who had married the dauphin Louis de Guyenne in the previous year, Christine states that she writes for the "*acroissement du bien et honneur* de toute femme, grande, moyenne, et petite" (emphasis added; 3) (*the increase in well-being and honor* of all women, high-born, middle class, and common). She organizes her treatise accordingly, with Book I addressed to princesses, Book II to ladies at court and on the manor, and Book III to all other women, including bourgeoises, wives of artisans and merchants, laborers, prostitutes, and the destitute. Christine repeats her goals in economic terms in Book I, Chapter 2: the Virtues speak on behalf of "le bien et accroissement de l'honneur et prosperité de l'université des femmes" (10) (the well-being and increase in honor and prosperity of the university of women). In each book, Christine demonstrates how female honor may be guarded and increased and how it may be lost in economic terms that are expressed both materially and metaphorically.

Book I, for the Princess, is dominated by a conflicted image of "tresor," as defined by two competing discourses. In material terms, "tresor" designates the personal store of riches, jewels, and accoutrements that princesses maintain for their pleasure and distinction; in moral and spiritual terms, it is the source of their potential damnation. These two views are articulated, respectively, by the voice of worldly Temptacion and the voice of Nostre Seigneur. Temptacion attempts to convince the princess, who reclines on a luxurious bed, that she should stake her happiness on material wealth, which can buy influence and security: "Si te convient mettre peine a amasser tresor afin qu'a ton besoing tu t'en puisses aidier. C'est le meilleur ami et le plus seur moyen que avoir puisses" (13) (You need to work to amass treasure so that you can help yourself with it when you need to; it is the best friend and the surest means that you can have.) In stern contrast, Nostre Seigneur warns that worldly pleasures are fleeting and that it is harder for a rich man to enter Paradise than for a camel to go through the eye of a needle (15). Earthly "tresor" is not delightful but "doloreux" because it is amassed at the expense of others:

> Ha! doloreux *tresor*! c'est chose comme impossible que tu puisses estre *amassé* sans le prejudice de plusieurs, a leur grant grief et extorcion, et tu le veulx assembler de la sueur de plusieurs gens, et contre leur voloir pour alouer mauvaisement et a ton singulier vouloir. Saches certainement, et ne doubtes du contraire, que l'avoir acquis et amassé indeuement, tu n'useras ja joyeusement, car la ou tu l'auras assemblé en entente de l'employer en aucunes choses a ton plaisir, Dieu t'envoyera d'austre costé tant d'aversité, ou de maladies ou d'aultres charges, qu'il convendra que *ce maudit tresor soit desployé et mis en usage doloreux*, tout au contraire de ce que tu pensoyes. (emphasis added; 16–17)

(Oh, painful *treasure*! It's impossible that you could be amassed without the harm of many, at their great pain and extortion, and you want to gather it from the sweat of many people, against their will and for your own desire. Know certainly, and don't doubt, that having amassed and acquired it unfairly, you will not use it joyfully, because wherever you have sought to use something for your pleasure, God will send you such adversity or sickness or other charge, that *this damnable trea-*

sure will be deployed and put to painful use, very much to the contrary of what you think.)

Nostre Seigneur's negative portrait of the princess shows a young lady beset by the temptations of her inherited wealth and poisoned by pride and idleness; she has nothing better to do than rest all morning and, after lunch, to "visiter les coffres"—her trunks laden with jewels and adornments (18). Such "treasure," amassed at the expense of others and extorted unjustly against the wishes of others at the will of the princess is indeed "douleureux," a burden on the princess and on those from whom it is unfairly acquired.

Christine converts such material "treasure" into a powerful economic metaphor for spiritual salvation in the opening pages of Book I, when the Virtues state that rather than amass such worldly treasures, the princess should store up the "tresors de l'ame" (10) which are the moral virtues, "plus nobles que richeces mondaines" and which will be served, like delicious foodstuffs, "premierement" to noble women (11). Although it may be extremely difficult for the rich to attain salvation, the wealthy lady can acquire spiritual treasure through acts of charity, by giving away superfluous goods that belong rightly to the poor. Whatever is given away in charity is like money put in savings, to be drawn on in the afterlife: "Tout ainsi l'avoir que l'en restraint de superflu estat pour donner aux povres et bien faire est *le tresor qui est mis a part en sainte huche*, qui sert aprés la mort et garde de l'exil d'enfer. . . . Thesaurisiez au ciel!" (emphasis added; 40) (Thus all the wealth that one keeps from spending on superfluous goods to give to the poor and do good is *the treasure that is put in a holy hutch*, which can be used after death and keeps one from the exile of hell. . . . Save up in heaven!). Accumulation of unnecessary and outrageous dress, jewels, accoutrements, and possessions beyond reason (43) is a major impediment to the acquisition and increase of spiritual "tresor." Christine urges that worldly gains be converted, through charity, into heavenly assets, for this "tresor" is the only one that can be carried into the afterlife. Each "bonne mainagiere" of all ranks—"la princepce et toute femme"—should attend to such spiritual "espargne" (savings).[13]

In advocating that the princess give alms for her spiritual welfare, the Virtues encounter a contradiction: the narrator imagines the princess asking, if one must not store up worldly treasure, how is it possible to have wealth to dispose of in alms (39)? Here, the moralist makes an important concession to the medieval class hierarchy: God does not order a lady to give up all her wealth to the poor, but rather permits her to keep what is necessary "pour son estat, et pour payer ses servans, faire dons quant il est expedient, et payer ce que est pris pour elle et ses debtes" (for her estate, and to pay her servants, to distribute gifts as necessary and to cover her purchases and debts) (39). Whatever she refrains from spending on her pleasures that exceed need—"superfluitez" such as "robes" and "joyaulx" more than appropriate for her station—will be converted into "treasure" in a celestial coffer and stored up in heavenly investment.

When Christine insists that the princess manage her financial resources prudently, she speaks not only to the nobility, but to all people who would live wisely ("toutes gens qui veulent vivre par ordre de sagece," 75). There is no "honte" (shame) in knowing about revenues and accounts and in observing bookkeeping practices. On the contrary, the princess should know about every aspect of the estate's financial practices; she should ensure that nothing will be extorted from the poor, that business dealings will be fair, that prices be just (75). The benefits of the princess's sound financial management thus extend throughout the community, and the example of her wise conduct applies to all.

Following the practices she has described for Charles V,[14] Christine recommends that the princess divide her wealth in five parts to be distributed, first in alms to the poor; second, in household expenses; third, to her officers and ladies-in-waiting; fourth, to foreign visitors or those deserving of special recognition; and finally, to her "tresor," from which she may spend "a sa plaisance ce qu'elle vouldra pour mettre en joyaulx, robes et autres abillemens" (75–6) (at her pleasure whatever she wishes on jewels, gowns and other clothing). As long as the "grande dame" ensures that her revenues from legitimate means cover her expenses and that no new taxes or loans—"faire finances estranges ou chevances non licites a grans domages et fraiz" (76) (make unusual financial arrangements or take unsuitable loans that would incur large losses and costs)—need be arranged, then the princess may enjoy her financial superiority. Christine's detailed advice about financial management constitutes the seventh and last teaching offered by Prudence Mondaine. Economic prudence is thus an essential means by which the princess may "acquerir" "los, gloire, renommee and grant honneur" in this world and "paradis" in the afterlife (76).

In stressing the princess's financial responsibility, Christine may have known that Queen Isabeau, following the King's declared incompetence in 1402, had financial authority in the realm and shared, with Louis d'Orleans, the responsibility of levying "aide" for war.[15] Christine was surely ignorant of the bottom line of Isabeau de Baviere's revenues and expenses, and she probably never surveyed the contents of the Queen's personal treasury, whose luxurious objects and splendid costumes surpassed those of earlier monarchs.[16] But Christine was surely aware of the Queen's extravagant tastes and her fondness for luxury,[17] and she condemns extortion, seizing of goods, and indebtedness—all means by which the nobility fed their insatiable thirst for sartorial extravagance. Christine upholds the principle of a certain degree of "tresor" as legitimate, as we've seen. Yet, she attacks both unjust means of acquiring wealth and extravagance consumption, especially sartorial excess.[18]

In her comments on financial management, Christine conflates material and metaphoric meanings of "tresor" so that economic and spiritual life are seen as intersecting. Similarly, when she addresses specifically moral behavior, she again uses economic terms to discuss women's proactive management. She adopts the Menagier de Paris's terminology when she describes women's greatest "treasure" as *bonne renommé*, but she portrays this as a changing commodity whose value women can increase:

> O le tres grant *tresor* a princepce ou haulte dame que bonne renommee! Certes, nul si grant en ce monde ne pourroit avoir, *ne que elle doye tant amer a amasser*; car le *tresor* commun ne la puet servir qu'environ elle, mais cellui de bonne renommee lui sert et pres et loing, *qui eslieve son honneur par toute la terre*. (emphasis added; 42)

(Oh, what a great *treasure* has the princess or high-born lady in a good reputation! She can surely have no greater in this world, *nor should she love to amass any treasure more*. For ordinary *treasure* can only help her in her immediate environment, but that of a good reputation serves her far and near, and *raises her honor all over the earth*.)

By charging high-born women with the management of their own accounts and by urging ladies to "increase" their moral and spiritual well-being, Christine advocates strategies of fiscal and social management that may easily be adapted by the ladies of the other estates. Christine's portrayal of women's economic life in Book I thus offers a complex view of late medieval society: it appears to uphold traditional distinctions of class and rank, and yet attacks abuse, extortion, and extravagance among the nobility; it conflates economic prudence with spiritual gain; and by urging all women to "increase" their moral and spiritual "treasure," it promotes women's active management of their material and their social life in all ranks—whose different effects and consequences Christine explores in Books II and III.

In Book II, the Virtues continue to deploy economic language as they address the two high-born, yet socially distinct classes of women: ladies of the court, who serve higher-born queens or princesses, and ladies on their own in great manor houses. The greatest asset of the former group is their reputation, which Christine defines as a precious commodity whose value women must maintain and increase by carefully limiting their social interactions.[19] As the Virtues explain, the more valuable a "beau tresor" one has, the more it must be cherished. A woman should not exchange her "tres grans tresors" (very great treasure)—her friendship or personal acquaintance—too freely. Rather, she should make it become a scarce commodity, so that it will be held in greater esteem:

> Or est il ainsi que *toute femme honourable, bonne et sage, doit estre reputee comme un beau tresor* et une notable et singuliere chose digne d'onneur et de reverence. Doncques, puisqu'elle est telle et y veult estre tenue, *il n'apertient point que trop grant marchié ne largece face de ses tres grans tresors*—c'est assavoir de l'acointance de son honnourable personne.... (emphasis added; 133)

(And so it is that *every honorable, good, wise woman should be valued like a beautiful treasure* and a notable thing, uniquely worthy of honor and reverence.

Thus, because this is how she is and wants to be regarded, *it is not appropriate that she trade and give away her very great treasures too liberally*—that is to say the acquaintance of her honorable person. . . .)

Christine takes up the classic notion of male moralists that woman's chastity is her greatest "tresor." But far from portraying women as no more than passive "objects" to be acquired by men as household treasures, Christine shows women as active managers of their own social accounts; the frugality that she exercises with her favors will only make her social worth greater in the eyes of those who esteem and perhaps desire her. Christine's use of economic language underscores the extent to which women are agents of the construction of their own social identity—which is, indeed, the theme of this section devoted to court life.

As she turns to address ladies on the manor, Christine's economic advice becomes more concrete. Because these women are often charged with managing the estate in their husbands' absence, they must be able to assume complete control of finances and "faire valoir leurs revenues et leurs meubles" (152) (to maintain the worth of their revenues and possessions). Women of this rank must know everything about the costs and revenues of the estate and must know how to admonish their husbands gently to live within their means and not incur debts (153). Christine expects them to understand the complicated system of rents and rights accruing from fiefs and other dependencies so that the lords of these domains cannot cheat them.

There is no "deshonneur" for these "dames et damesoilles" in being knowledgeable about accounts—"si ne lui sera point de deshonneur se elle se cognoist en comptes" (153) (it is no dishonor to her if she knows about the accounts)—to make sure that taxes are collected fairly and that the poor are treated with compassion rather than punished: "Au fait des amendes aux povres gens doint estre pour l'amour de Dieu plus piteuse que rigoureuse" (153) (Concerning fines levied on poor people may she for God's sake be more compassionate than rigorous). Again, Christine shows that women's prudent oversight of their own estate can effect the economic well-being of the community.

The economic role that Christine envisages for the "dames et damoiselles du manoir" exceeds active collection and management of traditional revenues. Ladies should also organize, supervise, and participate in the production of wool and textiles for household use and for sale, and they should supervise the cultivation of hemp and production of household linens (155–56). Christine emphasizes that the profits from such home industry may well exceed the customary rents from landholdings. Christine praises the resourcefulness of a contemporary, the Countess of Eu, who was not ashamed ("n'avoit point de honte") to participate in the "honneste labour de mainage" (156) (honest household work) and who managed to earn more "prouffit" from her work than she earned from "toute la revenue de sa terre" (all the income from her land). With such an example, Christine suggests that industrious women may have contributed significantly to the late medieval economy and that their industry may well have offset the decline in value of seigneurial rents for some noble families.

Christine discusses another way that women of this class may make accommodations to changing socioeconomic conditions and increase their "bien" and "honneur" (163). "Dames et demoiselles" who live in cities should not shun, out of false pride, the opportunity to marry wealthy commoners—clerks, officers of the crown, bourgeois, or merchants. Their new condition will bring them all the greater "honor" if they accept their status graciously, acting with humility before their husbands and treating others courteously and discreetly (164). Maintaining and increasing "honor" for women of the mid-level aristocracy—women in courts, women on manors, noble women who marry bourgeois—entails far more than remaining chaste or faithful. Increasing honor also entails domestic management and negotiation of social value, activities Christine often expresses in economic terms and as bound up with economic activity.

Turning at last to Book III, when the Virtues offer advice to wives of merchants and artisans, they do so almost exclusively as economic precepts that are both concrete and morally uplifting. Apart from a brief admonition to offer "amour et foy" to one's husband, Christine's prescriptions focus on financial management of the household and the workplace (which may be identical). Woman's primary role is to distribute household assets wisely and put them to good use, and to oversee her husband's revenues and spend them with discretion (173). Accordingly, as Christine explains throughout this book, the good wife will oversee wise expenditures, will perform careful accounting, will supervise the work of servants and the noise level of children, will see that chambermaids are occupied in clothwork when their chores are done, will ensure that fair prices are paid for services rendered, will caution husbands against risky business deals and bad loans, and, among other things, will maintain an impeccable linen closet, which, according to Christine, is "le plaisir naturel aux femmes" (176). Part Martha Stewart, part *Get a Financial Life*, Book III demonstrates in no uncertain terms that bourgeois "honor" is a carefully groomed system of appearances upheld by men but maintained by women, as summed up in the advice: "Doit estre soingneuse que son mary soit nettement tenus en robes et toutes choses, *car le net aournement du mary est l'onneur de la femme*" (emphasis added; 174). ([A good housewife] will make sure that her husband is neatly supplied in gowns and other things, *because the neat adornment of the husband is the honor of the wife.*)

Christine's emphasis on female honor is striking. In the *Menagier de Paris*, the housewife's appearance reflects the husband's standing and the wife provides for her husband's comforts;[20] here, it is the husband, carefully decked out by his wife, who brings honor to her. Christine shows, far more explicitly than her contemporaries, that bourgeois female "honor" entails efficient management of a domestic system, and that women are the prime commanders of such order.

Christine advocates a system in which women actively manage court and household economies and in which such economic activity is commensurate with their social identities. Revenues, expenses, gifts, donations, payment of debts, expenditures on items of necessity and luxury: in different ways, these economic activities constitute "tresaure" and "honor" for the different social classes Christine describes, and women are its active managers.

The domestic and political economy that Christine seeks to describe and to advocate is a stable and, in the moralist's view, a just one, as degrees of worldly "honor" are meted out to efficient domestic systems according to rank, "chascune a son estat," and since spiritual "tresor" awaits even the lowliest. But just as Christine's earlier advice to the Queen revealed anxiety about financial abuse in a system centered on personal morality, so in Book III does her description of merchant's wives and servants reveal a further underlying economic instability. If women are active traders in the marketplace of social honor and if their goal is to increase their "tresor," as Christine says repeatedly, then they may so manipulate its value as to unsettle its foundations. Women are those within the household who often oversee, if not control, the purse strings and who are charged with the social construction of honor. It follows, then, that women may be agents of disruption as well as agents of domestic stability. The extravagance of the Princess who indulges in jewels and new dresses presents a serious threat to her impoverished subjects, as we have seen in Book I. In Book III, the extravagance of a merchant's wife who wants to live like a princess presents a similarly alarming threat to the Queen.

In the third chapter of Book III, Christine rails against the sartorial extravagance of merchants' wives by describing an especially "outrageous" act of conspicuous consumption, namely the lavish adornment of a household for the lying-in of a retail merchant's wife (III.3, 183–8). This passage constitutes the longest extended description in the entire Book, Christine's most detailed analysis of material culture.[21] We hear about the home's architecture, its furnishings and draperies (decorated with the lady's "devise," as if she were nobility), its silver service, the mistress's gown and her bedclothes, and the estimated price of the hangings and the bedspread. In the midst of such calculated splendor, the expectant mother lies draped in silk, propped up on fine pillows with pearl buttons, and done up like a "demoiselle" (185). Although Christine decries this sight, its very excess makes it worthy of writing about ("digne d'etre mis en livre," 186) and, indeed, news of it travels all the way to the Queen's room, where its extravagance is denounced by those who declare first, that the Parisians have too much "blood" and are likely to fall ill from their excesses and second, that they should be taxed with "aucun aide" so that they not compete with the Queen (186).

The wife's "outrageous" bed echoes the princess's luxurious bed of temptation in Book I. Yet this bed is not a metaphor for idleness, but rather a concrete product of active commercial trade that is decked out in anticipatory celebration of a new life. Its creator seems to have taken Christine's precepts about self-fashioning very much to heart. Christine warns that there are limits to bourgeois self-advancement: the fancy "estats" or trappings of ladies cannot disguise the wife's "estat" or status as the spouse of a merchant, and of one who sells retail at that: she acquires not "pris" but "despris" by trying so hard (186). Just as she had earlier urged the princess to "thesaurisiez au ciel," converting excess wealth into alms so that charity will bring her salvation, so Christine exhorts the merchant's wife to reform her financial practice for social and spiritual gain. If she avoids "superfluitéz" she will prevent her husband from being assessed a new tax; if she gives her "grant richesse" away to the poor, she will be able to "achepter le champ dont l'Euvangile parle en parabole, ou est le tres grant tresor mucié" (187) (buy the field that the Gospel speaks of in the parable, where the very great treasure is hidden).

Yet even as Christine urges economic and moral reform within the traditional hierarchy, whereby the merchant's wife would not dress above her station, she vividly portrays the social vitality of the emergent merchant class that gives birth to a dynamic historic force—one supercharged with blood and portending violent social change—whose profits from trade create chambers that vie with the queen's. In the final book of *Trois vertus*, Christine admonishes middle- and lower-class women to respect traditional social categories in their management of household resources, yet she also reveals their power to disrupt and transform the social order through their economic agency. If the Princess who dresses extravagantly takes money from the poor and corrupts the moral order upon which the hierarchy rests, the bourgeoise who imitate the Princess in her dress threaten the system of distinction itself.

The last and briefest chapters of *Trois Vertus* address the moral and economic lives of those who possess the fewest material possessions yet may still earn worldly honor and spiritual treasure: widows, artisans' wives, servants, prostitutes, and the destitute. To each of these groups, Christine includes pertinent advice about revenues and expenses as an aspect of her counsel on social honor and moral virtue. Widows need to be savvy about debts, and aware of the expenses incurred in lawsuits; "femmes de mestiers" should help keep their husbands out of debt; servants must account honestly for expenses at market and must not steal food; prostitutes should not shun menial jobs such as washing in which they may earn honest money (215).

In the last chapter (13), when she addresses poor women, those who have no material resources, Christine shifts into allegory and speaks only of metaphoric "tresor." She invokes Dame Esperance, armed with Patience, bearing a shield of Foy to combat Impatience, which might prevent the poor from attaining heavenly "tresor" (222). If the destitute are patient in their poverty, and do not covet more than God offers, they will be richly rewarded: "Et par ceste voye pouuez acquerir plus noble possession et plus de richecese que Cm mondes ne pourroient contenir; et a tousjours durer" (224) (And by this path you may acquire more noble possessions and greater riches than a hundred thousand worlds could contain; and these will last forever). Christine here preaches resignation rather than social revolution and finds a solution to poverty only in the afterlife.[22] Yet by ending *Trois vertus* with a chapter dedicated to those who have nothing, she emphasizes their importance within the body politic and reminds her noble and bourgeois readers of their responsibility to be charitable. As she explores the relationship between female "honor" and household economies throughout the social order, Christine urges her readers to think about the relationship between moral and economic life within their own spheres and to reflect on the effects of their practices for others. Like a good *menagere* who shrewdly assesses and manages her estate, Christine astutely observes and attempts to regulate moral and economic life within the polis—the *université féminine*—so that its members will live virtuously and reflect the honor of womankind. Her book attempts to delimit and delineate moral virtues and values—to fix boundaries between husband and wife; lady and servant; princess and subject; subject and God—and to describe an ideal economy where goods and social honors circulate in proportion to their traditional values. In contrast to her male predecessors, Christine's notion of female "honor" is not static but dynamic; it accords to women an active role in negotiating and increasing their value. By teaching that each woman is the keeper of her own "tresor," and by demonstrating that women's financial activity has both personal and societal consequences, Christine invites women's participation in the economic and social transformations of late medieval France.

The *Trois vertus* is an important transitional work in the *oeuvre* of Christine de Pizan and in late medieval literature. It marks a transition from moral allegory to political theory in Christine's work, and it heralds the "self-fashioning" of Renaissance treatises on comportment. In a period of immense political uncertainty and demographic change, books such as Christine's articulated precepts of social and domestic order and conferred distinction and legitimacy on their noble patrons. For bourgeois readers, *Trois vertus* articulated an ethos of careful domestic management and moral self-improvement. The *Trois vertus* stands out among medieval didactic treatises for women as a female-authored text that recognizes women's significant contribution to medieval economic life and that portrays the economic, social, moral, and spiritual growth of individuals as integrally connected within all ranks to the welfare of the community.

NOTES

1. Christine de Pizan, *Le livre des trois vertus*, ed. Eric Hicks and Charity Cannon Willard (Paris: Champion, 1989). All subsequent references are to this edition; translations of this text and other primary sources are my own. Early studies include Mathilde Laigle, "*Le livre des trois vertus*" *de Christine de Pisan* (Paris: Champion, 1912); Charity Cannon Willard, "A Fifteenth-Century View of Women's Role in Medieval Society: Christine de Pizan's *Livre des trois vertus*," in *The Role of Women in the Middle Ages*, ed. Rosemarie T. Morewedge (Albany: State University of New York Press, 1975), 90–120; Josette A. Wisman, "Aspects

socio-économiques du *Livre des trois vertus* de Christine de Pizan," *Le Moyen français* 30 (1992): 27–43. For a comparison of *Trois vertus* with other conduct books, see Marie-Thérèse Lorcin, "L'Ecole des femmes, les devoirs envers le mari dans quelques traités d'éducation," *Cahiers du CRISIMA* 1 (1993), 233–48, and Rosalind Brown-Grant, *Christine de Pizan and the Moral Defense of Women: Reading Beyond Gender* (Cambridge: Cambridge University Press, 1999), 175–214. I thank Margarete Zimmermann for bringing to my attention recently two works I have not yet consulted: Claudia Probst, *Ratgeberbuch fuer die weibliche Lebenspraxis. Christine de Pizans 'Livre des Trois vertus' "* (Pfaffenweiler: Centaurus Verlag: 1996) and Sylvia Nagel, *Speigel der Geschlechterdifferenz. Frauendidaxen im Frankreich des Spaetmittelalters* (Stuttgart: J. B Meltzer Verlag, 2000).

2. On the literature of instruction for women, see Alice Hentsch, *De la littérature didactique au moyen âge s'adressant spécialement aux femmes* (Halle: Cahors, 1903; reprinted Geneva: Slatkine, 1975) and Diane Bornstein, *The Lady in the Tower: Medieval Courtesy Literature for Women* (Hamden, CT: Archon Books, 1983).

3. See Marie-Thérèse Lorcin, "Le *Livre des trois vertus* et le *sermo ad status*," in *Une femme de lettres au Moyen Age. Etudes autour de Christine de Pizan*, eds. Liliane Dulac and Bernard Ribémont (Orléans: Paradigme, 1995), 139–49.

4. See Liliane Dulac, "The Representation and Functions of Feminine Speech in Christine de Pizan's *Livre des trois vertus*," in *Reinterpreting Christine de Pizan*, ed. Earl Jeffrey Richards et al. (Athens: University of Georgia Press, 1992), 14–22.

5. Anatole de Montaiglon, ed., *Le Livre du Chevalier de la Tour Landry pour l'enseignement de ses filles* (Paris: Bibliothèque Elzévirienne, 1854); reprinted Millwood, NY: Kraus, 1982; Georgine E. Brereton and Janet M. Ferrier, eds., *Le Menagier de Paris* (Oxford: Clarendon Press, 1981). A modern French translation of the Brereton and Ferrier edition is provided by Karen Ueltschi, trans., *Le Mesnagier de Paris*, Lettres gothiques (Paris: Librairie Générale Française, 1994).

6. Brown-Grant, *Christine de Pizan and the Moral Defence of Women*, 200.

7. On the book's appeal to bourgeois as well as aristocrat readers, see Charity Cannon Willard, "The Manuscript Tradition of the *Livre des trois vertus* and Christine de Pizan's Audience," *Journal of the History of Ideas* 27.3 (1966): 433–44.

8. Previous studies touching on Christine's focus on economic issues in *Trois vertus* include Laigle, *Le livre des trois vertus*, especially pp. 263–319, and Wisman, "Aspects socio-économiques."

9. Cary J. Nederman, "The Expanding Body Politic: Christine de Pizan and the Medieval Roots of Political Economy," in *Au champ des escriptures: IIIeme Colloque international sur Christine de Pizan, Lausanne, 18–22 juillet 1998*, ed. Eric Hicks et al. (Paris: Champion, 2000), 385–97.

10. See Nederman, "The Expanding Body Politic," 386–93.

11. See "tresor," in Frédérick Godefroy, *Dictionnaire de l'ancienne langue française et de tous ses dialectes du IXe au XVe siècle* (Paris: E. Bouillon, 1902), 806–7.

12. Brereton and Ferrier, eds., *Le Menagier de Paris*, 48.

13. For a nuanced discussion of Christine's views on charity, see Giovanna Angeli, "Charité et pauvreté chez Christine de Pizan," in *Au champ des escriptures*, ed. Hicks, 425–38.

14. Christine de Pizan, *Le Livre des faits et de bonnes moeurs de Charles V*, XV.1. Cited by Laigle, *Le Livre des trois vertus*, 290.
15. See Laigle, "*Le Livre des trois vertus*," 267, and Jean Verdon, *Isabeau de Bavière* (Paris: Tallandier, 1981).
16. On Isabeau's treasury, wardrobe, and financial constraints, see Verdon, *Isabeau de Bavière*, 69–105.
17. On Isabeau's notoriety in promoting a new wave of fashionable extravagance, see H. Baudrillart, *Histoire du Luxe privé et public depuis l'antiquité jusqu'à nos jours*, vol. 3 *Le Moyen Age et la Renaissance* (Paris: Hachette, 1881), 280–319. On Christine's criticism of Isabeau de Bavière in the *Trois vertus*, see Julia M. Walker, "Re-politicizing *The Book of Three Virtues*," in *Au champs des escriptures*, ed. Hicks, 533–48.
18. Paradoxically, as I have argued, Christine attacks extravagant dress for all classes even as she unwittingly promotes fashion's appeal. See my "*Nouvelles choses*: Social Instability and the Problem of Fashion in the *Livre du Chevalier de la Tour Landry*, the *Ménagier de Paris*, and Christine de Pizan's *Livre des Trois Vertus*," in *Medieval Conduct*, ed. Kathleen Ashley and Robert L.A. Clark (Minnesota: University of Minnesota Press, 2001), 49–85.
19. On the importance of "bonne renomme" in conduct books, see Kathleen Ashley, "The *Miroir des bonnes femmes*: Not for Women Only?" in *Medieval Conduct*, ed. Kathleen Ashley and Robert L. A. Clark (Minneapolis: University of Minnesota Press, 2001), 97–102; and on reputation in the *Trois vertus*, see Thelma Fenster, "La Fama, La Femme, et la Dame de La Tour: Christine de Pizan et la Médisance," in *Au champ des escriptures*, ed. Hicks, 461–77.
20. One of the Menagier's first points concerns the necessity of dressing neatly, so that a woman will uphold her honor and the estate of her husband; *Le Menagier de Paris*, 9. The wife also plays a crucial role in keeping her husband warmly and neatly clothed, I.7, 98.
21. For a fuller discussion of this scene as it participates in Christine's critique of fashion throughout the book, see my "Nouvelles Choses," 75–9.
22. On Christine's attitudes toward the poor in her works, see Otto Gerhard Oexle, "Christine et les pauvres," in *The City of Scholars: New Approaches to Christine de Pizan*, ed. Margarete Zimmerman and Dina De Rentiis (Berlin: W. de Gruyter, 1994), 206–20.

8

Who's a Heroine?

The Example of Christine de Pizan

Thelma Fenster

The conventional French-language medieval heroine, linked overwhelmingly with the romance,[1] and diversely represented in work by Chrétien de Troyes, Thomas d'Angleterre, Jean Renart, and others, is not to be found in Christine de Pizan's courtly poetry. The shepherdess of the *Dit de la pastoure*, once expert at every task and "des bergieres l'adrece" (a model for all shepherdesses, ll.110–12),[2] who comes to lament that love is a very cruel adventure (l.2251), can at best be but a cautionary "exemplaire aux dames" (exemplar for ladies, l.53). The unnamed princess in the *Livre du duc des vrais amans*, once a model of aristocratic comportment, finishes her tale disgraced and filled with regret over her love affair, as does the Dame in the *Cent balades d'amant et de dame*. All lack the emotional courage to triumph over the erotic and sentimental forces pulling them away from their public, community responsibilities.[3] Although modern readers understand Christine's point—that private, illicit love, the kind celebrated in earlier romance, would inevitably distract women from the public activities that Christine thought useful and worthy, as well as crucial to a woman's personal glory—we may nonetheless feel uncomfortable at some level with those portrayals. The depiction of young females, by a female author, as persistently clueless victims without a shred of gumption may disappoint less restrained sensibilities than the medieval; and the depiction by earlier male authors of romance heroines who are often lively and resourceful (notwithstanding their occasional dishonesty for a higher cause) doesn't help. Can't we, after all, even have some version of a young, respectable married lady like Enide?[4] Which of Christine's female depictions can we *name*, as we can the canonical Enide, Iseut, or Liënor, or—to take an example closer to Christine's own epoch—Alain Chartier's epithetical heroine, the "belle dame sans merci"? Whom, in the end, do we remember?

115

Some would argue that the answer lies in Christine's writing in the "catalogues of women" tradition. Indeed, the *Cité des dames* (1405), although not the only text to do so, features many worthy heroines, such as Christian saints and Greco-Roman mythological figures. These heroines conform to at least one definition of a heroine as a "mythological or legendary" woman, with "the qualities of a hero" (see Note 1 of this chapter); and, the real Joan of Arc, a serendipitous figure whom Christine praises in poetry two decades after having written the bulk of her work, would seem to have confirmed that a woman could be a "hero." Whatever may be said about such heroines, they are nonetheless presented as exceptional women in part because they have "the qualities of a hero."

One inhabitant of the *Cité* stands out, however: she is the Sibyl, a widely known symbol of wisdom in the form of a woman, and thus a reasonable template for real women, among them Christine herself, as a number of earlier scholars have already established.[5] But in fact, the classical and medieval worlds knew many sibyls, and their characteristics did not necessarily remain discrete in popular—or even educated—minds. "The Sibyl" could be an amalgam of sibyls, a mixed bag of traits from both Jewish and Christian sibylline figures[6] that afforded medieval writers latitude in their depictions of her. Thus if Christine patterned her represented self after the Sibyl, it is also true that she redrew the Sibyl to suit the image she held of herself and of her own possibilities. For that project, not all aspects of the inherited sibyl figures were equally germane. But the sibyl's great age and mortality, the tradition of her books of prophecy, and above all, her emblematic voice, served the exemplary portrait Christine envisaged.

The sibyl Christine knew had been absorbed quite early into Christianity as a prophetess of Christ's coming,[7] and the clarity in her message, as opposed to the obscurity of her utterances in an earlier tradition, naturally became paramount. That idea is reflected in Boccaccio's *De claris mulieribus*, when the narrator says that Erythraea (Herophile) clarified "the secret of divine thought" foreshadowed by the symbols and "obscure utterances of prophets, or rather by the Holy Spirit speaking through the prophets."[8] The first time Christine mentions the Sibyl, in the *Epistre Othea* (1399–1400), she is the prophetess who announced Christ's coming to Caesar Augustus.[9] In the *Cité des dames*, based loosely on the *De claris mulieribus*, the allegorical figure named Droiture (Rectitude) explains that the sibylline prophecy of Christ's coming was clearer than ever before. Droiture says that Erithea (Erythraea), unlike earlier prophets who spoke "par figures et paroles obscures et couvertes" (through veiled and obscure figures and words), spoke "plainement" (plainly) about "le secret de la puissance de Dieu" (the secret of God's power).[10] Droiture says that "Sebile" is a title meaning "savant la pensee de Dieu" (knowing God's thinking), for the sibyl's prophecy came from the "pure pensee de Dieu" (God's pure thought). That new clarity, however, also made the Sibyl a more mundane teacher or counselor, replacing in important ways the older, more mysterious Sibyl, whose message required interpretation.

Among inherited literary portraits of the Sibyl, Virgil's was central. In Book Six of *The Aeneid*, the Sibyl is invaded by a divine message and utters her prophecy while in a frenzied trance. Still in the twelfth-century French adaptation of Virgil's epic, the *Roman d'Eneas*, she is described as frightening:

> tote chenue, eschevelee;
> la face avoit tote palie
> et la char noire et froncie;
> peors prenoit de son regart,
> feme sanblot de male part.
> (ll. 2268–72)[11]

(completely white-haired and disheveled;/her face was completely pale/and her flesh was black and wrinkled;/he took fright at a look from her,/she seemed an evil woman.) But in the same work, she is also said to know "fusique," "restorique," "musique," "dialetique," and "gramaire" (physics, rhetoric, music, dialectic, and grammar), and she practices "nigremance" (black magic, ll.2207–9)[12] as well.

A more sustained medieval reconceptualization of the Sibyl as learned is Bernardus Silvestris's *Commentary on the First Six Books of Virgil's Aeneid*. In Bernardus's interpretative essay, Aeneas brings his fleet to the "grove of Trivia," where the hero intends to study eloquence, reached through the three arts of grammar, dialectic, and rhetorical persuasion (33): the Sibyl is "divine counsel," but now she gains her knowledge through the effort of study (34). "Cume" (from Cumaean) in Greek means "honest dwellings," Bernardus says; these are the "philosophical arts," and they are called "dwellings" because "the Sibyl is in them" (35).[13]

The *Ovide moralisé*, the medieval rewriting of Ovid's *Metamorphoses*, adds to the mix an emphasis upon the Sibyl's mortality, which occupies seventy-two lines.[14] When a grateful Aeneas declares that he will worship the Sibyl as a goddess, she rejects his declaration, explaining that "Je sui une fame mortelz" (l.919). She then recounts to Aeneas how Apollo had granted her long life, but when she refused his amorous importuning, he declined to give her "pardurable joventé" (everlasting youth, l.950). Now she is an old woman whom no man will pick out ("choisira"), except "à la vois tant seulement/N'iere cogneüe autrement" (ll.970–72)[15] (only by her voice, she'll not be known otherwise). In the *Chemin de long estude*, Christine too tells her readers the story of the Sibyl's long life: as her body withers away from human sight, she says: "mais ma voix ilz ouoïent,/Qui trop durement leur plaisoit/Pour le voir quë el leur disoit" (ll.588–90) (but they heard my voice,/Which pleased them greatly/Because of the truth it told them).

In the *Cité des dames* once more, Christine does not miss a chance to emphasize the Sibyl's wise voice and therefore her value as a past and future counselor to rulers: Amaltheia (Almathee, Almathea), sibyl of Cumae, who sold books of prophecy to Tarquinius, was able to "conseiller et aviser non mie seulement un empereur a son vivant, mais si comme tous ceulx qui le monde durant estoient a avenir a Romme et tous les fais de l'empire" (*Cité des dames*, 226) (to counsel and advise not only an emperor during her lifetime, but all those [rulers] who were to come to Rome as long as the world lasts and all the things that would happen to the empire). This point, not one made by Boccaccio, is central to Christine's idea of the Sibyl,[16] for through the figure of the Sibyl, Christine is able to promote the role that women can play in public life. Nadia Margolis has already observed that in the *Epistre Othea* the Sibyl "predicts not only [the] triumph of *translatio studii* ... but also the growing role of women in shaping the New Order" ("Christine de Pizan," 363).

Christine's own fashioning of the Sibyl figure begins to take on prominence in the *Chemin de long estude* (1402). The Sibyl appears while Christine sleeps, as Lady Philosophy had appeared to Boethius in the *Consolatio philosophiae*:[17] "Une dame de grant corsage/Qui moult avoit honneste et sage/Semblant, et pesante maniere" (ll.459–61) (A woman of great importance [physical presence, size]/Who had a wise and noble/appearance, and a grave manner).

She is "simplement atournee" (simply dressed, l.446), which helps Christine to conclude that "Par semblant si fort et durable/Si sembla bien femme honorable:/Quoye, attrempee et de grant sens,/Et maistrece de tous ses sens" (ll.472–74) (By her strong and durable appearance/She indeed seemed an honorable woman:/Calm, measured, and wise,/And mistress of all her senses).

In that description, the Sibyl's corporeality, signaled by her "grant corsage," is striking. Her noble bearing and imposing proportions capture a plasticity that may well reflect her new popularity as a subject for religious sculpture.[18] (Bernardus Silvestris had also noted that the Sibyl was of "changing stature."[19]) Further, as "maistrece de tous ses sens," she is surely Christine's signature character.[20] And Christine adds that "point ne troubla/Mon courage pour son venir" (ll.476–77). (My thoughts were not at all troubled by her approach.) These details cannot help but suggest that Christine has portrayed Sibyl with an eye to remodeling the Virgilian Sibyl into a less fearsome figure, one more suited to inspiring confidence, both Christine's and her reader's.

That embodying of the Sibyl takes an even richer, more idiosyncratic turn in the *Duc des vrais amans*, a narrative poem composed between 1403 and 1405. Whereas in the *Chemin*, Christine portrays herself as a student and is narratively separate from the Sibyl, the prophetess turned pedagogue,[21] in the *Duc des vrais amans*, Christine herself assumes several identities. At the opening of the poem, Christine speaks in her own voice, as she does in many other works, saying that although reluctant to spin yet another love story,[22] she has yielded to the request of a nobleman to tell his story; at that point, she exits as narrator and speaks instead not just *for* the duke but *as* the duke, in his voice. Later, a character named Sebille de Mont Hault, Dame de la Tour[23] (Sybil of the High Mountain, Lady of the Tower), former governess to the princess-protagonist, writes a detailed letter of advice to the princess. The style of the letter (which is in prose), evokes that of the letters Christine wrote in her own name in the *Querelle de la Rose*[24]—its deeply committed tone, its advocacy, its questions directed at engaging the addressee, its tactful outrage and exclamations, all mark aspects of Christine's own diction. The letter recalls to readers just who has written this tale: a real author who slips into the voice of a male character, then resurfaces as a freshly redesigned Sibyl, who speaks for or is Christine herself.

In her letter, Sebille condemns the illicit romance, of course, fearing that the princess will lose her "bon los" (good reputation).[25] The medieval requirement of "bonne renommée" (good renown or reputation) is at stake here, the multivalent *fama* (one's reputation, but also "common knowledge" about a person held by others; "what people say"), certainly the princess's social capital.[26] But "what people say" is potentially chaotic, as indeed classical tradition and Chaucer described it (in the *House of Fame*), and as Christine well understood. Given the credence awarded to "common knowledge," it could also be dangerous: it is the Sibyl and her cave with its thousand mouths, its unstoppable message. Hearsay and rumor, in Hans-Joachim Neubauer's rich formulation, are not so much "what is said," but rather "what is said about what is said"; they take on a life of their own—"speak as if of their own accord,"[27] the identity of the source long since lost. Boundless and uncentered, talk arrives as a disembodied voice. But Sebille, now the new embodiment of the Sibyl's voice, the very example of self-control, has been "reconstructed" to confront and contain the older Sibyl's voice.

The princess is—or should be—an exemplar. Whether she likes it or not, she is especially susceptible to visual and other kinds of scrutiny. Her public will apprehend her first by sight, noting at once what she is wearing, how she gestures, and her facial expressions; then her public will note what she says. In that regard, Sebille advises:

> que elle ait contenance asseuree, coye, et rassise, et en ses esbatemens atrempee et sans effroy; rie bas et non sans cause; ait haulte maniere, humble chiere, et grant port; soit a tous de doulce response et amiable parole; . . . a estrangiers d'acueil seignori; parlant a dongier, non trop acointable, de regard tardive et non volage; . . . n'ait costume de souvent conseiller a estrange ne privé en lieu secret ne

a part . . . et ne die devant gens a personne quelconques, en riant, aucuns moz couvers que chacun n'entende. . . . (*Duc des vrais amans*, 172–3)

(let her have an assured, quiet, and calm demeanor, and be moderate in her amusements and not noisy; may she laugh quietly and not without cause; may she have a noble manner, humble countenance, and stately bearing; may she respond kindly to everyone, and with an agreeable word; may she welcome foreigners in a dignified manner, speaking with restraint and not too familiarly; may she reflect thoughtfully upon matters and not be flighty . . . ; let her never laugh and say in front of other people, to no matter what person, any veiled words not understood by all present. . . . *Duke of True Lovers*, 112–13.)

As that brief passage shows, the letter participates in the medieval mirror genre, to which it adds an implicit prophecy: personal ruin for the princess if she does not end her liaison with the duke. The prophecy of course comes to pass: the princess does not withdraw from her liaison with the duke, and thus is left undone at the end of the poem.

In all that, it may look as if Sebille advocates exclusively a program of restraint and self-denial for the princess; the reality is more complex. Especially noteworthy is Sebille's advice to women about speaking, for she admonishes the princess about inappropriate speech even as she urges appropriate speech upon her. The strategy in fact parallels what Christine says about speaking in her writings not intended for a specifically female readership. A particularly rich example lies in the *Livre de Prudence*.

Christine's understanding of right speaking depends upon inherited Greco-Roman concepts and upon avoiding the rather stringent Christian "sins of the tongue." In the *Livre de Prudence* (first entitled the *Prod'hommie de l'homme*, ca. 1402–1403), restraint in speaking is highly desirable, as is setting a good example through proper behavior; after all, "par le signe de la langue ou parolle se demonstre la sapience de l'omme" (by the sign of the tongue or word the wisdom of the man is demonstrated).[28] Any number of passages from *Prudence* could be quoted to show the source of much of Sebille's advice; one, in which moderation in all things is recommended, will have to suffice: "Tes gieux soient sans vilté et tes ris sans niceté, ta voix sans clameur. . . . Ris excessis, lesquieulx deffent l'autteur, sont messeans, et est signe de folie; voix haultaine est desplaisant, ou elle vient d'arogance, . . . , ou elle vient de faulte d'enseignement politique."[29] (Let your amusements be without baseness and your laughter without foolishness; let your voice be without loudness. Excessive laughter . . . is inappropriate and a sign of folly; a haughty voice is unpleasant, whether it comes from arrogance or whether it comes from a lack of political teaching.) The program outlined by Sebille de Mont Hault in the *Duc des vrais amans* strongly resembles the one in *Prudence*, as it adapts for women the general lines of advice in the *Prudence*. It also removes the cultivation of a public persona from an exclusively male group by articulating a parallel public role for women. To return to a point I raised earlier about Christine's failed heroines: here, just at the point at which the reader might yearn for a demonstration, even a fictionalized one, of how Sebille's program works, Christine stops. And the princess, too in love, never sustains the recommended comportment. Once a model for other women, she has lost her self-command: she is no longer "maistrece de tous ses sens."

On the other hand, Christine's writing, even her courtly writing, had implicit or explicit extratextual references, a thrust that had very early become the point of writing for Christine. It is not entirely impossible that the *Duc des vrais amans* had some relevance to the case of Queen Isabel of Bavaria (reigned 1385–1422), wife of King Charles VI. Given Christine's well-documented turn away from fiction generally, real women, with the potential for real accomplishments, would certainly have engaged her didactic impulse. A living noblewoman could conceivably influence events not yet concluded, and Christine would not have ignored the chance to form such a living exemplar. As Christine well understood, moreover, French political aspirations, once embodied in the person of King Charles V, sorely needed a royal example, which the ailing King Charles VI could not provide. Although Isabel could not replace her husband entirely, his infirmity placed a special burden on her to exemplify the French throne.

Christine's involvement with Isabel remains underexplored by modern scholars, as does the queen's *fama* and her ensuing historical *mala fama*. Historian Rachel Gibbons laments that, given Isabel's "high personal profile," she has been little studied, and she notes that "the few historians" who have looked into Isabel's history have concluded that "her infamous legacy is not deserved." There is no proof to date, for example, of the alleged love affair between the queen and the Duke of Orleans.[30]

Gibbons has observed that opinion about Isabel "tends to take a turn for the worse on all subjects, personal and public, around 1405."[31] Many of the accusations against the queen were reported by the Religieux de Saint-Denis in the prestigious *Grandes Chroniques de France*. In an entry for the year 1405, it is said that Isabel taxed the people harshly while spending too much on the luxury she enjoyed, she neglected her children and husband, and she and Louis d'Orléans cared only for pleasure. Significantly, the Religieux warns that Louis and Isabel had become objects of scandal for France and a laughing-stock among foreign states.[32]

Christine would certainly have heard the rumors about Isabel and Louis, yet she gives the queen an honored place in the *Cité des dames*. At first reading, the entry has a generic flavor; but then its denials of any crimes on Isabel's part, followed by assurances that she loves her subjects, begin to sound like rebuttals of quite pointed, though unarticulated, accusations against the queen that Christine's readers would certainly have known: "Et tout premierement ne sera pas refusee la noble royne de France Ysabel de Baviere, a present par grace de Dieu regnant, en laquelle n'a raim de cruaulté, extorcion ne quelconques mal vice, mais tout bonne amour et benignité vers ses subgés." (First of all, the noble queen Isabel of Bavaria will not be refused [a place in the city], [she who] reigns at present by the grace of God and in whom there isn't a bit of cruelty, extortion nor any horrible vice whatsoever, but complete love and kindness toward her subjects.)

Some readers of that passage believe that Christine was paying a debt to a patron.[33] But I would argue that Christine's aim is to offer the queen as a worthy exemplar,[34] in keeping with, but certainly surpassing in contemporary political importance, the catalogued women of the *Cité des dames*. Christine presses her wholly legitimate concern for the *appearance* of the royal house in the eyes both of its subjects and of foreigners—again the matter of *fama*, both the queen's and that of French royalty, from which Isabel's person was utterly inseparable. Thus in the *Epistre a la Reine*, dated October 5, 1405, at a particularly tense moment in relations between the Dukes of Orleans and Burgundy, Christine asked the queen to use her most powerful instrument, her voice, to bring peace to the kingdom. Then, when she turned to Isabel's relations with the French public, she urged Isabel to give to the French people "une piecete *de la parolle* et du labour de vostre hautesse et puissance" (a small bit *of the word* and work of your majesty and power; emphasis mine). And in a gesture reminiscent of Dante's belief that good acts would lead to good fame after death, Christine closed by asking God to give Isabel "gloire perdurable" (everlasting glory).[35] Isabel did try to effect a reconciliation, but her historical reputation has been anything but glorious.

The presumed date of 1403–1405 for the composition of the *Duc des vrais amans* offers a provocative coincidence with those events. If the poem had any relevance to them, it would have complemented Isabel's appearance in the *Cité* and the *Epistre a la Reine*, forming a group of at least three works, written at about the same time, in which Christine was thinking about the queen. If the *Duc des vrais amans* was a cautionary tale aimed not merely at the generality of noblewomen but also at Isabel in particular, then Christine would have been taking a two-pronged approach to the problem of the queen's reputation: first, she enhanced her image in the *Cité* and encouraged her to tend to matters of state in the *Epistre a la Reine*; second, she admonished her privately in the *Duc des vrais amans* with a tale whose characters are at several, exquisitely discreet removes from the queen and duke themselves but whose point—if indeed relevant to Isabel's activities—could not have been mistaken.

It may not have been possible to make a stellar example out of Isabel, but that did not dull Christine's abiding interest in the actuality of praxis, and in meditating on the uses of her writing. In the end, the "real" took precedence over fiction, as, in many ways, the present did over the past. Christine's own present/presence infiltrates her writing at almost every turn, as readers have often noticed. Michel Zink has called the writer's frequent self-representation in later French medieval literature the "mise en scène du moi,"[36] and Anne Paupert has pointed to Christine's contribution to that staging of the self: in addition to transposing that "moi" into the feminine, Paupert notes the unambiguous "je" of the poet in the lyric poetry, distinct from the "je" of the principal character; a clear "je" of the author in longer works of partial autobiographical content, such as the *Mutacion de Fortune*, the *Advision Cristine*, and the *Chemin de long estude*.[37] In addition to its possible extratextual gesture toward Isabel, the *Duc des vrais amans* offers a unique authorial representation, one that places the flesh-and-blood writer among her characters. In the character of Sebille, the distinctions among narrator, character, and author have become permeable, as a deliberate ambiguity arises around Sebille's voice. Christine—somewhat coyly, as it turns out—had led readers to believe that her own voice was to be effaced behind that of the duke, only to have it reemerge as Sebille's. That *fictionalization* of the writer's self, operating against Christine's increasing tendency to disdain fictionalized representation, puts the author into her work as an actor, in this instance as counselor to the royal princess, as if to stage an exploratory interaction with other characters.

Dante may have been "his own best hero," as has recently been repeated,[38] and it is tempting to call Christine her own best heroine, given that she is at the center of her writing, in one way or another. But the word heroine does not seem to apply to Christine's view of her female protagonists; instead, the concept of the exemplar, which could embrace both historical and contemporary women, seemed to hold greater meaning. Which exemplar, then, do readers remember best? Perhaps Christine herself. A woman—even a queen—could have done worse, the reader surmises, than take Christine as her sibylline example.

NOTES

1. Most recently, in the introduction to *Reassessing the Heroine in Medieval French Romance*, ed. Kathy M. Krause (Gainesville: University Press of Florida, 2001), which makes a systematic lexical distinction between the "female protagonists" of saints' lives and the "heroines" of romance. That application appears to have respected general dictionary definitions, such as this one in *Webster's Third New International Dictionary* (Springfield, MA: G. & C. Merriam, 1971): "Heroine: **1 a.** a mythological or legendary woman having the qualities of a hero; **b.** a woman admired for her achievements and noble qualities and considered a model or ideal; **2. a.** the principal female character in a drama, novel, story, or narrative poem; **b.** the central female character in an event, action, or period."

2. *Oeuvres poétiques de Christine de Pisan*, ed. Maurice Roy, SATF, 3 vols.; vol. 2, 223–94 (Paris: Firmin Didot, 1891).
3. Christine's three debate poems also present a negative view of sensual love; see Barbara Altmann's comments in her introduction to *The Love Debate Poems of Christine de Pizan: Le Livre du Debat de deux amans, Le Livre des Trois jugemens, Le Livre du Dit de Poissy* (Gainesville: University Press of Florida, 1998), 12, 27.
4. On Enide's gumption, see E. Jane Burns, *Bodytalk: When Women Speak in Old French Literature* (Philadelphia: University of Pennsylvania Press, 1993), 151–202; abridged in *Arthurian Women: A Casebook*, ed. Thelma Fenster (New York: Garland, 1995).
5. Jean-Claude Mühlethaler found that the narrator of the *Lamentations sur les maux de la France* approximated a prophet and that the narrator of the *Ditié de Jehanne d'Arc* constituted a clairvoyant witness (*témoin clairvoyant*): "Le Poète et le prophète: Littérature et politique au XVe siècle," *Le Moyen Français* 13 (1984): 37–57, at 42. Nadia Margolis remarked that Christine "took on the qualities of the Cumaean Sibyl, who led Aeneas to the underworld and who, in another thread of tradition, offered prophetic books to Tarquin the Proud": "Christine de Pizan: The Poetess as Historian," *Journal of the History of Ideas* XLVII (1986): 361–75; at 363. Kevin Brownlee subsequently proposed that Christine positioned herself as sibyl in the *Ditié de Jehanne d'Arc* (1429), prophesying all the good the Maid would do for France: "Structures of Authority in Christine de Pizan's Ditié de Jehanne d'Arc," in *Discourses of Authority in Medieval and Renaissance Literature* (Hanover: University Press of New England, 1989), 131–50; and Stephen Nichols has noted the "prophetic signature" of the *Ditié*, with Joan as the "prophet-figure" and Christine as the "prophetic voice": "Prophetic Discourse: St. Augustine to Christine de Pizan," in *The Bible in the Middle Ages: Its Influence on Literature and Art*, ed. Bernard S. Levy, Medieval and Renaissance Texts and Studies 89 (Binghamton: Medieval and Renaissance Texts and Studies, 1992), 51–76, at 70.
6. See the extensive discussion by Josiane Haffen in her *Contribution à l'étude de la Sibylle médiévale: Etude et édition du M.S. B.N., F. Fr. 25407, Fol. 160v-172: Le Livre de Sibile*, Annales littéraires de l'Université de Besançon (Paris: Les Belles Lettres, 1984), 11–49, as well as Bernard McGinn's "*Teste David cum Sibylla*: The Significance of the Sibylline Tradition in the Middle Ages," in *Women of the Medieval World: Essays in Honor of John H. Mundy*, ed. Julius Kirshner and Suzanne F. Wemple (Oxford: Basil Blackwell, 1985), 7–35. See also H. W. Parke, *Sibyls and Sibylline Prophecy in Classical Antiquity*, ed. B. C. McGing (London: Routledge, 1988), especially Chap. 8, "The Sibyl in Christian Literature," 152–73, which deals informatively with early Christian writing. For a recent discussion of Christine's use of classical myth in general, see Renate Blumenfeld-Kosinski, "Christine de Pizan: Mythographer and Mythmaker," in *Reading Myth: Classical Mythology and Its Interpretations in Medieval French Literature* (Stanford: Stanford University Press, 1997), 171–212.
7. In fact, the Sibyl appears early in Christian writing, partly, apparently, as a means of persuading non-Christians "to treat Christianity seriously on the strength of

Who's a Heroine? *125*

supposed echoes of Christian teaching in pagan authors," as H. W. Parke observes. Augustine's acceptance of the Sibyl, although lukewarm, "must have gone far to guarantee her credentials in the West" (Parke, *Sibyls and Sibylline Prophecies*, 164, 170). To Boccaccio, she seemed more an evangelizer of the early church than a pagan prophet. The christianized Sibyl is also treated, although more briefly, in "The Sibyl in the Medieval Tradition," Chap. 3 of William M. Kinter and Joseph R. Keller, *The Sibyl: Prophetess of Antiquity and Medieval Fay* (Philadelphia: Dorrance, 1967), 19–29. *La Città delle Dame*, ed. E. J. Richards, trans. (into Italian) Patrizia Caraffi. Biblioteca Medievale 2 (Milan: Luni, 1998), 220. That idea is the result of a christianized reading of Virgil's Fourth Eclogue as predicting the birth of Christ.

8. Giovanni Boccaccio, *Famous Women*, ed. and trans. Virginia Brown (Cambridge, MA.: I Tatti Renaissance Library, Harvard University Press, 2001), 86–87.
9. *Epistre Othea*, ed. Gabriella Parussa, Textes littéraires français (Geneva: Droz, 1999), 340–41 (all citations from this edition).
10. Later, however, in the *Chemin de long estude*, the Cumaean sibyl who guides Christine says that all ten sibyls (she was the seventh) predicted the coming of Christ: ed. Andrea Tarnowski, Lettres Gothiques (Paris: Livre de Poche, 2000), ll.528–34. P. G. C. Campbell believed that Christine had relied upon the story in Jacobus de Voragine's *Legenda aurea: L'Epître d'Othéa: Etude sur les sources de Christine de Pisan* (Paris: Honoré Champion, 1924), 78; cited in Margolis, 363.
11. This sibyl frightens Aeneas again when she raises her eyebrows, opens her deep eyes, and starts to speak (ll.2291–2294). See *Eneas: Roman du XIIe siècle*, ed. J. Salverda de Grave, Classiques français du Moyen Age, 2 vols. (Paris: Honoré Champion, 1985), 1.
12. The blurred lines between medieval prophetess and fay are discussed in Kinter and Keller, *The Sibyl: Prophetess of Antiquity and Medieval Fay*.
13. Bernardus Silvestris, *Commentary on the First Six Books of Virgil's Aeneid*, trans. Earl G. Schreiber and Thomas E. Maresca (Lincoln: University of Nebraska Press, 1979), 33, 34, 35, trans. from *Commentum super sex libros Eneidos Virgilii*.
14. P. G. C. Campbell was the first modern scholar to have investigated Christine's debt to the *Ovide moralisé, L'Epître d'Othéa*, 110–41.
15. "*Ovide moralisé*": *poème du commencement du quatorzième siècle*, ed. C. de Boer (Amsterdam: J. Müller, 1915–1938).
16. For other, important strands of stories centered on the Sibyl, see Haffen and see Gaston Paris, *Légendes du Moyen Age* (Paris: Hachette, 1904), 67–109.
17. In their introduction to Bernardus Silvestris's *Commentary on the First Six Books of Virgil's Aeneid*, Earl G. Schreiber and Thomas E. Maresca suggest that Bernardus's Sibyl "herself functions as and is to be understood in a way similar to Boethius's Lady Philosophy, guiding Aeneas to an understanding of his past mistakes," xxviii.
18. Parke notes that the sibyls became popular subjects for religious sculpture as of the thirteenth century, and were even more often portrayed by early Renaissance painters; Michelangelo painted five of the sibyls on the ceiling of the Sistine Chapel. By contrast, the sibyl was rarely represented in Greco-Roman art (*Sibyls*

and Sibylline Prophecies in Classical Antiquity, 170). Kinter and Keller find that Christine's depiction of the Sibyl in the *Chemin* is "merely a bas-relief symbol of wisdom and guidance," and they dismiss her for being "really based on Boethius's Dame Philosophy and not on Virgil" (*The Sibyl: Prophetess of Antiquity and Medieval Fay*), 35, 44, n. 17.

19. On Sybil's stature, see Silvestris's *Commentary* on Virgil's *Aeneid*, trans. Schreiber and Maresca, 44.
20. See Rosalind Brown-Grant, *Christine de Pizan and the Moral Defence of Women: Reading Beyond Gender* (Cambridge: Cambridge University Press, 1999). Christine also mentions twice that Sebille wore no crown and was not a queen; the Sibyl appears as a queen in the Hebraic strand of sibyl lore and in the legend of the Italian sibyl, a version of which would be written later by Antoine de la Sale in *Le paradis de la Reine Sibylle*. See also Gaston Paris, *Légendes du Moyen Age*, 67–109.
21. See Nichols's discussion of "mediated reading," especially 51–58.
22. On this, see Barbara Altmann, " 'Trop peu en sçay': The Reluctant Narrator in Christine de Pizan's Works on Love," in *Chaucer's French Contemporaries: The Poetry/Poetics of Self and Tradition*, ed. R. Barton Palmer, Georgia State Literary Series 10 (New York: AMS Press, 1999), 217–49.
23. Some historians would like to identify the "real" woman they believe Sebille represents in the *Duc des vrais amans*. In an article about Gabrielle de la Tour, oldest daughter of Bertrand V de la Tour, Colette Beaune and Elodie Lequain remark that the cultivated women of that family were so numerous that Christine de Pizan must have named Sybille de la Tour after them: "Femmes et histoire en France au XVe siècle: Gabrielle de la Tour et ses contemporaines," *Médiévales* 38 (Spring 2000): 111–36, at 126. (I thank Liliane Dulac for bringing this article to my attention.) And in an article published a year earlier, Françoise Autrand found that "Tout ce qui est dit d'elle [about the Dame de la Tour] est assez précis pour faire penser à un personnage bien réel," but the evidence she adduces is slim. Autrand does point out, however, that there were many families named Montaut or de la Tour, and she suggests that we would do better to look to Christine's three chapters in the *Cité des dames* devoted to the sibyl, "antique symbole de la sagesse féminine": "Christine de Pisan et les dames à la Cour," in *Autour de Marguerite d'Ecosse: Reines, princesses et dames au XVe siècle, actes du colloque de Thouars (23 et 24 mai 1997)*, ed. Geneviève et Philippe Contamine (Paris: Honoré Champion, 1999), 19–31, at 27–28.
24. See *Le Débat sur le Roman de la Rose*, ed. Eric Hicks (Paris: Honoré Champion, Bibliothèque du XVe siècle 43, 1977).
25. *Le Livre du duc des vrais amans*, ed. Thelma S. Fenster, Medieval and Renaissance Texts and Studies 124 (Binghamton: Center for Medieval and Early Renaissance Studies, 1995), 172; *The Book of the Duke of True Lovers*, trans. Thelma Fenster and Nadia Margolis (New York: Persea, 1991), 112.
26. See *Fama: The Politics of Talk and Reputation in Medieval Europe*, ed. Thelma S. Fenster and Daniel Lord Smail (Ithaca, NY: Cornell University Press, forthcoming).
27. Neubauer, *The Rumour: A Cultural History*, trans. Christian Braun of *FAMA: Eine Geschichte des Gerüchts* (Berlin: Berlin Verlag, 1998) (London: Free Association Books, 1999), 18.

28. Bibliothèque Nationale MS., f. f., 605, f. 6b.
29. Ibid., f. 11b.
30. Rachel Gibbons, "Isabeau of Bavaria Queen of France (1385–1422): The Creation of An Historical Villainess," *Transactions of the Royal Historical Society*, Series 6, VI (1996): 51–73; at 51. See also Rachel Gibbons, "Les conciliatrices au bas Moyen Age: Isabeau de Bavière et la guerre civile," in *La guerre, la violence et les gens au Moyen Age*, ed. Philippe Contamine and O. Guyotjeannin (Paris: Comité des travaux historiques et scientifiques, 1996), vol. 2, *La violence et les gens*, 23–34. For other recent defenders of Isabel, see the bibliography under Famiglietti; Kimm; Verdon, Grandeau; see also Jean Markale, A. Vallet de Virivilie, M. Thibault; Marie-Veronique Clin's recent book, *Isabeau de Bavière: La Reine calomniée* (Paris: Perrin, 1999) is based on these other sources.
31. Rachel Gibbons, "Isabeau of Bavaria Queen of France (1385–1422)," 57. After Philip of Burgundy's death in 1404, his son Jean (Jean sans Peur) became Duke of Burgundy and stepped up the campaign against Orleans.
32. According to the Religieux, the Augustinian monk Jacques Legrand, in a sermon preached before the queen, assured Isabel that people were talking about the disorderliness and dishonor of her court; should Isabel not believe him, she need only make the rounds of the city disguised as a poor woman and she'll hear it all herself. Michel Pintoin, *Chronique du Religieux de Saint-Denys, contenant le règne de Charles VI de 1380 à 1422*, ed. and trans. M. L. Bellaguet, introduction by Bernard Guenée (Paris: Comité des travaux historiques et scientifiques, 1994). In 1976 Nicole Grévy-Pons and Ezio Ornato showed persuasively that the "Religieux" was Michel Pointon; see Guenée's comprehensive introduction, i–lxviii. Briefer but more insulting were the accusations against the queen in the *Songe Veritable*, a political pamphlet in the form of an allegory probably written in 1406: *Le Songe véritable: Pamphlet politique d'un Parisien du XVe siècle*, ed. H. Moranville (Paris: n.p., taken from *Mémoires de la Société de l'Histoire de Paris et de l'Ile-de-France*, v. 17 (1890), 1891. Relying upon the reports of such personifications as Chascun (Everyman) and Commune Renommee (Common Knowledge; Public Opinion), the *Songe* accuses the king's uncle, Jean, Duke of Berry; the king's brother Louis; his queen, Isabel; and the king's powerful head steward/butler Jean de Montaigu. Although the *Songe* devotes a mere sixteen lines to addressing Isabel directly (ll.2387–52), it manages a low blow: Isabel is "Envelopée en laide peau" (l.2838), a line conventionally read as referring to her weight, although not without challenge. In sum, although many of the accusations brought against Isabel rehearse a rhetoric of misogyny, they have not inspired much modern reexamination.
33. See Jacques Lemaire, *Les Visions de la vie de cour dans la littérature française de la fin du Moyen Age* (Brussels: Palais des Académies; Paris: Klincksieck, 1994), 136.
34. On political exemplarity, see Kate Forhan, *The Political Theory of Christine de Pizan* (Brookfield, VT: Ashgate, 2002).
35. Angus J. Kennedy, "Christine de Pizan's Epistre à la Reine (1405)," *Revue des Langues Romanes* 92 (1988): 253–64, at 257–58.
36. See Zink, *La subjectivité littéraire* (Paris: PUF, 1985).

37. Paupert, "Le 'Je' lyrique féminin dans l'oeuvre poétique de Christine de Pizan," in *Et c'est la fin pour quoy sommes ensemble: hommage à Jean Dufournet: littérature, histoire et langue du Moyen Age*, ed. Jean-Claude Aubailly, Nouvelle bibliothèque du Moyen Age, 25 (Paris: Honoré Champion, 1993), 1057–71, at 1062.
38. Cover headline to Robert Pinsky's review of R. W. B. Lewis's *Dante* (New York: Lipper/Viking, 2001), *The New York Times Book Review*, July 29, 2001. By comparison, Pinsky notes in his review, Shakespeare said nothing about himself (9).

9

Le Livre de la cité des dames

Reconfiguring Knowledge and Reimagining Gendered Space

Judith L. Kellogg

Christine de Pizan's *Livre de la cité des dames* ranges extraordinarily far in its contexts. Drawing upon an encyclopedic recall of inherited tradition, it moves temporally throughout history and geographically from Christine's contemporary France to exotic and ancient realms on the borders of Christine's known world. Discussions invoke the earthly and divine. Issues are both personal and universal. Yet, remarkably, the place where such dynamic interaction unfolds never changes, for once Christine is led to the allegorical Field of Letters, all subsequent "action" in the work, the constructing and populating of the City of Ladies, takes place in that same spot. Consequently as Christine and her three divine mentors excavate and then build, they create new configurations of space. Christine is then able to analyze and transform the meanings of these configurations with a view to exposing the inequitable gendering of space, and subsequently to identify the spaces in which women can shift the balance of patriarchal power. By her relentless intellectual probing within the Field of Letters, she manages to evoke an array of lived spaces, query the correctness of perceived spaces, and envision newly conceived spaces.[1] These allegorical spaces defined and explored within Christine's City of Ladies provide a valuable context for exploring the gender implications of Foucault's observation that "Space is fundamental to any form of communal life; space is fundamental to any exercise of power."[2]

Roberta Gilchrist's archaeological studies of actual spaces inhabited by women have suggestive applications to Christine's metaphorical construction, leading to insights about the ways configurations of "landscapes, architecture and boundaries" result in "spatial maps" that "represent discourses of power based in the body."[3] This conjunction of space and the body is crucial for Christine. Within the *Cité des dames*, the body functions on multiple levels, including the body of knowledge and the body politic reconfigured by her city. Specifically, new formulations of knowledge create a political structure in which the marginalized become the center of the social system and responsible for its governance. Seen in this light, as we will see, her city represents a regendered body politic, which becomes literally embodied, for in the end, Christine's city is an idea meant to be "mapped" into individual female bodies—to be internalized to function as protection and fortification within the social spaces they actually inhabit.

The familiar passage that instigates Christine's initial building project describes her despair over being, as a woman, a "vile creature" (ville chose) and a "montrosit[y] in nature" (5) (monstre en nature, I.1, 44).[4] To console and instruct Christine, Lady Reason takes her into the Field of Letters to construct the marvelous city that will validate women's virtue, goodness, and strength, and showcase their fundamental contribution to the development of civilization. But before the building begins, they must excavate the space for the foundations. Reason, using "la pioche d'inquisicion" (I.8, 66) (pick of cross examination, 16), asks Christine to measure the misogynist authorities she has internalized against her own experience. In so doing, basketful by basketful, layers of misogynist misconception are removed so that the construction can be built on a true understanding of feminine nature. This dramatization of the rhetorical deconstruction on which her subsequent civic reconstruction program is based is a means, as Kathleen Biddick describes in another context, to provide clues "to the historical processes" that are invisible, "in order to make some category visible,"[5] the category in this case, of course, being misogyny.

The preparation of the allegorical space on which Christine de Pizan creates her City of Ladies does not simply involve digging and discarding, for the false assumptions are removed using an archaeological model. The purpose of an archaeological dig is to use the architectural configurations and material artifacts discovered to reconstruct painstakingly the beliefs and social structures that shape a civilization. This is metaphorically what Lady Reason does for Christine. The first basketful of dirt contains the response to the question, Why have men said such terrible things about women? Each additional layer removed is analyzed in terms of the ideological positions represented,[6] essentially pointing to the irrationality and arbitrary nature of the misogynist positions that are perpetuated as knowledge. This process thus represents the initial surveying and mapping of the social spaces inhabited by women in relationship to men, spaces over which men have been firmly in control. Given the denigratory and constricting attitudes toward women that this process unearths, Christine's use of spatial imagery illuminates the way that "structures of knowledge function as strategies of oppression."[7]

Significant here is that the removal of these layers of received authority also will outline the structure of the new edifice, for the new foundations, after all, will be placed in the negative space created. The previous structures will provide the outward shape, but the fact that traditional material will be reinscribed free of misogynist bias will fundamentally alter the meaning of the body of knowledge now placed in The Field of Letters. Christine's initial excavation project within the Field of Letters, by which she deconstructs the layers of misogynist bias that have been represented as knowledge, attests to her sophisticated understanding of the "process by which knowledge functions as a form of power and disseminates the effects of power."[8] Her entire work, in fact, is a sustained exploration of this process, for her intent is, by reconfiguring that knowledge, to subvert the "form of power" that misogyny has imposed on women, redirect that power, and disseminate the consequent positive effects to other women. Her method is to replace the faulty knowledge of inherited traditions through massive reeducation, drawing examples from an encyclopedic collection of material, including the traditional authorities of myth, history, Biblical material, saints' lives, and Christine's own contemporaries.[9]

Christine develops her project in three sections, and in each of these a specific allegorical figure serves as mentor. Lady Reason, Lady Rectitude, and Lady Justice reflect Christine's growing enlightenment, and represent the various kinds of conceptual structures that will be utilized for her building project. Reason, with her mirror, represents knowledge one can access through one's own experience, without the aid of Christian revelation. The examples Reason uses to excavate the Field of Letters and set the foundations in mortar are drawn from pagan myth, Old Testament stories, and familiar women's histories. Reason establishes the fact that women are smart, virtuous, and active contributors to the very foundations of civilized life. Rectitude focuses on moral issues and ethical concepts. With her ruler of righteousness, she measures the parameters of the city and builds fortifications, palaces, and houses. She builds from the examples of women who, faced with complex and difficult moral challenges, managed to make proper decisions. She insists that men are not simply unreasonable in devaluing women, but ethically wrong. Rectitude also begins to populate this magnificent city with exemplary pagan, Biblical, and living women. Justice, holding her golden vessel that measures each person's portion of blessedness, decorates the turrets and the high roofs, and introduces the queen and her entourage of female saints. She adds spiritual knowledge and the assurance that the city and the values it represents have divine approval. Although embodying Christian belief, in validating the pagan foundations on which the city is built, Justice reminds women that the community that binds them has been shared since creation, establishing that this is not simply a spatial structure, but a temporal edifice as well that provides women a collective history.[10] Margarete Zimmermann's nuanced discussion of the role of memory in Christine's city illuminates the complex role that history plays in configuring knowledge. In discussing the cosmic perfection of the city, Zimmerman establishes the framework of spiritual time:

> Son caractère de forteresse, sa beauté et surtout sa durée, qui la situe en un certain sens hors de la finalité du temps humain, aspect sur lequel Christine insiste tout particulièrement, en constituent les qualités principales. La stricte rationalité et la linéarité de sa construction renvoient à l'idéal d'un cosmos parfaitement structuré selon la volonté divine.[11]

(Its fortress-like nature, its beauty and especially its duration situate it, in a certain sense, outside the finality of human time—an aspect on which Christine puts particular emphasis—and constitute its principle qualities. The strict rationality and linearity of its construction reflect the ideal of a cosmos perfectly structured according to divine will.)

But in spite of the City's solidity and eternal character (existing always in the mind of God), because it is constructed in the context of human time, it also allows for a fluidity of memory that invites Christine to view recalled figures and events as representative of truths that transcend their historical moment. Christine, with the aid of her three allegorical mentors, does not so much create new knowledge or discover new truths; rather she simply remembers what women have accomplished and how they have conducted themselves throughout history. In so doing, she encourages other women to participate actively in the remembering with her. As Zimmermann says,

> Ainsi, l'espace imaginaire de la *Cité des dames* permet aux femmes de dialoguer avec l'ensemble des femmes de toutes les époques de l'histoire et constitue une sorte d'archive, un vaste lieu de mémoire où sont enregistrés et conservés les faits des "grandes dames exemplaires." (571)

(Thus the imaginary space of the *City of Ladies* allows women to enter into dialogue with all women of all periods of history and constitutes a sort of archive, a vast site of memory, in which are inscribed and preserved the deeds of exemplary great ladies.)

To recoup the full meaning of this "vaste lieu de mémoire," one must return to the Field of Letters, where history has been remembered badly. Here, Lady Reason goes beyond simply responding to individual misogynist claims, for she offers a careful analysis of the underlying bases of these attitudes. If she can refute the very assumptions on which men claim "knowledge" about women, then, of course, the entire misogynist argument crumbles. As the dialogue between Lady Reason and Christine develops, it becomes clear that men's faulty memories have led them to see women through the lens of a debased female body. This is clear from Christine's initial lament, for she closes with the summation, "me tenoie tres malcontente de ce que en corps femenin m'ot fait Dieux ester au monde" (I.1,46) (I considered myself most unfortunate because God had made me inhabit a female body in this world, 5).[12] Once Lady Reason begins to question this self-loathing, one of the first authorities that Christine confronts is Aristotle. She recalls that "quant il a assez parlé de l'impotence et foiblece qui est cause de former le corps femenin ou ventre de la mere, que Nature est aussi comme toute honteuse quant elle voit que elle a formé tel corps si comme chose imparfaicte" (I.11, 76–8) (after he has discussed the impotence and weakness which cause the formation of a feminine body in the womb of the mother, he says that Nature is completely ashamed when she sees that she has formed such a body, as though it were something imperfect, 23). But after examining the Biblical creation story of Adam and Eve, Reason returns authority to the female body by insisting, "Si n'ot pas honte le souverain ouvrier de faire et former corps femenin, et Nature s'en hontoyeroit?" (I.11, 78) (If the Supreme Craftsman was not ashamed to create and form the feminine body, would Nature then have been ashamed? 23).[13] Thus it becomes apparent that because Christine's paralyzing and self-destructive vulnerability as she begins her work is focused on her body, so must the female body be valorized for her to proceed.

As we examine Christine's attitude to the body, it is instructive to recall another familiar passage, the segment of the *Mutacion de Fortune* in which Christine allegorically describes the loss of her husband in a terrible ocean storm and the subsequent building project it necessitates, in this case the repair of her husband's ship.[14] As in the *Cité des dames*, this building project is precipitated by a moment of crisis and intense despair related to the vulnerability associated with her gender. In a powerful and dramatic passage, Christine weeps, rages, and wants to commit suicide, but is restrained by her responsibility to her household. In the midst of her intense grief, Lady Fortune takes pity on her and in one of Christine's most dramatic sequences, transforms Christine's body into that of a man. The physical changes are described graphically as Christine feels her body hardening and her voice deepening. She realizes that in order to negotiate the world alone, and especially since she will support her family by writing, she must acquire the discursive authority available almost exclusively to men in her society. Thus a male body becomes the symbolic cover that will allow her entry into the public world of patriarchal discourse. Once Christine has been transformed into her new male body, she picks up her hammer to rejoin the planks of the decimated ship so that she can sail into the world of male discursive privilege. As Marilynn Desmond notes, "She sees authorship as masculine performance, and in the *Mutacion de Fortune* she fashions her authorial identity accordingly."[15] However, in spite of her understanding that she must frame herself with a masculine authorial stance, she continues to see herself from a female subject position. Even given her newly authorized masculine voice, Christine continues to desire "to return as a woman and be heard" (v. 1397).[16]

This desire "to return as a woman and be heard" brings us back to the *Cité des dames* because the early interchange with Lady Reason, focusing specifically on misconceptions regarding the female body, can be seen imagistically as the point at which Christine allows herself the symbolic transformation back into the body of a woman, with a voice that *will* be heard. In returning authority to her female body, the symbolic direction of her movement changes as well. Her male body had enabled her to construct a ship to move out into the patriarchal world, into a space in which she is in many ways isolated from other women. However, the female body allows her to build an unmoving, centered enclosure to protect herself from the same world, while exploring its social dynamics. But the strength of her newfound feminine subjectivity comes not in isolation, but from creating an orderly and well-governed community available to all women. Such a community necessarily involves a political base, and here this feminine civic order can be usefully explored in terms of a body politic. And in fact, in close proximity to the period in which she was writing the *Cité des dames* (1405), she was also writing the *Livre du corps de policie* (1406–1407) along the traditional lines of a mirror for princes.[17] Briefly, the idea of the body politic goes back to the early Church and uses the organic image of the body to suggest the interrelatedness and reciprocity of all parts of a community. Paul says, "For just as in a single human body there are many limbs and organs, all with different functions, so we who are united with Christ, though many, form one body, and belong to one another as its limbs and organs" (Epistle to the Romans 12:4–5). Paul's analogy was adapted by medieval political theorists, who argued that as each part of the body must be healthy for the whole to thrive, so must each segment of a community perform its proper function to ensure communal well-being. The most influential work in this tradition is John of Salisbury's twelfth-century *Policraticus*, which establishes the analogy of the head as the ruling figure, the Prince. In his model, the upper body and limbs represent the aristocracy, those who must maintain order. The soul is the Church and the feet are the peasantry. Although Christine attributes her model to Plutarch, she is clearly influenced by John of Salisbury, using a similar three-part overall structure, while, however, diminishing the importance of the Church.

Not surprisingly, the *Corps de policie* and the *Cité des dames* share many of the same emphases. Each depicts the well-run society and provides a civic model for good governance. Each emphasizes the interdependence of all the parts. Certainly, the *Cité* shares the essential idea of community that Nederman describes in the *Corps de policie* as "inclusive, reciprocal, and interdependent."[18] Whereas the *Corps de policie* provides a mirror for Princes, one can call the *Cité* a mirror for women. And here one might recall that Lady Reason's emblem is a mirror, suggesting that the self-reflexivity of those in control leads to the harmony of an enlightened community. Further, the *Corps de policie* is written to edify the sovereign, with continual attention to his education and that of his nobles. Likewise, most of the *Cité de dames* is organized around the education of the narrator. In both works, all the classes are involved, although in the *Cité des dames*, all the citizens are female. In addition, in each work, the social model is hierarchical. In the *Corps de policie* we find the traditional model, with the levels differentiated by estate. However, in the *Cité des dames*, Christine discards a hierarchy based

Le Livre de la cité des dames

strictly on class, because virtuous women of all estates are included. Instead, she moves from pagan foundations to increasingly spiritual contexts. Although different classes are acknowledged, in each work, a royal figure is at the center of political power. In the *Corps de policie*, the Prince is both the literal and figurative head of the body politic, whereas in the *Cité des dames*, Christine culminates her project with a Queen, the Virgin Mary, as ruler and head (specifically using the corporeal language, *chief*) of the body politic. Mary herself asserts, "Si suis et seray a tousjours chief du sexe femenin" (III.1, 432) (I am and will always be the head of the feminine sex, 218). That this political organization is a natural one is further indicated by Mary's statement that "ceste chose fu dés oncques en la pensee de Dieu le Pere" (III.1, 432) (This arrangement was present in the mind of God the father from the start, 218).[19]

All the similarities suggest Christine's conscious modeling of the *Cité des dames* on the ideal of a feminine body politic. However, one significant difference in the structure of the two works suggests a redirected emphasis, for the order in which the hierarchies are elaborated is reversed. In the *Corps de policie*, Christine's discussion follows the traditional order, beginning, as does John of Salisbury, with the head (the Prince) and working down to the lower classes, who constitute the belly, legs, and feet. She emphasizes the importance of maintaining the health and well-being of the lower classes. Here, Christine explicitly recognizes how crucial the foundation of the community is to the whole, stating that, "il me semble que il sont les sousteneurs et ont la charge de tout le seurplus du dit corps, par quoy ont mestier d'avoir force et puissance de porter la pesanteur des autres parties" (it seems to me that they are the support and have the burden of the rest of the body, thus they need the strength and power to carry the weight of the other parties).[20] Although the lower classes provide the solid foundation on which the entire body politic depends for support, they are relegated to the end of the work, because, as essential as they are, they are also the least powerful political entity. In the *Cité*, however, Christine emphasizes the degree to which strong foundations are essential to the cohesiveness of the body politic, for she begins from the bottom, working up through a complex set of hierarchies. And basic to her foundations are assumptions based on a reformulated corporeal image of the head in relationship to the body that entirely upsets traditional gender associations.

An often invoked image legitimizing male authority was that of the man as head and intellect, ruling over the woman as body and carnality. Blamires summarizes the oppressive consequences of this model:

> The *caput/corpus* paradigm had been consolidated with harsh rigour in some patristic contexts. St. Jerome argued at one point that a wife not "subject to her head" or husband commits a crime of blasphemy as great as that committed by a man who fails to be "subject to Christ." The paradigm's ostensibly unchallenged status

enabled later writers to use it as if it constituted definitive proof of male *auctoritas in praesidendo*.[21]

But early in the *Cité des dames*, Reason establishes that the fundamental assumptions on which this paradigm is based are simply wrong. The problem for women is that they lack education, not intellect. She says, "se coustume estoit de mettre les petites filles a l'escole et que suivamment on les feist apprendre les sciences, comme on fait au filz, qu'elles apprendroient aussi parfaictement et entendroient les soubtilletéz de toutes les ars et sciences comme ilz font" (I.27,150–52) (if it were customary to send daughters to school like sons, and if they were then taught the natural sciences, they would learn as thoroughly and understand the subtleties of all the arts and sciences as well as sons, 63). In fact, she suggests the truly destabilizing idea that women may be intellectually superior to men precisely because of the differences in their bodies, saying "de tant comme femmes ont le corps plus delié que les hommes, plus faible et moins abile a plusieurs chose faire, de tant ont elles l'entendement plus a delivre et plus agu ou elles s'appliquent" (I.27,152) (just as women have more delicate bodies than men, weaker and less able to perform many tasks, so do they have minds that are freer and sharper whenever they apply themselves, 63). It is only a few logical steps from there to reach the conclusion that women can govern admirably, that is, that they can occupy the metaphorical position of head in the body politic.

Thus we have the parameter for the entire building project set in mortar—for these lower walls define the configurations of space within which the regendered body politic will be established. The good governance of the city will thus be supported and maintained by capable women who now are associated with the intellectual qualities of head in relationship to men, who in their physical strength are associated with body. Appropriately, this first section describes a series of remarkable pagan and euphemerized mythological women who create a social structure based on feminine intellect, imagination, moral strength, and insight. Christine's women are not simply able and active participants in maintaining their community; they are responsible for creating the technological and institutional foundations of civilized life. For instance, Ceres, with her invention of plowing and the sowing of seed, provides the basis for social organization and creates the possibility for community among people who had traditionally lived scattered. Isis not only invents an alphabet and devises horticulture, but she also teaches the Egyptians to live according to the law ("a vivre par ordre de droitture," I.36,176). Minerva contributes a Greek script, numbers, and such basic skills as woolen fabrication, cartmaking, and the making of armor. In addition she taught men how to deploy their armies and invented chivalry, the institution fundamental to the medieval social order. In Christine's vision then, these women and their achievements constitute the building blocks that make cultural, social, and political communal structures possible, and thus they are essential to shaping her own historical moment.

That Christine's building blocks are organized on the model of a *"cité"* rather than, for instance, a religious community, tells us much about the social space she envisions, for a *cité* was the political space that afforded the most fluid social possibilities for its citizens. As Richards has recently pointed out, "a city in the late Middle Ages represented as a legal entity a far more open model of political freedom than any other legal corporation."[22] Richards is careful to insist that Christine has chosen the city as a paradigm "for its symbolic freedom" as a place in which ideally "life is conducted according to order of law, *par ordre de droit*" (228, 229). In fact, living as she did in a time marked by urban strife and factionalism, Christine understood the limitations of actual cities well enough, as she demonstrates in the *Corps de policie*. Thus "her view of the City was more directly influenced by legal commentaries on the *civitas* and the concern for a secure defense than by the social historical realities within the city itself. A human city, as opposed to an allegorical one, was still far from perfect" (231). The situation for women in cities was particularly deplorable. As Jo Ann McNamara asserts, the ideology of urban life "imaged a broad womanless space wherein men became not only free but commensurable: equal to one another in their masculinity."[23] Increasingly, women were silenced and enclosed, and thus "women, by their absence from serious places where men could control and use them to celebrate masculinity, helped to establish male commensurability" (McNamara, 151). As Hanawalt observes, in the medieval world, space is increasingly divided by gender: "women occupied rooms, houses, quarters in the cities and villages, while men's activities took them farther abroad to streets, highways, fields, cities, oceans, battles, and council tables" (*Medieval Practices of Space*, x). This increasing physical constriction of women well illustrates Elizabeth Grosz's contention that "the enclosure of women in men's physical spaces is not entirely different from the constraint of women in men's conceptual universe."[24]

McNamara points to the dynamic by which, as growing cities created new professional categories to maintain and order the social fabric, women were progressively excluded from public responsibilities:

> Women found that, as society became more institutionalized, their place within it became ever more confined and stereotyped. New professions generated by the church, secular government, and towns were not readily pinned to masculine warrior qualities. The new identities had to be gendered as well as classed, which meant that men had to prove women's incapacity to carry out public professional responsibilities by developing arcane skills that mysteriously qualified them to *man* the offices of the opening bureaucracy. (144)

This is the very dynamic that Christine repeats, but redirects in building her city. Christine must do her own regendering of identities and responsibilities that had been relegated as exclusive male enterprises, but without subverting the legal underpinnings of civic life.[25] No wonder the first building blocks placed in the freshly excavated Field of Letters are exempla of women who, besides being valiant chivalric warriors, are learned and able civic leaders such as Thamiris, Zenobia, and Artemisia, who represent the very roles from which women are excluded in Christine's own society. Her first building block, Semiramis, is even a city builder herself who "enforça et refist la cite de Babiloine ... de merveilleuse force et cruauté" (I.15,108) (reinforced and built the strong and cruel city of Babylon, 39).[26]

In presenting these impressive women whose roles mirror those normally occupied by men in actual society, Christine is able to use the legal model for the city as a place affording autonomy and political freedom. She then adapts it, using regendered assumptions of women's capabilities, thus forming the social blueprint from which she builds. Marilynn Desmond also points to the tangible importance of the city in Christine's own experience where, given the disruption of the Hundred Years War between France and England, she "grew into adulthood in a culture poised and prepared for invasion." In addition to the legal and cultural contexts for the city, her work reflects "the political and social understanding of the city as a unit of defense." Desmond points out that the "military practices of the English focused attention on cities, resulting in a war marked less by decisive battles between armies than by sieges of cities and walled towns." Thus, the "French landscape was transformed by ... defensive measures aimed at turning urban settlements into walled fortresses" (*Reading Dido*, 207). The focus here is on the defensive aspect of cities, a concern that certainly resonates in the *Cité des dames*. In her initial conversation with Christine, Lady Reason insists on the fundamental defensive purpose of this building project. It is necessary precisely because the men who are supposed to be women's great protectors have failed miserably. That the Field of Letters is not simply a place to create an intellectually enlightened building ground, but also a battlefield in which women are assailed by "envieux ennemis et l'oultrage des villains" (I.3, 54), is reinforced at the end of Christine's work, when she again insists that women take a defensive stance in their relations with men; she says, more particularly: "fuyez, fuyez la fole amour dont ilz vous admonnestent" (III.19, 50) (flee, flee the foolish love they urge on you!, 256). The city becomes a place in which women are thus protected not only from misogynist thinking, but also from men's actions—from the "engins estranges et decevables" (III.19, 502) (strange and deceptive tricks, 256) that men use to hunt and trap women.

Thus the building of the city is framed with comments pointing to the defensive needs of women within a misogynist culture, beginning with Reason's insistence that women cannot depend on men to protect them, and ending with Christine's caution concerning men's predatory tendencies. The central section, recounting the actual city building, repeats this insistence, for it begins and ends by describing two specific communities that are organized with specific defensive concerns in mind: that of the Amazons and that of the city's inhabitants. Early in her work, Christine establishes Amazon society as exemplary (I.16–19), recounting how this heroic secular community prospered for 800 years. In this society, women defended themselves by an aggressive military organization, modeled on that of the knights of Christine's own society. Yet however admirable this Amazon society may have been, it was not complete. Ultimately women must move beyond a chivalric model to the more permanent, peaceful, and self-sufficient "nouvel royaume de Femenie" (II.12, 250) (New Kingdom of Femininity, 117), realized in the newly perfected and divinely sanctioned City of Ladies. However, as harmonious as the metaphorical community may be, Lady Justice's last speech highlights the inescapable fact that a crucial aspect of the city is defensive, for it must function as "non mie seulement le refuge de vous toutes, c'est a entendre des vertueuses, mais aussi la deffence et garde contre voz ennemis et assaillans" (III.24, 498) (not only a refuge for you all, that is, for virtuous women, but also the defense and guard against your enemies and assailants, 254).

However, even Lady Justice's final words of caution do not diminish the magnificence of the edifice that Christine has created and the space it offers women to see one another freed of the veil of misogynist distortion. Patterned as it is on Augustine's City of God, this final city transcends the limitations of earthly cities in its reflection of divine harmonies. As we have seen, the process of building to this point has been meticulous and systematic. Thus we can see that the glorious culminating moment of the *Cité des dames*, the enthronement of the Queen, is founded on the initial valorization of the female body—literally (no longer seen as grotesque) as well as in the figurative modes of the body of knowledge (where women's strength, virtue, and ingenuity are remembered) and the body politic (with a woman as head and ruler). The result is a place where Christine can assure women that "a grant honneur vous toutes, celles qui amez gloire, vertus et loz, povez estre hebergees, tant les passees dames, commes les presentes et celles a avenir, car pour toute dame honorable est faicte et fondee" (I.19, 498) (all of you who love glory, virtue, and praise may be lodged in great honor, ladies from the past as well as from the present and future, for it has been established for every honorable lady, 254). It is a place "si reluisant que toutes vous y povez mirer" (I.19, 498) (so resplendent that you may see yourselves mirrored in it, 254).

But given the euphoria of the city's perfection, Christine's ending is troubling. For Christine concludes by reminding women that once the final steps in building are completed and the queen is triumphantly placed, they must return to their actual lives. That leaves unanswered the important question of how this city can in the end affect women's daily circumstances. Where, in fact, is this marvelous city? Where are the defensive walls? Where is the *space* in which the regendered body politic can be maintained? Allegorically, the city is built in the Field of Letters, but what is the impact of this new body of knowledge for actual women?

Clearly the city has to be built within the consciousness of each individual woman.[27] And here, discussion of the part one's culture plays in the construction of subjectivity is useful.[28] Although few would now contend that the "humanist subject" arrived in Western culture only in the Renaissance, the terms of that debate are instructive for understanding how subjectivity is formed within specific historical contexts. David Aers asserts that one would fail to develop "the interiority" necessary to think of oneself as a "free subject" only in "a culture free from commodity production, free from economic instabilities, class conflicts, political struggles and free from any ideological contests."[29] This certainly does not describe Christine's culture. In fact, Aers contends, interiority existed well before the fifteenth century, exemplified in Augustine (183). Aers argues that early modernists can locate the beginning of human subjectivity in the Renaissance only by creating a medieval culture with "no puzzled selves conscious of tensions between self and received norms, roles and expectations in changing communities. No Langland, no Petrarch, no Chaucer, no Margery Kempe" (193), and certainly, no Christine de Pizan. In arguing for medieval subjectivity, Lee Patterson describes the "process of self-construction" as "the dialectic between an inward subjectivity and an external world that alienates it from both itself and its divine source."[30] This dialectical model accurately describes the narrative structure of the *Cité des dames*, for Christine's starting point is the attempt to resolve the discrepancy between her perception that God has created a "vile" piece of handiwork in having created women (her initial "inward subjectivity") and the alienation from the divine source apparent in the inference that God has somehow made a mistake. As the work progresses in dialectic fashion, with Christine posing successive questions based on false concepts learned from her "external world," one can see that Christine, in building her city, is also reconstructing a self.[31] In creating her text, Christine becomes both the author and subject of the work, for the substance of the text becomes the reconstruction of the creator of the text.

As Christine reconstructs her subject position in the course of building her textual city, so her female reader also reconstructs herself in the act of reading the text. To return to Gilchrist's archaeological model, in laying out her repository of newly configured knowledge, Christine maps out the metaphorical spaces that women can internalize within their own experience. Ultimately, the space in which the city is built must be within each woman. The spatial maps must become a part of the subject position that each woman takes into the world, where they can be used, parallel to the maps of the material culture, "to construct, maintain, control, and transform social identity" (44). Otherwise Christine's advice to women to return even to violent and abusive husbands would be seen as the failure of the city to make any difference. After noting that not all women have bad husbands, she directs those women not so lucky to be humble and patient: "Et celles qui les ont divers, felons et reveschez, mettent peine tele en endurant que

Le Livre de la cité des dames   *141*

elles puissant convaincre leur felonnie et les ramener, se elles pevent, a vie raisonable et debonaire" (III.19, 500) (And those women who have husbands who are cruel, mean, and savage, should strive to endure them while trying to overcome their vices and lead them back, if they can, to a reasonable and seemly life, 255). Christine does not do this naïvely, for she has amply recounted the horrors of living with such men. Lady Rectitude had earlier asked her whether she recalled the women

> qui usent leur lasse de vie ou lien de mariage par durté de leurs maris en plus grant penitence que se elles fussent esclaves entre les Sarrasins? Dieux! quantes dures bateures, sanz cause et sans raison, quants laidenges, quantes villenies, injures, servitudes et oultrages y sueffrent maintes bonnes preudes femmes, qui toutes n'en cryent pas harou. (II.13, 254)

(who because of their husbands' harshness spend their weary lives in the bond of marriage in greater suffering than if they were slaves among the Saracens? My God! How many harsh beatings—without cause and without reason—how many injuries, how many cruelties, insults, humiliations, and outrages have so many upright women suffered, none of whom cried out for help? 119.)

Christine's final advice places women squarely back into the spaces configured by men—not only occupied by abusive husbands, but also laced with what she has described as the seductive "traps" in which women can be enclosed if they do not enclose themselves self-reflexively within the city. Presumably, Christine herself will return from this vision into the same enclosed space where she began, her *"cele"* (I.1, 40), with Matheolus still beside her. Her city does not make his voice disappear, but only allows her a different relationship to it. Given the real social constraints of women's lived lives, the body politic must reside within Christine as within every other citizen of her city. Thus at the same time that she directs women back to their marginalized social position, she can also reassure them that her city can remain both a refuge and a defense.

Christine de Pizan's *Cité des dames* incorporates extraordinarily rich intersections of ideas relating female bodies, the construction of knowledge, social space, and female subjectivity. In her work, Christine inscribes within female bodies an internalized discourse of power afforded by a regendered body politic built upon a newly configured body of knowledge based on overturning of traditional images of male as head and intellect and of female as body and flesh. This suggestive layering of corporeal images makes clear what critics have described as the "embodied nature of consciousness."[32] The incisiveness of Christine's analysis is largely afforded by the care with which she validates her initial assumptions concerning female virtue and talent. Her initial excavation has functioned remarkably like current archaeological practice, as described by Gilchrist:

Archaeology may be seen as central to a discourse of space and the body, since space reproduces social order and sometimes acts as a metaphorical extension of the body. Here the constitution of the subject is considered through the relationship of material culture and space to the human body. (45)

Thus we see how Christine, by beginning with careful archaeological preparation, defines a space in which to create an intricately designed city. By exploring how the meaning of that space shifts as Christine proceeds with her project, we can better understand how medieval women envisioned and metaphorically negotiated their material world in order to carve out workable subject positions, given the constraints unearthed by the initial archaeological project.

NOTES

1. For a developed discussion of these spatial distinctions, see Henri Lefebvre, *The Production of Space*, trans. Donald Nicholson-Smith (Oxford: Blackwell, 1991). Barbara Hanawalt and Michel Kobialka encapsulate Lebfevre's distinctions, describing the "triad of *spatial practice* (perceived), which embraces production and reproduction of each social formation, *representations of space* (conceived), which are tied to the relations of production and to the order, hence knowledge, that these relations impose, and *representational spaces* (lived), which embody complex symbolism dominating, by containing them, all senses and all bodies" (italics in original text), "Introduction," *Medieval Practices of Space*, ed. Barbara Hanawalt and Michel Kobialka (Minneapolis: University of Minnesota Press, 2000), ix–xviii, citation ix.
2. Michel Foucault, "Space, Knowledge, and Power," in *The Foucault Reader*, ed. Paul Rabinow (New York: Pantheon, 1984), 239–56, citation 252.
3. Roberta Gilchrist, "Medieval Bodies in the Material World: Gender, Stigma and the Body," in *Framing Medieval Bodies*, ed. Sarah Kay and Miri Rubin (Manchester: Manchester University Press, 1994), 41–63, 45.
4. French citations are from Christine de Pizan, *La Città delle dame*, ed. Earl Jeffrey Richards, trans. Patrizia Caraffi (Milano: Luni Editrice, 1997). English citations are from *The Book of the City of Ladies*, trans. Earl Jeffrey Richards (New York: Persea, 1982).
5. Kathleen Biddick, "Genders, Bodies, Borders: Technologies of the Visible," *Speculum* 68 (1993): 389–418, citation 390.
6. The *Cité des dames* is, of course, not the first work in which Christine defends women against misogynist claims, and does so not simply to rehabilitate the image of women, but with a larger political vision as well. See Helen Solterer, "Christine's Way: The *Querelle du Roman de la Rose* and the Ethics of a Political Response," in *The Master and Minerva: Disputing Women in French Medieval Culture* (Berkeley: University of California Press, 1995), 151–75, for a particularly good discussion of the way the Querelle de la *Rose* and the *Chemin de long estude* established Christine's insistence that "defamatory language [was] a potential threat to the commonweal" (153), for it marked a dangerous ethical failing in men generally.

7. Laurie Finke, *Feminist Theory, Women's Writing* (Ithaca, NY: Cornell University Press, 1992), 5.
8. Michel Foucault, "Questions on Geography," in *Power/Knowledge: Selected Interviews and Other Writings 1972–1977*, ed. Colin Gordon (New York: Pantheon, 1980), 63–77, citation 69.
9. Maureen Quilligan discusses the medieval distinction between an *auctor* (one who is respected as an authority) and a *compilator* (whose endeavor was to arrange inherited material in a meaningful order), suggesting that Christine positions herself as a *compilator* (*The Allegory of Female Authority: Christine de Pizan's Cité des Dames* [Ithaca: Cornell University Press, 1991], 31–40). This allows her, even though a woman, to place herself in the influential company of writers such as Jean de Meun, Boccaccio, and Vincent of Beauvais. Her role as one responsible for ordering material works meshes well with the archaeological model of one who also systematically analyzes the meanings of layers of artifacts. The spatial and material aspects of this model are even more explicitly suggested by Joel Blanchard, "Compilation and Legitimation in the Fifteenth Century: *Le Livre de la Cité des Dames*," in *Reinterpreting Christine de Pizan*, ed. Earl Jeffrey Richards (Athens and London: University of Georgia Press, 1992), 228–49, who describes the "scraps, fragments, and pieces" (243) out of which her work is constructed, and remarks, "Through the means of compilation, the transfer of one text into another corresponds to an architectural gesture" (229). For a general discussion of the distinction between an *auctor* and a *compilator*, see A. J. Minnis, *Medieval Theory of Authorship: Scholastic Literary Attitudes in the Late Middle Ages*, 2nd ed. (Philadelphia: University of Philadelphia Press, 1988).
10. It is helpful to see these three sections as conforming to an exegetical, mythographic model, where, as meanings move from literal (*texte*) to moral (*glose*) and spiritual (*allegorie*) levels, they are seen to coexist as different facets of an unchanging, universal, atemporal truth. This is a model with which Christine was experienced, for she used it in her *Epistre Othea* (c. 1400). For a fuller discussion of Christine's use of a mythographic method in the *Cité des dames*, see Judith Kellogg, "*Le Livre de la Cité des Dames*: Feminist Myth and Community," *Essays in Arts and Sciences* 18 (1989): 1–15.
11. Margarete Zimmermann, "Utopie et lieu de la mémoire feminine: *la Cité des Dames*," in *Au champ des escriptures*, ed. Eric Hicks (Paris: Champion, 2000), 561–80, citation 570.
12. Although she does not discuss Christine, Laurie Finke describes graphically the kinds of ideas that Christine has internalized: "The grosser, more material aspects of 'the body' were displaced onto the 'grotesque body.' Women . . . were constructed by the dominant culture as the grotesque body, the low other, whose discursive norms include heterogeneity, disproportion, a focus on gaps, orifices, and symbolic filth. The grotesque body is at once feminized, corrupt, and threatening; it is a reminder of mortality, imperfection, and the wretchedness of human existence." See Finke, "The Grotesque Mystical Body: Representing the Woman Writer," in *Feminist Theory, Women's Writing* (Ithaca: Cornell University Press, 1992), 75–107, citation 88.

13. For a still classic overview of the way Christine's own progress from being an "immasculated" reader and writer (one who has internalized a male perspective) toward becoming a writer with a confident feminine authorial stance, see Susan Schibanoff, "Taking the Gold Out of Egypt: The Art of Reading as a Woman," in *Gender and Reading: Essays on Readers, Texts, and Contexts*, ed. Elizabeth A. Flynn and Patrocino P. Shweikart (Baltimore: Johns Hopkins University Press, 1986), 83–106. For a specific discussion of this passage, particularly the way Christine uses theological arguments to counter the misogynist loathing of the female body, see Rosalind Brown-Grant, *Christine de Pizan and the Moral Defence of Women: Reading Beyond Gender* (Cambridge: Cambridge University Press, 1999), 151–55; in her comparisons between Christine's use of certain stories and those of Petrarch and Boccaccio, Brown-Grant also demonstrates how Christine rehabilitates and reclaims the female body (along with female language) as a site of virtue (167–73). Quilligan has a particularly good discussion of the way, in the third part of the *Cité*, in discussing female saints, Christine manages to make the tortured but resisting female body a locus of power.
14. For a fuller discussion of this passage, see Judith Kellogg, "Transforming Ovid: The Metamorphosis of Female Authority," in *Christine de Pizan and the Categories of Difference*, ed. Marilynn Desmond (Minneapolis: University of Minnesota Press, 1998), 181–94.
15. Marilynn Desmond, *Reading Dido: Gender, Textuality, and the Medieval Aeneid* (Minneapolis: University of Minnesota Press, 1994), 195.
16. *The Writings of Christine de Pizan*, ed. Charity C. Willard (New York: Persea, 1994), 127.
17. For good discussions of Christine's formulation of the body politic, see Kate Langdon Forhan, "Polycracy, Obligation and Revolt: The Body Politic in John of Salisbury and Christine de Pizan, in *Politics, Gender, and Genre: The Political Thought of Christine de Pizan*, ed. Margaret Brabant (Boulder: Westview, 1992), 33–52; and Kate Langdon Forhan, "Reflecting Heroes. Christine de Pizan and the Mirror Tradition," in *The City of Scholars: New Approaches to Christine de Pizan*, ed. Margarete Zimmermann and Dina De Rentiis (Berlin and New York: Walter de Gruyter, 1994), 189–96. For a fuller discussion of the larger political context in which Christine uses the mirror tradition and the concept of the body politic, see Kate Langdon Forhan, *The Political Thought of Christine de Pizan* (Ashgate, 2002). For a brief introduction to the intellectual history of the concept of the body politic, see Ernst Kantorowicz, *The King's Two Bodies: A Study in Medieval Political Theology* (Princeton: Princeton University Press, 1957), 207–31.
18. Cary Nederman, "The Expanding Body Politic: Christine de Pizan and the Medieval Roots of Political Economy," in Hicks, 383–97, citation 388.
19. This valorization of the divine aspects of Christine's city reflects the influence of Augustine's *City of God*, which lends moral and religious authority to Christine's city. Lady Justice explicitly recalls Augustine in her concluding remarks, as she turns the city over to Christine, "finished perfectly and well enclosed" (254) (clos, parfaicte et bien fermee, III, xviii, 496) echoing Augustine with "*Gloriosa dicta sunt de te, civitas Dei.*" For an excellent discussion of Christine's use of Augus-

tine, see Lori J. Walters, "La réécriture de saint Augustin par Christine de Pizan: De la Cité de Dieu à la Cité des Dames," in Hicks, 197–218.
20. Christine de Pizan. *The Book of the Body Politic*, trans. Kate Langdon Forhan (Cambridge: Cambridge University Press, 1994), 90–1. French edition, *Le Livre du corps de policie*, ed. Angus J. Kennedy (Paris: Champion, 1998), 91.
21. Alcuin Blamires, "Paradox in the Medieval Gender Doctrine of Head and Body," in *Medieval Theology and the Natural Body*, ed. Peter Biller and A. J. Minnis (York: York Medieval Press, 1997), 27. Given the binary nature of Western thought, this is a dichotomy that has remained in place to this day, and even one perpetuated, as Elizabeth Grosz contends, by some feminists. See Grosz, *Volatile Bodies* (Bloomington: Indiana University Press, 1994).
22. Earl Jeffrey Richards, "Where Are the Men in Christine de Pizan's City of Ladies? Architectural and Allegorical Structures in Christine de Pizan's *Livre de la Cité des dames*," in *Translatio Studii*, ed. Renate Blumenfeld-Kosinski, Kevin Brownlee, Mary B. Speer, and Lori J. Walters (Amsterdam: Rodopi, 1999), 221–43, 230.
23. Jo Ann McNamara, "City Air Makes Men Free and Women Bound," in *Text and Territory: Geographical Imagination in the European Middle Ages*, ed. Sylvia Tomasch and Sealy Giles (Philadelphia: University of Pennsylvania Press, 1998), 143–58, citation 144.
24. Elizabeth Grosz, *Space, Time, and Perversion: Essays on the Politics of Bodies* (London: Routledge, 1995), 123. In a more extreme version of this general idea, Grosz comments, "In seeking to take up all (social) space themselves, in aspiring to occupy not only the territory of the earth, but also that of the heavens, in seeking a dominion from the earth to the sky, men have contained women in a deathlike tomb" (122).
25. Christine's continuing concern that women see themselves as civic and public is suggested in her following work, *Le Livre des trois vertus*, where she translates the lessons implicit in the *Cité des dames* into practical terms. There, she addresses her audience as "citoyennes de vertu" (9); see Christine de Pizan, *Le Livre des trois vertus*, ed. Charity Cannon Willard and Eric Hicks (Paris: Champion, 1989).
26. Marilynn Desmond, *Reading Dido*, elaborates on the theme of female builders of cities, noting that "Dido's identity as a city builder makes her central to the allegorical program of the textual city under construction in the first two books of the *Cité des dames*. Christine's interest in recontextualizing and retelling Dido's story in relation to the founding of Carthage foregrounds the thematic value of cities as a cultural construct central to French consciousness at the start of the fifteenth century" (203).
27. Quilligan sees Christine's "ultimate subject in the *Cité* to be the creation of female subjectivity" (237). She earlier (5) offers Catherine Belsey's useful observation that "in post-structuralist analysis ... subjectivity is not a single unified presence but the point of intersection of a range of discourses, produced and reproduced as the subject occupies a series of places in the signifying system, takes on the multiplicity of meanings language offers," from "Disrupting Sexual Difference," in *Alternative Shakespeares*, ed. John Drakakis (London: Methuen, 1985), 166–90, 188.

28. This discussion takes into account Louis Althusser's fundamental observation that the term "subject" has both a personal and a political component, for it means both "1) a free subjectivity, a center of initiative, author of and responsible for its actions; 2) a subjected being, who submits to a higher authority, and is therefore stripped of all freedom except that of freely accepting his submission." See "Ideology and Ideological State Apparatuses," in *Lenin and Philosophy* (New York: Monthly Review Press, 1971), 127–86, citation 182. Felicity Nussbaum's exploration of subjectivity, *The Autobiographical Subject: Gender and Ideology in Eighteenth-Century England* (Baltimore: Johns Hopkins University Press, 1989), has clear applications to Christine as well, for she sees possibilities for developing altered subjectivities in the tensions and contradictions between ideologies (36). This describes Christine's progress from one who "misrecognizes" herself as a loathsome creature to one who turns that misapprehension into the production of new knowledge. I would especially like to thank Martha Wall for useful discussions of these issues.
29. David Aers, "A Whisper in the Ear of the Early Modernists; or, Reflections on Literary Critics Writing the 'History of the Subject,'" in *Culture and History 1350–1600: Essays on English Communities, Identities, and Writing*, ed. David Aers (Detroit: Wayne State University Press, 1992), citation 181.
30. Lee Patterson, *Chaucer and the Subject of History* (Madison: University of Wisconsin Press, 1991), quotations from 11 and 8.
31. See Sandra Hindman for a discussion of the way the illuminations of the *Cité des dames* reinforce the connection between the "enterprises of authoring and building." "With Ink and Mortar: Christine de Pizan's *Cité des dames* [An Art Essay]," *Feminist Studies* 10 (1984): 457–77, citation 465.
32. Sarah Kay and Miri Rubin, eds., "Introduction," in *Framing Medieval Bodies* (Manchester: Manchester University Press, 1994), 1–9, citation 7.

III
Christine's Writings

10

Love as Metaphor in Christine de Pizan's Ballade Cycles

Tracy Adams

Christine de Pizan's "Seulete suy, et seulete vueil estre" epitomizes the late fourteenth-century ballade, a form that works by transferring its subjectivity to its listeners or readers and guiding them through the collective expression of a single emotion.[1] The narrator of "Seulete suy" laments being left by her beloved in a series of three seven-line stanzas, plus envoi, which, except for the first line of the envoi, all begin with the haunting "Seulete suy." The impression of sorrow deepens with each incantation; each line adds a nuance to the emotion.[2] By the end of the ballade, the idea of bereavement has been exhausted.

Perdurably moving as a expression of the pain of being abandoned by a lover, "Seulete suy" assumes added meaning as an element in the life narrative elliptically recounted in Christine's first lyric cycle, the *Cent balades*. As part of a fiction controlled by Christine's poetic presence, the poem is infused with her personal narrative of misfortune and, ultimately, consolation.[3] "Seulete suy," which in another context would be a typical late fourteenth-century love lyric, assumes a place in the universal dialectic between mutability and eternity that Christine sets up in her ballade cycles, and it therefore takes on a grandeur that a love lyric, by virtue of its self-reflexivity, would not ordinarily possess on its own.[4] In numerous spots throughout her ballade cycles, Christine the narrator refers to the experience of love, but only to insist upon her present distance from it. Thus she differs utterly from the narrators of contemporary love lyric cycles, and not only because of her gender.[5] Participating in Christine's story of consolation, the forlorn narrator of "Seulete suy" signifies human helplessness in the face of worldly change; yet she holds out the promise of eventual comfort through the transcendence of worldly pleasures.

"Seulete suy," then, must be read as a product of two distinct poetic functions, the lyric and the narrative, for Christine's personal narrative lends significance to her individual lyrics, creating an architecture that controls her three major cycles. The first part of this chapter will be devoted to exploring how each of Christine's cycles represents a different manifestation of her personal narrative's paradigmatic rendering of sorrow. Then I will consider the relationship between Christine's lyric corpus and the rest of her work, reexamining in particular the relationship between her love lyrics, with their stories of loss and comfort, and her "feminist" writings, a relationship that has received critical attention in recent years.

But before exploring her ballade cycles, I would like to note some of the formal aspects of Christine's poetry important to understanding her particular contribution to the lyric cycle. Had she produced none of her long allegorical or political works, Christine de Pizan would still be known today as a major lyric poet. She began her writing career as a lyric poet with the *Cent balades*, composing the individual lyrics for this cycle between 1394 and 1399 and collating them in manuscript form by 1402.[6] She went on to compose two more ballade cycles, *Autres balades* and the *Cent balades d'amant et de dame*, as well as a collection of *rondeaux* and one of *virelais*.[7] In addition, following the fashion of her day, she composed two narrative pieces with lyric inserts, the *Dit de la pastoure* and *Le Livre du duc des vrais amans*. In her narrator persona Christine deems her lyric work less worthy than her allegorical and political narratives and states that she had intended to abandon lyric production altogether when she turned her talents to weightier themes. However, her patrons requested more, according to her narrator persona, and she complied. For example, in the prologue to her last major ballade cycle, the *Cent balades d'amant et de dame*, ca. 1410, she claims to have taken on writing of the work reluctantly at the request of a patron, as an *amende* for having written earlier that love was to be avoided.

And yet although she feigns a lack of interest in composing lyrics, she continues to produce them throughout much of her career. This continued activity and the sheer volume of her output suggest that despite the disavowals of her narrator, Christine found that medium apt for conveying a particular perspective. Christine's output of more than 300 ballades, seventy rondeaux, twenty virelais, and various lais and complaintes, although not as large as the outputs of Machaut, Froissart, or Deschamps, was substantial, and, as a great experimenter with stanza length, verses, and rhyme scheme, she left a corpus of tremendous formal variety.[8]

Christine's favorite lyric form was the ballade, a form that during the course of the fourteenth century overtook the longer, more fluid chanson as the most popular vehicle for personal expression among poets.[9] Already from the mid-thirteenth century, forms that were relatively fixed gained in popularity over flexible ones as the *puys*, literary organizations that conducted poetic contests, began to regulate closely the rules to which the poems they judged had to adhere. Codified along with other major lyric types by Guillaume de Machaut and later by Eustache Deschamps, the ballade became the preferred form of the *Cour amoureuse* of Charles VI and was cultivated by a great number of poets, including, besides Machaut and Deschamps, Froissart, Villon, and Marot. Its popularity plummeted during the sixteenth century under the regime of the Pléiade, who relegated it to the ragbag of unworthy medieval poetic forms. Along with the rondeau, virelai, and chant royal, Joachim du Bellay dismissed the formerly esteemed ballade as one of the "episseries qui corrumpent le goust de notre langue" (strange spices corrupting the taste of our language).[10]

The move toward more rigid codification, however, was mitigated by a fourteenth-century development. Somewhere between the end of Machaut's career and the beginning of Christine's, the ballade, along with other lyric forms, detached itself definitively from music, and when Deschamps composed the *Art de dictier* in 1392, he distinguished between "musique artificiele" and "musique naturele," meaning, in the first instance, the kind that is sung, and in the second, the kind inherent in the rhythm of spoken words.[11]

The new distinction between artificial and natural music affected the poetic tradition that Christine inherited in two principal ways. First, it reversed the trend begun in the thirteenth century toward a tightening of the rules of composition. The ballade's symmetry derived from the music that had once governed its repetitions. Traditionally it had contained three stanzas of eight to ten lines with identical rhyme schemes, each stanza leading to the same refrain, generally one line long. The stanza length often matched the number of syllables in each line. The rhyme patterns varied, with ballades tending to be built on three or four rhymes, with the same scheme repeated in each stanza. But freed from the metrical constraints imposed by music, the ballade became more flexible in the lengths of its lines and stanzas, and the envoi, the half-stanza in which the Prince of the *puy* was addressed, formerly associated with the chant royal, became common.[12]

Second, this distinction gave rise to a new lyric voice. In *La Subjectivité littéraire*, Michel Zink describes the contrast between sung poetry, with its standard form and impersonal narrator, and recited poetry, whose narrator represents himor herself as a personalized individual. Separated from music, the ballade became more suited to personalized expression. Zink writes, "Une poésie chantée, qui est une poésie de la formalisation rhétorique et de la généralisation éthique, s'oppose à une poésie récitée, qui est une poésie de l'anecdote du moi" (48) ("Sung poetry, which is a poetry of rhetorical formalization and ethical generalization, contrasts with recited poetry, which is a poetry of the anecdote of the self").[13]

Chronological examinations of lyric poetry show a trend toward the personalized narrator beginning already in the thirteenth century: the lyric *je*, which in the grand chant courtois had exteriorized the common human fund of joy and pain without drawing attention to its own individual subjectivity and without entering into dialogue with the beloved, begins to give way to a more individualized narrator capable of engaging in dialogue. This evolution was speeded along by the separation of lyric poetry from music, a strongly ritualistic element.

Christine's ballade cycles bear the imprint of a literary subjectivity—a recognizable *je* with historical specifications. Furthermore, her ballades demonstrate what Jacqueline Cerquiglini has called a "pluralisation des voix," dialogues among different speakers, a phenomenon that with the addition of personal anecdotes has the effect of rendering a lyric *je* more concrete.[14] In these characteristics Christine follows in the footsteps of Machaut, whose narrative persona inserts lyrics into his *dits* and furnishes them with a history, a specific origin. In addition, as Lori Walters has shown, Christine follows Petrarch of the *Rime Sparse*, whose work was well known among writers at the French court at the end of the fourteenth century. Christine's use of male and female voices in dialogue suggests that she was influenced by poem 23 of the *Rime Sparse*, a dialogue between a man and a woman in love, and, like Petrarch, in her cycles she uses love to discuss universal verities. Writes Walters, "As early as the *Cent balades*, Christine builds upon Petrarch's sublimated recasting of Ovidian myth in order to raise her own personal story to the level of universal history."[15] Another model would have been suggested by the *Livre des cent balades*, a team effort of Jean le Seneschal, Boucicaut le Jeune, Jean de Cresecque, and the Count of Eu, who created a cycle entirely of lyric verse, complete with plot, in 1389 or 1390, about ten years before Christine's first cycle.[16] Thus Christine's ballade cycles fall within a tradition of the personalized narrator who may or may not recount a coherent narrative, but whose life story provides an architecture for a group of poems.

In fact, the *Cent balades* do not recount a coherent narrative of a single character. Rather, as James Laidlaw has written, several narrative units covering diverse themes are apportioned among different poetic voices. Thus along with lyrics attributable to Christine's voice exist what Laidlaw has called *balades de personnages*.[17] Still, as I will attempt to demonstrate in what follows, a fundamental coherence resulting from Christine's narrative presence underlies the discrete units of this cycle.

In the first ballade of the *Cent balades* Christine establishes the personal narrative from which the following ballades, and, indeed, much of her future writing will derive meaning. Requested to write some "beaulz diz," she complies, but emphasizes that she does not personally feel the joy she recounts in her lyrics: "Peine y mettray, combien qu'ignorant soie . . ." (1.7) (I will exert myself, however much I lack the feelings myself). The reason for her lack of joy she explains in the third stanza of the poem: the death of her beloved several years earlier.

> Et qui vouldra savoir pour quoy efface
> Dueil tout mon bien, de legier le diroye:
> Ce fist la mort qui fery sanz menace
> Cellui de qui trestout mon bien avoye;
> Laquelle mort m'a mis et met en voye
> De desespoir. . . . (ll.17–22)

(And those who wish to know why sorrow obliterates/everything for me, I will tell them simply:/Death struck without warning the one who was everything to me/and this death has put me on the road to despair. . . .)

Historical fact accords with Christine's description of her sorrow, for she lost her husband in 1390. But historical accuracy aside, representing herself as a mourning widow is strategic for at least two reasons. First, although her present indifference toward love guarantees her a respectability and a measure of objectivity, she understands the intensity of love because she has experienced it herself. As a widow she writes both within and without, and the importance of this liminal stance to her narrative self-authorization has been skillfully described by critics.[18]

But second, Christine's personal experience of the devastating force of Fortune becomes a type for unhappiness of all varieties, uniting them all—from the personal misery of love gone awry to France's suffering because of the madness of Charles VI (ballade 95)—under the general problem of the mutability of earthly pleasures. Her paradigm of sorrow, one she evokes again and again, not only in the *Cent balades*, but throughout her corpus, is the anxiety of "not knowing," of hovering between desperate hope and the increasingly certain fear that all is lost.[19] Although she never reveals precisely how she received news of her husband's death, it is known that Christine's husband died in Beauvais while traveling with the royal court, and the image of an impatiently waiting and increasingly fearful Christine adds a special poignancy to her repeated depictions of lovers waiting and to her lyrics' repeated exhortations not to depend on Fortune.

In the *Cent balades*, Christine writes lyrics of the variety popular at court, but in framing them as she does within her personal history, she creates a narrative that distinguishes them from other lyrics of her time. Her persona possesses a depth and courage one does not find in the typical suffering lover. Whether she is complying with the requests of her audience or bowing to the blows of Fortune, the voice who describes herself as "seulete" never lets her audience forget that she complies of her own free will, having considered her options. Christine is patiently obedient because she *chooses* to be; she is as worthy of admiration as of pity. In ballade 20, she pauses to wonder how she could possibly be able to compose pretty rhymes when after ten years she has still not come to terms with the loss of her husband: "Quant des ans a près de dix/que mon cuer ne fu joyeux?" (When for nearly ten years/my heart has not been joyous?) In lines 15–18 she offers an answer to her own question. She cannot. Instead of creating beautiful lyrics, she expresses the sorrowing state of her own heart in her lyrics.

Si ay bien droit se je dis
Mes plains malencolieux;
Car en tristour est toudis
Mon dolent cuer. . . . (ll.15–18)

(Thus it is right if I recount/my melancholic complaints; for my grieving heart/is in complete sorrow.)

When the next ballade seems to change direction, then, recounting the tentative beginnings of a woman's love for one who is "courtois et debonaire" the reader recognizes that within the framework provided by Christine's narrative, the love is inevitably doomed. And indeed the story suggested by the ensemble of ballades 21 to 49 is one of sadness and separation. Readers cannot avoiding feeling a connection between Christine's loss and the frightened female voice awaiting the return of her already overdue lover:

> En grant desir attendoie
> Le terme que m'aviez mis
> De retourner, mais ma joye
> Tourne en dueil: tout est cassé
> Le bon espoir que j'avoye,
> Puis que le terme est passé. (ballade 38, ll.2–7)

(In great longing I awaited/the date that you had given me/for your return, but my joy/is turning into sorrow: completely destroyed/is the pleasant hope I used to have/since the date has passed.)

The *Cent balades* do not leave the audience without comfort, however. The specific details of Christine's tragic experience interact with the pain of her *personnages* to create an impression of universality, a fund of loss that all share. Poems bitterly bemoaning Fortune punctuate the cycle, with 12 and 13 expressing outrage. But her anger fades with 16, where she strikes a more resigned tone, noting in the refrain that whatever happens, "c'est souverain bien que prendre en pascience" (l.8) (it is a sovereign good to face [hardship] with patience) and with references such as these, she offers a constant counterpoint to her narratives of loss. If certain of her individual characters suffer the pain of love gone wrong, her lyric presence insists upon the possibility and indeed the necessity of patiently mastering Fortune. The last three ballades before the final ballade, the celebrated ballade 100 in which she reveals her identity ("En la centiesme entierement/En escrit y ay mis mon nom") (in the hundredth/I have written my entire name), review her major themes of consolation. Ballade 96 reminds the audience that true *bonté* is worth more than riches. Ballade 97 draws upon Boethius as an authority to persuade the audience to shun Fortune in favor of Nature. Here the narrator stresses the dangers of Fortune, whose goods "sont si legiers/Qu'on n'en devroit a nul fuer avoir cure" (ll.3–4) (are so fickle/that one should in no way even worry about them), as Boethius pointed out in his book. Ballade 98 emphasizes the importance of wisdom, and ballade 99 leads the cycle back to God: "si doit on toutevoie/Soy retourner vers Dieu" (thus should we all/turn ourselves towards God).

Nor do the *Cent balades* draw a distinction as to gender in their recounting of sad love stories. The men of this cycle are as unhappy as the women.[20] Christine construes the sadness of love as part of the universal human condition. Love is to be enjoyed, like other earthly pleasures, but recognized for what it is: transitory. It must be let go when it disappears. Filled with narratives of pain and suffering, thus, the *Cent balades* nonetheless offers its own transcendent approach to consolation.

A second cycle, referred to in Roy's edition as *Autres balades*, gathers fifty-three lyrics (in certain manuscripts only twenty-nine) together in a somewhat looser construction, but one that like the *Cent balades* sets up a narrative based on the theme of earthly mutability. The *Autres balades*, however, thematize a new aspect of this narrative. Although love lyrics figure in this collection, a more important source of lyric interaction with the narrator's history can be found in the numerous poems Christine dedicates to her patrons and potential patrons. After singing the importance of *bonté* over riches in the first ballades, she begins to court the powerful, addressing Charles d'Albret in ballades 2 and 3 (and later in 21). Ballade 15 to an unnamed "Seigneur" opens with a cajoling tone barely masking desperation: "Mon cher Seigneur, vueilliez avoir pitié/Du povre estat de vostre bonne amie,/Qui ne treuve nulle part amistié" (ll.1–3) (My dear lord, please have pity/for the poor state of your good friend). Other addressees of the *Autre balades* include Isabeau of Bavière, Marie of Berry, and Jean de Werchin. Like the lady asking her lover for a sign of affection, Christine offers flattering words to those from whom she seeks aid. Interspersed among the love lyrics, Christine's poems to her patrons reflect the abjectness of the love lyrics with their appeals to figures they cannot fully trust. Christine seldom mentions her less reliable patrons by name for obvious reasons, but the Duke of Orleans seems to have treated her with less concern than she thought she merited.[21] The warmth she expresses in 19 of the *Autres ballades* towards that "Prince excellent ou il n'a demesure" (Excellent and moderate Prince) takes on a pathetic color when the reader knows that Louis in fact proved negligent toward her.

Throughout the *Autres balades*, Christine relies upon mythological references to universalize her situation of helplessness.[22] In ballade 14 she invokes Pallas to send her comfort in the face of Fortune.

> Viegne Pallas, la deesse honourable,
> Moy conforter en ma dure destresce,
> Ou mon anui et peine intolerable
> Mettront a fin ma vie en grant asprece.
> Car Fortune me cuert sure
> Qui tout mon bien destruit, rompt et deveure.... (ll.1–6)

(Let Pallas, the honorable goddess, come/to comfort me in my terrible distress,/where my worry and intolerable grief/will bring my life to a violent end./For Fortune, who has destroyed, broken and devoured everything of mine/surely chases me....)

Her personal situation, which she implicitly poses as a paradigm for the poor and downtrodden, achieves a grand pathos by its insertion in the Greek cosmology. Moreover, throughout the cycle, she creates a contrast between worldly riches and true wealth, which is based upon *bonté*. Financially dependent and worthy of pity, she nonetheless presents a powerful figure as one who has overcome fickle Fortune by drawing on her own inner resources.

Of the three cycles, the *Cent balades d'amant et de dame* possesses the most fully developed narrative. A dialogue consisting of 100 ballades (plus a final *lay* that brings the total to 101), exchanged between two lovers (with an intervention by Amour and by a narrator who may not be identical with the lady in the *Lay Mortel* with which the cycle ends), this cycle dramatizes a tragic love story, uncovering in minute and painful detail the dynamics of an inherently unequal relationship, that is, a relationship between someone who leads a full life of movement and travel, and someone who waits at home, someone for whom the love affair represents the center of her existence.[23] A young man falls in love and presents his pleas for love in return to a woman who initially refuses. She is unable to resist him, however, and falls in love herself, early in the exchange.

In her first responses to the lover's pleas, the lady insists that she has no interest in love at all: "Car vous ne autre je ne vueil amer brief" (2, l.8) (For, in short, I do not wish to love you or anyone else). The lover eventually grows desperate at the lack of response, and he turns to Amours for help. "Elle me fait enragier" he complains, because "plus apperçoit mes plours,/Moins conte en tient. . . ." (9, ll.9–11) (She drives me mad/ . . . the more she notices my tears,/the less she cares). The God of Love, convinced of the lover's sincerity, seals the lady's fate. She is not responding as a proper woman should, Amours tells her, and he castigates her for her arrogance.

> Trop est folle ta vantise,
> Ma fillette belle et gente,
> Qui cuidiez qu'en telle guise
> Amours te lait ta jouvent
> Passer, sans avoir entente
> Aux plaisans biens amoureux. (10, l.1–6)

(Your arrogance is foolish/my beautiful and refined girl/who believes that in such a fashion/Love will allow your youth/to pass without your paying any mind/to the sweet experience of love.)

The lady thus falls prey to a power greater than herself. Once seduced, she enjoys long stretches of happiness. But in Christine's love stories, happiness never endures. Ubiquitous *médisans* (gossips) damage the lady's happiness, for because of them her lover sometimes fails to come to her: she complains that they "avoient broyé/Encontre nous dur buvraige" (58, ll.15–6) (have stirred up/harsh rumors about us).

Still, the affair brings mutual pleasure and excitement throughout the majority of the cycle. Although the lovers weather separations brought about by the man's military obligations, they rejoice at passionate reunions. But an ominous tone is struck by the lover in the seventy-fourth ballade. "Car je me doubt que un autre mieulx vous plaise" (1.3) (For I fear that someone else pleases you more than I do) he confesses. Something has passed between them, for in the previous ballade the lady's refrain had been, "Et te promès a amer d'amour ferme" (1.7) (And I promise to love you steadfastly). An unspoken dialogue, an anxious subtext, governs the lyrics from this point on, and the reader cannot know whom to believe. Is the lover growing colder, or is it merely the perception of the lady? Is her dramatic death of lovesickness based on an error of perception? From the seventy-fourth ballade on the lady aims increasingly anguished accusations at her lover, but he denies them all. Who is the more believable witness?

The tragic ending of the *Cent balades d'amant et de dame* is the unavoidable outcome of love as Christine naturalizes it in the figure of Amours. The lady is seduced by someone whose sincerity seems assured within the framework of the lyric collection. Indeed, the lover of the *Cent balades d'amant et de dame* appears to be one of the loyal lovers Christine's God of Love praises in the *Epistre au dieu d'Amour*, one of the "vrays loyaulx servans" (1.6) (true loyal servants), for the lover's appeal is underwritten by the God of Love himself.[24] Making good on his promise that lovers who are "humbles et doulx, jolies et assesmez,/Fermes et francs" (ll.79–80) (humble and gentle, attractive and talented,/steadfast and honest) will be rewarded, the God of Love seems a reasonable witness to the lover's loyalty in the *Cent balades d'amant et de dame*.

But the lady can never establish beyond a doubt that her lover is loyal, and the opportunity for betrayal coupled with the impossibility of knowing whether it has taken place is the problem Christine exposes in the *Cent balades d'amant et de dame*. The text offers limited evidence, reflecting the limits of the lady's knowledge, and provides no positive proof of the lover's motivation, one way or another. Furthermore, the lover is plagued with doubts himself, voicing his own suspicions that the lady is unfaithful to him. He hints that her laments mask a dishonest game, demanding, "Sont ce des jeux dont vous savez jouer?" (93, 1.7) (Are you playing games?) Whatever the truth, the lady's situation reenacts Christine's paradigm of sorrow, the seemingly endless wait, a function of the impossibility of determining her lover's feelings.

This cycle seems to arise out of a sense that courtly values, the norms governing behavior among members of the court, were in the process of breaking down. This sense was shared by many of Christine's contemporaries. As Poirion has written of poets of her period, "A la fin du XIVe siècle, la poésie courtoise, jusqu'àlors tendue vers la joie dans l'élan mystique de l'espérance, se laisse plus souvent envahir par la douleur et le désepoir. L'effort volontaire et collectif d'initiation à une vie meilleure semble s'être brisé devant l'obstacle d'insurmontables souffrances" (548) (At the end of the fourteenth century, courtly poetry, which until then had taken as its theme the joy caused by the mystical elation of hope, begins to be infused with the sorrow of despair. The voluntary and collective effort to initiate a better life seems to have crumbled in the face of insurmountable suffering). Christine's ballades, like those of her contemporaries, describe sorrow and demonstrate pessimism toward the possibility of happiness, in love or in other endeavors. And yet on the strength of her lyric persona, Christine creates a framework within which her sad love lyrics take on an aura of universal suffering. Like the other pessimistic mininarratives recounted in the *Cent balades* and the *Autres balades*, the story of the lady's demise achieves its full meaning as part of the inevitable passing of all earthly pleasures.

Recent criticism has suggested that Christine's love lyrics, particularly those of the *Cent balades d'amant et de dame*, be read as subversively critical of the conceptions of love they take as their point of departure.[25] Evoking the disastrous consequences of love from a feminine perspective, her lyrics have been said to provide a corrective to the masculine views of love prevalent in the love lyric. It is important to note, however, that the terrible effects of love Christine describes do not arise from male deception. Rather, Christine's ladies suffer because they are unable to verify their lovers' true feelings. In her love poetry, Christine hardly ever shows ladies being abandoned by their lovers. More often—certainly in the ballade cycles—neither readers of Christine's love works nor the victims of love in the works possess enough information to understand for certain whether abandonment has taken place. In these multivalent works, for every doubt the ladies dramatize, the texts offer male voices objecting. In the lyric cycle most obviously dramatizing the lady's unhappiness, the *Cent balades d'amant et de dame*, the lover is still declaring his innocence in ballade 99, the ballade just before the one in which the lady reports herself to be on the very verge of expiring. He protests: "D'elle veoir, ce dist, suis nonchalant/Pour autre amer, dont forment se douloit./Mais elle a tort. . . ." (130, ll.8–10) (She says that I don't care whether I see her/because I love someone else, which causes her great pain./But she is wrong. . . .). Constrained to conceal their love affairs and therefore unable to gain adequate assurances of each other's fidelity through regular communication, Christine's courtly lovers, men and women, suffer constantly the anguish of not being able to gauge their partner's state of mind.

The woman's agonizing wait for someone upon whom she is utterly dependent is not a critique of love as it was expressed by male courtly writers of the fourteenth and fifteenth centuries. Certainly the wait represents an unpleasant element of love in an age in which women lack independence, but the sorrow of love is a metaphor rather than the actual problem Christine confronts. The anxiety of Christine's ladies gains its full relevance against the more general backdrop of a fear common to women of Christine's time, and one that she herself experienced firsthand—the fear of being dependent upon the whims of an utterly arbitrary power.[26] The deaths of her male protectors from Charles V to her father to her husband marked Christine's passage from security to a terrified helplessness. Dependent upon the fickle desire of beings who were sometimes kind, loyal, and even lavishly rewarding, but who sometimes withdrew financial support for no apparent reason, she manifests her feelings about her humiliating but necessary submission to patrons in many places in her writings.

Documenting Christine's increasing self-awareness as a writer, Deborah McGrady describes the difficulties of Christine's early years, exacerbated as they were by the fifteenth-century transformation of the old system of literary patronage. Whereas earlier writers had been able to hope for sustained support from a single patron and sometimes a court position, writers of the later Middle Ages faced a different system. The flourishing preprinting book trade, coupled with "historical shifts in the cultural priorities of French nobility prompted writers and bookmakers to distribute their manuscripts to a larger buying audience."[27] Christine thus could not enjoy the lifelong patronage of one generous patron, but had to market her work to a diverse audience. McGrady notes the problems this transformation caused for writers such as Christine: "The wider dissemination of texts to multiple patrons . . . had a secondary impact on patronage dynamics, not mentioned by scholars, in that it encouraged noble figures to collect examples of diverse writers, rather than support the literature of a select few. Consequently, many writers, especially Christine, lacked a source of consistent and substantial support from a single patron" (197).

This lack of consistent support sent Christine scrambling for patrons. In number 22 of the *Autres balades*, she solicits Louis, Duke of Orleans, to find a position at court for her son, who had recently returned from England.

> Et si vous viens donner d'amour esprise
> Le riens qui soit que doy plus chier avoir
> Et soubzmettre du tout a vo franchise,
> Si le vueilliez, noble duc, recevoir.
> C'est un mien filz. . . . (ll.7–11)

(And so I have come, filled with love, to offer/the thing I hold dearer than anything on earth/and to submit it entirely to your good will/if you would like to have it./It is my son. . . .)

She gives the details of her attempts to place her son in the *Advision Cristine*, writing:

> Si lui quis maistre grant et puissant qui de sa grace le retint. Mais comme la petite faculté du jeune enfant fust pou apparant en la multitude des grans de sa court, tousjours a ma charge convint que son estat fust soustenu sanz de son service tirer aucun fruit./Et ainsi me desherita Fortune d'un de mes bons amis et d'un de mes bons espoirs.[28]

(I sought a great and powerful master for him who graciously retained him. But as the abilities of the young child were not very striking in the throng of important people at his court, I always had to maintain his position at my own expense without drawing any benefit from his service. In this way, Fortune cut me off from one of my good friends and one of my hopes.[29])

As we learn from the *Advision*, her son later appears at the court of Philippe le Hardi, rather than that of the Duke of Orleans. Moreover, the *Dit de la Rose*, dedicated to Louis, disappears from her collections after 1402: a silent indication of her disappointment at his neglect of her?

The theme of dependence upon an arbitrary authority underlies Christine's unpleasant experiences as a widow trying to feed her family. It also colors her descriptions of contemporary politics, of the French people's dependence on the unreliable nobility. As Christine uses her autobiography as a medium to focus and illuminate the terrible events of early fifteenth-century France, so the uncertainty that shadows her lyrics takes on a more horrifying aspect in her writings on the civil unrest of her time. At many points Christine refers to the terrible situation hanging over the heads of the French people of the first decade of the fifteenth century, of an impending war whose outcome could only be disastrous for all involved. In the power vacuum created by the incapacitating mental illness of Charles VI, the Duke of Orleans and Queen Isabeau on one hand and the Duke of Burgundy on the other, entered into a long-term struggle for control, with the welfare of the French people apparently the least of their priorities.[30] The French depended completely upon the wills of a group of leaders dedicated to self-advancement, and Christine's fear of their capriciousness manifests itself in several works addressed to potential intercessors. Like the lady dependent upon Amour, Christine addresses her pleas to a capricious mediator who may or may not reward her efforts. In her *Epistre a la reine*, Christine begs Isabeau to intercede to gain peace between Charles VI and the Duke of Orleans. The figure she creates of Isabeau upon her throne, "seant en vostre trosne royal couronné de honneurs," utterly oblivious to the horrors taking place around her, is subversively unflattering. But Isabeau, like Amour, is capable of changing the wills of others, if she so chooses. And thus Christine begs for her intervention, as the lover begs aid from Amour. She writes:

> Pour ce, haulte Dame, ne vous soit grief oïr les ramentevances en piteux regrais des adouléz supplians Françoys, a present reampliz d'affliccions et tretresse, qui a humble voix plaine de plours crient a vous, leur souveraine et redoubtee Dame, priant, pour Dieu mercy, que humble pitié vueille monstrer a vostre begnin cuer leur desolacion et misere, par cy que prouchaine paix entre ces .II. haulz princes germains de sanc et naturelment amis, mais a present par estrange Fortune meuz a aucune contencion, ensemble veuilliez procurer et empetrer.[31]

(For this reason, High Lady, do willingly hear the complaints and pitiful regrets of the suffering and suppliant French people now full of affliction and sadness, and who cry with tearful voices to you, their supreme and revered lady, praying, by the mercy of God, that a humble pity may show to your tender heart their desolation and misery, so that you can procure and obtain peace soon between these two princes of the same blood and who are loved ones by nature, but who are at present brought to a quarrel by strange Fortune.)

Later, in the *Lamentacion sur les maux de la France*, Christine begs the Duke of Berry to intervene to talk common sense into the warring factions, both of which are willing to destroy France because both think their victory is assured. An outcome is never guaranteed, she argues, but subject to the whims of Fortune. And even victory comes with a terrible cost, she continues, supplying a list of classical examples of kings who may have won battles, but for whom the victory was Pyrrhic. Surely God's attitude toward battle is clear, she points out, for even those who win lose more than they gain. The Duke Christine addresses is as all-powerful as Amour, equally capable of bringing peace or war. But her urging that he put aside his own interests to help the country avoid war is ultimately futile, for the Duke is as amoral as Amour. The people of France are completely subject to the whims of quarrelling royal relations. "Sont-ils or aveuglez, comme il semble," she demands, "vos peres de la congregacion francoise, soubz les quelz ayolz seullent estre gardez, deffenduz et nourriz les multitudes des enfans de la terre jadiz beneuree... ?"[32] (Are the fathers of your French assembly now blind, as it seems, under whose eyes the numerous children of a land once blessed, were protected, defended and nurtured...?).

The popular success of Christine's lyric poetry speaks for itself. And yet, this is a genre she claims never to have valued, for she relegated her lyric activity to the order of triviality. Still, she returned to the lyric form throughout her career. Her dismissive attitude toward the love lyric, thus, need not be accepted at face value. In describing lyric activity as trivial, it is likely that she is signaling her readers to look beyond the "trivial" matters of love recounted therein: they are more than love lyrics, she is saying. To return to the ballade "Seulete suy," nothing in its contents implies that its subject is a widow mourning her husband. The subject might just as well be a woman abandoned by her lover. Removed from its narrative context, this ballade represents one of the "ditz d'amours" Christine was requested by "aucunes gens" to compose, as she relates in the first ballade of the *Cent balades*.

But within the greater architecture of that cycle, "Seulete suy" transcends the status of a pleasantly sad lyric of failed love. It becomes instead part of the universal story of the world under the reign of Fortune. This world, like love, is overwhelmingly beautiful. But like love it is transitory. The only defense against loss in this world is the cultivation of personal goodness and honor, the *bonté* Christine opposes to earthly riches. Christine as lyric narrator, fully cognizant of the terrible power of human love, celebrates and laments it in equal measure, describing its effects as both sublime and horrifying, and holding up the danger of its loss as a metaphor for life in the mutable world.

NOTES

1. On the poetic effects of the ballade form see Daniel Poirion, *Le Poète et le prince*: *L'évolution du lyrisme courtois de Guillaume de Machaut à Charles d'Orléans* (Paris: Presses Universitaires de France, 1965), 374–91.
2. All citations from the *Cent balades* and *Autres balades* are taken from *Oeuvres poétiques de Christine de Pisan*, ed. Maurice Roy, Vol. 1 of 3 (Paris: Firmin Didot, 1886–91), I. "Seulete suy" is ballade 11 of the *Cent balades*, p. 12 in Roy. Citations from the *Cent balades d'amant et de dame* are taken from Jacqueline Cerquiglini's edition (Paris: Union Générale d'Editions, 1982). On the ritualistic aspect of the lyric, see Roland Greene, *Post-Petrarchism: Origins and Innovations of the Western Lyric Sequence* (Princeton: Princeton University Press, 1991). He describes the dialectical tendencies contained within the lyric as follows. As for its generalizing tendencies, he writes, "the nature of lyric's ritual dimension, simply stated, is to superpose the subjectivity of the scripted speaker on the reader . . ." (5). This tendency he opposes to a fictive element, an "implicit plot that unfolds within a hypothetical world" (11). Roger Dragonetti has described the lyric's abstract qualities in his conclusion to *La technique poétique des trouvères dans la chanson courtoise* (Bruges: De Tempel, 1960), 539–80. Medieval lyric poets did not seek to create a work of great originality. Rather they sought to "discover" a poem in a common theme through which they reaffirmed the shared values of their audience. See also Paul Zumthor, *Essai de poétique médiévale* (Paris: Editions du Seuil, 1972), 189–284.
3. See Michel Zink, *La Subjectivité littéraire* (Paris: Presses Universitaires de France, 1985) for the background on the development of literary subjectivity through the thirteenth century.
4. On the poetic effects of Christine's narrative presence in her ballade cycles, see Barbara K. Altmann, "L'Art de l'autoportrait littéraire dans les *Cent ballades* de Christine de Pizan," in *Autour de Christine de Pizan*, ed. Lilian Dulac and Bernard Ribémont (Orléans: Paradigme, 1995), 327–36; "Last Words: Reflections on a 'Lay mortel' and the Poetics of Lyric Sequences," in *Christine de Pizan and the Medieval French Lyric*, ed. Earl Jeffrey Richards (Gainesville: University Press of Florida, 1998), 83–102; and "Through the Byways of Lyric and Narrative: The *Voiage d'oultremer* in the Ballade Cycles of Christine de Pizan," in *Studies in Honour of Angus J. Kennedy*, ed. John Campbell and Nadia Margolis (Amsterdam: Rodopi, 2000), 49–64.
5. See Barbara K. Altmann, " 'Trop peu en sçay': The Reluctant Narrator in Christine de Pizan's Works on Love," in *Chaucer's French Contemporaries: The Poetry/ Poetics of Self and Tradition*, ed. R. Barton Palmer (New York: AMS Press, 1999), 217–49. Altmann describes the crucial differences between Christine and Machaut as narrators of love lyrics.

6. See Roy, I, v–xxi and James C. Laidlaw, "Christine de Pizan—A Publisher's Progress," *Modern Language Review* 82 (1987): 35–75.
7. On the *Autres balades* as a cycle see Félix Lecoy, "Notes sur quelques ballades de Christine de Pisan," in *Fin du Moyen Age et Renaissance: Mélanges de philologie française offerts à Robert Guiette* (Anvers: Nederlandsche Boekhandel, 1961), 107–14.
8. On Christine's innovations see Suzanne Bagoly, "Christine de Pizan et l'art de 'dictier' ballades," *Moyen Age* 92 (1986): 41–67. For a comparison of Christine's experimentations with those of her contemporaries see Poirion, 382–91.
9. The other two poetic forms Christine relied upon most frequently were the rondeau and the virelai. The rondeau, like the ballade, originated as a dance form, but it was shorter and more repetitive, built on two rhymes and usually consisting of three sections of two to six lines. The beginning of the first stanza was repeated at the end of the second and third stanzas. Too short to allow thematic development, the form at its best immortalized one striking image. The virelai enjoyed a period of fame during the fourteenth century, then faded, leaving only a few traces by the fifteenth century. Flexible compared to the other fixed forms, the virelai was built on a variable number of stanzas containing three rhymes each, with a refrain beginning the poem and repeated every other stanza.
10. *La Deffence et Illustration de la Langue Françoyse*, ed. Henri Chamard (Geneva: Slatkine Reprints, 1969), 202–3. On the popularity of the ballade in general see Poirion's Chapter 9.
11. *Oeuvres complètes de Eustache Deschamps*, ed. Marquis de Queux de Saint-Hilaire and Gaston Raynaud, 11 vols. (Paris: Firmin Didot, 1878–1903), Vol. 7, 270–1.
12. On Christine's use of the envoi, see James C. Laidlaw, "The *Cent balades*: The Marriage of Content and Form," in *Christine de Pizan and the Medieval French Lyric*, ed. Earl Jeffrey Richards (Gainesville: University Press of Florida, 1998), 53–82.
13. Michel Zink, *The Invention of Literary Subjectivity*, trans. David Sices (Baltimore: Johns Hopkins University Press, 1999), 38.
14. "*Un Engin si soutil.*" *Guillaume de Machaut et l'Ecriture au XIVe siècle* (Geneva: Slatkin, 1985), 91.
15. Lori Walters, "Chivalry and the (En)Gendered Poetic Self. Petrarchan Models in the '*Cent balades*,' " in *The City of Scholars: New Approaches to Christine de Pizan*, ed. Margarete Zimmermann and Dina De Rentiis (Berlin: Walter de Gruyter, 1994), 43–66. Margarete Zimmermann has proposed another lyric sequence that may have served as a model for Christine, Boccaccio's *Elegia de Madonna Fiammetta*. See her "Les *Cent balades d'amant et de dame*: Une Réécriture de *L'Elegia de Madonna Fiammetta* de Boccace?" in *Autour de Christine de Pizan*, ed. Lilian Dulac and Bernard Ribémont (Orléans: Paradigme, 1995), 337–46.
16. Laidlaw, "Marriage of Content and Form," 60–2.
17. As Laidlaw states, "Dans Chantilly, Musée Condée 492 on trouve la rubrique, 'Balade de personnages' (fol. 4c): par contre, Paris, Bibliothèque Nationale, fonds français 12779 met 'balades' au pluriel: 'Balades de personnages' (fol. 3c). La

rubrique s'applique-t-elle à la seule ballade 12 ou à une suite de ballades de longueur indéterminée? Les recueils du duc de Berry et de la reine Isabelle ne nous aident pas à trancher la question, car, la ballade 12 n'a pas de rubrique" (98). Laidlaw analyzes the *Cent balades* as a cycle in "L'unité des 'Cent balades,' " in *The City of Scholars: New Approaches to Christine de Pizan*, ed. Zimmermann and De Rentiis, 97–106 and in "The *Cent balades*" cited above, Note 12. See also Kenneth Varty's introduction to his anthology of Christine's poetry, *Christine de Pisan's Ballades, Rondeaux, and Virelais: An Anthology* (Leicester: Leicester University Press, 1965).

18. See Kevin Brownlee's "Discourses of the Self: Christine de Pizan and the Rose," *Romanic Review* 79 (1988): 199–221 and "Widowhood, Sexuality and Gender in Christine de Pizan," *Romanic Review* 86 (1995): 339–53. See also Lori Walters, cited above, Note 15.

19. Ballades 3, 7, 25, 27, 28, 30, 31, 32, 33, 34, 35, 36, 38, 39, 40, 41, 42, 43, 44, 45, 46, 47, 55, 56, 57, 62, 63, 70, 71, 72, 73, 74, 75, 76, 80, 82, 83, 84, 85 (although here anticipation rather than fear is the predominant note), 87, 88, and 95 all treat the theme of waiting from some angle. The last four ballades put the pain of waiting into perspective by calling on the audience to renounce earthly comforts in favor of spiritual ones.

20. See for example ballades 65, 68, 70, 72, 75, and 84, which express a man's request for love. Of course his tone is never as nervous as the female voice, because as a man, he has the "right" to make his request directly and is thus spared some of the uncertainty his female counterpart must undergo.

21. Charity Cannon Willard, *Christine de Pizan: Her Life and Works* (New York: Persea Books, 1984), 155–56. See also 22 of *Autres balades*, in *Roy*, cited above, 232–33.

22. As Lori Walters has written of Christine's use of myth in lyric, "she proposes the alternative of considering universal history through the mythic constructs based upon her own experience" (46–47).

23. On the relationship between the *Lay mortel* and the body of the *Cent balades d'amant et de dame* see Altmann, "Last Words: Reflections on a 'Lay mortel' and the Poetics of Lyric Sequences."

24. Thelma Fenster and Mary Carpenter Erler, eds. and trans., *Poems of Cupid, God of Love* (Leiden: Brill, 1990).

25. See Deborah Hubbard Nelson, "Christine de Pizan and Courtly Love," *Fifteenth Century Studies* 17 (1990): 281–89. Also, see Christine McWebb, "Lyrical Conventions and the Creation of Female Subjectivity in Christine de Pizan's *Cent ballades d'amant et de dame*," in *Christine de Pizan and Medieval French Lyric*, ed. E. Jeffrey Richards (Gainesville: University Press of Florida, 1998): 168–83. See also Charity Cannon Willard's "Lover's Dialogues in Christine de Pizan's Lyric Poetry from the *Cent ballades* to the *Cent ballades d'amant et de dame*," *Fifteenth Century Studies* 4 (1981): 167–80.

26. In her work on the continuity of Christine's personal narrative, Anne Paupert describes how Christine's lyric subject of the earliest poetry is taken up and amplified in the later works, culminating in the *Advision:* "Le récit autobiographique de l'*Advision* est aussi le point d'aboutissement d'une demarche qui

trouve son point de départ dans les tout premiers poèmes et s'est poursuivie sous diverses formes dans plusieurs oeuvres" (71). "'La Narracion de mes aventures,' des premiers poèmes à l'*Advision*: l'élaboration d'une écriture autobiographique dans l'oeuvre de Christine de Pizan," in *Au champs des escriptures*, ed. Eric Hicks (Paris: Champion, 2000). See also by Paupert "Le 'je' lyrique féminin dans l'oeuvre de Christine de Pizan," in *Et c'est la fin pourquoi sommes ensemble: Hommage à Jean Dufournet*, ed. Jean-Claude Aubailly (Pairs: Champion, 1993), vol. 3, 1057–71. Barbara K. Altmann has also analyzed the autoportrait of Christine's *Cent ballades* as "un prototype sur lequel se modèlent toutes les représentations de Christine à suivre" in "L'Art de l'Autoportrait Littéraire," 328.

27. Deborah McGrady, "What is a Patron? Benefactors and Authorship in Harley 4431, Christine de Pizan's Collected Works" in *Christine de Pizan and the Categories of Difference*, ed. Marilynn Desmond (Minneapolis: University of Minnesota Press, 1998), 195–214, at 197.

28. Quotation taken from Christine Reno and Liliane Dulac, *Le livre de l'advision Cristine* (Paris: Honoré Champion, 2001), 3.XI, 113.

29. Translation from Glenda K. McLeod, trans., *Christine's Vision* (New York and London: Garland, 1993), 121.

30. Charity Cannon Willard's quotation of chronicler Jean Juvenal des Ursins captures the helplessness of the people of France in the face of the overtly personal rivalry and self-interest among the dukes: "If they had wished to pay attention to the contents of this in a good policy and government for the kingdom, affairs would have gone well. But it was useless to preach, for the lords and those who surrounded them paid no attention and thought only of their particular interests." *Christine de Pizan*, 156.

31. The quotation and translation are both from *The Epistle of the Prison of Human Life with An Epistle to the Queen of France and Lament on the Evils of the Civil War*, ed. and trans. Josette A. Wisman (New York and London: Garland, 1984), 72 and 73, respectively.

32. *Epistle* 84, translation 85. Margarete Zimmermann describes the similarity between the voluntarily marginalized female voice of *Lamentacion* and that of Christine's early poems, but demonstrates that the voice of the *Lamentacion* takes on important new features as well, becoming an "*au-dessus de la mêlée*, the position of an individual in need of this solitude in order to contemplate her times." "Vox Femina, Vox Politica: The *Lamentacion sur les maux de la France*," in *Politics, Gender & Genre; The Political Thought of Christine de Pizan*, ed. Margaret Brabant (Boulder: Westview Press, 1992), 113–27, at 119.

11

The *Querelle de la Rose* and the Ethics of Reading

Marilynn Desmond

> A letter does not always arrive at its destination, and from that moment that this possibility belongs to its structure, one can say that it never truly arrives, and that when it does arrive its capacity not to arrive torments it with an internal drifting.
> JACQUES DERRIDA, *THE POSTCARD: FROM SOCRATES TO FREUD AND BEYOND*

EPISTOLARY RHETORIC AND THE *QUERELLE*

In 1401–1402, Christine de Pizan contributed three letters to the *Querelle de la Rose*, an epistolary debate on the ethical implications of reading Jean de Meun's portion of the *Roman de la Rose*.[1] As a collection of letters, the *Querelle de la Rose* enacts all the interpretive difficulties that epistolary rhetoric might pose: although these letters would appear to have arrived at their destinations, these epistles throughout are animated by rhetorical refusals; they are read by interloping readers and redirected to readers other than their addressees. For instance, Christine enters the debate in the summer of 1401 when she sends a letter to John de Montreuil, Provost of Lille, in which she criticizes a treatise he had authored in praise of the *Rose*. Christine comments that this treatise, although forwarded to her by Montreuil, was neither addressed to her nor did it require a response ("combien que a moy ne soit adreçant ne response ne requiert," 12). Nonetheless, she sends Montreuil a letter in which she offers a sustained critique of his position on the *Rose*. Although Montreuil never responds directly to Christine's letter, he writes several more letters to various people regarding the *Rose*. However, a few months later, Gontier Col responds critically to Christine's critique of Montreuil in two separate letters addressed to Christine. In his first letter, Gontier Col requests a copy of her "invective" on the *Rose*, and he expresses his dismay that she dared to challenge the authority of Jean de Meun. Gontier Col demands that Christine retract her argument, even before he has read her letter. A few days later, having read her letter, he puts his case even more forcefully in a second letter to her: "t'ay ... exortee, avisee et priee de toy corrigier et admender de l'erreur manifeste, folie ou demence a toy venue par presompcion ou oultrecuidance et comme femme passionnee en ceste matiere" (23) (I have ... exhorted, advised and prayed you to correct and amend your obvious error, the madness or lunacy that has come over you, from self-conceit or overweening pride, and like a woman impassioned in this matter.)[2] At this point, Christine responds directly to Gontier Col.

In early 1402, she collected her two letters and Gontier Col's two letters—but omitted Montreuil's—in a dossier she called the "epistres du debat sus *le Roman de la Rose*." She composed two cover letters for this dossier, one addressed to Queen Isabeau and one to the Provost of Paris, Guillaume de Tignonville. The *querelle*, however, was not to be neatly closed with the completion of this initial dossier. In May 1402, Jean Gerson—chancellor of the university of Paris—authors a treatise against the *Rose*, and several months later Pierre Col, brother of Gontier Col, writes to Christine to point out once more that her reading of the *Rose* was erroneous. In response to Pierre Col's letter, Christine composes a long detailed reply in which she reiterates and develops the views expressed in her earlier two letters. As this schematic outline of the *Querelle* shows, Christine addressed one letter to Montreuil, one to Gontier Col, and one to Pierre Col; each letter repeats or expands on the previous letter. In addition she wrote two cover letters for the dossier on the debate, and this dossier was included in the first edition of her collected works in June 1402. She later expanded the dossier to incorporate her letter to Pierre Col, and this expanded dossier appears in both the Duke's and Queen's manuscripts of her collected works. Other documents related to the *Querelle* include letters by Montreuil and sermons by Gerson; more tangential documents include several poems by Christine, including the occasional pieces entitled the *Epistre au dieu d'Amours* and the *Dit de la Rose*.[3]

Like most medieval letter collections, the epistles in the *Querelle* are simultaneously personal and public, so that the texture of each letter works against its arrival at a single destination.[4] In addition, the *Querelle* demonstrates the reach of the Latin rhetorical tradition into vernacular practice, as vernacular letters generally followed the epistolary convention of letter compositions as codified in the *ars dictaminis*.[5] Epistolary discourse—whether Latin or vernacular—enacted social hierarchy in its *salutatio*: according to the *ars dictaminis*, the *salutatio* is structured according to the social significance of the office—or lack of office—held by both sender and addressee.[6] For a woman such as Christine—excluded by her gender from occupying any clerical office—epistolary rhetoric required her to acknowledge both her own lack of position as well as the authority of her male interlocutors whose offices authorized their social and intellectual status. This rhetorical inequity accounts for the tone of self-deprecation in her initial letter addressed to Montreuil "de par moy Cristine de Pizan, femme ignorant d'entendement et de sentement legier—pour lesquelles choses vostre sagesce aucunement n'ait en despris la petitesse de mes raisons, ains vueille supploier par la consideracion de ma femmenine foiblece" (12) (from me, Christine de Pizan, a woman untutored in judgment, and of frivolous sense, on account of which factors may your wisdom not in the least despise the smallness of my arguments, but rather take into consideration my feminine weakness). Such *salutatio* is conventional; nonetheless, such expression of *humilitas* could be disabling for a woman composing a letter to intervene in a *disputatio* with clerical figures.

When she collected the epistles that had circulated in the first stage of the *Querelle* and dedicated them to Queen Isabeau, Christine explicitly published all of them under her signature. In addressing the Queen, Christine articulates an empowering "destination" for her critique of the *Rose*, a destination that did not require that she perform a debilitating *salutatio* to a clerk: this dedicatory letter to Isabeau revises the social structure of the *Querelle* because Christine addresses another woman, a woman of higher rank rather than a clerk. In her letter to the Queen, moreover, Christine characterizes her subject position as a woman writing in defense of women. This rhetorical framework allowed her to refuse the anger of Gontier Col and deflect the "destination" of his critical letters. Having authorized her agency as a letter writer in addressing the Queen, Christine expresses no self-abasing discourse in her subsequent letter to Gontier Col, which she composed several months after the composition of the cover letter to Isabeau. Instead her letter to Col identifies the rhetorical violence of his two letters to her: "O clerc subtil d'entendement philosophique, stilé es sciences, prompt en polie rethorique et subtile poetique, ne vueilles par erreur voluntaire repprendre et reprimer ma veritable oppinion justement meue pour tant se elle n'est a ta plaisance" (24) (O clerc discerning in philosophical judgment, well versed in learning, quick with polished rhetoric and subtle poetics; do not try by a capricious distortion to criticize and put down my legitimate opinion, justly conceived, simply because it does not please you). She describes his letters as injurious ("injurieuses," 25), although she declares that she does not feel any sting from his criticism: "saiches de vray que ce ne tiens je a villenie ou aucun repprouche" (25) (You should know truly that I have not taken it as an insult nor as any sort of reproach). She stands her ground with the statement: "Si ne cuides aucunement moy estre meue ne desmeue par legiereté, par quoy soye tost desditte—ja soit ce que en moy disant vilenie me menaces de tes subtilles raisons" (26) (Don't think me to be in any way moved or deterred through fickleness, so that I could be soon overruled, although while saying offensive things to me, you threaten me with your clever discourse). In his demand that Christine correct ("corrigier") herself, Col deploys the power relations implicit in epistolary rhetoric as codified in the *ars dictaminis*.[7] But because Christine writes to Gontier Col and the queen simultaneously as part of her dossier on the *Rose*, she articulates a destination for her letter that authorizes her rejection of the subject position he identifies for her.

Christine also sent the dossier of letters to Guillaume de Tignonville, the Provost of Paris, and she composed a cover letter to him, asking him to judge the debate and rule in her favor: "proprement eslire le bon droit de mon oppinion" (7) (to appropriately recognize the justice of my opinion). Guillaume de Tignonville was a minister in the *cour amoureuse* from its inception in 1400; his role as one of the twenty-four ministers in the literary and poetic court dedicated to upholding the honor of women made him an appropriate adjudicator of the *Querelle*.[8] Yet although the letter to the Queen characterizes Christine's intention in the debate as the defense of women[9]—the ostensible purpose of the *cour amoureuse*—the letter to the provost appeals instead to his wisdom and sense of justice. Guillaume de Tignonville's textual orientation was philosophical and ethical: he had translated the *Dicta philosophorum*, a text of ethical proverbs. In sending the dossier to Guillaume de Tignonville, Christine implicitly frames the issue in the *Querelle* as a question of the ethics of reading Jean de Meun's *Roman de la Rose*.

CHRISTINE AND THE ETHICS OF READING THE *ROSE*

The epistles in the *Querelle* participate in a century-long tradition of literary and textual responses to the *Rose*; nonetheless, the rhetorical skirmishes in the *Querelle* tend to obscure the interpretive performances of these letters as readerly engagements with Jean de Meun's text.[10] Although Christine, Montreuil, and the Col brothers disagree about the value of the *Rose*, they all share the same assumptions regarding the purposes of literary texts. A. J. Minnis has demonstrated that both sides of the *Querelle* consider that the *Rose* must be read for its *utilitas*: "its usefulness in behavioral and pedagogic terms," an assumption that emerges from their shared premise that "poetry showed its audience both what to do and what to avoid."[11] In addition, as Mary Carruthers has shown, texts acquire their ethical urgency through their memorability, and highly memorable texts encourage readers to imitate the actions represented therein.[12] The more memorable a text, the more it would need to be evaluated for its potential impact on the behavior of readers. In her letter to Montreuil, Christine comments that her memory of the *Rose* poses an ethical problem: "Neantmoins demoura en ma memoire aucunes choses traictees en lui que mon jugement condempna moult" (13) (Nevertheless there remained in my memory some things treated there that my judgment condemned greatly). In her letter to Gontier Col, Christine summarizes her anxiety about the ethical implications of the *Rose* when she concludes that it is a "perverse exortacion en tres abhominables meurs confortant vie dissolue" (26) (a wicked exhortation to abominable conduct, endorsing the dissolute life).

Christine's critique of the *Rose* emphasizes that Jean de Meun defames the female sex by portraying women as deceitful and wanton. In this respect, Christine considers the *Rose* to be an instance of injurious language, as Helen Solterer has shown.[13]

But beyond the verbal violence of the text, Christine also evaluates the *Rose* specifically for its material impact on the lives of married women. In her letter to Montreuil, she criticizes Jean de Meun for suggesting that wives deceive their husbands, and she states "a quelle bonne fin pot ce estre, ne quel bien ensuivre? N'y sçay entendre fors empeschement de bien et de paix, et rendre les maris qui tant oyent de babuises et fatras, se foy y adjoustent, souspeçonneux et pou amant leurs femmes" (18) (What good purpose could it have, and what good could come of it? All I expect from it is the obstruction of happiness and peace, and it makes husbands who hear such babbling and rubbish, if they give it any credence, suspicious and less loving to their wives). Not only might the *Rose* lead to marital discord by encouraging husbands to mistreat their wives, but many women already endure difficult marriages: "Et pluseurs qui ont esté cause du reconciliement de leurs maris, et porté leurs affaires et leurs secréz et leurs passions doulcement et secretement, non obstant leur feussent leurs maris rudes et mal amoureux" (19) (And [there are] many [women] who have been instrumental in obtaining absolution for their husbands and who put up with their affairs and their secrets and their passions quietly and discreetly, even if their husbands were brutal and unloving to them). Such comments illustrate the ethical premises of reading that Christine articulates and develops in her three letters in the *Querelle*: Christine evaluates reading practices for their potential to have a material impact on the lives of contemporary, married women. And in such a context, the most troubling aspect of the allegory of the *Rose* is the violent nature of erotic desire, and the potential for this violence to materialize as wife abuse.

The issue of erotic violence hovers over the *Querelle*, but it takes vivid shape in Christine's final letter, addressed to Pierre Col. This letter, however, is especially haunted by the possibility that it might not arrive: its tone of exasperation and its repetition of earlier statements all suggest that Christine was aware that her earlier letters had not truly reached their destinations. Given the failure of her previous letters to "arrive," Christine takes pains to explain in detail issues that she had treated more generally in the earlier two letters, so that the letter to Pierre Col can almost be read as a gloss on her earlier two letters. In this letter, she takes exception to Col's assertion that the *Rose* could have a beneficial effect on the reader; Col had reported that a male reader found that the *Rose* had cured him of lovesickness. Christine's retort specifically evokes the conduct of a more violent reader:

> Et je te diray ung aultre exemple sans mentir, puis que nous sommes es miracles du *Roman de la Rose*: je oy dire, n'a pas moult, a .i. de ces compaingnons de l'office dont tu es et que tu bien congnois, et homme d'auctorité, que il congnoit ung home marié, lequel ajouste foy au *Roman de la Rose* comme a l'Euvangile; celluy est sonverainnement jaloux, et quant sa passion le tient plus aigrement il va querre son livre

et list devant sa fame, et puis fiert et frappe sus et dist: "Orde, telle come quelle il dist, voir que tu me fais tel tour. Ce bon sage homme maistre Jehan de Meung savoit bien que femmes savoient fere!" Et a chascun mot qu'il treuve a son propos il fiert ung coup ou deux du pié ou de la paume; si m'est advis que quiconques s'en loe, telle povre famme le compere chier. (139–40)

(And I will tell you another true example, since we are on [the subject of] the miracles of the *Romance of the Rose*. I heard not long ago from one of the members of the profession to which you belong, with whom you are well acquainted, a man of authority, that he knew a married man who put as much faith in the *Romance of the Rose* as in the gospel. This man is often jealous, and when his passion takes hold of him most intensely, he goes to find his book and reads it in front of his wife, and then he strikes and hits her, and says "Filthy thing" [you are] just like what he says; it is true that you play such tricks on me. This good wise man, Master Jean de Meun, knew full well what women could do." And at each word that he finds to his purpose, he strikes her once or twice with his foot or with his hand. So it seems to me that no matter who may praise [this book], unfortunate women such as this one pay dearly for it.)

This is the only time during the *Querelle* that Christine describes a scene of reading, and this narration of wife abuse clarifies how the *Rose* might encourage husbands to mistreat their wives. How has her reading of the *Rose* led her to view the *Rose* as a text that legitimates violence against women?[14] Indeed one programmatic strand in the *Rose* recirculates Ovidian discourse on violence, especially from the *Ars amatoria*, so that the *Rose* can be read as a thematic demonstration of the efficacy of violence for the male heterosexual. What happens if, following Christine's critique, we read the *Rose* for its *utilitas* as a manual of violence?

In Jean de Meun's portion of the *Rose*, the representation of erotic violence is most blatantly deployed in the discourse of Ami, whose advice to the lover includes the long ventriloquized speech of the Jaloux. Ami quotes almost 900 lines of direct discourse, of a "typical" speech of a stereotypically jealous husband, the Jaloux; this speech vigorously rehearses a performance of verbal abuse that is crude and offensive. For hundreds of lines, the Jaloux complains that his wife, like all women, is incapable of chastity. He reiterates misogynous and misogamous *exempla* and he repeatedly and abusively accuses his wife of infidelity. After Ami has finished quoting the verbal abuse of the Jaloux, he depicts a chilling scene of physical abuse:

Lors la prent espoir de venue
cil qui de mautalant tressue
par les treces et sache et tire,
ront li les cheveus et descire

The Querelle de la Rose *and the Ethics of Reading* 173

li jalous, et seur li s'aourse,
por noiant fust lions seur ourse,
et par tout l'ostel la traïne
par corrouz et par ataïne,
et la ledange malement;
ne ne veust, por nul serement,
recevoir excusacion,
tant est de male entencion,
ainz fiert et frape et roille et maille. (ll.9331–43)[15]

(Then perhaps, boiling with rage, he takes her there and then by the hair and pulls her and tugs her, tearing and rending her locks in his jealousy, setting upon her (a lion attacking a bear is nothing in comparison), dragging her all through the house in his anger and fury and insulting her cruelly. Whatever she swears, he bears her such ill will that he will accept no excuses; instead he strikes her and beats her and flogs her and thrashes her.[16])

Eventually the neighbors arrive and separate the Jaloux from the wife once he has exhausted himself in beating her. This vivid combination of verbal abuse followed by physical violence animates the advice of Ami, and physical violence appears to be the final consequence of verbal abuse.

The Jaloux, however, is rhetorically bracketed by Ami as a negative *exemplum*: Ami asserts that such an abusive husband will only alienate his wife, who might even plot to poison him. From the behavior of the Jaloux, Ami draws the lesson that the husband should treat the wife as his equal: the behavior of the Jaloux is so vividly described in order for Ami to satirize the Jaloux as a brute whose strategy will destroy eros. Having dismissed the Jaloux, Ami proceeds to tutor the lover in the more subtle approaches to erotic success in the quest for the rose. But several hundred lines after Ami has dismissed the behavior of the Jaloux as ineffective, the discourse of the Vieille returns us to this scene. The Vieille makes a long speech addressed to Bel Acueil on the ways in which women might pursue and manipulate men with maximum financial gain and minimum emotional risk. Despite this highly cynical context and purpose, the Vieille closes her speech with a subjective gloss on the erotic value of violence:

Onc n'amoi home qui m'amast;
mes se cil ribauz m'antamast
l'espaule, ou ma teste eüst quasse,
sachiez que je l'en merciasse.
Il ne me seüst ja tant batre
que seur moi nou feïsse enbatre,
qu'il savoit trop bien sa pes fere,
ja tant ne m'eüst fet contrere.

Ja tant ne m'eüst maumenee
ne batue ne trahinee,
ne mon vis blecié ne nerci,
qu'ainceis ne me criast merci
que de la place se meüst;
ja tant dit honte ne m'eüst
que de pes ne m'amonetast
et que lors ne me rafetast:
si ravions pes et concorde (ll.14461–14477)

(I never loved a man who loved me, but if this wretch had hurt my shoulder or cracked my skull, I tell you I would have thanked him for it. However much he beat me, I would still have had him fall upon me, for he was so good at making peace, whatever hurt he might have done me. However badly he treated me, beating me and dragging me about, hurting my face and bruising it, he would always beg my forgiveness before he left. However humiliating his language to me, he would always sue for peace and then take me to bed, and so there was peace and harmony between us once more.)

This "confessional" moment revises the earlier representation of violence as brutish when deployed by the Jaloux. From the female perspective voiced by the Vieille, violence can be eroticized if a violent lover knows how to follow blows with sexual caress. The Vieille catalogues a set of injuries that is very similar to those suffered by the Wife at the hands of the Jaloux: a broken shoulder or cracked skull and a face cut and bruised from the effects of being dragged and struck. Although the Vieille describes violent actions that are remarkably close to the violence perpetrated by the Jaloux, she interprets this violence as desire, and she concludes her speech with the assertion that a good lover can effectively deploy violence as part of eros.

As the text of the *Rose* develops and elaborates on the discourse and rhetoric of eros, the category of erotic violence becomes refined, and in the process, the lover-narrator learns how and when to deploy violence to maximum erotic effect. In such a context, the problem with the Jaloux is not the fact of his violence but the fact that his violence is too crude to be erotic. Motivated by possessiveness, the Jaloux is as jealous of the jewels and furs he buys his wife as he is of her. By contrast, the Vieille, in tutoring Bel Acueil, normalizes erotic violence when she instructs the lover on the effective use of violence to enthrall rather than alienate the object of his desire. By her account, the lover can best achieve his erotic dominance through a more disinterested brutality than that exhibited by the Jaloux. Indeed, the teachings of the Vieille anticipate the violent conclusion of the poem where the connection between violence and eros is made explicit. Kathryn Gravdal sees the violent conclusion of the allegory as emblematic of the desire articulated in the poem: "The 'seduction' of Rose—the courtly lady—is depicted blatantly as the rape of a virgin . . . a scene which asserts the violence at the heart of male seduction and courtly love."[17]

Christine repeatedly states that she is critical only of certain parts of the *Rose* ("trop traicte deshonnestment en aucunes pars," 13), and she specifically criticizes the figures of Raison, Genius, the Vieille, and the Jaloux; however, she repeatedly names the figures of the Vieille and the Jaloux in her letters. Both the Vieille and the Jaloux are assessed for their exemplarity, their effect on the conduct and ethics of specific readers:

> quel horribleté! quel deshonnesteté! Et divers reprouvéz enseignemens recorde ou‧ chapitre de la Vieille! Mais pour Dieu! qui y pourra noter fors ennortemens sophistez tous plains de laidure et toute vilaine memoire? . . . Et a quel utilité ne a quoy prouffite aux oyans tant oïr de laidures? Puis ou chapitre de Jalousie, pour Dieu! quelx grans biens y peuent estre notéz, n'a quel besoing recorder les deshonnestetés et laides paroles qui asséz sont communes en la bouche des maleureux passionnéz d'icelle maladie? Quel bon exemple ne introducion puet estre ce? (15)

(What atrocity! What dishonor! And the malicious, despicable teachings recorded in the chapter of the Vieille! By God! What can one observe there except sophistical advice full of abuse and utterly repulsive recollection? . . . And for what *utilitas* or for what profit do listeners hear such abuse? Then in the chapter on Jealousy, by God! What great good can be discovered there, what need is there to record the dishonorable and abusive words that are so common in the mouth of those unhappy ones afflicted with this malady? What good model or example could this be?)

In pairing the Vieille and the Jaloux in this passage, Christine questions the *utilitas* of the desire they perform in relation to one another in the allegorical reiterations of the *Rose*. Because the Vieille concludes her speech in the *Rose* by celebrating the efficacy of erotic violence, she becomes an *exemplum* of female conduct and experience that ultimately eroticizes the sort of violence performed by the Jaloux. In her critique of the Jaloux, Christine acknowledges that his is not the normative voice in the text, but she nonetheless judges his performance in the context of the ambient culture, as she says in her letter to Montreuil: "Et la laidure qui est recordee des femmes, dient pluseurs en lui excusant que c'est le Jaloux qui parle, et voirement fait ainsi comme Dieu parla par la bouche Jeremie. Mais sans faille, quelxque addicions mençongeuses qu'il ait adjoustees, ne peuent—Dieu mercy!—en riens amenrir ne rendre empirees les conditions des femmes" (15) (And as for the vile nature that is there accorded to women, many say in excusing him [Jean de Meun] that it is the Jaloux who speaks, and indeed that [Jean de Meun] does exactly what God does in speaking through the mouth of Jeremiah. But without fail whatever deceitful additions he may have added, thank God, they cannot make worse the condition of women). When Christine later in her letter to

Pierre Col cites the specific case of a contemporary Jaloux who justifies his conduct by reference to the *Rose*, she clarifies her anxiety about the way the Jaloux speaks of women as vile and deserving of abuse. Christine identifies the *exempla* of the Vieille and the Jaloux as a form of "laidure" (insult/abuse), precisely because readers could appeal to the *Rose* to authorize wife abuse.

That the *Rose* implicitly poses the issue of violence within heterosexuality becomes evident in Gerson's more normative reactions to the *Rose*. Early in 1403, partially as a response to Pierre Col's praise of the *Rose* in his second letter, Gerson preached a series of sermons on the seven deadly sins.[18] These sermons—preached in the vernacular—were designed to reach a popular audience and to address issues of everyday conduct for Parisian Christians.[19] Gerson's sermon on marital chastity, delivered on January 7, 1403, explicitly identifies domestic violence as part of the conduct of marriage. In his sermon, Gerson suggests that violence is inherent in marriage when he pragmatically encourages women to steer clear of angry husbands. He asserts that the husband must use physical and psychological violence responsibly: "S'elles sont juenes, le mary les peut chastoier, premierement de paroles doulcement, puis des verges" (If the wife is young, the husband may chastise her, first gently with words, then with rods).[20] To Gerson, violence is a standard component of marriage, and the ethical issues it raises involve the appropriate levels of force in a given context.

The letters in the *Querelle* are not the only occasion when Christine addresses issues of wife abuse. For instance, in the third section of her conduct book for women, the *Livre des trois vertus*, she speaks of the "amor et foy" (love and faith, 172) that wives owe their husbands; she asserts that wives must be governed by their husbands, whether their husbands are "paisibles ou rioteux" (peaceful or quarrelsome, 172).[21] Christine points out that many wives who had endured the mistreatment of their husbands reaped their rewards as widows because their abusive husbands repented of their wrongs on their deathbeds and left all their worldly goods to their long suffering wives. Such advice in the *Trois vertus* is striking in its utterly pragmatic approach to wife abuse; this advice echoes very similar comments at the end of the *Livre de la cité des dames*. Christine's acceptance of wife abuse in the *Cité des dames* and the *Trois vertus* stands in stark contrast to her critique of domestic violence in the epistle she wrote to Pierre Col.

Wife abuse was part of the quotidian reality negotiated by married women in late medieval Paris; James Brundage comments on the ubiquity of domestic violence in the years for which legal records survive: "marital violence ... appears to have been remarkably common in the purlieus of Paris between 1384 and 1387."[22] Christine's scattered references to wife abuse demonstrate her awareness that many married women lived with the threat or the fact of wife abuse. But because husbands had a legal right—and in Gerson's terms, a moral responsibility—to "discipline" their wives within limits, Christine could not address the problem of physical violence in marriage as a moral issue, nor even an issue of appropriate conduct within marriage. But in the course of the *Querelle*, Christine manages to develop a critique of domestic violence as an issue in the ethics of reading. As Solterer has demonstrated, Aristotle's *Ethics*, known to Christine in Nicole Oresme's French translation, offered a paradigm for connecting learning and study to ethical questions of social utility.[23] Such an ethical framework makes it possible for her to articulate a connection between wife abuse and reading practices by questioning the purpose to which a reader might put sections of the *Rose*, specifically the sections that eroticize violence. Indeed, the persistence with which she interrogates the *Rose* in relation to erotic violence suggests that she sees violence against women as the ultimate test of an ethics of reading any given text.

Unlike a sermon or a conduct book—both of which reinforce the status quo—the rhetorical strategies of an epistle offer an opportunity to sustain a critique of cultural practices such as reading and sexuality. Christine's three contributions to the *Querelle* suggest that the epistolary format allowed her to articulate an interpretive—rather than moral—approach to the problematics of erotic violence. As these letters develop Christine's subject position as a critical reader, they adopt an antagonistic tone toward the *Rose* and its author, Jean de Meun. Although modern scholars have often been put off by what they see as Christine's irreverent attitude toward Jean de Meun,[24] Christine's antagonistic stance ought to be recognized as a strategic engagement with the authoritative status of the text of the *Rose*. Doris Sommer sees antagonism as a constitutive feature of an ethical reading: "Antagonism, to put it simply, is built into the asymmetries between texts and readers . . . the operative esthetic for antagonistic, or politely off-putting, postures includes a set of conventions for reminding powerful interlocutors of the inequalities they would rather forget. And the name for these literary and locutionary conventions is what we popularly call 'attitude.'"[25] Modern readers of Christine's contributions to the *Querelle de la Rose* might find in Christine's "attitude" an eloquent statement of late medieval interest in the ethical implications of reading practices. Such an inquiry, however, requires that we read Christine's epistles in relation to their intertext, the *Roman de la Rose*. Likewise, Christine's analysis of the *Rose* needs to be distinguished from Gerson's, her more reactionary ally, who did not always share her assumptions, as his acceptance of wife abuse makes clear.[26]

Much recent scholarship suggests that many texts in Christine's corpus address issues that Christine initially raises in the letters she wrote during the *Querelle de la Rose*.[27] But the social and rhetorical limitations of the epistolary format made it difficult for such antagonistic letters to "truly arrive at their destinations," in the Derridean sense of the phrase. We should not allow the consequent "internal drift" of these epistles to obscure the critical issues that emerge from this literary debate that proved so formative to Christine's authorial development as well as to the early modern *Querelle des femmes*.[28]

NOTES

1. For an edition of the documents in the *Querelle*, see Eric Hicks, *Le Débat sur le Roman de la rose* (Geneva: Slatkine Reprints, 1996); for a narrative of the *Querelle*, see Charity Cannon Willard, *Christine de Pizan: Her Life and Works* (New York: Persea, 1984) 73–90; see also Eric Hicks, "Situation du débat sur le *Roman de la Rose*," in *Une femme de lettres au Moyen Age. Etudes autour de Christine de Pizan*, ed. Liliane Dulac and Bernard Ribémont (Orleans: Paradigme, 1995): 51–67; Pierre-Yves Badel, *Le Roman de la Rose au XIVe siècle: Etude de la réception de l'oeuvre* (Geneva: Droz, 1980), 411–91; Eric Hicks and Ezio Ornato, "Jean de Montreuil et le débat sur le *Roman de la Rose*," *Romania* 98 (1977): 34–64; 186–219. For a translation of many of the documents in the *Querelle*, see Joseph L. Baird and John R. Kane, *La Querelle de la Rose: Letters and Documents*, Chapel Hill, North Carolina Studies in the Romance Languages and Literatures, no. 199 (Chapel Hill, 1978).

    For studies of Christine's role in the *Querelle*, see Kevin Brownlee, "Discourses of the Self: Christine de Pizan and the *Rose*," *Romanic Review* 59 (1988): 213–21; Karen Sullivan, "At the Limit of Feminist Theory: the Architectonics of the *Querelle de la Rose*," *Exemplaria* 3 (1991): 435–65; Helen Solterer, *The Master and Minerva: Disputing Women in French Medieval Culture* (Berkeley: University of California Press, 1995), 151–75, and "Fiction vs. Defamation: The Quarrel over the *Romance of the Rose*," *Medieval History Journal* 2 (1999): 111–41; Rosalind Brown-Grant, *Christine de Pizan and the Moral Defence of Women: Reading Beyond Gender* (Cambridge: Cambridge University Press, 1999), 7–51; Earl Jeffrey Richards, " '*Seulette a part*'—the 'Little Woman on the Sidelines' Takes up her Pen: The Letters of Christine de Pizan," in *Dear Sister: Medieval Women and the Epistolary Genre* (Philadelphia: University of Pennsylvania Press, 1993), 139–70.

2. The translations from the letters in the *Querelle* are my own, with the assistance of Barbara Altmann.

3. The *Epistre au dieu d'Amours* and the *Dit de la Rose* are generally not considered to be part of the *Querelle*. For a schematic chronology of the documents and events in the *Querelle*, see Hicks, *Débat*, lii–liv.

4. See Giles Constable, *Letters and Letter Collections* (Turnhout: Brepols, 1976): "in the Middle Ages, letters were for the most part self-conscious, quasi-public literary documents, often written with an eye to future collection and publication" (11).

5. Martin Carmago, *Ars dictaminis, ars dictandi* (Turnhout: Brepols, 1991).

6. Giles Constable, "The Structure of Medieval Society According to the *Dictatores* of the Twelfth Century," in *Law, Church and Society: Essays in Honor of Stephan Kuttner*, ed. Kenneth Pennington and Robert Somerville (Philadelphia: University of Pennsylvania Press, 1977), 253–67.

7. On the use of the term "corriger," see Karen Sullivan, "The Inquisatorial Origins of the Literary Debate," *Romanic Review* 88 (1997): 1–26.

8. On the *cour amoureuse* see Carla Bozzolo and Hélène Loyau, *La cour amoureuse dite de Charles VI*, 2 vols. (Paris: Le Léopard d'Or, 1982, 1991); Daniel Poirion,

Le Poète et le prince: L'évolution du lyrisme courtois de Guillaume de Machaut à Charles d'Orléans (Paris: Presses Universitaires de France, 1965), 37–9; Arthur Piaget, "La cour amoureuse, dite de Charles VI," *Romania* 20 (1891): 417–52. Montreuil and the Col brothers were also members of the *cour amoureuse*.

9. On the *Querelle* and the tradition of the defense of women, see Alcuin Blamires, *The Case for Women in Medieval Culture* (Oxford: Oxford University Press, 1997).

10. See Badel, 135–206; see also Sylvia Huot, *The Romance of the Rose and its Medieval Readers: Interpretation, Reception, Manuscript Transmission* (Cambridge: Cambridge University Press, 1993), 22–7.

11. A. J. Minnis, "Theorizing the *Rose*: Commentary Tradition in the *Querelle de la Rose*," in *Poetics: Theory and Practice in Medieval Engish Literature*, ed. Piero Boitani and Anna Torti (Cambridge: D. S. Brewer, 1990): 13–36; "Latin to Vernacular: Academic Prologues and the Medieval French Art of Love," in *Medieval and Renaissance Scholarship*, ed. Nicholas Mann and Birger Munk Olsen (Leiden: E. J. Brill, 1997), 154–86. For a further discussion of the implications of the academic prologues, see Rosalind Brown-Grant, 7–51.

12. See Mary Carruthers, "Memory and the Ethics of Reading," in *The Book of Memory: A Study of Memory in Medieval Culture* (Cambridge: Cambridge University Press, 1990), 156–188.

13. Helen Solterer, "Flaming Words: Verbal Violence and Gender in Premodern Paris," *Romanic Review* 86 (1995): 355–78.

14. Few studies of the *Querelle* actually consider the texts in relation to the *Rose*; for a discussion of Christine's reading of the *Rose*, see Sylvia Huot, "Seduction and Sublimation: Christine de Pizan, Jean de Meun and Dante," *Romance Notes* 25 (1985): 361–73.

15. The text of the *Roman de la Rose* is taken from Félix Lecoy, *Le Roman de la Rose*, 3 vols. (Paris: H. Champion, 1966).

16. Translations for the *Roman de la Rose* are taken from *The Romance of the Rose*, trans. Frances Horgan (Oxford: Oxford University Press, 1994).

17. Kathryn Gravdal, *Ravishing Maidens: Writing Rape in Medieval French Literature and Law* (Philadelphia: University of Pennsylvania Press, 1991), 68.

18. See Louis Mourin, *Jean Gerson: Prédicateur français* (Bruges: De Tempel, 1952), 138–48.

19. As Eric Hicks says, "Les sermons de la série *Poenitemini* témoignent de l'intérêt soutenu du public comme de l'actualité des problèmes" (*Débat*, 1).

20. Jean Gerson, *Oeuvres complètes*, ed. P. Glorieux, vol. 7 (Paris: Desclée, 1968), no. 375, 862.

21. Christine de Pizan, *Le Livre des Trois Vertus: édition critique*, ed. Eric Hicks and Charity Cannon Willard (Paris: H. Champion, 1989); for a translation: Christine de Pisan, *The Treasure of the City of Ladies*, trans. Sarah Lawson (New York: Penguin, 1985), 145.

22. James Brundage, "Domestic Violence in Classical Canon Law," in *Violence in Medieval Society*, ed. Richard W. Kaeuper (Woodbridge: Boydell Press, 2001), 191.

23. Solterer, *Master and Minerva*, 156–62.

24. See D. W. Robertson Jr., *A Preface to Chaucer: A Study in Medieval Perspectives* (Princeton: Princeton University Press, 1963), 361–64; John V. Fleming, *The "Roman de la Rose": A Study in Allegory and Iconography* (Princeton: Princeton University Press, 1969); David F. Hult, "Words and Deeds: Jean de Meun's *Roman de la Rose* and the Hermeneutics of Censorship," *New Literary History* 28 (1997): 345–66.
25. Doris Sommer, "Attitude, Its Rhetoric," in *The Turn to Ethics*, ed. Marjorie Garber, Beatrice Hanssen, and Rebecca L. Walkowitz (London: Routledge, 2000), 204.
26. For a recent example of this tendency, see Hult.
27. See Solterer, *Disputing Women* 163–75; Rosalind Brown-Grant, *Christine de Pizan and the Moral Defence of Woman*; see also Marilynn Desmond and Pamela Sheingorn, *Myth, Montage and Visuality in Late Medieval Manuscript Culture: Christine de Pizan's Othea* (Ann Arbor: University of Michigan Press: 2002).
28. See Joan Kelly, "Early Feminist Theory and the *Querelle des Femmes* 1400–1789," *Signs* 8 (1982): 4–28.

12

The Lessons of Experience and the *Chemin de long estude*

Andrea Tarnowski

THE PROLOGUE AND "FIRST BEGINNING"

The *Chemin de long estude* opens in fits and starts, beginning once, twice, and then again before it finds its way. Christine de Pizan presents three liminary scenes, then binds them together in a single narrative; each of the three continues, however, to influence her story. Like variously colored threads running through a single piece of cloth, these beginnings signal themes that will remain distinct throughout the poem, while all work to create the whole.

It takes some time to reach the Long Road of Learning. The author leads the reader along a trio of paths, three avenues that offer as many prospects, all useful during the journey. First, the prologue evokes the dilemma of combining womanhood and authorship. Although one reason Christine enjoyed a renaissance of critical interest in the twentieth century was that she was the first French woman to earn her living as an author, she often seems uneasy claiming the authority to write. Widowed at twenty-five, she devoted most of her adult life to reading and study, but clearly wondered whether this was sufficient to adopt the voice of a *clerc*. She was thirty-eight when she dedicated the *Chemin de long estude* to King Charles VI in 1402:

> A vous, bon roy de France redoubtable [. . .]
> Mon petit dit soit premier presenté,
> Tout ne soit il digne qu'en tieulx mains aille (vv.9, 12–13)[1]

(Good and mighty King of France,/my little poem goes first to you,/though it is not worthy to rest in your hands.)

These lines convey not only conventional humility, the modesty required of an author addressing a powerful patron, but also genuine timidity on Christine's part. She begs the king not to fault her for being presumptuous; she is well aware that her womanhood is an "indignite" (v.28). Because her status is precarious, she has recourse to the old idea that truth can be found in what the humble say: "de simple personne/Peut bien venir vraye raison et bonne" (vv.53–4). The *Chemin de long estude*, which presents the narrator undertaking a voyage destined to fill the gaps in her knowledge, is thus at once a *mise en scène* of the uncertainty Christine feels about her ability, or her right, to write like the erudite men of her day, and the remedy for the same uncertainty: making the trek will supply her with the knowledge, and thus the confidence, necessary to produce her work.

The voyage in quest of knowledge, which will see Christine sojourn in faraway countries and witness exotic marvels, climb through the skies and observe the course of planets, is at the same time an experience, a (fictional) lived reality. The narrator perceives the world through her five senses, instead of approaching it only by way of books. Christine's faith in the teachings of experience helps her attempts to write, lifting the double barrier of gender and lack of scholarly training. To the extent that Christine proclaims the primacy of experience, she anticipates, and neutralizes, objections to her career as an author. From the start, she privileges her own feelings, making them a foundation of her work. In the *Cent balades* (c. 1399), she notes her readership's taste for courtly poetry and light-hearted verse, only to declare that her widowhood must supply the matter for her compositions: "De ce feray mes dis" (balade I, v.23).[2] She cannot write without revealing her heart. Over the years, she turns away from lyric to favor allegory and prose; her writerly stature increases; she becomes a confirmed author; she overlays her work with multiple proofs of erudition. Yet she continues to call on experience. When composing the *Livre de la cité des dames* in 1405—the work that will ensure her renown in the twentieth century—she undertakes to denounce the misogyny of certain authors by reflecting on her own heart-held convictions. Are women truly inconstant, deceitful, and grasping, as their detractors posit? Although Christine will eventually refute these accusations with numerous counterexamples drawn from books, she begins by reflecting what she knows on her own, without the help of authorities. The evidence of experience is cited first.[3]

Strengthened by experience, still unsure of her learning, such is the Christine who dedicates the *Chemin de long estude* to Charles VI and the princes of the blood. This work marks an intermediate phase in Christine's *oeuvre*, one in which she assigns herself a dual function: that of fictional character and producer of texts. In the early *Cent balades*, Christine occasionally seems to be writing despite herself; although she draws material from her own experiences, she does not feel the need to assert a singular, inner identity, to identify the contours of her own persona. At the beginning of the *Cent balades*, she affirms that she is writing solely at the behest of her audience, "pour acomplir leur bonne voulenté" (*balade*

I, v.8). This line constitutes the refrain of the first ballade, a reiteration of the distance Christine feels before the "necessity" of writing. Her tone changes in 1399, when she composes the *Epistre au dieu d'Amours*: there she takes up one of the causes that will make her a prolific author, denouncing with great energy those who would speak ill of women.[4] But she places her exhortations in the mouth of Cupid, thus maintaining a certain distance from her poem. The character of the God of Love acts as a screen and an alibi; Christine does not use her own voice. In the *Epistre Othea* (ca. 1400), she tries her hand at a new genre, the mirror of the prince, destined to inculcate virtue in future kings.[5] The prologue in the *Epistre Othea* is quite similar to that of the *Chemin* in accenting Christine's inferiority and ignorance. But unlike the rest of the *Chemin*, the *Epistre Othea* provides no direct corrective to this self-denigration. Christine maintains that the goddess Othea has sent a letter of advice to prince Hector; Christine's only role has been to "versify" the text the goddess has supplied. Although Christine's composition does in fact bear witness to her considerable learning, she never admits to scholarly purpose. Within the framework of the *Epistre Othea*, she is loath to lay claim to her own powers.

The *Dit de la Rose* (February 1402), written just a few months before the *Chemin de long estude*, makes use of a narrative structure that Christine will recycle in large part in the latter work.[6] Christine is chosen to accomplish a mission. The *Dit de la Rose* opens with a banquet in which Christine takes part; over the course of the meal Dame Loyauté arrives, announcing the creation of a new Order devoted to the honor and protection of ladies. Everyone swears fealty. But once the banquet finishes, the guests go home, and Christine goes to bed, Loyauté returns to visit her alone. She says she comes on behalf of Amour, her superior in the gods' hierarchy.[7] Christine will be asked to find recruits to the new Order among the ladies of the world; she will be a propagandist or a missionary. Loyauté entrusts her with a parchment containing the Order's statutes, and when Christine awakes, she is convinced that her vision of Loyauté was real because the parchment lies at her bedside. The document's presence both inside and outside the dream is analagous to Christine's; she is both a character in and the author of her tale. She exercises a more active control over the development of the *Dit de la Rose* by placing herself within it. In addition, the Order, although created and instituted by Amour to demand the defense of ladies, bears literary witness to Christine's moral and political concerns. As author and character, a poet of dreams and a committed thinker, Christine establishes a symbiosis of experience and imagination. Nevertheless, the narrative *mise en scène* limits her role: it is Amour who writes the documents concerning the Order, and Loyauté who gives them to Christine. The latter's job consists wholly of spreading the good news. In later works, Christine will no longer designate others as "responsible" for her ideas, but the time to declare her own complete authority has at this point not yet arrived.

Other facets of the *Dit de la Rose* show how the *Chemin* will stand in contradistinction to its predecessors. We mentioned that the poem initially unfolds during a banquet, and then continues in the intimate setting of Christine's bedroom. Life in a community or social group opens the first poems; in contrast, at the beginning of the *Chemin*, Christine is alone. She is free of the constraints and artifice of the court. In her lyric and courtly work, Christine indulges in anagrams to reveal her name obliquely: *creintis* (fearful) is the rearrangement of letters she finds to communicate something of her feelings in the *Epistre au dieu d'Amours* and the *Livre du dit de poissy*.[8] In the *Dit de la Rose*, the anagram reappears, and this time Christine isolates the *cri* her name contains, as if to fight the muffling of her voice.[9] Her defense of women must be heard, even though in this text her ideas remain embellished by literary device. In the *Chemin*, such indirect declarations lose their relevance; Christine stops hiding and begins to speak in her own name.

Nevertheless, Christine does not name herself in the *Chemin*. She does not have the courage to say, as she does in the *Ditié de Jehanne d'Arc* at the end of her career, "je, Christine."[10] She comes out from behind the screen of word games, but does not proclaim her identity outright. The *Chemin* still resolves the question of the author's place in the text by making Christine an apprentice. She speaks of herself in the first person, but when she is addressed, it is by the name "daughter" ("Fille," v.490). She needs a spiritual mother; her guide, the Sibyl, appears one evening at her bedside, as Loyauté had done in the *Dit de la Rose*. The Sibyl will protect her, will take her to see the world and visit the skies; it thus falls to the Sibyl to be the first to speak.

Replacing Loyauté with the Sibyl moves the narrative from the courtly realm to that of scholarly knowledge and philosophical speculation. When Loyauté comes before Christine, she calls her "amie," a term from the courtly vocabulary. Her speech at the banquet is couched in the form of three ballades and a rondeau, poetic genres tailored to a noble audience (Loyauté stops using such fixed formulas when she is alone with Christine to advocate the Order of the Rose; thus, in their private discussion, the essential idea of defending women is privileged over the artifice of form). Loyauté is a pure allegory in the tradition of the first *Roman de la Rose*; that is, she is a personified quality, an idea without further dimension. Sent by the god Amour, she embodies a virtue that all members of the new Order must show; she represents what human beings must aspire to. In contrast, the Sibyl traces her heritage along another literary line that hearkens back to the *Inferno* and the *Aeneid*.[11] Virgil and Dante introduced her into readers' consciousness; her character is well known and recognizable; her voice resonates with echoes from the past. When Christine introduces the Sibyl into the *Chemin*, she calls on a preexisting entity, rather than simply constituting a character by way of a name-shell, as with Loyauté. The Sibyl does not by definition *contain* a principle that must influence everything she touches; rather, she is a means for Christine to acquire on her own, by experience, knowledge she has previously lacked. The Sibyl answers directly to God, rather than to Amour—another sign of the new nature of Christine's quest. Christine attempts to understand the world, and, to the extent possible, the divine; she will no longer limit herself to the closed circle of the court.

It is precisely because Christine loves learning that the Sibyl singles her out, saying:

> Et pour le bien de ton memoire,
> Que voy abille a concevoir,
> Je t'aim, et vueil faire a savoir
> De mes secrés une partie. (vv.498–501)

(And for the treasure of your memory,/whose capacity I see,/I love you, and want to share with you/a portion of my secrets.)

Christine already possesses the quality that makes her worthy of the Sibyl's visit. Desire for knowledge will act as her motivation, her raison d'être, and also her passkey into the realm of writers; erudition will provide a solid base for a woman's claim to the status of author. In the analagous passage of the *Dit de la Rose*, the moment when Loyauté appears at Christine's bedside, we learn that the goddess loves Christine for resembling her in virtue: "[elle] ... m'ama ... et me clama/Sa belle suer de cuer eslit" (vv.271–3) (she ... loved me well ... and called me her/Sister in sensibility). Christine's loyalty is further defined when she claims friendship with the ever-pure Diana: "je suis a Dyane amie" (v.280). Thus, loyalty coupled with chastity, perhaps even loyalty *as* chastity, will make Christine a worthy helpmeet in publicizing the new Order. We remain in the realm of the heart, and the regulation of its affairs in a court setting. When the Sibyl comes to Christine in the *Chemin*, the context is new, despite the structural similarities of the visitation scenes.

Both the *Chemin* and the *Dit de la Rose* announce enterprises that will concern a considerable audience: nobles loyal to their ladies in the *Dit* and the world at large in the *Chemin*. The second scenario, in which Christine witnesses a debate about ideal princely qualities that she must then report to Charles VI, will receive further attention below. Suffice it to say for the moment that the *Chemin* adds the function of secretary, or scribe, to that of messenger. The statutes for the Order of the Rose are handed to Christine complete and ready for distribution; in the *Chemin*, her task extends to preparing the document she must present to the king. She transcribes the debate while it is taking place; at the end, when the assembly is looking for someone to write out the proceedings, she steps forward to say the job is already done. That Christine—character and author—combines these noted "minutes" with the description of her world travels to constitute the king's manuscript again places Christine both inside and outside her poem. But this time, the stakes are higher than in the *Dit de la Rose*: not only do Christine and her character meld, but they do so by means of writing. The pure fiction of the Christine character's debate transcription is tied to the half-fiction of the voyage; although the journey itself is imaginary, its narration exists as the work of Christine the author; Christine de Pizan has penned it in her own study. Travel narrative and dream debate record are tied together by a historically dated introduction that comprises both the dedication to Charles VI and the writer's self-description. In drawing up the transcription of the debate, recounting her voyage, and suggesting, timidly but undeniably, that she is the author of the ensemble, Christine tests the possibilities of her vocation. From one angle and then another, she defines herself, for herself, by writing.

STARTING AGAIN: READING, CELESTIAL TRAVEL, AND A DEBATE

The preceding remarks focus on a reading of the *Chemin*'s prologue. The first approach to the poem is shaped by the motifs of experience, gender, and literary creation. This path leads to a second, which marks Christine's real entry into her text.[12] The author crafts the offering she will make her protector; the narrator now carefully prepares the story about to unfold. The Christine the reader hears in these verses is both a liminary and a mediating figure; she stands between historical reality and literary vision, bridging the two with her pen. At first, however, other authors' writing will be privileged, as befits Christine's apprentice status.

She again starts off with a declaration of powerlessness. Her first verses invoke "La Fortune perverse" (v.61), that figure of the arbitrary who respects neither merit nor virtue, but chooses instead to provoke ruin at whim, without regard for logic or duty. Fortune has imposed a crushing weight on Christine's life, and the latter is at a loss as to how to fight the unjustifiable. She laments her husband's death, recalls the idyll they lived together, and, overcome by nostalgia, returns to her original subject to heap curses on Fortune. Her past experience and present unhappiness thus underpin the *Chemin*; they form the departure point of a linear trajectory that will describe, step by step, an intellectual development. To lift Christine out of her despair, the things of the mind must progressively replace those of the heart and body. She first tries to take leave of her sadness by leafing through "escriptures/De diverses aventures" (vv.175–76). But reading brings no comfort. Does the word "aventures" suggest that the tales Christine initially chooses are, for example, courtly romances, stories of a handsome knight who endures multiple trials for the love of his lady? Does Christine judge this particular form of literary fare too light to cure her ills? The *Chemin* goes no further in its evocation of "aventures," but in mentioning a reading experience she then rejects, Christine catches the reader's attention and awakens curiosity. Perhaps this aborted reading signals her dismissal of the courtly ethic, and gauges a distance from her first authorial incarnation as a courtly poet.[13] Her redemption, her reconciliation with the human condition, will depend on texts of another order.

Still looking, then, for something to read, she takes up another work, and this time, it soothes. The second book, just like the second path of access to the *Chemin*, is the right choice. Both begin Christine's transformation, in the same way that the work of producing the *Chemin* in its entirety launches the author on the second and most important stage of her career. For Christine, beginning again means improving. The text that helps her effect this change is Boethius's *Consolation of Philosophy*.[14] It fortifies her against Fortune's attacks, reminding her to raise her eyes beyond the earthly. She must cast off her despair by renouncing personal ties and dedicating herself to a life of study and meditation turned toward God. She will evolve from an inconsolable widow into a woman of aspiring mind and spirit, always striving to learn more. This, then, is the *Chemin*'s first literary model; Christine announces from the beginning that she will pattern herself after scholars and philosophers. Throughout the poem, she will collect such models to strengthen her claim to the status of serious author. But Boethius remains an important reference, not only because Christine remodels aspects of the *Consolation of Philosophy* for her own work,[15] but because Boethius, like Christine, was faced with the problem of transmuting one type of experience into another, of reenvisioning the earthly on another plane.

We should keep in mind that in enriching her poem with books, Christine expands her experience as well. She sees no opposition between writing and living; she can advocate the primacy of experience, and, at the same time, find her greatest satisfaction in the written word. Like her predecessor Boethius, she feels compelled to find another, greater, more lasting meaning in what goes on around her; whether as a traveling protagonist in the *Chemin* or a developing author, Christine is a perpetual pilgrim, an idealist and moralist with her sights set beyond the visible. Life on earth requires defending oneself against the blows of Fortune, becoming invulnerable to the vicissitudes of existence, depending only on what is certain. Books are a source of enduring truth, which no sudden circumstance can alter. But although Christine does seek certainty, she tries to hold it within the confines of earthly life. Ultimately more active than contemplative, she chooses the path of letters without yielding to the temptations of abstraction.

Proof of this comes at the end of the verses devoted to Boethius. Calmed and comforted by her reading, Christine recalls the late hour, decides to retire for the night, and says her prayers. Such details of daily life punctuate her work, always replacing it in the context of lived experience. The touches that reveal Christine in all her humanity—asking for a candle once darkness falls, hitching up her skirts so as to be able to match the Sibyl's pace—gentle the rhetoric of the text. However many authors or *exempla* she cites, Christine reinserts them into a life substantial in its everyday dimensions. At the end of the *Chemin*, when Christine comes out of the dream that has taken her around the world and through the skies, the author conveys the feeling of a real awakening, at home; the celestial vision yields to the familiar, as Christine hears her mother knock on the door and call her, surprised that her daughter is still in bed so late in the morning. The poem, linear in tracing a progressive change and a growing assurance on the part of both author and character, follows at the same time a circular course: it returns, in the end, to sensations and experiences common to all.

The second beginning, the avenue that describes an individual's intellectual sojourn, sets up the part of the *Chemin* in which the Sibyl serves as Christine's guide (vv.451–2494). It can be tempting to focus only on this section of the poem, which is more approachable than others. It tells a story that satisfies the reader's taste for narrative: Christine sets out on her journey, marvels at the world's curiosities, and trembles with fear before strange perils. She lives out her apprenticeship. Biography mixes with fiction, relaying information about the historical Christine de Pizan while maintaining Christine as a literary character. Yet the verses that describe Christine's travels represent less than a third of the poem. We must take the rest into account to do justice to the whole. The voyage ends when Christine has covered the globe and explored five of the ten concentric circles that make up the heavens. Christine's mortal state and limited speculative powers prevent her from climbing higher than the circle of the firmament, located halfway between earth and the realm of the divine.[16] At this mid-point of the skies, she makes a stop that will last the length of her dream and of the poem—a space of several thousand verses. She becomes a spectator at a celestial debate, no longer the protagonist-voyager but now an unobtrusive witness. The reader does not, and indeed, cannot pay attention to her; she has no role to play. She does act as scribe for the debate, but we do not know this while the discussion is taking place; we learn it only at the very end of the text. It is worth emphasizing that for most of the poem, the author focuses the reader's attention on a situation that has no intrinsic connection with Christine's destiny. What we have called the narrative path is exchanged for a closed, static space: that of the debate. The reasons for what seems to be a change in the author's perspective, a shift in her objectives, demand elucidation. Once again, the tripartite beginning of the poem can provide answers.

The third, as-yet-unexamined route opens before the reader once Christine is in bed for the night. Although she had been heartened after reading Boethius, she is quickly assailed again by sadness as she awaits the arrival of sleep. The cause is no longer her own unhappy circumstances, or the arbitrary powers of Fortune as they apply to her life. On the contrary; at issue now is the world at large, and the say human beings have, or do not have, in their own destiny. Christine reflects on the various conflicts destroying the world, and on humankind's incapacity to live in peace. Some of her worries refer to a specific historical event, such as the Church torn asunder by competing papal claims in the Great Schism of 1378–1417 (vv.371–77). But she emphasizes more the general nature of human quarrels, their intensity and ferocity, born of lust for wealth and power. Mortals are capable of better behavior; they anger their Creator by yielding to baser instincts; and yet they are not motivated to reform, do not try to hew to virtue. Although Christine is engaged in these somber reflections, the Sibyl appears at her bedside, and the preliminaries to the voyage come to an end (v.450).[17]

The Sibyl's arrival thus takes place in an atmosphere of discord. Christine paints a picture of social chaos, and leaves this image before her reader at the very moment she is about to undertake her voyage of education. Disorder and dispute are the given problems; the rest of the poem will logically be obliged to suggest solutions. Although the *Consolation of Philosophy* serves as a remedy to Christine's initial suffering, and introduces the spirit of curiosity in which she will pursue her quest, the antidote to larger social conflicts remains to be discovered. Personal progress is easier to define and realize than the improvement of society at large. But it is precisely the question of social progress that occupies the center of the *Chemin*; this is the problem the poem as a whole seeks to resolve.

The term "progress" is no doubt an anachronism, the sign of a contemporary mindset that inevitably associates the passage of time with improvement. Christine does not offer anything new in the way of social structure or theory; what she wants is to *re*establish harmony, rather than to find an original means of constituting it. At times she emphasizes the corruption of human nature, the inexpungible faults that have been man's undoing since Eden; at other moments she concentrates on the woes of her own epoch, a period of decline in contrast to other ages that were admirable in their respect for virtue. But whether Christine's nostalgia is expressed in theological or historical terms, the necessity of reforming the world remains.

At the celestial assembly, Christine again finds herself in a social space, but one much different from that of the *Dit de la Rose*. The pretext for dialogue is no longer a noble banquet, but a true "parlement." Mère Nature files a complaint against human beings at the court of Dame Raison (a gesture that recalls, among other texts, Alan of Lille's *Plaint of Nature*).[18] There follows a lawyers' debate, sustained by examples. A verdict is in order on the issue of which single man might be a sufficient paragon of human qualities to govern the world. Four ladies, Noblesse, Chevalerie, Richesse, and Sagesse, oppose each other in the discussion, each one supporting a candidate who embodies her particular characteristic. The ladies accuse one another of causing the world's troubles, defending their respective points of view; their royal status in no way inhibits rough-and-tumble verbal exchange. Although the debate unfolds in ethereal surroundings, it has a human character and reflects human conflicts.

The debate's cosmological setting highlights the discord that reigns on earth; its arguments are formulated not in the fifth-circle firmament, but four levels below, in the first heaven, known as "air." Air arches above the globe, but remains visible from the earth; this is a sign that it is subject to change and corruption. It occupies a moral status halfway between the human habitat's materiality and the higher heavens' purity. Having pursued the immutable divine as far as her body's limits will allow, Christine redescends to a realm more familiar to mortal creatures.

The disorder of this place contrasts with the planetary harmony Christine has just admired. Men are destroyed by chronic conflicts, whereas everlasting peace reigns above. In the firmament, Christine admired the stability of the planetary orbits, the fixed relation of each to the other (vv.1785–2020). Order and beauty prevailed for as far as the eye could see, and would endure for longer than the mind could imagine. The heavens offered a model for earthly affairs; the question that underlay contemplation of such an ideal was how men might be led toward the same kind of perfection.

Although betraying human characteristics, the debate in Dame Raison's court maintains a distinctly literary nature. The *Chemin de long estude* is torn between an acute awareness of the real and a desire to transform and control the same. In this respect, the poem is itself an intermediate work—not only because it combines traits of two distinct periods in the author's career, or because it manifests Christine's writerly hesitations, but because it presents literary credentials in the service of practical goals. The way Christine uses the allegorical ladies in the debate illustrates this point. The four queens have more substance—more personality, we might say—than, for example, Dame Loyauté in the *Dit de la Rose*. The latter's function is simply to announce a virtue essential to the new Order, based on the principle of loyalty, whereas the former show character in their argumentation with their sisters. At the same time, however, these ladies preserve their basic literary dimension, that of allegories; they are figures that substitute for an idea. They officially *embody* a notion; they need neither to prove it by their words and gestures nor to communicate it actively to the reader. They mark a place in the realm of the mind; they are not developed, complex personae. In both the story and the structure of the *Chemin*, they play a role apart; unlike the Sibyl, or allegorical figures in the author's later work—particularly Raison, Droiture, and Justice in the *Cité des dames*—they do not communicate with Christine. The narrative that concerns Christine is interrupted in order to yield the floor to the ladies; they are not conscious of their visitor's presence. Neither Christine the apprentice nor, for that matter, Christine de Pizan can affect them; the task of representing an idea goes hand in hand, at least theoretically, with the obligation to represent it continuously, and always in the same manner, independently of any interaction with or intervention from the outside. The attraction of allegory, and one reason it was such a popular trope at the end of the Middle Ages, is precisely that it offers certainty. It declares itself invulnerable to the vicissitudes of life; this, as we saw in Christine's complaints against Fortune, was one of the great aspirations of a troubled and tumultuous epoch.

Although the example of the *Dit de la Rose* gives us a rich range of prefigurations for the *Chemin*, that of the *Cité des dames* shows where Christine's reflections led her several years after the *Chemin* was complete. When composing the *Cité des dames* in 1405, the author felt surer of what she had to write. This time, it is the allegories who visit Christine in order to lift her out of deep discouragement, due, as it happens, to the misogyny she perceives in the writing of respected authors. Raison, Droiture, and Justice act as authorities, godmother figures similar to the Sibyl in the *Chemin*. But their goal is not to guide Christine out of ignorance; they come, on the contrary, to make her reflect on what she already knows. The *Cité des dames* gives the importance of experience its full expression. Christine reasons by herself, using the knowledge she possesses. Nothing comes to her from the outside, except the pretext for expressing her thoughts. Alternating between the authority of learned figures and that of the thinking, sentient individual, the *Cité*'s structure mimes the dynamic relation the author conceives between erudition and experience. Christine's sadness has its source in a book; then this feeling is attenuated by a conscious review of her own experience; gradually, finally, it dissipates entirely in the face of text-based examples of virtuous women. Writing initially provokes a feeling of betrayal, but subsequently provides happy confirmation of Christine's own ideas; only experience, the middle term between two presentations of writerly authority, allows Christine to distinguish between the true and the false. Experience can either undo or guarantee the claims of the written word; it is in any case more reliable. Writing and living are more imbricated in the *Cité* than in the *Chemin de long estude*; Christine no longer distinguishes thematic paths, stressing either one value or the other; instead, she implicates both in every section of her text.

One might argue that in the *Cité* as in the *Chemin*, there are authoritative guides: in this case, Raison, Droiture, and Justice, all exemplars of virtuous women. They are the ones who do the talking; most of the text is made up of their speeches. But in this work, Christine is far from being a passive listener: she calls on the ladies and questions them, asking them to clarify one point or another. The reader cannot forget Christine; she remains a strong presence throughout. Instead, the three allegorical ladies' contours blur somewhat; because the author lets them enumerate their proofs of feminine virtue without always specifying which figure is speaking, the ladies' individuality is diminished. Although Christine engages in dialogue with each lady in turn, the group's collective function is more important: they are there to stimulate, and respond to, Christine's questions. The *Cité des dames* always takes its protagonist into account, unlike the *Chemin de long estude*. Because Christine never disappears from the scene, the reader is more willing to consider the allegories' examples as the author's work; that is, the work itself, as writerly composition, is made more visible. The ladies' speech becomes the textual city the author builds, rather than remaining a series of individualized discourses. Although Christine continues to employ allegories in the *Cité*, maintaining the notion of their superior authority to emphasize her own ideas, the ladies are less distant and independent than their counterparts in the *Chemin*.

They are less allegorical. Instead of privileging allegory's lofty, truth-bearing status, Christine accents her own ability to execute her work.

In both texts, however, the task consists more of remodeling than inventing. Christine reflects her era in regarding compilation and revision of earlier authors as a standard mode of composition.[19] She cites her sources for the examples offered by the allegorical ladies in both the *Chemin* and the *Cité*: Valerius Maxiums, Cicero, and Seneca in the *Chemin* and Boccaccio in the majority of instances for the *Cité*.[20] In the *Chemin*, we find not only a greater number of authorial sources, but also a more explicit desire to list them. Noblesse, Chevalerie, Richesse, and especially Sagesse multiply name-references in order to strengthen their arguments; their declarations regularly begin with the phrase "Si dit (author's name) que. . . ." Christine de Pizan mentions these authors as much for their own degree of fame as for the value of the stories she is recycling. Stating a source adds another pillar to the structure of the poem, supporting the verses and lending them solidity. Christine is eager to use her forefathers as references, positing a continuity between their writing and her own.

The *Cité des dames* relies on its sources in a more subtle, less anxious manner. Christine draws on *exempla* from Boccaccio's *De claris mulieribus (Des cleres et nobles femmes* in an anonymous translation from 1401): the original vignettes are sometimes ironic and ambiguous, suggesting that celebrated women are not necessarily very admirable. Christine rewrites these legends so as to make their heroines fully worthy of praise. Mythical and historical figures are portrayed in a particularly flattering light: for example, Christine excuses the queen of Babylon Semiramis for incestuous relations with her son, protesting that at the time there were no written laws forbidding such intermarriage.[21] The use Christine makes of Boccaccio has at least as much to do with her advocacy of the feminine cause as it does with fame of the Italian author. When she cites his name—which she continues to do, despite the fact that names are less present in the *Cité* than in the *Chemin*—it is more to signal her subtle attacks on this predecessor than to bask in his reflected glory. The ways in which Christine modifies material from *De claris mulieribus* are more substantial than we might think, given Boccaccio's towering reputation. At least we may say that this reputation is evoked to suggest the skill of the rising author ready to revise it, rather than to prove that Christine knows Boccaccio's work.

Christine's use of allegories and authorities characterizes both the *Chemin* and the *Cité*, while distinguishing one from the other. The different emphases placed on these elements indicate the extent to which each text *says* rather than *does*: in the *Chemin*'s debate, the author announces the allegories' presence, presents their points of view, and declares her references, whereas in the *Cité*, building a city for virtuous women is both an architectural metaphor and the movement of writing that reasons out, develops, and connects ideas. The *Chemin*'s allegories are supposed to guarantee an effective text simply because they appear; the *Cité* sets allegorical rhetoric into motion.

The Lessons of Experience and the Chemin de long estude

Yet action is the presumed goal in the *Chemin de long estude*, which seeks, as we recall, a remedy to the general discord among human beings. The assembly decides to elect a single, perfect man to shoulder the task of bringing about peace. The static nature of the poem's language thus seems somewhat at odds with its political objective. This less-than-ideal fit is manifest in the debate's inconclusive result: the parliament cannot reach a consensus on the right man.[22] The allegorical ladies speak, the assembly deliberates, and still no clear decision emerges. One might say that Noblesse, Chevalerie, Richesse, and Sagesse have debated around a void; no man materializes to fulfill all the criteria of perfection. Human reality clashes with the allegorical ladies' claims, which are supposed to generate truth in the same way that their names guarantee their nature. There is no one to occupy the designated place of the perfect prince, precisely because such a prince does not exist; he can be described, but not embodied. The *Chemin de long estude* recognizes this. To end the celestial debate on earthly issues, Christine de Pizan provokes the necessary aporia, allowing the literary ideals of her poem to run up against their own limits.

Although the perfect prince is absent, Christine does not leave her poem completely open; she sketches out an arc of closure, returning to statements made at the very beginning of the *Chemin*. In her praiseful dedication to Charles VI, Christine had drawn him into the story she was about to recount, telling him he was invited to judge a "grant debat" (v.46). An assembly on high was appealing to him as a "fontaine vive/de souverain sens" (vv.47–8) (a flowing fountain of sovereign wisdom). At the end of the text, when the heavenly gathering no longer knows how to proceed, Christine comes back to her early evocations of the king's role: instead of designating the best candidate to rule the world, she refers the debate to the King of France. This roundabout approach to the question of an impeccable monarch necessitates several comments. First, removing the debate from the skies to have it judged on earth implies Christine's preference for practical, concrete, human solutions to problems that plague human beings. Often torn between a desire for a transcendent ideal and a need to relate the real, Christine ultimately sides with the pragmatists. We may question the wisdom of submitting to a man a debate about man's inability to live in peace; Mère Nature travels to Reason's court—and thus acts as catalyst for the speeches that follow—specifically to complain about this fatal human flaw (vv.2627–94). Yet symbolically, the ending Christine creates corresponds to her principles. Man must govern himself; a debate among allegories should not, by itself, solve the problems of the world below. Experience again prevails over theory. It is interesting to note in passing that Maître Avis, who wears a lawyer's robes (vv.6227–9) is the allegorical figure who suggests sending the debate down to earth. His name designates him as a representative of opinion rather than as an immanent virtue; Avis thus serves as an excellent intermediary, or middle term, between celestial certitudes and the disorder of men.

Second, we should emphasize that in asking Charles to act as judge, the author evades any notion that he could be a candidate. He is not the required perfect prince. Christine calls the French court "souveraine," but will not go so far as to conflate Charles with the ideal monarch discussed in the assembly; it would be too easy to discover the ideal in what is already, as she herself says, the most brilliant court in the world's most glorious nation. The historical reason for Christine's reserve is surely the king's insanity, which prevented him, despite all good intentions, from being a model ruler.[23] But beyond this fact, there subsists Christine's conviction that man can never fully embody an idea. Those who pursue a perfect union of the two are destined always to fall short of their goal.

This should not discourage aspiration, however; from early in her career, Christine composed mirrors for the prince to review the traits of the accomplished monarch and supply real rulers with examples to imitate. The *Epistre Othea* addressed Charles VI's younger brother Louis d'Orléans, exhorting him to behave irreproachably. The *Chemin de long estude* also participates in the mirror genre, even though its hybrid composition, at once dream vision, travel narrative, and debate poem, also gives it a place in other categories of medieval literature. The fullest expression of Christine's interest in describing the perfect prince is the *Livre des fais et bonnes meurs du sage roi Charles V*, written in 1404.[24] It was not the last work in which Christine undertook to educate her royal readers, but it is no doubt the text that best captures her cast of mind. The *Charles V* offers at once a catalog of perfections and the portrait of a historical figure. More than twenty years after Charles V's death, Christine sets out to praise him, and follows literary protocol so well that her admiration sometimes risks seeming merely conventional. But only sometimes: Charles's personal qualities, his subtlety and prudence, do indeed emerge from the anecdotes Christine recounts and the numerous examples she gives. She speaks from memory, from experience, having known the king in her youth. She puts her knowledge to good use, and projects her experience on the intangible, unchangeable image of the king as he should always be. For Christine, the great advantage of this text over her other mirrors is that it concerns the past. Charles did once exist; all that is required is to fit his being to a certain enduring concept of monarchy. Christine is not looking, here, to reform the present, or, except indirectly, to ensure the future; there is no void that needs filling. She seeks instead to coordinate two images that are *already* compatible because immobilized by time: one a life gone by and one a constant ideal. The central absence around which the four ladies debate in the *Chemin de long estude* is filled from the beginning in the *Charles V*. The author breathes more easily, freed from the painful necessity of putting aside an ideal in favor of the human.

The *Chemin de long estude* may well contain the seed for the *Charles V* in Sagesse's speech praising the late king (vv.5001–46). The nostalgic verses Christine devotes to Charles V provide a significant counterpoint to the song of sorrow in which she recalled her husband at the beginning of the poem. The solitary widow lamented the companion who had loved her tenderly; the author, in the voice of the supreme virtue Sagesse, proffers her admiration for the king. The course of the poem has indeed taken the reader from the realm of the personal to that of the political, from the injustices of life to the compensations accessible to all who would observe and reflect. The memories Christine evokes are almost all linked to the king's love of knowledge; she praises his expertise in philosophy and astronomy, and speaks warmly of his practice of commissioning translations of Latin works into French, "Pour les cuers des François attraire/A nobles meurs" (vv.5024–5) (To draw Frenchmen's hearts/to noble behavior). Charles's qualities correspond to those Christine seeks with greatest ardor: books and study have shaped her to now affect her fellow Frenchmen's destiny, urging them to attend to the issue of virtuous government.

The end of the *Chemin de long estude* is as abrupt as its beginning was sinuous. In just a few dozen verses, Christine is chosen as messenger to the French court, submits her transcription of the debate for Dame Raison's approval, accepts jewels in compensation, descends from the sky, thanks the Sibyl, and finds herself abed in the morning light (vv.6329–98). The conflicts that had preoccupied her the previous evening, the somber thoughts that had pursued her into the night, dissipate in the bright face of the day. Christine has gained strength from new knowledge and experience. She has explored an idea of considerable societal importance, and yet she returns *in fine* to the heart of her family, woken from her dream by "la mere qui la porta" (v.6395) (the mother who carried her). Neither character nor author yet knows what "verdict" Charles VI may render, but the fiction of the *Chemin* has laid the groundwork for the writer's real participation in the great questions of her era.

NOTES

1. All quotations from this text are from Tarnowski, ed. and trans., *Le Chemin de longue étude* (Paris: Livre de poche, 2000). All translations are my own unless otherwise indicated.
2. Maurice Roy, ed., *Oeuvres poétiques de Christine de Pisan*, 3 vols. [Paris: Firmin Didot (SATF), 1886–96]; *Cent balades*, I:1–100.
3. See Renate Blumenfeld-Kosinski, "Christine de Pizan and the Misogynistic Tradition," *Romanic Review* 81 (1990): 279–92. Reprinted in *The Selected Writings of Christine de Pizan*, ed. Renate Blumenfeld-Kosinski, trans. Renate Blumenfeld-Kosinski and Kevin Brownlee, Norton Critical Edition (New York: W.W. Norton, 1997), 297–311. For the *Livre de la Cité des dames*: Middle French edited text by Earl Jeffrey Richards in *La Città delle Dame* (Milan: Luni Editrice, 1997), rev. ed. 1998. Modern French translation with introduction by Thérèse Moreau and Eric Hicks, *Le Livre de la cité des dames* (Paris: Stock, 1986). *The Book of the City of Ladies*, trans. Rosalind Brown-Grant (Harmondsworth: Penguin, 1999). *The Book of the City of Ladies*, trans. Earl Jeffrey Richards (New

York: Persea, 1982), rev. ed. with introduction by Natalie Zemon Davis (New York: Persea, 1998). See the *Cité des dames*, I.1.1–I.2.2.
4. An edition and English translation of the *Epistre au dieu d'Amours* can be found in Thelma S. Fenster and Mary Carpenter Erler, eds., *Poems of Cupid, God of Love* (New York: E.J. Brill, 1990), 33–89. For an earlier edition, see Roy, *Oeuvres poétiques*, 2:1–27; an English translation also appears in Blumenfeld-Kosinski and Brownlee, *Selected Writings*, 15–28.
5. Gabriella Parussa, ed., *Christine de Pizan. Epistre Othea*, Textes Littéraires Français, 517 (Geneva: Droz, 1999).
6. An edition and English translation of the *Dit de la Rose* appears in Fenster and Erler, *Poems of Cupid*, 91–131. See also Roy, *Oeuvres poétiques* 2: 29–48.
7. The greatest divinity is of course God himself, as Loyauté declares in two passages: "Je suis la deesse loyale/De la haulte ligne royale/De Dieu, qui me fist et fourma" (vv.299–301) (I am the faithful goddess of/The high and royal lineage/Of God, who formed and fashioned me), and "mon maistre/Amours, qu'au monde Dieu fist naistre" (vv.401–2) (Love, my lord,/Whom God has brought into the world). Christine is unbothered by the copresence of allegorical or mythological deities and the Christian God on a single scale of importance.
8. In the *Epistre au dieu d'Amours*, "creintis" appears only in ms. D, at the end of the poem, "between [Cupid's] signature couplet and Explicit." See Fenster and Erler, 79. "Creintis" appears in the Roy edition of *Oeuvres poétiques*, 2:27. In the *Livre du dit de Poissy* we find: "Du derrenier ver de cuer loyal et fin/Me nommeray ... creintis (vv.2069–70, 2075). In Barbara K. Altmann, ed., *The Love Debate Poems of Christine de Pizan* (Gainesville: University Press of Florida, 1998). See also Roy, *Oeuvres poétiques*, 2:159–222.
9. "S'aucun en veult le nom savoir,/Je lui en diray tout le voir:/Qui un tout seul cry crieroit,/Et la fin d'aoust y mettroit,/Se il disoit avec une yne,/Il sauroit le nom bel et digne" (vv.645–50) (If someone wants to know her name/I'll tell the truth of it complete:/If he would say a single cry,/Then add the month of August's end,/And if he said it with an een/He'd know the fine and worthy name).
10. This is the first verse of the poem. See *Christine de Pisan. Ditié de Jehanne d'Arc*, ed. and trans. Angus J. Kennedy and Kenneth Varty, Medium Aevum Monographs, 9 (Oxford: Society for Mediaeval Languages and Literatures, 1977). An English translation appears in Blumenfeld-Kosinski and Brownlee, *Selected Writings*, 253–62.
11. On Christine de Pizan and Dante, see in particular Earl Jeffrey Richards, "Christine de Pizan and Dante: A Re-examination," *Archiv für das Studium der Neueren Sprachen und Literaturen* 222 (1985): 100–11; and Sylvia Huot, "Seduction and Sublimation: Christine de Pizan, Jean de Meun, and Dante," *Romance Notes* 25 (1985): 361–73.
12. When she moves from the dedication to Charles VI to the poem's introduction, Christine also changes meter, from decasyllables to heptasyllables.
13. For an essay discussing Christine's anticourtly stance even while she was engaged in writing courtly poetry, see Barbara K. Altmann, "Trop peu en sçay: The Reluctant Narrator in Christine de Pizan's Works on Love," in *The Poetry/Poetics of Self and Tradition*, ed. R. Barton Palmer (New York: AMS Press, 1999), 217–47.

14. *De consolation philosophiae/The Consolation of Philosophy*, trans. with introduction and notes by Patrick Gerard Walsh (Oxford: Clarendon Press; New York: Oxford University Press; 1999).
15. For example, Lady Philosophy's visit to Boethius in his prison, recycled in the Sibyl's appearance in Christine's study. For a detailed discussion of Christine's debt to Boethius, see Glynnis Cropp, "Boèce et Christine de Pizan," *Moyen Age* 87 (1981): 387–417.
16. With this obstacle, the author again recalls the constraints of the human condition; we have only to think of Dante, for whom both Hell and Heaven open their gates, to see how acutely aware Christine is of her own weakness.
17. Christine finishes her moral commentary at v.450, but subsequent verses introduce the Sibyl of Cumae and recount her life's story; the Sibyl and Christine actually depart on their travels at v.700.
18. *De planctu naturae/The Plaint of Nature*, trans. and commentary by James J. Sheridan (Toronto: Pontifical Institute of Mediaeval Studies, 1980).
19. See Joël Blanchard, "Compilation et légitimation au XVe siècle," *Poétique* 74 (April 1988): 138–57.
20. On Christine's debt to Boccaccio, see Patricia A. Phillippy, "Establishing Authority: Boccaccio's *De claris mulieribus* and Christine de Pizan's *Le Livre de la cité des dames*," *Romanic Review* 77 (1987): 167–93.
21. See Liliane Dulac, "Un mythe didactique de Christine de Pizan: Semiramis ou la veuve héroïque," *Mélanges de philologie romanes offertes à Charles Camproux* (Montpellier, 1978): 315–45.
22. Gilbert Ouy and Christine M. Reno have recently argued that Charles VI's younger brother, Louis d'Orléans, was Christine's preferred candidate for the office of universal monarch. See "Où mène le *Chemin de long estude*? Christine de Pizan, Ambrogio Migli, et les ambitions impériales de Louis d'Orléans (A propos du ms. BNF fr. 1643)," in *Christine de Pizan 2000, Studies on Christine de Pizan in Honour of Angus J. Kennedy*, ed. John Campbell and Nadia Margolis (Amsterdam: Rodopi, 2000), 177–95.
23. By 1402, Charles had already suffered bouts of insanity for a decade.
24. Suzanne Solente, ed., 2 vols., Société de l'Histoire de France (Paris: Honoré Champion, 1936, 1940). Reprinted as 1 vol. (Geneva: Slatkine, 1977). Modern French trans., *Le Livre des faits et bonnes moeurs du roi Charles V le Sage*, Eric Hicks and Thérèse Moreau, Série Moyen Age (Paris: Stock, 1997).

13

The *Livre de l'advision Cristine*

Liliane Dulac and Christine Reno

The *Livre de l'advision Cristine* presents something of a paradox: although its autobiographical content is familiar to anyone who knows about Christine, the work itself has never enjoyed significant popularity, even though, as Charity Cannon Willard opined with good reason, it is the most interesting of her allegories.[1] Only three manuscripts of the *Advision* have come down to us, compared with the more than fifty of Christine's allegory on knighthood, the *Epistre Othea*, and the twenty-seven of the *Cité des dames*, which has had a particularly wide readership in modern English translation.[2] All three of the surviving *Advision* manuscripts date from the work's composition in 1405 or 1406.[3] Among its early owners were the constable Charles of Albret, cousin to King Charles VI and a faithful supporter of Christine,[4] either or perhaps both Louis d'Orléans and Jean de Berry, and almost certainly John the Fearless, Duke of Burgundy (*Advision*, XLIII–XLIX).

Some later readers and/or collectors of the *Advision* can be identified with more certainty from roughly 1420 through the nineteenth century. Charles d'Orléans had in his extensive library the earliest surviving manuscript, Paris, BnF fr. 1176. Philip the Good of Burgundy, son of John the Fearless, owned the second oldest *Advision* copy, Brussels B.R. 10309 (*Advision*, XLIII–XLIX). The latest surviving *Advision* manuscript, ex-Phillipps 128, the only one to contain the interpretative preface Christine wrote shortly after the work,[5] was owned by two prominent eighteenth- and nineteenth-century collectors, the Duke de La Vallière and Sir Thomas Phillipps; it is currently in private hands.[6]

Succeeding generations of the House of Savoy also owned at least one copy of the *Advision*, whose original owner was quite possibly Bonne, daughter of Count Amadeus VII, who married her illegitimate half-brother in 1405, and whose library contained a codex titled the "romancium de Crestina."[7]

199

Finally, the Renaissance author Anne de Graville (d. ca. 1540), who had more than a casual interest in Christine, owned an *Advision* that no evidence can connect to any of the surviving copies but that became part of the impressive collection of her son-in-law Claude d'Urfé (1501–1558), greatgrandfather of the celebrated author of the pastoral l'*Astrée*.[8]

Divided into three stages of a journey framed by a dream, the *Advision* is structured by the peregrinations of the narrator "Cristine." At the outset, "Cristine's" spirit, released in her sleep, encounters a fantastical giant with a head beyond the clouds, a belly that encompasses the earth, piercing eyes, and a moaning voice; the letters on his forehead identify him as "Chaos." Beside him stands an even more gigantic female shadow bearing a crown (identified in the preface as Nature), who works tirelessly to keep Chaos supplied with food. Nature makes a new body for "Cristine's" spirit by mixing four ingredients, gall, honey, lead, and feathers.[9] The new "Cristine" is "cooked" in Chaos's mouth, then swallowed into his enormous belly. Journeying through Chaos's entrails, she travels with her "guardians" to the land of the great crowned lady "Libera" (France), whose reputation draws them to her.[10] Libera takes the young foreigner into her confidence, describing her history and current woes in the form of allegories. The first recounts the history of the "golden tree" of French monarchs, set in a garden filled with whimsical fauna including birds of prey who spring from butterflies, lionesses, worms, and a chameleon. The second allegory bemoans the imprisonment of the virtues Reason, Chivalry, and Justice by Fraud, Luxuria, and Avarice and the plague of a pernicious wind: Pride.[11] Reason is locked in a tower whose windows Fraud stuffs with moss so that the resplendent light of her mirror cannot shine through. Chivalry is lulled into torpor by Luxuria, who sings to her while scratching her head;[12] weakened Justice lies on a couch, her scales and measuring implements useless at her side. Libera expresses her fear that divine retribution for her children's evil ways is close at hand, and confers on "Cristine" the mission to act before they bring about her ruin.

The next two stages of "Cristine's" journey take her to the University of "the second Athens," where she encounters another fantastical figure, Dame Opinion. Like Nature, Opinion is gigantic and incorporeal, yet composed of myriad shadows of different sizes and hues. Christine watches tiny shadows swoop among the clerics who are deep in debate, alighting by their ears as if to give advice. Opinion, like Libera, has a very long tale to tell "Cristine," and proceeds to recount her influence on human history. She claims responsibility for all human error since Adam, including heresies, political rivalries, ludicrous alchemical experiments, and erroneous philosophical theories; however, she is also instrumental in all human accomplishments. Despite her dubious record, Opinion promises she will not lead "Cristine" astray as long as she follows the guidelines of "loy, raison et vray sentement" (law, reason and true judgment) (*Advision*, 89).[13]

The Livre de l'advision Cristine 201

"Cristine" leaves Opinion to follow an abbess guide to a beautiful room at the top of the university tower, where sweet female voices draw her to the inner sanctum of Lady Philosophy. She is literally knocked over by the blinding light that shines from Philosophy and her brilliant retinue, but quickly recovers and launches into a lament of her misfortunes. Philosophy responds with a lengthy lesson in moral fortitude and wisdom that is structured along the lines of Boethius's *Consolation of Philosophy* and illustrated with dozens of quotations from the *Consolation*, the Fathers of the Church, later Christian authorities, pseudo-Aristotle, and Seneca.[14] "Cristine" listens intently and thanks Philosophy, whom she addresses as "Sainte Theologie" (Holy Theology), for the wisdom she has imparted. The dream journey ends abruptly with a comparison of the three parts of the work to a diamond, a cameo, and a ruby.[15]

AN AUTOBIOGRAPHY?

Despite the fact that the word "autobiography" was not coined until the nineteenth century[16] and critical hesitancy over the possibility of autobiography in the Middle Ages,[17] the *Advision* has most often been associated with the autobiographical genre. In recent updates of a textbook that has been widely used for decades in American university classrooms, it is clearly the *Advision* that is referred to as "her autobiography."[18] Anne Paupert characterizes the *Advision* as "le premier véritable récit autobiographique de quelque ampleur en langue française" (the first real autobiography of some length written in French) ("Christine et Boèce," 658). More specifically, the *Advision* has been characterized as an intellectual autobiography,[19] and as portraying the author's spiritual development;[20] it has been varyingly seen as casting the author as a female suffering figure,[21] and as presenting her as nurturer and healer.[22]

Art and literary history lend credence to an autobiographical interpretation. As Charity Cannon Willard reminds us, the *Advision* can be read in the light of the development of portrait painting in the late medieval period.[23] It is, in addition, roughly contemporary with three early autobiographical accounts by women in England and Spain. In her *Showings*, Julian of Norwich (d. 1413) dictated, over the space of about twenty years, two separate versions of the mystical visions she had had in 1373 at the age of thirty, revealing many personal details in the process.[24] Margery Kempe (1373–ca. 1438) dictated first partially, then in a revised, complete version, her worldly and spiritual journey. Margery's incomparable life story unfolds against a richly textured backdrop of family life, failed business ventures, pilgrimages domestic and foreign, extreme personal eccentricities, and uncomfortable encounters with the guardians of orthodoxy.[25] In Castile, Leonor López de Córdoba dictated sometime after 1412 a brief account of her life, which has the distinction of being the first autobiography written in Spain and the first Spanish work by a known woman. Structuring her narrative around the deaths of her father, brother, and son, López de Córdoba leaves a testimony to her family's honor and her profound piety.[26]

Christine, a professional writer, shapes information about herself in a much more artful form than her contemporaries, developing her self-portrait on two levels. A detailed autobiography takes up nearly half the third part of the work, where the narrator "Cristine" relates to Lady Philosophy/Theology a life story that biographers have retold for centuries as that of Christine de Pizan.[27] "Cristine" describes her birth in Venice, her father's and maternal grandfather's positions as Venetian advisors, her father's decision to accept an invitation to Charles V's court, and the family's eventual move to Paris. She recounts her happy, ten-year marriage to an educated nobleman from Picardy and the birth of their three children, then enumerates a string of misfortunes and personal tragedies: the king's death, her father's financial difficulties and physical decline, and her young husband's sudden demise from the plague. She recounts the financial woes that ensued, her loneliness, impatience, a bout of serious illness, exasperation over being the target of romantic gossip,[28] and her proud struggle to maintain her dignity. She relates how she turned to study and writing, and boasts of the number of both works and quires she has produced, explaining how they led to a promising situation for her son in England, invitations for her to the courts of England and Milan, and patronage in France and Burgundy. Finally, she tells of her continuing financial hardships after the death of her benefactor Philip the Bold, and the heavy responsibility of supporting an extended family and trying to provide comfortably for her elderly mother.

This detailed autobiographical narrative is anticipated at various stages of "Cristine's" allegorical journey. For example, the narrator, toward the beginning of her encounter with Libera, refers cryptically to her own move to Paris, the "second Athens," with her guardians—"ceulz qui m'avaient en bail" (*Advision*, 15). "Cristine," like Christine de Pizan, is a writer (*Advision*, 16), and is appointed by Libera to be her "antigraphe" or scribe.[29] On the second leg of the allegorical journey, the narrator is identified as the author of the *Mutacion de Fortune* (*Advision*, 77), as one of the parties in the *Rose* quarrel (*Advision*, 87), and as a writer whose works are considered somewhat abstruse (*Advision*, 88). Dame Opinion connects the narrator with a notable event in Christine de Pizan's family history, the correspondence between her father and the alchemist "Maistre Bernart," Bernard of Treviso.[30] In the "consolation" Lady Philosophy/Theology delivers to "Cristine," she mentions aspects of Christine de Pizan's life, including a daughter who took the veil at Poissy, a son of about twenty who is gifted in letters and has a passion for learning (*Advision*, 120–24). Finally, narrator and author coalesce in the rapid conclusion of the allegorical journey: the transition words "Ainsi me depars de mon advision . . ." (*Advision*, 142) ("Thus I leave my vision. . . . , *Christine's Vision*, 143) are spoken by the author who then compares the three parts of her work to three jewels. Unlike the end of the allegorical journey in the *Chemin de long estude* in which the dreamer Christine quickly climbs down Sibyl's ladder and back into her own bed, the allegorical journey of the *Advision* leaves the narrator suspended as it were in the framework of the narrative, having merged with the author of whom she was all the while an alias.

Christine de Pizan adds further complexity to the autobiographical portrait in the *Advision* by typologizing it according to certain literary and historical figures and a social group. Thus, "Cristine" is represented as following in Dante's footsteps at the very beginning of the journey. The opening words of the *Advision*, "Ja avoye passé la moitié du chemin de mon pelerinage," echo the opening of the *Commedia* "Nel mezzo del cammin di nostra vita."[31] More explicitly and more fully, Christine portrays herself, particularly in the third part of the work, as a feminine counterpart to Boethius who is also instructed by Lady Philosophy. Her life story is introduced by the heading "La Complainte de Cristine a Philosophie" (Christine's Complaint to Philosophy), and one of the rubrics for Lady Philosophy's reply is "Le Confort de Philosophie" (Philosophy's Consolation).[32] In the course of her account, the narrator casts herself in the tradition of much larger icons of suffering: Job and Jesus Christ (*Advision*, 59–62).[33] Finally, in presenting herself as a courageous widow pursued by adversity, she describes her trials as representative of those besetting other widows, thus folding her individuality into a social category.[34]

Despite the tendency to shape her life story in terms of figures and categories, the portrait of an individual emerges quite distinctly and in remarkable detail from the pages of the *Advision*: that of the author. It is not by chance that Christine's name appears in the title of the work, and that the reader's interest is focused on her at the outset by the familiar miniature that depicts her at work at her writing table.[35]

POLITICAL INTERPRETATIONS

A small number of critics have deemphasized the autobiographical elements of the *Advision* in favor of a political interpretation. Joël Blanchard, although not denying the importance of the autobiographical aspects of the work, has described them as valorizing the figure of the poet and, in that way, authorizing the writer's entry into the arena of political discourse.[36] Pointing out the continuity of the *Advision*'s autobiographical narrative with both the *Mutacion de Fortune* and the *Chemin de long estude*, Blanchard sees this narrative as ultimately metaphorical and representative of the poet whose function is to embrace and give expression to the entire universe: "Le regard du poète, au lieu de se porter sur lui-même, se porte sur l'universel" (The poet is not concerned with himself but with what is universal).[37]

MIRROR FOR THE PRINCE?

Rosalind Brown-Grant, noting the prominence of the image of the mirror in the *Advision*, argues that the work is more specifically understood as belonging to the genre of mirror for princes, in which the princely reader is invited to imitate the lessons learned by the figure of the narrator: "Thus, far from being of simply autobiographical interest, *L'Avision* shows Christine, as exemplar, demonstrating to the prince how to look into the self as if in a mirror to see that self anew."[38] Brown-Grant expands this interpretation in her recent book. She argues that just as in the *Epistre Othea*, the knightly reader is encouraged to accept the glosses of the stories involving female characters, so too in the *Advision*, Christine downplays her gender in order to set herself up as a moral role model for the king. She points out how the figure of the widowed Christine who has suffered a decline in fortunes parallels the situation of the bereft Libera, who has enjoyed better days under wiser rulers. The parallel is made even further, Brown-Grant astutely demonstrates, by the way Christine, after describing the reign of the vices of Fraud, Lust, and Avarice in the nation, depicts herself as victimized in her own life by individuals who have fallen prey to these same vices. Brown-Grant places Christine among medieval proponents of the "rhetorical" school of political philosophy, like Brunetto Latini, who believed that individual morality was the basis of good government.[39]

Although the "mirror for princes" genre traditionally involves quite straightforward and detailed prescriptions for moral and even physical behavior, it did allow for considerable latitude, as Jacques Krynen demonstrates in his comprehensive analysis of late medieval examples of the genre.[40] Indeed, Christine wrote several sorts of mirrors. The *Epistre Othea* is a book of advice for knights. Her *Livre des fais et bonnes meurs du sage roi Charles V*, ostensibly a memorial to Charles V, is also a book of advice on kingship for his grandson Louis de Guyenne, and adapts much material from the French translation of the quintessential mirror for princes, Giles of Rome's *De regimine principum*.[41] The *Livre de Prod'hommie de l'homme/Livre de prudence*, based ultimately on a sixth-century precursor of the mirror for princes genre, Martin of Braga's *Formula honestae vitae*, describes the virtues appropriate to those in power. The *Livre de la paix*, as Christine states unambiguously in the preface, is a book on good governance addressed to the dauphin and sometimes regent Louis de Guyenne in a brief period of civil calm (*Livre de la paix*, 57). The *Livre du corps de policie* is a mirror of conduct meant for all of civil society, conceived as parts of the social body.[42] Finally, the *Livre des trois vertus* is a "mirror" of conduct written for women of all stations, from princesses to prostitutes, as is made explicit in the introductory title chosen by its translators, "A Medieval Woman's Mirror of Honor."[43] Thus, it is not unreasonable to hypothesize that Christine meant her *Advision* as a kind of mirror for princes as well, albeit of an atypical sort.

POLITICAL DREAM?

Christiane Marchello-Nizia associates the *Advision* with another category of political works that it perhaps fits more closely, the political dream, represented by Philippe de Mézières's *Songe du Vieil Pelerin* (1386–1389),[44] Honoré Bouvet's *Apparicion Maistre Jehan de Meun* (1398), the anonymous *Songe veritable* (1406), and Chartier's *Quadrilogue invectif* (1422).[45] As Marchello-Nizia points out, the political "dream" can focus on political theory or political criticism, explain the source of current woes, or suggest political solutions, as does Philippe de Mézières in advocating a new crusade.

The *Advision* exhibits most elements of the typology Marchello-Nizia sets forth: it opens with the framework of the narrator falling asleep and dreaming, presents the various sites visited in the dream as distinct entities bearing little apparent connection with each other, and casts the narrator in the guise of the "scripteur" (scribe) of the dream. By having all political criticism originate, at least formally, from the interlocutors "Cristine" encounters—it is Libera who reveals the vices of those in power and fears their downfall in prophetic terms, and Opinion who points out the dangers of factionalism—the author takes advantage of the freedom of expression allowed by the genre. The fiction of having her ideas "revealed" by prestigious figures rather than simply emanating from her lends authority to them and provides something of a shield.

One major feature distinguishes the *Advision* from other political dreams, however: that is the prominence of the narrator. In the typology that Marchello-Nizia sets forth, the dream-narrator is always a very discrete presence, and occasionally is not even identified. In the *Advision*, on the contrary, the narrator "Cristine" remains in the forefront; her life story occupies nearly half the concluding part of the work, and her allegorical journey appears central to the work's interpretation.

THE INTERPRETIVE PREFACE TO THE *ADVISION CRISTINE*

In fact, both autobiographical and political interpretations of the *Advision* are supported, but not unambiguously, in the preface Christine wrote for the work. Critics have not sufficiently appreciated that the preface is written as a gloss on the first part of the work only; it is introduced as a "Glose sur la premiere partie de ce present volume" (Gloss on the first part of this volume) and begins "Pour ouvrir la voie a declairier les choses soubz figures dictes en la premiere partie de ce livre, laquelle appert aucunement obscure.... (*Advision*, 9) (To open the way toward declaring those things said by means of figures in the first part of this work, which appears somewhat obscure....) ("The Preface to the *A-C*," 209). The gloss interprets the first part in three ways, according to the macrocosm, the individual, and the kingdom of France (*Advision*, 12).

This juxtaposition of the macrocosmic and microcosmic is, of course, commonplace in the exegetical tradition in which allegory features so prominently. When we look at the details, however, the explicit emphasis on the political interpretation in an allegorical schema is unusual for the period (although political writing certainly is not). Equally remarkable is a conflation of the autobiographical and the universal in the use of the second category of the individual. For in the illustrations of what that term means, both Christine as an individual and mankind are presented as the signifiers:

> Par ce que Cristine dit ou .IIIe. chappitre que son esperit estoit par les mains de l'ombre gecté en la gueule de l'image et puis en espace de temps trait hors en ung petit corps qui chiet ou ventre tant qu'il pouoit se sousteni et aler, se puet clerement entendre la naissance et premiere nourriture et de elle et semblablement de toute creature humaine. (*Advision*, 5)

(By what Christine says in the third chapter with regard to her spirit, which was thrust into the belly of the figure by the shade [i.e., Chaos] and a while later taken out in a small body which fell into the belly of the said figure, and then was nourished by the servant of the said shade until it was able to sustain itself and move about on its own, can be clearly understood her birth and early nourishment, and likewise that of every living creature, "The Preface to the *A-C*," 211.)

In addition to the elasticity of her first category, another noteworthy feature of Christine's schema is the permeability of her categories. Her individual glosses sometimes conflate her own life with that of the French nation. For example, the supposedly political interpretation of chapter four explains: "Moreover, this same fourth chapter can signify how Christine was transported with her parents as a child into France from the land of Lombardy, where she was born, as she explains more fully hereafter in the third part, the beauties of which land she saw and speaks about in literal fashion, as well as the ruins which followed upon the wars" ("The Preface to the *A-C*," 213 and *Advision*, 6). The political gloss of the following chapter translates thus: "Likewise, it can signify how Christine was already grown when she became aware of the customs of France, and was able to speak of them" ("The Preface to the *A-C*," 215 and *Advision*, 7). In these supposedly political interpretations, the narrator/author takes center stage from the political situation she purports to be explaining.

At first glance, the three-tiered interpretive scheme Christine sets up for the first part of the *Advision* in the preface appears comparable to the three levels of meaning on which the entire *Epistre Othea* is constructed: literal ("text"), moral ("gloss"), and spiritual ("allegory")—the miniatures accompanying each chapter of the *Othea* adding another potential hermeneutic dimension. It is doubtful, however, that the triple interpretation of the first part of the *Advision*, even with the ambiguities that are evident in the individual explanations, could be sustained for every chapter of the second and third parts. For despite the continuity of the framework of the dream journey and the presence of allegorical figures in each part (Dame Opinion for the second and Lady Philosophy/Theology in the third), the second and third parts are written in much more direct language than the first, whose cryptic language readily lends itself to multiple meanings. In particular, the many chapters of the second part that follow almost word for word Christine's main philosophical source, Aquinas's *Commentary on the Metaphysics of Aristotle*, the very detailed narration of numerous events in Christine's life, and the litany of dozens of quotations from the Church Fathers that Lady Philosophy delivers would not easily open up to sustained multiple layers of interpretation. Indeed, the special nature of the first part of the work is suggested in the concluding comparison of the three jewels: the first part of the *Advision* is like a diamond that can either be admired separately or mounted in a setting (*Advision*, 142).

There is, in fact, another kind of allegorical practice that Christine suggests to her readers, not connected with perceiving clearly defined multiple meanings but rather with acceding to "secretes sciences" (secret knowledge) and "pures veritéz" (pure truths) that lie behind the veil of "parole couverte" (covered language) (*Advision*, 3). The final image of the work, which compares the third part to a precious ruby "that becomes more and more pleasing the more one gazes upon it" (*Christine's Vision*, 143), seems an invitation to contemplate the work in an effort to discover a significance that is not immediately obvious.

SELF AND STATE

As the trilevel gloss for the first part of the *Advision* might suggest, the work's political intent seems clearest in the first stage of the journey where the narrator learns the history of the French monarchy and the current vice-ridden state of society. This political content is recapitulated briefly in the second part (*Advision*, 79–81) in which Dame Opinion recalls France's factional woes and Fraud's reign over the forces of Reason. Moreover, as a number of critics have noted, the author's self-representation suggestively parallels that of the French nation: both Libera and "Cristine" are bereft widows whose sufferings are described in detail with particular intensity; both have enjoyed happier times; both are searching for a better existence, although "Cristine," in coming to writing, has already taken an important step forward (*Advision*, 12). The narrator, depicted as a foreign-born writer, is the most positive figure to emerge against the backdrop of social decay and political turmoil painted by Libera and later evoked by Opinion, the best hope for positive change. The role that the *Advision* reserves for her appears even more striking in the light of the political debate in the slightly earlier *Chemin de long estude* over the qualities best suited for political leadership. Whereas in that latter work the narrator's role seems limited to submitting the debate to the French princes, in the *Advision* it is "Cristine" who appears destined to resolve the political crisis. Finally, "Cristine's" autobiographical complaint is clearly linked to the nation as a whole, as it is motivated by a perceived lack of human and social support, as Christine emphasizes by inserting the only poem the *Advision* contains, the sixth of her *Autres balades*, which describes the plight of widows in the face of the indifference and even the malice of the powerful: nobles, clerics, knights, judges, officials, and royal princes.[46]

In relation to the political turmoil described by Libera and briefly recalled by Opinion, the narrative suggests positive development in its upward trajectory to the top of the tower of Libera's University where Philosophy's study is located. The political dilemma that is evoked so powerfully in the first part of the work seems to open up, in the third, to the hope of some spiritual resolution. Indeed, as the work progresses, various images lead us to a certain sense of transcendence. One critic located this movement in the progression of the three principle allegorical figures Nature, Opinion and Philosophy, depicted as "successively more serene" and "more chaste."[47] One could add that the fantastical elements associated with the main figures of the first two parts, for example Chaos's inestimable size and insatiable appetite and Opinion's composing parts, both beautiful and horrible, and of every conceivable shape, size, and color, do not appear in the third part of the work, as if to indicate the superiority of philosophical/theological knowledge over the creations of the imagination.[48] Images of light also mark the progress of "Cristine's" journey, beginning with the light of Reason that is totally blocked by Fraud, to the shadowy light of Opinion to the bright light of the richly painted room where her abbess guide leads her, to the blinding light that throws her to the floor in a faint when Philosophy's door is opened. It is in terms of light that she expresses the value of the knowledge Philosophy/Theology has imparted: "The blessed Doctor Saint Jerome, who so dearly loved you, says of you and once again in your praise, 'Just as the shadows of night do not darken the brilliance of the stars of heaven, so no worldly [iniquity] can darken the souls supported in the firmament of Holy Theology' " (*Christine's Vision*, 143).[49] Moreover, the allegorical journey brings about the narrator's own growth: symbolically reborn by Nature's magical ingredients, she is depicted in the first part as mainly a witness to Libera's tale of woes, at the end of which she is entrusted with a mission; on the second stage of her journey, she engages with Opinion in more of a dialogue, and in a way displaces the clerics who were initially shown debating; in the third part, she takes over center stage to recount her life as a prelude to receiving Philosophy/Theology's lessons of wisdom. She is, at the end of her allegorical journey, in a position analogous to that of the king, the possessor of superior wisdom that the narrator acknowledges, in fact, as universal:

You [Philosophy/Theology] are ethics because you teach the good and honorable life, or loving what should be loved, which is God and one's neighbor. These things, Theology, you yourself reveal in the sciences of ethics and physics. You are logic because you demonstrate the light and truth of the just soul. You are the study of politics because you teach the virtuous life, for no city is better protected than by the foundation and water of the faith and by the firm agreement to love the common good, which is true and supreme.... (Christine's Vision, 142)

The autobiographical and political dimensions of the *Advision* are thus inextricably linked to such a degree that it is impossible to classify the work neatly according to a single genre that would exclude or downplay the importance of one or the other. Furthermore, although the depiction of the political horizon in the *Advision* is bleak, the figure of the woman writer who emerges and the political role she designates for herself are far from traditional and far from pessimistic. The confidence Christine invests in her self-portrayal can be read as a promise of her astonishing activity, particularly in the field of political writing, in the years to follow.

NOTES

1. The *"Livre de la Paix" of Christine de Pisan*, ed. Charity Cannon Willard (The Hague: Mouton, 1958), 15. Two critical editions of the *Advision* exist: *Lavision-Christine*, ed. Sister Mary Louis Towner (Washington, DC: Catholic University of America Press, 1932, reprinted New York: AMS Press, 1969) and *Le Livre de l'Advision Cristine*, ed. Christine Reno and Liliane Dulac (Paris: Honoré Champion, 2001), henceforth cited as *Advision*. All quotations are taken from this edition. The work has been translated into English by Glenda K. McLeod under the title *Christine's Vision* (New York and London: Garland, 1993) and into Dutch: *De Droom van Christine*, trans. Albertine Ponfoort (Rotterdam: Historische Uitgeverij Rotterdam, 1995). Anne Paupert will soon publish a modern French translation, *La Vision de Christine, Le Moyen Age et la femme; voix poétiques, utopiques et amoureuses*, ed. Danielle Régnier-Bohler in the Bouquins collection published by Robert Laffont.
2. More than fifty thousand copies of Earl Jeffrey Richards's translation, *The Book of the City of Ladies* (New York: Persea Books, 1982, 1998), have been sold to date; we thank Prof. Richards for communicating this information. In 1999, Rosalind Brown-Grant published a British translation under the same title in the Penguin Classics series.
3. Christine gives the date 1405 in the third part of the *Advision*, Chap. 10; since the year began at Easter according to the Julian calendar used at the time, this would place it between April 19, 1405 and April 10, 1406, Easter falling that year on April 11.
4. Approximately a dozen books, including *"La Vision de Cristine,"* are listed in the inventory of Charles of Albret's library drawn up in 1409, two years before his

death. See Henri Stein, "La Bibliothèque du Connétable d'Albret à Sully-sur-Loire (1409)," *Le Bibliographe Moderne* 6 (1902): 91–3. Charles of Albret also owned a copy of the *Debat de deux amans*, Brussels, B.R. 11034, that contains a dedicatory poem to him, one of three poems Christine wrote in his honor. See Maurice Roy, ed., *Oeuvres poétiques de Christine de Pisan*, I (Paris: Didot, 1886), 208–11, 231.

5. The preface is written in a separate quire of six folia in this manuscript and dated twenty-eight years into the Schism. See Christine Reno, "The Preface to the *Avision-Christine* in ex-Phillipps 128," in *Reinterpreting Christine de Pizan*, ed. Earl Jeffrey Richards et al. (Athens and London: University of Georgia Press, 1992), 207–27. This article will hereafter be cited as "The Preface to the *A-C*."

6. Guillaume Debure, *Catalogue des livres de la bibliothèque de feu M. le duc de La Vallière*, I, 2 (Paris, 1783), no. 1327 and *The Phillipps Manuscripts; Catalogue Librorum Manuscriptorum in Bibliotheca D. Thomae Phillipps, Bt.* (Impressum Typis Medio-Montanis, 1837–1871, reprinted London: The Holland Press, 1968), no. 236.

7. Gianni Mombello, "Christine de Pizan and the House of Savoy," trans. and ed. Nadia Margolis, in *Reinterpreting Christine de Pizan*, 187–93 and Sheila Edmunds, "The Medieval Library of Savoy, II: Documents," *Scriptorium* 25 (1971): par. 96, m. Because, as Mombello mentions, many of the Savoy manuscripts fell victim to the political turmoil of the sixteenth century and a fire in 1667, it is quite possible that the Savoy *Advision* was lost. But it is not impossible, given that the Savoy manuscript contained the preface, that it survived and was acquired by Sir Thomas Phillipps several hundred years later.

8. In addition to the *Advision*, Anne de Graville owned two copies of the *Mutacion de Fortune* and one of the *Livre des trois Vertus*. See Myra Dickman Orth, "Dedicating Women: Manuscript Culture in the French Renaissance, and the Cases of Catherine d'Amboise and Anne de Graville," *Journal of the Early Book Society* 1 (1997): 23 and 27, n. 6.

9. Sylvia Huot interprets this scene in light of medieval notions of creation and procreation in "Seduction and Sublimation: Christine de Pizan, Jean de Meun, and Dante," *Romance Notes* 25 (1985): 361–73.

10. The figure of Libera has attracted a good deal of critical attention. See Liliane Dulac, "A propos des représentations du corps souffrant chez Christine de Pizan," in *Mélanges de langue et de littérature françaises du Moyen Age offerts à Pierre Demarolle*, ed. Charles Brucker (Paris: Honoré Champion, 1998), 313–24 and, by the same author, "La représentation de la France chez Eustache Deschamps et Christine de Pizan," in *Autour d'Eustache Deschamps. Actes du Colloque du Centre d'Etudes Médiévales de l'Université de Picardie-Jules Verne, Amiens, 5–8 novembre 1998*, ed. Danielle Buschinger (Amiens: Presses du Centre d'Etudes Médiévales, Université de Picardie-Jules Verne, 1999), 79–92; see also Thierry Lassabatère, "La personnification de la France dans la littérature de la fin du Moyen Age. Autour d'Eustache Deschamps et Christine de Pizan," in *Contexts and Continuities: Proceedings of the IVth International Colloquium on Christine de Pizan (Glasgow 21–27 July 2000)*, ed. Angus J. Kennedy in collaboration with

Rosalind Brown-Grant, James C. Laidlaw, and Catherine Müller and published in honour of Liliane Dulac (Glasgow: University Press, 2002), 3 vols., 483–504. We thank the author for showing us a copy of his paper prior to publication.

11. See Jean-Louis G. Picherit, "Les Références pathologiques et thérapeutiques dans l'oeuvre de Christine de Pizan," in *Une femme de lettres au Moyen Age*, ed. Liliane Dulac and Bernard Ribémont (Orléans: Paradigme, 1995), 233–44.

12. On the importance of gestures in Christine's work, see Liliane Dulac, "La Gestuelle chez Christine de Pizan: quelques aperçus," in *Au Champ des escriptures*; *IIIe Colloque international sur Christine de Pizan, Lausanne 18–22 juillet 1998*, ed. Eric Hicks et al. (Paris: Honoré Champion, 2000), 609–26.

13. Armand Strubel makes a number of pertinent remarks on Opinion in his article "Le Style allégorique de Christine," *Une femme de lettres au Moyen Age*, 357–72. Roberta Krueger detects a strong undercurrent of doubt not only in Opinion, but in all of Christine's female authority figures. See "Christine's Anxious Lessons: Gender, Morality, and the Social Order from the *Enseignemens* to the *Avision*," in *Christine de Pizan and the Categories of Difference*, ed. Marilynn Desmond (Minneapolis: University of Minnesota Press, 1998), 16–40.

14. The majority of these quotations, aside from those from Boethius, are taken from an early fourteenth-century preacher's compilation, Thomas of Ireland's *Manipulus florum*. See *Advision*, XXXIII–XXXIV. Earl Jeffrey Richards argues for Christine's direct knowledge of at least some of the Church fathers in "In Search of a Feminist Patrology: Christine de Pizan and 'Les Glorieux Dotteurs,' " in *Une femme de lettres au Moyen Age*, 281–95. On Christine's use of Boethius, see the landmark article by Glynnis M. Cropp identifying which translations of the *Consolation of Philosophy* Christine knew: "Boèce et Christine de Pizan," *Le Moyen Age* 87 (1981): 387–417. Benjamin Semple analyzes Christine de Pizan's adaptation of Boethius in the context of medieval philosophical and religious thought in "The Consolation of a Woman Writer: Christine de Pizan's Use of Boethius in *Lavision-Christine*," in *Women, the Book and the Worldly. Selected Proceedings of the St. Hilda's Conference, 1993*, ed. Lesley Smith and Jane H. M. Taylor (Woodbridge: D.S. Brewer, 1995), 39–48 and "The Critique of Knowledge as Power: The Limits of Philosophy and Theology in Christine de Pizan," in *Christine de Pizan and the Categories of Difference*, 108–27.

15. For an interpretation of these images in the context of the allegory, see Liliane Dulac, "Travail allégorique et ruptures du sens chez Christine de Pizan: *L'Epistre Othea*," in *Continuités et ruptures dans l'histoire et la littérature: Colloque Franco-Polonais 9–14 février 1987, Montpellier*, ed. Dominique Triaire (Paris: Honoré Champion, 1988), 30.

16. The word is first attested in English in 1809 and in French in 1836. See Alain Rey, *Dictionnaire historique de la langue française*, I (Paris: Le Robert, 1992), 223.

17. Critical opinion ranges from Georg Misch's inclusive use of the term in the *Geschichte der Autobiographie* to Eugene Vance's DeManian musing over whether autobiography can exist at all, in "Augustine's Confessions and the Grammar of Selfhood," *Genre* 6 (1973): 2, 6. Other important studies include Leo Spitzer, "Note on the Poetic and the Empirical 'I' in Medieval Authors," *Traditio* 4 (1946): 414–22; Mary Martin McLaughlin, "Abelard as an Autobiographer,"

Speculum 42 (1967): 463–88; Paul Zumthor, "Autobiography in the Middle Ages?," trans. Sherry Simon, *Genre* 6 (1973): 29–48; Evelyn B. Vitz, "Type et individu dans 'l'autobiographie' médiévale," *Poétique* 24 (1975): 426–45; and Laurence de Looze's *Pseudo-Autobiography in the Fourteenth Century* (Gainesville: University Press of Florida, 1997). Philippe Lejeune, whose yardstick of the "autobiographical pact" is widely accepted by critics of modern literature, states categorically that his notion cannot be applied to first-person narratives prior to Rousseau's *Confessions*; see *Le Pacte autobiographique* (Paris: Seuil, 1975): 13–4. Nonetheless, two Christine scholars show how Christine's construction of the "I" conforms to Lejeune's parameters. See Jean-Philippe Beaulieu, "*Lavision Christine* ou la tentation autobiographique," *Littératures* 18 (1998): 20 and Anne Paupert, in "Christine et Boèce: de la lecture à l'écriture, de la réécriture à l'écriture du moi," *Contexts and Continuities*, 645–62. We thank Anne Paupert for showing us her article prior to publication.

18. C. Warren Hollister, *Medieval Europe: A Short History*, 8th ed. (Boston: McGraw-Hill, 1998), 369. It is interesting to note that Christine's nutshell paragraph is larger than Chaucer's and Villon's.

19. Christine McArdle Reno, *Self and Society in L'Avision-Christine of Christine de Pizan*, Ph.D. dissertation, Yale University, 1972, p. 7 and Anne Paupert, " 'La Narracion de mes aventures,' des premiers poèmes à l'*Advision*: élaboration d'une écriture autobiographique dans l'oeuvre de Christine de Pizan," *Au champ des escriptures*, 54.

20. Sr. Mary Louis Towner, the work's first editor, saw the three stages of the narrator's journey as analogous to three stages in the author's life: "the material, the intellectual, and that of divine things" (47).

21. Renate Blumenfeld-Kosinski, "Christine de Pizan et l' (Auto) biographie féminine," in *Mélanges de l'École française de Rome, Italie et Mediterranée* 113 (2001): 1–15. We thank the author for sending us her article prior to publication.

22. Claire Le Brun-Gouanvic, "L'écriture médecine: une relecture de l'*Avision Christine* (1405)," in *Dans les miroirs de l'écriture. La Réflexivité chez les femmes écrivains d'Ancien Régime*, ed. Jean-Philippe Beaulieu and Diane Desrosiers-Bonin (Montreal: University of Montreal, 1998), 9–20.

23. Willard, *Christine de Pizan: Her Life and Works* (New York: Persea, 1984), 163.

24. Julian of Norwich, *Showings*, trans. Edmund Colledge and James Walsh (New York: Paulist Press, 1978).

25. *The Book of Margery Kempe*, trans. B.A. Windeatt (London: Penguin, 1994).

26. Amy Katz Kaminsky and Elaine Dorough Johnson, "To Restore Honor and Fortune: 'The Autobiography of Leonor López de Córdoba,' " in *The Female Autograph: Theory and Practice of Autobiography from the Tenth to the Twentieth Century*, ed. Domna C. Stanton (Chicago: University of Chicago Press, 1987), 70–80.

27. As early as 1717, Boivin le Cadet paraphrased the *Advision* account step by step, interspersing long quotations from the work in his "Vie de Christine de Pisan, et de Thomas de Pisan son père," in *Mémoires de Littérature, tirez des registres de l'Académie Royale des Inscriptions et Belles Lettres* (Paris: Imprimerie Royale, II, 1736), 704–14.

28. Gianni Mombello engagingly traces the survival of the legend into the eighteenth century in "J.-M.-L. Coupé e H. Walpole: Gli amori di Christine de Pizan," *Studi francesi* 46 (1972): 5–25.
29. The term "antigraphe" has been the object of considerable critical speculation involving notions of "writing against." See Christine Moneera Laennec, *Christine antygrafe: Authorship and Self in the Prose Works of Christine de Pizan, with an Edition of B.N. Ms. 603, Le Livre des fais d'armes et de Chevallerie*. 2 vols., Ph.D. dissertation, Yale University, 1988: I, abstract, 4, 74, 211; and Andrea W. Tarnowski, "Perspectives on the *Advision*," in *Christine de Pizan 2000: Studies on Christine de Pizan in Honour of Angus J. Kennedy*, ed. John Campbell and Nadia Margolis (Amsterdam, GA: Rodopi, 2000), 113. "Antigraphe," derived from the Latin "antigraphum" and ultimately from the Greek where the preposition "anti" is not necessarily oppositional, means scribe, secretary, and by extension, writer. See Joël Blanchard and Michel Quereuil, *Lexique de Christine de Pizan* (Paris: Klincksieck, 1999), 24. We note that before Christine, Dante, in the *Divine Comedy*, had described himself as the scribe of truths revealed by Beatrice (*Purg.* XXXIII, 52–7 and *Par.* I, 27), and that Christine's original choice of words in the earliest *Advision* manuscript, Paris BnF f.fr. 1176, was "philographe." See *Advision*, 16.
30. See Christine de Pizan, *Le Livre des fais et bonnes meurs du sage roy Charles V*, 2 vols., ed. Suzanne Solente (Paris: Champion, 1936), I, xi–xiv.
31. The parallel, mentioned by many commentators, was first noted by Arturo Farinelli in *Dante e la Francia dall'età media al secolo di Voltaire*, 2 vols. (Milan: Hoepli, 1908), I, 181. The *Advision* mentions Dante specifically in the first part (I, 16) when Fraud is equated with the Geryon (see *Inf.* XVI and XVII). As Earl Jeffrey Richards points out, Christine was the first French writer to actually incorporate elements of the *Commedia* in her work. "Christine de Pizan and Dante: A Reexamination," *Archiv für das Studium der neueren Sprachen und Literaturen* 222, Band 137 (1985): 100–11.
32. In addition to Anne Paupert's article "Boèce et Christine," see Joël Blanchard, "Artefact littéraire et problématisation morale au XVe siècle," *Le Moyen français* 17 (1985): 7–27.
33. See Mary L. Skemp, "Autobiography as Authority in *Lavision-Christine*," *Le Moyen français* 35–6 (1996): 23–4.
34. Kevin Brownlee interprets this self-presentation as a strategy of self-authorization in "Widowhood, Sexuality, and Gender in Christine de Pizan," *Romanic Review* 86 (1995): 343–53. It is also, however, a remarkable social critique.
35. Paris, BnF fr. 1176 f. 1r, Brussels, B.R. 10309 f. 1r, and ex-Phillipps 128, f. 7r.
36. Joël Blanchard, " 'Vox poetica, vox politica': l'entrée du poète dans le champ politique au XVe siècle," in *Actes du Ve colloque international sur le Moyen Français, Milan 6–8 mai 1985* (Milan: Vita e Pensiero, 1986), 39–51.
37. Joël Blanchard, "Christine de Pizan: les raisons de l'histoire," *Le Moyen Age* 42 (1986): 417–36 (435).
38. Rosalind Brown-Grant, "*L'Avision Christine*: Autobiographical Narrative or Mirror for the Prince?," in *Politics, Gender & Genre: The Political Thought of Christine de Pizan*, ed. Margaret Brabant (Boulder, Oxford: Westview Press, 1992), 108.

39. Rosalind Brown-Grant, *Christine de Pizan and the Moral Defence of Women: Reading Beyond Gender* (Cambridge: Cambridge University Press, 1999), 119.
40. Jacques Krynen, *Idéal du prince et pouvoir royal en France à la fin du Moyen Age (1380–1440)* (Paris: Picard, 1981).
41. Christine de Pisan, *Le Livre des fais et bonnes meurs du sage roy Charles V*, ed. Suzanne Solente (Paris: Honoré Champion, 1936), lxii–lxvi.
42. Christine de Pizan, *Le Livre du corps de policie*, ed. Angus J. Kennedy (Paris: Honoré Champion, 1998. Etudes christiniennes no. 1), xi.
43. Christine de Pizan, *A Medieval Woman's Mirror of Honor: The Treasury of the City of Ladies*, trans. Charity Cannon Willard, ed. Madeleine Pelner Cosman (New York: Persea and Bard Hall Press, 1989).
44. The imperfect nature of classifications is demonstrated by the fact that Mézières's work, which fits quite well into the schema of the "songe politique," is also considered by Krynen, and rightly so, as an example of the "mirror of princes." See Jacques Krynen, 57–60.
45. Christiane Marchello-Nizia, "Entre l'histoire et la poétique: le 'Songe politique,' " *Revue des Sciences Humaines*, 55 (July–September 1981): 39–53.
46. See Liliane Dulac, "Thèmes et variations du *Chemin de long estude à l'Advision-Christine*: remarques sur un itinéraire," in *Sur le chemin de longue étude. Actes du colloque d'Orléans juillet 1995*, ed. Bernard Ribémont (Paris: Honoré Champion, 1998), 85–6.
47. Maureen Slattery Durley, "The Crowned Dame, Dame Opinion, and Dame Philosophy: the Female Characteristics of Three Ideals in Christine de Pizan's *L'Avision Christine*," in *Ideals for Women in the Works of Christine de Pizan*, ed. Diane Bornstein (Detroit: Michigan Consortium for Medieval and Early Modern Studies, 1981), 42.
48. See Liliane Dulac, "Sur les fonctions du bestiaire dans quelques oeuvres didactiques de Christine de Pizan," in *"Rien ne m'est seurs que la chose incertaine." Etudes sur l'art d'écrire au Moyen Age offertes à Eric Hicks par ses anciens élèves et ses amis*, ed. Jean-Claude Mühlethaler and Denis Billotte (Geneva: Slatkine, 2001), 181–94.
49. See *Advision*, 141, and Andrea Tarnowski, 112.

14

"Nous deffens de feu, . . . de pestilence, de guerres"

Christine de Pizan's Religious Works

Maureen Boulton

The religious works of Christine de Pizan—her three *Oroisons*, the *Sept psaumes allegorisés*, the *Epistre de la prison de vie humaine*, and the *Heures de la contemplacion sur la Passion*—have recently been the focus of excellent work by Charity Cannon Willard, Liliane Dulac, Gérard Gros, Nadia Margolis, and Lori Walters, who have related them to the political and feminist themes of her other works.[1] It now remains to begin setting these works into the wider contexts of late medieval devotional practices and the vernacular religious literature related to them: a task that can only be begun in this chapter.

One of the distinctive features of late medieval society was the intensity of religious feeling among the laity. This intensity often focused on Christ's humanity, especially His suffering, in new devotions and in a form of piety often termed "affective," in which emotion became a means of advancing toward spiritual perfection.[2] Affective piety found expression in virtually all the arts, including a wealth of texts, both in Latin and the vernacular, devoted to recreating the Passion of Christ in terms calculated to heighten the emotional response of the audience. Such texts might be either heard or read, or both. The effect of public sermons, for example (such as Jean Gerson's on the Passion), enthusiastically received among the laity, was often prolonged through reading and meditation.[3] Indeed as opportunities for lay religious experience expanded in this period, even lay people tied to an "active" secular life expressed an interest in contemplation, previously restricted to monks and mystics.[4]

For any investigation of affective devotion or lay meditation in this period, the principal sources are devotional treatises, religious narratives, sermons, and prayer books written in the vernacular. Unfortunately, most of these works in French remain unedited and virtually unknown to literary scholars.[5] Although religious questions have recently moved closer to the center of critical attention in medieval studies, vernacular religious works still fall outside the literary canon, and are also little read by historians and theologians. In this chapter I will first argue the centrality of religious questions to Christine's work, and then try to relate each of her religious works to the themes of affective and meditative piety. In the conclusion, I will examine the relationship between the narrator and her audience.

Given the importance of religion and of religious texts to most of her contemporaries, it can hardly be surprising that Christine took an active interest in religious questions throughout her literary career. The three verse prayers were written early, during a prolific period (1402 or 1403)[6] in which she also composed the *Dit de la Rose*, the *Epistres sur le debat du Roman de la Rose*, the *Mutacion de Fortune*, and the *Livre des trois jugemens*. A few years later, in 1409—the same year that saw the completion of the *Cent balades d'amant et de dame*—Christine wrote her meditation on the Penitential Psalms. This work was composed just after the *Livre de Prudence* and just before the *Lamentacion sur les maux de France*. In her final years of retreat at the convent of Poissy, Christine produced the *Epistre de la prison de vie humaine* and the *Contemplacion sur la Passion*, as well as the more famous *Ditié de Jehanne d'Arc*. Clearly religion was of central importance to Christine's vision of the world.

Indeed, although it is not often remarked, Christine's interest in religion also manifests itself in works not primarily religious in intention. In her biography of *Charles V* (1404), Christine devoted several chapters to her subject's religious life, which included daily assistance at mass, reading the Hours, and devotion to several saints.[7] Similarly, two chapters of the *Livre du corps de policie* (1406–1407) are devoted to the religious formation of the prince.[8] In the *Livre de la cité des dames* (1404–1405), Christine presented the Virgin Mary as the Queen of the new kingdom, and devoted the final part of the book to the stories of female saints.[9] The *Livre des trois vertus* (1405) continued the work of the *Cité des dames* by providing practical and religious advice to women of different social ranks. In contrast to clerics writing for laywomen (including her sometime ally Jean Gerson), Christine adapted her instructions to the different social spheres that women occupy.[10] Although she considered the "active" life the only one possible for her mainly noble and princely audience, she wrote sympathetically about the contemplative life, which gave a taste of the joys of Paradise, and enabled one to see God through contemplation.[11]

BOOKS OF HOURS

Of the various types of devotional work available to the laity in Christine's lifetime, the most common and most influential was the type of prayer book usually called the "Book of Hours," which first appeared in the thirteenth century and became increasingly common into the sixteenth century. Widely owned by literate people of all ranks, Books of Hours were especially common in the court circles in which Christine lived and worked, and most of her patrons are known to have owned one or more copies, often sumptuously illustrated.[12] It is only natural, therefore, that the prayers and offices included in the Book of Hours provide the principal intertext for Christine's religious works. Because their texts are less familiar to us than their illustrations, it will be useful to describe the contents of such books before discussing their influence on Christine's thought.

From the thirteenth through the sixteenth century, the Book of Hours was one of the most popular platforms for lay devotion. Composed of elements borrowed from the monastic Breviary (always including the Calendar, the Little Office of the Virgin, Penitential Psalms with the Litany, Suffrages, and the Office of the Dead, and often including in addition the Office of the Cross, Marian prayers, and Joys of the Virgin), the Book of Hours presented an abridged form of liturgical prayer suitable for laypeople.[13] It consisted mainly of the later accretions to the divine office, and omitted the numerous variations dependent on the liturgical calendar. Nevertheless the Book of Hours made accessible to a layperson a traditionally monastic method of prayer.

In the Office of the Virgin—the most important element of a Book of Hours—the devotional text is divided into seven sections (including psalms, hymns, lessons, prayers, verses, and responses), each assigned to a different hour of the day (Matins, Prime, Terce, etc.). The periodic interruption of the ordinary tasks of daily life to read or recite these texts was a deliberate attempt to sanctify secular time. Nevertheless, the essence of this type of prayer was not the mechanical repetition of the same words each day, but the effort enjoined on the pious reader to use the texts as a basis for meditation, particularly on the events of Christ's life. In illustrated Books of Hours, the program of illustrations served to guide the content of that meditation. Thus, by reading a devotional text, devout persons could recreate in their minds the holy events of the past, and become witnesses and even participants in those events.[14]

Also essential to a Book of Hours were the so-called Penitential Psalms. The Psalms in question (Psalms 6, 31, 37, 50, 101, 129, and 142 of the Vulgate) were thought to have been written by David in repentance of his murder of Uriah, and were meant to express sorrow for sin and to ask for pardon.[15] They were invariably followed by a Litany: an ancient form of liturgical prayer that seeks the intercession of a series of saints.

The Office of the Dead in a Book of Hours was identical to the office of that name in the Breviary. It consisted only of Vespers, Matins, and Lauds, and whereas its Psalms offered comfort to the bereaved, its nine lessons from the Book of Job presented an allegory for the trials of earthly life and the pains of purgatory. Praying the Office of the Dead made it possible for the living to help the dead, for it was considered the most effective way to reduce their time in Purgatory.[16]

Among the items commonly included in a Book of Hours are the Marian prayers "Obsecro te" and "O Intemerata," as well as a prose prayer, often in French ("Douce dame de misericorde"), based on the Joys of the Virgin.[17] The Hours of the Cross, which were frequently included in Books of Hours, comprise seven short sections each containing a hymn, an antiphon, and a prayer. Several Books of Hours also contain French poems entitled the "Heures de la Croix" that evoke rapidly the events of the Passion.[18]

The influence of this style of periodic prayer on other forms of devotion reveals itself in a series of texts in which a meditation on the Passion is structured according to the hours. The best known of these are doubtless the *Meditationes vitae Christi* and the *Vita Christi* of Ludolphus of Saxony, but the source of Christine's *Heures de contemplacion* may have been the *Meditatio de passione Christi per septem diei horas* attributed to Pseudo-Bede.[19] These works are central to the tradition of affective piety in the later Middle Ages, and are notable both for their insistence on the humanity of Christ and for their direct appeals to the emotions of their readers.

Even this brief description of the principal contents of a Book of Hours will recall the titles of several of Christine's religious works: the *Sept psaumes* (which includes a Litany), the *Heures de contemplacion*, and the *Quinze joyes Nostre Dame*. I shall now examine each of Christine's works in greater detail, in the order of their composition, and indicate more precisely the influence upon them of Books of Hours and other religious ideas and practices they represent.

THE *OROISONS*

Christine's three "Oroisons" share several characteristics that set them off from her other religious works. All three are written in stanzaic verse rather than prose and all three were included in the manuscripts of her collected works, the so-called "Livre de Christine," the Duke's manuscript, and the Queen's manuscript.[20] A distinctive feature of their form is the use of the incipit of a Latin prayer ("Ave Maria" or "Pater Noster") as a refrain after each stanza. This striking intrusion of the official liturgical language may be an imitation of the treatment of the invitatory (Psalm 94), where pairs of psalm verses are punctuated with the beginning of the Ave Maria.[21] As in many of her works, Christine used the first person for her prayers. In this way she mediated her readers' prayers to the Virgin (Gros, 101), but also made it possible for a reader to appropriate her words.

The *Oroison Nostre Dame* comprises eighteen douzains, most beginning with an invocation to the Virgin and ending with a petition. The opening stanza of the poem is a virtual paraphrase of the beginning of the Marian prayer "O Intemerata": "O immaculate virgin, blessed for eternity, unique and without equal, virgin Mother of God, Mary temple of God, most full of grace . . . ."[22] This is the most learned of Christine's prayers, with all but two stanzas containing references to Church Fathers: Bernard (ll.11, 26, 99, 135, 159, 171), Jerome (ll.39, 87, 111, 195), Augustine (ll.51, 75), Ambrose (l.62), Cassiodorus (l.123), and Anselm (ll.147, 208). What begins as "ma priere" (l.5) widens to "nous" in the second stanza and again at the end (ll.23, 216). Although she began by praying for "toute crestienté" (l.9), it is clear by the middle of the poem (l.140) that her chief concern was for her adopted kingdom of France, and she prayed for it to be delivered from torment (l.156). The objects of Christine's prayer are organized hierarchically: naming the Church in the second stanza and prelates in the third, she then catalogued the various levels of French society, from the king (stanza 4) and the extended royal family (stanzas 5–11), the kingdom of the French (stanza 12), including knights (stanza 13), clergy and bourgeois (stanza 14), laborers (stanza 15), those who have died (stanza 16), "le devot sexe des femmes" (stanza 17), before ending with a petition for herself and her friends. In her careful adaptation of the petition to the circumstances of the party named, Gros has observed the lucidity of a moralist unafraid of pointing out failings and weaknesses (103).

The *Quinze joyes Nostre Dame* is a brief verse prayer of sixteen decasyllabic quatrains, one for each joy after the introductory stanza. Christine's source was certainly the prose prayer (*Douce dame de misericorde*) commonly copied in Books of Hours, for she followed very closely both its form (the prayer is punctuated by the phrase "Ave Maria gratia plena" after each joy) and its sequence of joys.[23] In versifying the prayer, Christine produced a poem of extraordinary concision and stylistic variation, and gave the intrusive Latin prayer a formal function in her poem by using it as a refrain for each stanza. The departures from the source were the result of deliberate choices. Instead of the Passion, named as the eleventh "joy" in the prose prayer,[24] Christine evoked Christ's resurrection (ll.45–8). Because her source used this event as the twelfth joy, she changed the emphasis in her next stanza from the resurrection to Mary's joy at seeing her risen Son ("la joye plainiere/Qu'a Pasques eus quant ton filz t'apparu/Ressuscité . . . ," ll.48–51). A mother herself, Christine clearly found it impossible to imagine the Virgin considering her Son's crucifixion as joyful, and compensated by dividing the undeniable joy of resurrection into two stages. Christine's treatment of the petitions is also interesting. Where the prose prayer in the Hours consistently asks the Virgin's intercession with her Son for a spiritual gift—to find Christ in tribulation, to be moved or illumined by Him—Christine addressed herself directly to the Virgin requesting her pity (l.13), help (ll.18, 37), comfort (l.33), and protection (ll.21, 28, 31, 31). She ended with a prayer that the root of sin be removed and replaced by redemption (ll.63–4)—a request that many of her countrymen would have found completely appropriate for Queen Isabeau, who would have read it in her copy of Christine's works.

The *Oroison Nostre Seigneur* is another series of quatrains each devoted to a single event, but it is more than three times as long as the *Joyes*, and its recurring Latin refrain prayer is the *Pater Noster*. The *Oroison* is a meditative prayer, an act of recollection that requests fervor, forgiveness, and salvation by recalling to Christ the stages of His act of redemption. In retracing the entire life of Christ, from the Incarnation to Pentecost, some incidents (e.g., Annunciation, Nativity, Pentecost) are repeated from the *Joyes*, but the focus of each scene has shifted from the mother to her Son. The central and longest section of the prayer (vv.49–216) is an affective meditation on the Passion that deliberately engages the emotions of the person praying by dwelling on the physical suffering.[25] The passage of time is drastically slowed in the Passion section, a feature emphasized by allusions to the canonical hours of Matins, Terce, None, Vespers, and Compline (vv.61, 110, 185, 206, 214). Incomplete as they are, the references are nonetheless sufficient to evoke an office such as the Hours of the Cross, and they would also encourage the reader to associate the Passion with the daily ringing of the bells.

THE *SEPT PSAUMES ALLEGORISÉS*

Christine's *Sept psaumes*, written for Charles III (the Noble) King of Navarre, begins abruptly after a rubric announcing the title, but not the author, of the work.[26] There is no prologue to introduce or dedicate the work, and it is only at the end of the seventh Psalm that Charles is identified. Christine's discretion enabled other readers to appropriate to themselves the psalmist's words and her meditations upon them. This wider audience is made explicit in the final paragraph: "tous ceux et celles qui par devocion la diront ou orront" (152) (all those who with devotion say it or hear it).

In Christine's treatment each verse is translated, then supplied with a meditative paragraph that echoes the language of the psalm. The first part either restates or responds to the psalm verse, and the remainder of the paragraph is a petition. By interweaving psalm and meditation, Christine inscribed into her text the kind of meditative prayer associated with the monastic practice of the divine office, where psalmody provided the basis for personal meditation.[27]

The first three psalms are treated fairly briefly, and each petition is a prayer for forgiveness. The treatment of the last four psalms is more complex because each verse is paired with a series of other references. Psalm 50 is the pivot of the composition, and its opening verse announces the new organization. This meditation asks for pardon, but goes on to beg the grace to avoid sin, to govern the senses, to obey the commandments, to believe the articles of faith, and to receive the gifts of the Holy Ghost. In the succeeding verses, the articles of the Athanasian Creed serve as invocations to God and are paired with the seven deadly sins and their contrary virtues, and with a formula for confession according to the senses.

The final three psalms are unified by systematic recollection of the events of the life of Christ, and by a hierarchical set of prayers for the kingdom of France. Psalm 101 (which contains the events from the Annunciation to the Carrying of the Cross) names the first three Hours, and also lists the Ten Commandments and the Gifts of the Holy Ghost before praying for the upper strata of the kingdom in the order of the Seven Corporal Works of Mercy. In this psalm and the next Christine named the king and queen, the University of Paris, the nobility, the royal officers, bourgeois, merchants, farm workers, and serfs in a hierarchal set of prayers that recalls the *Oroison Nostre Dame*. Psalm 129 meditates on the Crucifixion and on four of the last words, while praying for the lower orders of French society. Psalm 142 evokes the rest of the Passion through the Hours of None, Vespers, and Compline before concluding with Pentecost. The prayers accompanying this Psalm are the most general, but paradoxically they are also the most personal. In praying for all Christians as well as for the unconverted, Christine prayed for herself along with the old, and those in trouble; remembering the sick, she prayed for health, and finally asked that her enemies might be converted into friends. In keeping with the treatment of the Penitential Psalms in Books of Hours, Christine ended her composition with a French version of the Litany of the Saints, in which a long list of Apostles, Martyrs, Confessors, and Virgins were asked for prayers, implicitly reinforcing the petitions that accompany the psalm verses.

The diverse elements of the Christian religion—articles of faith, lists of sins and virtues, the Commandments, and the life of Christ—are thus skillfully blended into a complicated tapestry that unites the four final Psalms. However abstruse the numerical lists may seem to modern readers, for medieval Christians they were the stuff of daily life.[28] Christine's innovation was to turn a review of the basic elements of religion into an impetus for a series of prayers that embraced the entire social structure of the French kingdom, even as it reflected on the humanity of God.

EPISTRE DE LA PRISON DE VIE HUMAINE

The *Epistre de la prison de vie humaine* was written between 1416 and 1418 at the request of an unknown (presumably deceased) patron, and was finally dedicated to Marie de Berry the duchess of Bourbon and daughter of the Duke of Berry. It is not always considered with the religious works: with its inclusions of pagan and secular sources as well as patristic ones, it has been seen as humanist rather than religious in inspiration.[29] Nevertheless, Christine's purpose in writing her epistle was to inculcate the virtue of humble patience as a consolation for loss and a remedy for excessive sorrow. Although Marie is the primary *destinataire* of the *Epistre*, Christine envisaged a wider audience of all those who have suffered losses similar to Marie's, for her prologue mentions "queens, princesses, baronesses, ladies and young girls of the noble royal blood of France, and in general most of the ladies-in-waiting who have been stricken by this pestilence in this French kingdom" (2–3).

The *Epistre* is divided into thirteen chapters, including a prologue explaining the metaphor of the prison and a conclusion. The body of the letter presents five reasons to cultivate patience in the face of the death of loved ones: (1) that they died honorably; (2) the dead are freed from the troubles and perils of earthly life (Chapter 3); (3) all men are mortal (Chapter 4); (4) that everyone has sources of comfort that should be cultivated (Chapter 7); and finally, (5) that those who have died well are rewarded (Chapter 9). The nature of that reward is described in Chapters 10 to 12, which celebrate the joys of Paradise. Chapters 5 and 6 interrupt the sequence of reasons to give a detailed analysis of patience and its opposite. The early sections of the letter, with a preponderance of classical examples, are almost stoic in their emphasis, whereas almost all of the citations in the final chapters are scriptural or patristic. Perhaps the most interesting chapter is the eighth, in which Christine addressed Marie directly, reminding her of the consolation she can find in her family. She used the interrogative form insistently: "Aprés ces choses, les biens de fortune dont tu as largement, sont-ilz a oublier? Et de quoy te plains? N'es-tu de haulx parens . . . ?" (42) (After these things, should the gifts of fortune, of which you have a great amount, be forgotten? Are you complaining? Are you not of great lineage . . . ?) The effect of these repeated questions is to shake Marie out of the lethargy of her sorrow, before urging her to consider the plight of those less fortunate than herself.

The purpose of the *Epistre* is firmly therapeutic; Christine recommended patience and hope in God as a "remede" and a "medicine" (2, 22, 24) against the sickness and infirmity of excessive sorrow. Patience is a "treasure" and the "fountain of virtues" (30). But Christine also developed a thread of military images, which would have resonated with her audience. She presented human life not only as a prison (6, 10, 16), but as a battle (24) that must be fought by knights (30). In this context, patience is also a shield (24). In the final chapter, she concluded with the reminder that Marie's beloved dead would profit more from alms, prayers, and good works than they would from tears, thus implicitly encouraging such practices as offering masses for the dead and reciting the Office of the Dead.

At the end of the work, in explaining the delay in completing it, Christine referred to the "grans ennuis et troubles de courage" (66–7) (the great worries and troubles of courage) that overwhelmed her and impeded her writing. Although we have no indication of the nature of these troubles, Christine must have suffered personally some of the distresses for which she offered comfort. She thus identified herself with her audience, sharing a composition that may have formed part of her own recuperation.

HEURES DE CONTEMPLACION

Christine returned to the themes of loss and consolation when she composed the *Heures de contemplacion sur la Passion* at some point between 1418 and 1429—perhaps after the death of her son in 1425.[30] In contrast to the humanist tone of the *Epistre*, this work is an affective meditation on Christ's Passion, divided into sections according to the monastic hours. The text, which survives in two manuscripts, was not dedicated to a patron, but the Paris manuscript bears a rubric addressing "des dames et damoiselles et generalement de toutes femmes adoulees" (the ladies and young ladies and generally all sorrowing women). The opening section is an epistolary address to her audience, "toutes du femenin sexe" (all of the feminine sex) who have suffered from the tribulations caused by the War with England. Referring to earlier work in the same vein (apparently the *Epistre*), she developed her therapeutic image and presents the *Heures* as "suppelative medecine" (superlative medicine) and offers "la recept du precieux beuvraige" (the recipe for the precious draft) that will benefit both body and soul. The work is a "fountain" (f. 114B) for those in need of patience. By following the course of meditation, Christine's audience would gain the bodily comfort of patience, and also earn spiritual merit from compassion for the sufferings of Christ. Thus the *Heures* are at once a continuation of, and a response to, the *Epistre*. Having observed that prayers are more useful than tears to the deceased (*Epistre*, 66), she provided an act of prayer in her later work. She acted on her earlier advice that sorrowing women console themselves by thinking of Christ's suffering (*Epistre*, 24) by seeking consolation for herself and for her readers in an extended meditation on the Passion.

In addition to ordering her meditation according to the hours of an office, Christine marked each section with a "verset" and quoted the phrase "Deus in adjutorium" or its French equivalent, from Psalm 69 (ff. 116B, 122B, 125C, etc.). Beginning with the events of Holy Thursday for Compline, the text continues through Matins, Prime, Terce, Sexte ('Midi'), None, and Vespers to end with Christ's burial on the evening of Good Friday in a second Compline. Despite its form, the source of the *Heures* is not an office from a Book of Hours, but rather seems to depend on the *Meditatio passionis Christi per septem diei horas* of Pseudo-Bede, a devotional meditation on the passion probably composed in the early fourteenth century.[31]

After the prologue, Christine turned away from her audience to recreate through memory and imagination the events of the Passion. Not content with a simple recollection, she projected herself into the scenes she created, as a witness or even as a participant. For example, in recounting Christ's withdrawal with Peter, James, and John to the Mount of Olives, she prays: "O mon Seigneur, plaise toy que je soie le quart disciple monté en esperit avec toy!" (O my Lord, may it please you for me to be the fourth disciple, raised up in spirit with you).

She spoke in her own voice and addressed herself passionately to the apostles, to Christ, to the Virgin.

Only when she has evoked the Virgin's sorrow at the death of her Son does Christine break this inward concentration to address her audience: "Dames contemplatives et entre vous du devost sexe des femmes" (f. 135D) (Contemplative ladies and those of you of the devout sex of women). She invites them to pity the Virgin's pain and to pray to share it. Through this exercise, the sorrow for their own losses may be transformed into compassion for the suffering savior that will lead to their union with Him.[32]

CONCLUSION

Not surprisingly, some of the salient characteristics of Christine's other writings are also found in her religious works. As elsewhere in her *oeuvre* she showed a concern for the fate of women, discernible in the special mentions in the *Oroison Nostre Dame* and the *Sept psaumes*, as well as in the addresses to her audience of sorrowful ladies in the *Epistre* and the *Heures de contemplacion*. Similarly her adoptive country, the "royaume de France," which was a central concern of many of her works, is the object of her prayers from the *Oroison* to the *Heures*. Although the *Heures de contemplacion* is her fullest expression of the meditation according to the Hours, both the *Oroison Nostre Seigneur* and the *Sept psaumes* attest to this interest earlier in her career.

Although Christine articulated each of her religious works through the first-person "I," the status of the speaking subject changed from one to the next. In the early *Oroisons*, she provided words for the Duke of Berry, Queen Isabeau, and her other readers. In the epilogue to the *Sept psaumes*, the author identified herself as "moy pecharesse qui l'ay compilee" (me, the sinner who has compiled it), and requested prayers at her own death. Her attention turned less toward her patron or audience than toward the whole kingdom, for which she prayed and perhaps represented in her prayers for forgiveness. Still speaking in the first person in the *Heures*, Christine turned away from her intended female audience to recount the narrative of the Passion in the second-person singular, addressing herself to Christ and the Virgin. Despite the shift of focus, the effect of this strategy was to identify Christine more closely with her audience: no longer its intermediary, she became its representative.

In all of her religious works Christine worked with known materials—the essential elements of Catholic doctrine, lists of virtues and vices, gifts of the Holy Spirit, works of mercy, the words of the psalter, the meditative program of the Book of Hours. What she brought to each work was an originality of form and treatment, a new combination of elements, and a particular refinement or vigor of expression. When coming to Christine's compositions after reading similar works, the attentive reader is struck more by the innovations she made than by the similarities to her predecessors. In each of these works we meet an artist at prayer.

NOTES

1. Gérard Gros, " 'Mon oroison entens . . . ' Etude sur les trois opuscules pieux de Christine de Pizan," *Bien dire et bien aprandre. Revue de médiévistique*, 8 (1990): 99–112 (104). Nadia Margolis, "La Progression polémique, spirituelle et personnelle dans les écrits religieux de Christine de Pizan" and Charity Cannon Willard, "Christine de Pizan's Allegorized Psalms," in *Une femme de lettres au Moyen Age. Etudes autour de Christine de Pizan*, ed. Liliane Dulac and Bernard Ribémont (Orléans: Paradigme, 1995), 297–316 and 317–324; Liliane Dulac, "Littérature et dévotion: à propos des *Heures de Contemplacion sur la passion de Nostre Seigneur* de Christine de Pizan," in *Miscellanea Mediaevalia. Mélanges offerts à Philippe Ménard*, ed. Jean-Claude Faucon (Paris: Champion, 1998) t. I, 475–84; Lori Walters, "The Royal Vernacular: Poet and Patron in *Charles V* and the *Sept Psaumes allégorisées*," in *The Vernacular Spirit*, ed. Renate Blumenfeld-Kosinski, Nancy Warren, and Duncan Robertson (NY: Palgrave, 2002) 145–182.
2. Thomas H. Bestul, *Texts of the Passion. Latin Devotional Literature and Medieval Society* (Philadelphia: University of Pennsylvania Press, 1996), 34–6. For works in French, see my "La Passion pour la passion: les textes en moyen français," *La Recherche: Bilan et Perspectives. Le Moyen Français* 44–45 (2000): 45–62.
3. J. Leclercq et al., *The Spirituality of the Middle Ages* (New York: Seabury, 1968), 481–505; *Prier au Moyen Age. Pratiques et Expériences (V^e–XVe siècles)*, ed. Nicole Bériou, Jacques Berlioz, and Jean Longère (Paris: Brepols, 1991), especially 34–41, 201–25.
4. For a general introduction, see R. N. Swanson, *Religion and Devotion in Europe, c. 1215–1515* (Cambridge: Cambridge University Press, 1995), especially 92–135; Edmond-René Labande, *Spiritualité et vie littéraire de l'Occident Xe-XIVe siècles* (London: Variorum Reprints, 1974), 145–64, 172–79. In medieval writing on this subject, meditation refers to an activity of mind that may be undertaken by anyone, whereas contemplation refers to the state of mystical union with God that may result from meditation.
5. The pioneering work of Geneviève Hasenohr is the exception, and essential to any study of religious literature in late medieval France: "Aperçu sur la diffusion et la réception de la littérature de spiritualité en langue française au dernier siècle du Moyen Age," in *Wissensorganisierende u. wissensvermittelnde Literatur im Mittelalter*, ed. Norbert Richard Wolf (Wiesbaden: Reichert, 1987), 57–90; "La littérature religieuse," *La littérature française aux XIVe et XVe siècles. GRLMA* VIII.1 (Heidelberg: Winter, 1988): 266–305; "Place et rôle des traductions dans la pastorale française du XVe siècle," Geneviève Contamine, ed., *Traduction et traducteurs au Moyen Age* (Paris: Editions du CNRS, 1989), 265–75; "Aspects de la littérature de spiritualité en langue française (1480–1520)," *Revue de l'histoire de l'église de France* 77 (1991): 29–45; "Religious Reading Amongst the Laity in

France in the Fifteenth Century," in *Heresy and Literacy 1000–1530*, ed. Peter Biller and Anne Hudson, Cambridge Studies in Medieval Literature 23 (Cambridge: Cambridge University Press, 1994), 205–21.
6. "L'Oroyson Nostre Dame," "Les XV Joyes Nostre Dame," "Une Oroyson de Nostre Seigneur," in *Oeuvres poétiques de Christine de Pisan*, vol. 3, ed. Maurice Roy (SATF; Paris: Firmin Didot, 1896), 1–26; ii–iii (on date).
7. *Le Livre des fais et bonnes meurs du sage roy Charles V*, ed. S. Solente (Paris: Société de l'Histoire de France, 1936–40), especially I.15–16, 33–34; III.71.
8. *Le Livre du corps de policie*, ed. Robert H. Lucas, Textes littéraires français 145 (Geneva: Droz, 1967), I. Chapters 7–8.
9. See Earl Jeffrey Richards, trans., Christine de Pizan. *The Book of the City of Ladies* (New York: Persea, 1982), 369.
10. Ibid., pp. 121–122, 194, 209, 218–219. On other guides for women, see Geneviève Hasenohr, "La vie quotidienne de la femme vue par l'Eglise" in *Frau und spätmittelalterlicher Alltag. Sitzungsberichte der Österreichischen Akademie der Wissenschaften*, phil.-hist. Klasse, 473 (1986): 19–101.
11. Eric Hicks and Charity Cannon Willard, *Christine de Pizan. Le Livre des Trois Vertus. Edition critique* (Paris: Champion, 1989), I.6: "car il sent ja et gouste des gloires et joyes de Paradis, c'est assavoir il voit Dieu en esperit par contemplacion" (23).
12. *La Librairie de Charles V* (Paris: Bibliothèque Nationale, 1968), Nos. 126, 129, 133, 171, 174, 175. For the Duke of Berry's copies, see Millard Meiss, *French Painting in the Time of Jean de Berry. The Late Fourteenth Century and the Patronage of the Duke* (London: Phaidon, 1967; 2nd ed. 1969), 309–17: the Belles Heures; Grandes Heures, Très Belles Heures, Petites Heures, Arsenal, 650. A. Vallet de Viriville, "La Bibliothèque d'Isabeau de Bavière, reine de France," *Bulletin du bibliophile*, 14 (1858): 663–87 (669–72).
13. V. Leroquais, *Les Livres d'heures manuscrits de la Bibliothèque nationale*, 2 vols. (Paris: Protat, 1927), 1, xiv–xxxii; Roger S. Wieck, *Time Sanctified. The Book of Hours in Medieval Art and Life* (London: Sotheby's, 1988), 157–67.
14. Eric Inglis, *The Hours of Mary of Burgundy. Codex Vindobonensis 1857, Vienna, Österreichische Nationalbibliothek* (London: Harvey Miller, 1995), 20.
15. French versions of the Penitential Psalms occur in several manuscripts: for details see Keith V. Sinclair, *French Devotional Texts of the Middle Ages. A Bibliographic Manuscript Guide* (Westport, CT: Greenwood Press, 1979, 1982, 1988), Index.
16. Roger S. Wieck, *Painted Prayers. The Book of Hours in Medieval and Renaissance Art* (New York: Braziller, 1997), 117–18.
17. Leroquais, 2, 310–11.
18. For French versions of the Office in prose and verse, see Sinclair, *French Devotional Texts*, Index.
19. For editions and bibliography on these works, see Bestul, *Latin Passion Narratives*, 186–92.
20. On these different collections, see James Laidlaw, "Christine de Pizan—An Author's Progress," *MLR* 78 (1983): 432–50; and "Christine de Pizan—A Pub-

lisher's Progress," *MLR* 82 (1987): 35–75, especially 68–75 for details of the contents. The *Oroyson de Nostre Seigneur* is the first of the additional works in L¹ (Chantilly, Musée Condé, 492–93), but is not found in L² (Paris, BnF, f.fr. 12779). In A² (London, Brit. Libr., Harley 4431), it precedes the other two prayers and bears a slightly different title ("Une oraison de la Vie et Passion de Nostre Seigneur").

21. Although not mentioned by Leroquais or Wieck, the invitatory is treated in this way in the modern Breviary, as well as in three fifteenth-century manuscripts that I have consulted: Vienne, ÖNB, 1857, ff. 57v–58r ("Ave Maria gracia plena dominus tecum" occurs after vv.2, 4, 7, 9, 11); Notre Dame, IN, University of Notre Dame Libr., MS. 4, ff. 50r ("Ave Maria" alternates with "dominus tecum"); University of Notre Dame, MS. 35, f. 34v ("Ave Maria gratia plena dominus tecum" or "dominus tecum").

22. *Hours of Mary of Burgundy*: "O intemerata et in eternum benedicta/singularis atque incomparabilis virgo dei genitrix Maria gratissimi dei templum . . ." (f. 24ʳ⁻ᵛ).

23. Although there were earlier verse treatments of the theme, they are significantly longer and present a different sequence of events and petitions; for other Joys of the Virgin, see Ruth J. Dean and Maureen Boulton, *Anglo-Norman Literature. A Guide to Texts and Manuscripts*, Occasional Publications 3 (London: Anglo-Norman Text Society, 1999), Nos. 740–767.

24. "[Q]uant votre doux fils souffrit mort et passion pour nous racheter": A. Wilmart, "Les Quinze Joies de Notre-Dame," *Vie et les arts liturgiques* 9 (1922): 302–7; for versions from other manuscripts, see Leroquais, *Les Livres d'heures*, II, 310–11; and Herman Suchier, "Les XV Joies Nostre Dame," *Zeitschrift für romanische Philologie* 17 (1893): 282–85. Cf. the list given by Wieck, *Time Sanctified*, 103.

25. Some of the graphic details of the crucifixion (e.g., stretching Christ's arms and legs to reach the holes for the nails, ll.125–36) probably come from the Passion section of Ludolphus of Saxony's *Vita Christi*. Ludolphus de Saxonia, *Vita Jesu Christi ex evangelio . . .*, ed. L.-M. Rigollot, 4 vols. (Paris: Victor Palme and Rome: Congregation of the Propagation of the Faith, 1870), especially, vol. 4, Chapter lxiii, p. 566.

26. Ruth Ringland Rains, *Les sept psaumes allégorisés of Christine de Pisan. A Critical Edition from the Brussels and Paris Manuscripts* (Washington, DC: Catholic University of America Press, 1965). Only two manuscripts were known to the editor, but Charity Cannon Willard has drawn attention to a third (Brussels, Bibl. Roy., IV. 1093): "Christine de Pizan's Allegorized Psalms," 324 n. 14.

27. Jean Leclercq, *Aux Sources de la spiritualité occidentale. Etapes et constantes* (Paris: Cerf, 1963), especially 285–303, "Culte liturgique et prière intime dans le monachisme au moyen âge."

28. All of these items were included by Jean Gerson in his "A.B.C. des simples gens," in *Jean Gerson. Oeuvres Complètes*, vol. 7 *L'Oeuvre française*, ed. P. Glorieux (Paris: Desclée, 1966), 154–57.

29. Willard, *Christine de Pizan. Her Life and Works* (New York: Persea, 1984), 203. On the sources, in addition to the edition by Josette A. Wisman, *Christine de*

Pizan. *The Epistle of the Prison of Human Life*, Garland Library of Medieval Literature, 21A (New York: Garland, 1984), see also S. Solente, "Un traité inédit de Christine de Pisan. *L'Epistre de la prison de vie humaine*," *Bibliothèque de l'école des chartes* 85 (1924): 263–301.

30. Willard, *Christine de* Pizan, 202–3. I am enormously grateful to Mme Liliane Dulac for her generosity in allowing me to use the unpublished text of her forthcoming edition of this work.

31. See Maureen Boulton, "Christine's *Heures de la Contemplacion de la Passion* in the Context of Late Medieval Passion Devotion," in *Contexts and Continuities: Proceedings of the IV International Colloquium on Christine de Pizan (Glasgow 21–27 July, 2000)*, ed. Angus J. Kennedy in collaboration with Rosalind Brown-Grant, James C. Laidlaw, and Catherine Muller, and published in honour of Liliane Dulac (Glasgow: University Press, 2002), 3 vols., vol. 1, 99–113.

32. See Leclercq, *The Spirituality of the Middle Ages*, 440–43; cf. Gerson's works on contemplation written in French for his sisters: "La Montaigne de Contemplation," "Mendicité Spirituelle," edited in Glorieux, *Jean Gerson*, 16–55, 220–80.

IV
Christine's Books

15

Christine and the Manuscript Tradition

James Laidlaw

Christine de Pizan's works are extant in some 200 manuscripts, nearly all copied in Northern France and the Low Countries during the fifteenth or early sixteenth centuries.[1] Fifty of these manuscripts were produced in Paris between 1399 and 1418 by the author's "scriptorium," the group of scribes and artists whom Christine engaged to make copies of her works. This chapter will center on these "autograph manuscripts" or "presentation copies," as they are generally known; a complete list of them will be found in the Appendix.

The remaining manuscripts, some 150, date from after 1418 when Christine fled from Paris, following the Burgundian invasion. Although these later copies have generally attracted less attention from specialists, they provide evidence of the continuing interest that the reading public took in her writings. This interest was selective, however, reflecting tastes very different from those of today. The texts most popular with later readers were educational works such as the *Epistre Othea* and the *Enseignemens moraux*, both directed primarily at young men, and the *Livre des trois vertus*, written to instruct women in their duties and responsibilities. The *Livre de la cité des dames*, celebrating women's achievements down the ages, was also widely read, as was the *Livre des fais d'armes et de chevalerie*, a treatise on warfare. Other works seem to have been quickly forgotten: Christine's poetry was rarely copied in the years after her death, and prose works such as the *Livre de l'advision Cristine* or the *Livre de la paix* attracted little attention.

THE AUTOGRAPH MANUSCRIPTS

The fifty manuscripts so far identified as autographs are linked by three features—contents, decoration, and scribal hands—which show them to be the products of Christine's scriptorium. Forty-four contain a single work by her; only six contain a collection. In all these manuscripts the focus is on Christine, works by other writers being almost entirely absent; the only exceptions are BnF, f.fr. 580,[2] a miscellany that includes the *Epistre a la reine Isabeau*,[3] and the collections of Christine's works, almost all of which contain the *Epistres du debat sur le "Roman de la Rose,"* and thus two short letters by Gontier Col that set Christine's contributions to the debate in a wider context.[4]

Each of these manuscripts, whether it contains a collection or a single work, was planned by Christine with a particular patron in mind. Some copies were commissioned and some were offered as gifts. In return Christine hoped to receive payment, perhaps a sum of money, perhaps a piece of plate: the accounts of Philip the Bold and John the Fearless, Dukes of Burgundy, give details of such payments to her.[5]

Before the extant presentation copies are examined in more detail, reference must be made to those that have been lost. Just how many we will never know. There are references in the *Advision* to copies made for foreign princes; Christine highlights the books she sent to England on two occasions, first the many *livres et dictiez* (books and poems) she gave to the Earl of Salisbury who had found a place in his household for Christine's son, Jehan de Castel, and then the books she presented to Henry IV of England to help secure Jehan's return to France;[6] none of these copies is known to exist today. Library catalogues are another source of information about volumes that have disappeared, for example, the copies of the *Epistre Othea* and the *Livre des fais et bonnes meurs du sage roi Charles V*, which Christine presented to the Duke of Berry; both were last recorded in the inventory of the Duke's effects made in 1416.[7] Again, there is the large collection of Christine's poetical works that formed part of the Burgundian library until at least 1731, but has not been heard of since.[8] Although we may lament the loss of so many presentation copies, it is fortunate that as many as fifty have survived. They greatly outnumber the surviving presentation copies of the works of Christine's contemporaries, such as Machaut, Froissart, Deschamps, Mézières, or Chartier; none of them combined the roles of writer and publisher in the way that Christine did.

THE IMPORTANCE OF THE AUTOGRAPH MANUSCRIPTS

Christine's autograph manuscripts make up a unique linguistic corpus. The texts they contain are authoritative, corrected by the writer herself. The vocabulary is extremely rich, reflecting the breadth of Christine's reading and the unusually wide range of subjects that she treats. Her works therefore provide an exceptional resource for the study of early fifteenth-century French.[9]

Authors do not change: like her counterparts in any age, Christine knew the tyranny of the deadline and was never entirely satisfied with anything she had written. Her writings evolve: as new presentation copies were prepared, she took the opportunity to amend her works, sometimes adding new thoughts, sometimes finding a more felicitous form of words. And so we must distinguish between different editions of her lyric poetry, of the *Epistre Othea*, and the *Mutacion de Fortune*, to give only three examples.[10]

Christine lived and worked in Paris at a time of exceptional activity and creativity in the book trade. In the earliest years of her publishing career her financial resources were limited. As she made her name, she could afford to be more ambitious, to employ artists of higher quality, to move "up-market." It is therefore important to appreciate the extent to which Christine's skills and resources as author and publisher develop and increase between 1399 and 1418. In sum, her autograph manuscripts are extremely significant, from whichever point of view we approach them, whether as linguists, literary scholars, art historians, or codicologists.

CHRISTINE'S PUBLISHING CAREER

The earliest works of Christine de Pizan that can be dated are a ballade written in 1395 or 1396 and a rondeau composed two years later.[11] By 1398 her poetry had become sufficiently well known for it to attract the attention of the Earl of Salisbury who had come to Paris to negotiate payment of the dowry of the Princess Isabelle who had married Richard II of England two years before. Christine describes her encounter with him in the *Advision*:

> Environ ce temps, comme la fille du roy de France fust mariee au roy Richart d'Engleterre, vint par de ça a celle cause ung noble conte dit de Salsbery. Et comme icellui gracieux chevalier amast dictiez et lui meismes fust gracieux dicteur, aprés ce qu'il ot veu des miens dictiez, tant me fist prier par plusieurs grans que je consenti . . . que l'ainsné de mes filz . . . alast avec lui oudit païs d'Engleterre. . . . [12] (112)

(About this time, since the daughter of the King of France had been married to King Richard of England, a noble earl named Salisbury came over to France on that account. And since that gracious knight loved poetry and was himself a graceful poet, after he had seen some of my poems, he besought me with so many gifts and promises that I agreed . . . that my eldest son . . . should go with him to the said country of England. . . .)

The fact that Salisbury had *seen* pieces of Christine's verse is a clear indication that her works were circulating in manuscript in 1398. None of these early copies is known to survive.

The oldest extant copies of Christine's works date from the years 1399 to 1403. A copy of the *Epistre Othea*, now BnF, f.fr. 848, was completed about 1400, and may very well be the volume that Christine presented to the Duke of Orléans.[13] The work is made up of a Prologue and 100 Texts, each accompanied by a Gloss and an Allegory. The layout in MS 848 is modeled on the biblical and theological manuscripts of the period: the scribe transcribed each Text in the center of the page, and used a smaller hand to copy the associated Gloss and Allegory in columns that frame the Text. However, the Glosses and Allegories vary so much in length that it proved impossible to present them in regularly shaped columns. MS 848 contains other examples of inexperience or poor planning. The work is illustrated by six neat miniatures in grisaille.[14] The first (f. 1r) precedes the Prologue and shows Christine kneeling to present her book to the Duke of Orleans. The other five, which take Texts 1–5 as their subjects, are not positioned to best advantage. Those that illustrate Texts 1 and 2 show Othea presenting a book to the young Hector, and *Attemprance* (Temperance) examining a clock; they are juxtaposed above the first line of Text 1 (f. 2r). The miniatures depicting Texts 3–4 (f. 2v) are also set side by side above part of Text 1, but have been transposed: King Amos dispensing justice (Text 4) is on the left; Hercules, representing force (Text 3) is on the right. The final miniature that presents Text 5 (f. 3r) is positioned above part of Texts 1 and 2. The very few ornamented initials and borders are positioned in the first four folios of the manuscript: thus, all the significant decoration is concentrated at the beginning of the work.

The preparation of copies of Christine's narrative poems, some of her earliest works, proved to be a more straightforward operation. Two autograph manuscripts of the *Debat de deux amans* (BnF, f.fr. 1740 and BR[15] 11034) date from the years 1399–1404; in both manuscripts the poem is introduced by a relatively unsophisticated miniature in grisaille. The Brussels manuscript, made for the Sire d'Albret, is the more elaborate: the opening line of verse is highlighted by an introductory "champie" initial and a short border composed of "vignettes";[16] the text is punctuated by four smaller, intermediate champie initials.[17] In the Paris copy the initials are less elaborate: the introductory and intermediate initials are in plain colors, set off with flourished penwork. An unillustrated copy of the *Dit de la pastoure* (BnF, f.fr. 2184) may have been completed soon after the poem itself was composed in May 1403.

The first collection of Christine's works, the *Livre de Cristine* (Christine's Book), survives in two copies, BnF, f.fr. 12779 and Chantilly, Musée Condé 492–493. Because of the table of contents in the Chantilly MS we know when the *Livre* was begun and completed: "Cy commencent les rebriches de la table de ce present volume, fait et compilé par Cristine de Pizan, demoiselle. Commencié l'an de grace mil.ccc.iiij^{xx}.xix. Eschevé et escript en l'an mil.Quatrecens et deux, la veille la nativité Saint Jehan Baptiste"[18] (Here begin the rubrics of the table of contents of this present volume, made and compiled by Christine de Pizan, a noble lady. Begun in the year of grace 1399 [o.s.].[19] Completed and copied in the year 1402, on the eve of the nativity of St. John the Baptist [23 June]). Both copies of the *Livre* were subsequently enlarged under Christine's direction. The *Dit de la pastoure*, composed in May 1403, is the first of five works, dating from 1403 to 1405, that were added to the Chantilly MS. By contrast the Paris MS contains only one additional work, the *Dit de la pastoure*.[20] The catalogue of the library at Blois made for Charles d'Orléans in May 1417 lists a copy of the *Livre de Cristine* made for Valentina, Duchess of Orléans, who died in 1408, but there is no way of telling if either of the surviving copies once belonged to her.[21]

In their original state, the two manuscripts were virtually identical in format and decoration. Each was made up of three sections: lyric poetry, narrative verse, and moralizing and didactic works, making a total of nineteen items. The layout in double columns is well proportioned, and the texts have been neatly and carefully copied. The collection is illustrated by twelve small colored miniatures that are competent rather than distinguished;[22] the flourished introductory and intermediate initials are similar in style to those in MS 1740, the less elaborate copy of the *Debat de deux amans* discussed earlier.[23] The layout of the *Epistre Othea* shows that Christine had learned by experience: the six miniatures have the same subjects as in MS 848, but they are now in the correct order and each one precedes the Text it illustrates; the presentation has been much improved, for the Glosses and Allegories now follow the Texts to which they relate. In sum, the two surviving copies of the *Livre* are well presented, stylish rather than luxurious; they show Christine using a limited budget to advantage.

In *French Painting in the Time of Jean de Berry* (1974), Millard Meiss examines the miniatures that illustrate the presentation copies of the *Epistre Othea*, the *Mutacion*, and the *Cité des dames*. His discussion of MS 848, the earliest known copy of the *Epistre Othea*, centers on the miniature that features *Attrempance* (Temperance) standing by a clock to which the text makes no reference. As Meiss points out, that inconsistency is remedied in the revised text of the *Epistre Othea*, which was included in the *Livre*. He explains what must have happened and, in so doing, paints Christine to the life:

> What, however, brought the clock into fr. 848? Certainly explicit instructions of Christine, who perhaps wrote this manuscript herself and certainly supervised its illustration. She formulated the analogy, in other words, after writing the text of fr. 848 but before she gave instructions to the illuminator. She incorporated the explanation of the new iconography in her text when, shortly afterward, she revised the *Epître*....[24]

Christine was an author who frequently changed her mind, had second thoughts, and recast her texts. Most importantly, she was under constant pressure, working to deadlines. It was inevitable that mistakes would occur.

In the *Advision*, written three years after the *Livre* was completed, Christine makes a second reference to the year 1399:

> Adonc me pris a forgier choses jolies, a mon commencement plus legieres, et tout ainsi comme l'ouvrier qui de plus en plus en son euvre se soubtille comme plus il la

frequente, ainsi tousjours estudiant diverses matieres, mon sens de plus en plus s'imbuoit de choses estranges, amendant mon stille en plus grant soubtilleté et plus haulte matiere, de | puis l'an mil .III^{c}IIII^{xx}. et .XIX. que je commençay jusques a cestui .IIII^c. et .V. ouquel encore je ne cesse, compillés en ce tendis .XV. volumes principaux, sans les autres particuliers petis dictiez, lesquelz tout ensemble contiennent environ .LXX. quaiers de grant volume, comme l'experience en est manifeste.[25] (111)

(And so I began to forge pretty things, lighter ones when I began, and just like the craftsman who becomes more and more subtle in his craft the more he practises it, so by always studying diverse subjects, my mind became more and more imbued with new and rare things, amending my style to make it more subtle and its subject-matter more lofty, from the year 1399 [o.s.], when I began, until this year 1405 [o.s.] when I have not stopped, fifteen principal works having been compiled in this space of time, not to mention the other separate small poems, which all together comprise about seventy quires of large format, as can be clearly seen.)

Christine sees 1405 (o.s.)[26] as a turning point: for her the previous six years have been a time of gradual change, when she moved from lighter subjects to the more demanding material that has become her chief concern. Her words are those of an experienced author and publisher who takes pride in the fifteen major works she has to her credit, plus a number of smaller items.

How are we to interpret the reference to the seventy quires of large format occupied by her collected works? Is Christine thinking of a collection in active preparation as she writes? Probably not: the Duke's and the Queen's MSS, the two largest collections extant, which both date from after 1405, contain only forty-seven and fifty-two quires, respectively. Could she be looking back to separate volumes produced in the previous six years and totaling the number of quires taken up by each individual work? Although that possibility cannot be excluded, it is more likely that Christine is referring to her "file-copies," her equivalent of the "livre ou je met toutes mes choses" (the book in which I put all my things), kept by Guillaume de Machaut, her illustrious predecessor.[27]

Between 1399 (o.s.) and 1405 (o.s.) Christine published a number of substantial works that are certainly included in the seventy quires to which she refers. The *Livre du chemin de long estude*, completed on 20 March 1403, is extant in the four separate presentation copies listed in the Appendix; the poem is also one of the additions made to the Chantilly copy of the *Livre*, and was included in the later Duke's and Queen's MSS. The frontispieces that introduce the four separate copies are almost certainly the first such examples commissioned by Christine.[28] The miniatures are, however, in grisaille, not in color as they had been in the *Livre*, and they cluster at the beginning of the poem in much the same way as the illustrations to the copies of the *Epistre Othea* discussed earlier. Christine's budget was still limited.

Christine and the Manuscript Tradition

By the end of 1403, however, when she completed the *Mutacion*, Christine's fortunes had improved sufficiently to allow her to commission copies of her new poem that are more elaborate than any of her previous productions. The frontispieces are more graceful, and the ornamented initials are of higher quality. Where some presentation copies of the *Chemin de long estude* have flourished initials in plain colors, the copies of the *Mutacion* make consistent use of champie initials, more elaborate and thus more costly. Christine could also afford to engage an artist who showed greater imagination and originality than any of the painters she had previously employed. This artist illustrated four manuscripts of the poem: BR 9508, the copy given to the Duke of Burgundy on 1 January 1404; The Hague, Koninklijke Bibliotheek 78 D 42, the Duke of Berry's copy presented to him in March 1404; Chantilly 494; and the ex-Phillipps MS, now in a private collection in Germany.[29]

Shortly after 1405 Christine entrusted the same artist with the more important task of illustrating a new collection of her works, which was acquired by the Duke of Berry in 1408 or early in 1409.[30] For this lavish volume Christine commissioned no less than 128 miniatures, and chose to highlight the *Epistre Othea*, which is illustrated by 101 miniatures.[31] For that reason Meiss gave the miniaturist the name of "Master of the *Epître d'Othéa*." Although the largest part of the illustrative program was entrusted to the *Epître* Master and his workshop, the Duke's MS also includes miniatures by the Saffron Master and by the Egerton Master or his workshop.[32]

The *Cité des dames*, completed between 1405 and 1406, contains the oft-quoted passage in which Christine celebrates the skills of Anastaise, a Parisian artist who specialized in painting decorative borders and the backgrounds for miniatures, and from whom she had commissioned *vignetes*:

> Mais a propos de ce que vous dites de femmes expertes en la science de painterie, je congnois aujourd'uy une femme que on appelle Anastaise qui tant est experte et apprise a faire vigneteures d'enlumineure en livres et champaignes d'istoires qu'il n'est mencion d'ouvrier en la ville de Paris ou sont les souverains du monde qui point l'en passe ne qui aussi doulcement face fleureteure et menu ouvrage qu'elle fait ne de qui on ait plus chier la besongne, tout soit le livre riche ou chier, que on a d'elle qui finer en peut. Et ce scay je par experience, car pour moy mesmes a ouvré d'aucunes choses qui sont tenues singulieres entre les vignetes des autres grans ouvriers.[33]

(But concerning what you say about women skilled in the art of painting, I know today a woman called Anastaise who is so expert and skilled in making illuminated vignette borders in books and miniature backgrounds that there is no craftsman known in Paris, where the very best in the world are to be found, who surpasses her or who does floral motifs and detailing as delicately as she does, or whose work is held in higher regard, however elaborate or expensive the book may be, if one can manage to secure her services. And I know this by experience, for she has made for me certain things which are considered to be outstanding when compared with the vignettes of the other great craftsmen.)

Art historians have tended to focus on the miniatures in the presentation copies, and to pay much less attention to other decorative components—frontispieces, borders, decorated initials, and paragraph marks. And yet they were important to Christine, as she makes clear in the tribute she pays to Anastaise. The frontispieces and decorative borders in the Duke's and particularly the Queen's MS are more assured and more elaborate than those in the earlier autograph manuscripts. Were they drawn and painted by Anastaise? We may never know.[34]

While the Duke's MS was in preparation, Christine engaged a still more talented painter. The Master of the *Cité des dames*, as Meiss calls him, continued to work for Christine until at least 1411. With his workshop, he was responsible for the miniatures in three separate manuscripts of the *Cité des dames* (BnF, f.fr. 1178 and 1179; BR 9393) and in the copy (BnF, f.fr. 607) that forms the final part of the Duke's MS;[35] a striking feature of these four copies is the frontispiece, which incorporates a miniature extending over two columns.[36] The *Cité des dames* workshop was also responsible for the miniatures in the second edition of the *Mutacion* (Munich, Bayerische Staatsbibliothek gall. 11 and BnF, f.fr. 603)[37] and for almost all the illustrations in the Queen's MS. That collection, commissioned by Queen Isabeau around 1410, is decorated even more lavishly than the Duke's MS: it contains 132 miniatures, of which 101 are once again inspired by the *Epistre Othea*.[38] Where the Duke's MS has a single frontispiece, illustrating the beginning of the *Cent balades* (f. 1r), the Queen's MS has two: the first (f. 3r) highlights the *Prologue* and incorporates a two-column miniature showing Christine presenting her book to Queen Isabeau; the second (f. 4r) sets off the first page of the *Cent balades*. The five illustrations in the Queen's MS that were not painted by the *Cité des dames* workshop are ascribed by Meiss to the workshop of the Bedford Trend Master.

The period between 1399 and 1411 was extremely productive, as the list of autograph manuscripts indicates; there was scarcely a year in which Christine did not complete and publish at least one new work. By 1411 the seventy quires to which she referred with pride in 1405 (o.s.) must have increased to a hundred or more. The pace slackens after 1411, for we know of only two works written by her between 1412 and 1418. The worsening political situation in France was a major factor, as Christine tells us herself. She began to write the *Livre de la paix* in September 1412 after the Peace of Auxerre, but stopped three months later, when civil war threatened once more. She did not resume until after the Peace of Pontoise, concluded in September 1413, and completed the work early in 1414.[39] Alas, Christine's pleas for peace went unheard: civil war, then national war, resumed, culminating in the French defeat at Agincourt in October 1415.

The last significant date in Christine's publishing career is 20 January 1418 (n.s.), when she completed the *Epistre de la prison de vie humaine*. The closing lines in the only surviving manuscript, an autograph copy, are addressed to Mary of Berry, Duchess of Bourbon. Christine apologizes for the delay in completing the *Epistre*:

> Escript à Paris par moy Cristine de Pizan, ton humble et obeissant, suppliant humblement que à mal tu n'aies ne moins gré ne m'en saches se plus tost n'as de moy eue ceste present epistre, laquelle ta benignité vueille en gré recevoir, et me soit du default de tant y avoir mis, quoyque dès pieça elle feust pour toy en ma pensée, s'il te plaist, souffisant excusacion pluseurs grans ennuis et troubles de courage, qui à cause de maints desplaisirs qui depuis le temps que je le commençay, qui fut dès pieça, ont mon povre entendement, pour sa foiblece, tenu si empeschié en tristes ymaginacions et pensées qu'il n'a esté en ma puissance de plus tost l'avoir achevé que à cestui .xx. jour de janvier l'an mil CCCCXVII.[40]

(Written in Paris by me, Christine de Pizan, your humble and obedient servant, humbly beseeching you that you should not take it ill nor be less gracious to me if you have not had this present epistle from me sooner. May you in your kindness be graciously pleased to receive it, and may the fault of having taken so much time over it, although the epistle was ready in my thoughts for you, be sufficiently excused, so please you, by the many great troubles and woes which, since I started it—and that was some time ago—have kept my poor mind, on account of its feebleness, so preoccupied with sad imaginings and reflections that it has not been in my power to complete the epistle before this 20th day of January 1417.)

On 29 May 1418, just over four months later, Paris was captured by the forces of the Duke of Burgundy. Having been forced to flee the capital, the Dauphin Charles set up an alternative administration south of the River Loire. Christine for her part sought refuge in the abbey where she was to remain for the next eleven years, as she tells us in the *Ditié de Jehanne d'Arc*, written on 31 July 1429:

> Je, Christine, qui ay plouré
> XI ans en abbaye close,
> Où j'ay tousjours puis demouré
> Que Charles (c'est estrange chose!),
> Le filz du roy, se dire l'ose,
> S'en fouÿ de Paris de tire,
> Par la traïson là enclose,
> Ore à prime me prens à rire.

(I, Christine, who have wept for eleven years in a walled abbey where I have lived ever since Charles [how strange this is] the King's son—dare I say it—fled in haste from Paris, I who have lived enclosed there on account of the treachery, now, for the first time, begin to laugh.[41])

The *Ditié de Jehanne d'Arc* is one of only three works by Christine that do not survive in an autograph manuscript. The other two are a letter criticizing the *Roman de la Rose* that she sent to Jean de Montreuil[42] and the *Heures de contemplacion de la Passion*, written perhaps in 1422, and certainly after the *Epistre de la prison de vie humaine*.[43] The copy of the *Epistre* is the last known production of Christine's scriptorium, which, it must be presumed, ceased operations in the early summer of 1418. We know from other sources how severely the Parisian book trade was disrupted by the Burgundian invasion.

THE EVOLVING TEXT

Sister Mary Louis Towner's critical edition of the *Advision* (1932) is based on BnF, f.fr. 1176 and Brussels 10309.[44] Comparison of her two sources led her to conclude that MS 10309 contains "a second, or revised edition [of the text] for which Christine herself is responsible."[45] That important observation attracted little attention, and it was not until 1967, when Gianni Mombello published his monumental study of the textual tradition of the *Epistre Othea*, that scholars began to realize the extent to which the texts of Christine's works evolve. Meiss provided confirmatory evidence when he discussed the appearance of the clock in the *Epistre Othea* and also pointed to the existence of a second edition of the *Mutacion*.[46] My review of Christine's progress as a writer, published in 1983, took as its starting point Christine's ballades and rondeaux, and showed that, like the *Advision*, the *Epistre Othea*, and the *Mutacion*, the lyric poems had also gone through different editions.[47] In an unpublished dissertation on the *Cité des dames* completed in 1974, Monika Lange identified three redactions of the text. Her conclusions went largely unnoticed until their importance was highlighted by Earl Jeffrey Richards in his edition of the work and in a stimulating article on the challenges faced by the editor of the *Cité des dames* and indeed any Christine text.[48]

It is now generally accepted that as new presentation manuscripts of her works were prepared, Christine revised the texts to be included; all her works effectively go through successive editions. That being so, it is essential that the editor of any work by Christine should privilege the last version known to have been copied under her supervision.[49] For very many of her writings the Queen's MS represents Christine's last word. The recently published editions of her love debates, the *Cité des dames*, the *Epistre Othea*, and the *Chemin de long estude*, are all based on the Queen's MS.[50]

AUTOGRAPH MANUSCRIPTS

In his comments about the clock in the *Epistre Othea*, quoted earlier, Meiss speculated that BnF, f.fr. 848 might be in Christine's own hand, echoing Charity Cannon Willard who a decade earlier had suggested that BnF, f.fr. 580 (*Epistre a la reine*) might well be an autograph manuscript.[51] In an important article published

Christine and the Manuscript Tradition

in 1980, Gilbert Ouy and Christine Reno reviewed more than twenty of the presentation copies and showed that they were all copied by one or another of three scribes whom they named "P," "R," and "X." (The same three scribes were also responsible for virtually all the manuscripts that have been added to the list since then.) The X hand is encountered most often and R and P are found less frequently. Ouy and Reno also demonstrated the extent to which the scribes cooperate, citing manuscripts in which two of the three worked together: one copied the text; the second made smaller but no less important contributions, adding rubrics, inserting a table of contents, making corrections, or inserting passages that had been omitted.[52]

Ouy and Reno paid particular attention to the many corrections found in the presentation copies. Some are careful, made by the scribe in a text hand; others are less neat, penned in a rapid, cursive hand. These last are generally small corrections, the insertion or the substitution of a single word, or a minor adjustment to spelling. There are occasional examples of more substantial corrections made in this hand: one such is in the Brussels copy of the *Mutacion* in which an octosyllabic couplet has been inserted at the foot of a page.[53] The cursive correcting hand is also responsible for a large number of marginal instructions. Particularly striking examples are to be found in BnF, f.fr. 1643 (*Chemin de long estude*) in which the correcting hand has indicated where additional miniatures should be positioned in a projected copy of the poem. A typical formulation reads: "[C]y soit laisié espace [pour] faire histoire" (Leave space here for a miniature).[54]

Ouy and Reno's discussion of corrections of this type leads them to two significant conclusions: first, that scribe X used an elegant text hand when transcribing text, rubrics, or running titles, but chose a rapid cursive hand to make the small corrections just described or to write instructions; second, that scribe X is to be identified with Christine de Pizan herself. In other words an apparently conventional statement of the type "Escript à Paris par moy Cristine de Pizan" (Written in Paris by me, Christine de Pizan), as found at the end of the *Epistre de la prison de vie humaine*,[55] is on occasion to be taken literally. And so the presentation manuscripts copied by X are to be seen as autographs in the fullest sense of that term.

There are specimens of the cursive correcting hand in virtually all the fifty manuscripts listed in the Appendix. The hand is in part that of a proofreader. Scribes were expected to check what they had written, but that was a task that would also—and quite naturally—fall to the author. The cursive hand is also in part that of a publisher, witness the marginal instructions in BnF, f.fr. 1643 just discussed. Only Christine herself could so consistently have combined the role of proofreader and publisher, and so the cursive correcting hand is certainly to be identified with Christine de Pizan.

Can we be sure that Christine was responsible for both the cursive correcting hand and the neat X hand? The X hand is consistently neat and controlled; the cursive hand is rapid, to the point of being scrappy on occasion. Would scribe X, whose professional skills are so evident, have been capable of making what are very often inelegant cursive corrections? There is also the question of time: could Christine have found the time to copy so many manuscripts in the midst of all her other activities? These problems will remain unresolved until further evidence is found, or until the research on pattern recognition that is being carried out in other fields, principally in areas of forensic inquiry, can be applied to codicology.

Since Ouy and Reno published their article in 1980, more autograph manuscripts have been identified and others perhaps remain to be discovered. More is known about Christine's scriptorium, the result of research on the preparation of the autograph manuscripts and in particular the ways in which the quires are signed: some quires are signed twice or, exceptionally, on three occasions; some are signed in black ink, some in red, some with a stylus, some with Roman numbers, some with Arabic; and the signatures are not always in alphabetical order.[56] What lies behind these overlapping systems is not yet fully understood.

Spelling is another focus of recent research. Ouy and Reno's article, published in 1988, on the orthographic variations in three autograph manuscripts describes "Christine's hesitations."[57] Hesitations between *peut* and *puet*; *plain* and *plein*; *noblece, noblesce,* and *noblesse* are only three examples. These questions have been taken up again more recently by Gabriella Parussa and Richard Trachsler who reach different conclusions.[58]

THE *ALBUM CHRISTINE DE PIZAN*

A comprehensive examination of *all* the autograph manuscripts is required if we are to achieve a fuller understanding of how Christine's scriptorium operated during the years 1399 to 1418. The *Album Christine de Pizan*, which is being prepared jointly by Ouy, Reno, and myself, will include a detailed description of each manuscript, taking account of the features known to be characteristic of the presentation copies. Close attention is being paid to scribal hands, the object being to identify the copyist(s) and to determine how the processes of transcription and correction were organized. Which version of Christine's work(s) does the manuscript contain? Were text, rubrics, and item numbers all copied at the same time? How extensively has the text been corrected, and by whom? Who was responsible for the tables of contents provided for longer works, and at what stage were they inserted?

In describing how each manuscript is illustrated, account must be taken of all the elements included in the decorative program devised by Christine and the artists she engaged. Miniatures require close attention, but not to the neglect of frontispieces, borders, rubrics, initials, and paragraph marks. The aim is not only to determine how text and decoration interrelate but also to judge how successful the scriptorium was in integrating the operations of transcription and illustration.

All this codicological and art historical information must be interpreted, together with the available literary evidence, before the copies of a particular work can be compared one with another and their precise relationship determined.

Brought to a successful conclusion, the *Album* will enormously increase our understanding of Christine de Pizan's career as writer and publisher. Were it possible to consult the author herself, she would no doubt stress the need for patience and perseverance, and might even cite the *enseignement moral* she fashioned for her son, Jehan de Castel:

> Se tu veulz en science eslire
> Ton estat par les livres lire,
> Fays tant, et par suivre l'estude,
> Qu'entre les clers ne soyes rude.[59]

(If you wish to increase your scholarly standing by reading books, ensure—above all by following a program of study—that you do not appear untutored in the company of the learned.)

APPENDIX

Presentation Copies Containing One Work by Christine

The works are arranged in chronological order, so far as it is possible to do so. The date quoted is the date of the work in question, and not the date of the manuscript(s) that contain it.

Debat de deux amans (1399–1400): BR 11034; BnF, f.fr. 1740. Each copy is illustrated by a single miniature in grisaille.

Epistre Othea (ca 1400): BnF, f.fr. 848, 1187. MS 848 contains six miniatures in grisaille.

Livre du chemin de long estude (1403): BR 10982, 10983; BnF, f.fr. 1188, 1643. The copies are illustrated by four, five, or six miniatures in grisaille; the spaces intended for five miniatures in MS 1643 have been left blank.

Dit de la pastoure (1403): BnF, f.fr. 2184, which has no illustrations.

Livre de la mutacion de Fortune (1403): BR 9508; Chantilly 494; Germany, Private Collection (Ex-Phillipps MS 207, owned later by Sir Sydney Cockerell, then by M. Pierre Bérès); The Hague, Koninklijke Bibliotheek 78 D 42; Munich, Bayerische Staatsbibliothek gall. 11; Paris, BnF, n.a.fr. 14852 (fragment of two folios). The complete copies are illustrated by four, six, or seven miniatures.

Livre des fais et bonnes meurs du saige roy Charles V (1404): Modena, Biblioteca d'Este α.n.8.7; BnF, f.fr. 5025, 10153; Vatican City, Biblioteca Apostolica Vaticana, Reg. lat. 920. None of the manuscripts is illustrated.

Epistre a la reine Isabeau (1405): BnF, f.fr. 580, fols 53r–54v, illustrated by a single miniature in grisaille.

Advision Cristine (1405 [o.s.]): BR 10309; BnF, f.fr. 1176; Paris, Private Collection (Ex-Phillipps MS 128). Each copy is illustrated by a single miniature.

Livre de la cité des dames (1405–1406): BR 9393; Arsenal 2686; BnF, f.fr. 1178, 1179, 24293. MS 2686 has no illustrations; MS 1179 has one miniature; the other copies are illustrated by three miniatures.

Livre des trois vertus (1405–1406): Boston, Public Library 1528; BL, Additional MS 31841; BnF, n.a.fr. 25636. Each copy is illustrated by a single miniature.

Livre de la prod'hommie de l'homme (1405–1406): Vatican City, Biblioteca Apostolica Vaticana, Reg. lat. 1238, which has no illustrations.

Livre du corps de policie (1406–1407): Besançon, Bibliothèque Publique 423; Chantilly 294; Arsenal 2681; BnF, f.fr. 1197. MS 2681 has one illustration, the others have none.

Livre de Prudence (1407): BR 11065–11073, which has no illustrations.

Sept psaumes allegorisés (1409–1410): BR 10987; BnF, n.a.fr. 4792; Coulet & Faire MS.[60] Each copy is illustrated by a single miniature.

Lamentacion sur les maux de la France (1410): BnF, f.fr. 24864, which has no illustrations.

Livre des fais d'armes et de chevalerie (*ca* 1410): BR 10476, illustrated by a single miniature.

Livre de la paix (1412–1414): BR 10366, illustrated by a single miniature.

Livre de la prison de vie humaine (1418): BnF, f.fr. 24786, which has no illustrations.

Presentation Copies Containing a Collection of Christine's Works

The dates quoted for the collected manuscripts are the years when the collection was in preparation. Each collection is treated here as a single manuscript, even if it is now bound or catalogued as more than one volume.

Chantilly 492–493 (1399–1405): the *Livre de Cristine*, a collection of nineteen works, mostly in verse, completed in June 1402 and illustrated by twelve miniatures; five works were added in stages between 1403 and 1405 and illustrated by thirteen further miniatures; now bound in two volumes.

Leiden, Bibliotheek der Rijksuniversteit, Ltk 1819: an incomplete folio containing part of the *Livre de la cité des dames*, which a running title shows to have been item 27 in a large collection.

BL, Harley MS 4431 (1410–1411): the Queen's MS, commissioned by Isabeau de Bavière; a collection of thirty works in verse and prose, completed in 1410 or 1411; illustrated by 132 miniatures; now bound in two volumes.

BnF, f.fr. 603 (1410–1412?): the *Livre des fais d'armes et de chevalerie*, illustrated by four miniatures, followed by the *Livre de la mutacion de Fortune*, illustrated by seven miniatures.

BnF, f.fr. 835, 606, 836, 605, 607 (1408–1409): the Duke's MS, perhaps intended for the Duke of Orleans (1407), acquired by the Duke of Berry in 1408 or 1409; a collection of twenty-six works in verse and prose; illustrated by 128 miniatures; now catalogued (and bound) as five separate volumes.

BnF, f.fr. 12779 (1399–1403): the *Livre de Cristine*, completed in June 1402, a collection of nineteen works, mostly in verse, now illustrated by eight miniatures, some having been lost or removed; one narrative poem, illustrated by a single miniature, was added, probably in 1403.

NOTES

1. Details of all the manuscripts can be found in Angus J. Kennedy, *Christine de Pizan: A Bibliographical Guide* and *Christine de Pizan: A Bibliographical Guide—Supplement I* (London: Grant & Cutler, 1984 and 1994).
2. Paris, Bibliothèque nationale de France, fonds français, abbreviated "BnF, f.fr."
3. See Charity Cannon Willard, "An Autograph Manuscript of Christine de Pizan?," *Studi Francesi* 27 (1965), 452–57; a black and white reproduction of f. 53r follows p. 456.
4. BnF, f.fr. 603 and the Leiden fragment are the only collected manuscripts that do not contain the *Epistres du debat sur le "Roman de la Rose."*
5. Pierre Cockshaw, "Mentions d'auteurs, de copistes, d'enlumineurs et de libraires dans les comptes généraux de l'état bourguignon (1384–1419)," *Scriptorium* 23 (1969), 122–44 (items 52, 64, 68, 72, 76, and 81).
6. *Christine de Pizan: Le livre de l'advision Cristine*, ed. Christine Reno and Liliane Dulac (Paris: Champion, 2001), 111–13.
7. *Inventaires de Jean duc de Berry (1401–16)*, ed. Jules Guiffrey, 2 vols. (Paris, 1894–1896), I, Items 943 and 949 (pp. 247, 249).
8. [Jean Barrois], *Bibliothéque* (sic) *protypographique, ou Librairies des fils du roi Jean, Charles V, Jean de Berri, Philippe de Bourgogne et les siens* (Paris: Treuttel et Würtz, 1830), n°s 679, 940, and 1665 (pp. 117, 150, and 238).
9. On Christine's language, see the Christine de Pizan Database: www.arts.ed.ac.uk/french/christine.
10. See G. Mombello, *La tradizione manoscritta dell' 'Epistre Othea' di Christine de Pizan. Prolegomeni all'edizione del testo* (Turin: Accademia delle Scienze, 1967); Millard C. Meiss, *French Painting in the Time of Jean de Berry: The Limbourgs and their Contemporaries*, 2 vols. (London: Thames & Hudson, 1974), I, 9–10, 291; J. C. Laidlaw, "Christine de Pizan—An Author's Progress," *Modern Language Review* 78 (1983), 532–50; *Christine de Pizan: Epistre Othea*, ed. Gabriella Parussa (Geneva: Droz, 1999), 87–101.
11. See *Œuvres poétiques de Christine de Pisan*, ed. Maurice Roy, 3 vols. (Paris: Firmin Didot, 1886–96), I, 10, 147. In the ballade Christine laments the death five years earlier of her husband, Jean de Castel; the rondeau was composed seven years after his death. Jean de Castel died in October or November 1390.
12. *Grans* could signify either "important people" or "gifts, promises." Because it is unlikely that Salisbury would have made his request through intermediaries, the second sense has been preferred. It is, however, better attested in Middle English than in Middle French. For details of Salisbury's mission see J. C. Laidlaw, "Christine de Pizan, the Earl of Salisbury and Henry IV," *French Studies* 36 (1982): 129–43.
13. For a detailed discussion of this and other copies of the work see Mombello, *La tradizione manoscritta*, and Parussa, *Epistre Othea*.

14. The first five miniatures are reproduced in Sandra L. Hindman, *Christine de Pizan's "Epistre Othéa": Painting and Politics at the Court of Charles VI* (Toronto: Pontifical Institute of Mediaeval Studies, 1986), plates 1–3; plate 2 shows how the manuscript is laid out. See also Meiss, *French Painting*, II, plate 129, for a reproduction of the second and third miniatures.

15. Brussels, Bibliothèque royale Albert 1er, abbreviated "BR."

16. "Champie initials are gold on a rectilinear ground . . . , generally two-color, with filiform patterning in white or another color" [Richard H. Rouse and Mary E. Rouse, *Manuscripts and their Makers: Commercial Book Producers in Medieval Paris 1200–1500*, 2 vols. (London: Harvey Miller Publishers, 2000), II, 359]. Vignettes are slender stalks bearing leaves of vine and/or ivy that grow from an initial or baguette (see Note 28), turning either upward or downward.

17. The miniature, introductory initial and border, and the opening lines of the poem are reproduced in color in *The Love Debate Poems of Christine de Pizan: "Le Livre du Debat de deux amans"; "Le Livre des Trois jugemens"; "Le Livre du Dit de Poissy,"* ed. Barbara K. Altmann (Gainesville: University Press of Florida, 1998), plate 1.

18. Chantilly 492–493, f. 1v. The *Livre* is so called because item 19, *Les Quinze Joyes de Nostre Dame rimees*, ends "Explicit le livre de Cristine" in BnF, f.fr. 12779 (f. 156c).

19. In Christine's day the calendar used by the French court ran not from 1 January to 31 December, but from Easter Day until the following Easter Eve. For her the year 1399 therefore began on Sunday 30 March 1399, Easter Day, and ended on Easter Eve, Saturday 17 April 1400. The abbreviation "o.s." (old style) indicates a date expressed in the terms of that older calendar; "n.s." (new style) marks a date adjusted in line with today's practice.

20. For a more detailed discussion of the two copies of the *Livre* and their later enlargement, see J. C. Laidlaw, "Christine de Pizan—A Publisher's Progress," *Modern Language Review* 82 (1987), 35–75 (42–52, 68–9).

21. "Le livre de Cristine fait pour feue madame d'Orléans, couvert de rouge marqueté" (Christine's Book made for the late Duchess of Orléans, bound in stamped red leather). L. Delisle, *Le Cabinet des manuscrits*, 3 vols. (Paris: Imprimerie nationale, 1868–1881), I, 105–08 (106).

22. The Chantilly copy contains the complete set of miniatures. In its present state BnF, f.fr. 12779 contains only eight of the illustrations, the other four having almost certainly been removed; see Laidlaw, "A Publisher's Progress," 47.

23. See Meiss, *French Painting*, II, plate 128, which shows one of the miniatures illustrating the *Epistre Othea* in Chantilly 492, together with part of a flourished introductory "E" and a portion of text. The color plate of BnF, f.fr. 12779, f. 40r, included in *Les plus beaux manuscrits des poètes français* (Paris: Robert Laffont, 1991), 40, illustrates the pleasing design of the *Livre* and its use of flourished initials alternately in red and blue.

24. Meiss, *French Painting*, I, 34; II, plates 127–29.

25. See also the long note to this passage (p. 180).

26. The year 1405 (o.s.) began on Sunday 19 April 1405 and ended on Saturday 10 April 1406. See Note 19.

27. Sarah Jane Williams, "An Author's Role in Fourteenth Century Book Production: Guillaume de Machaut's 'Livre ou je met toutes mes choses,'" *Romania* 90 (1969): 433–54.
28. The frontispiece is an elaborate page, designed to set off the beginning of a literary work. An essential component is the baguette, a staff or rod extending the length or the breadth of the page. Like Aaron's rod in the Old Testament (Numbers, 17:8) the baguette is fruitful, producing vignettes. The frontispiece is generally made up of three baguettes, two vertical and one horizontal, which combine with an overarching canopy of vignettes to enclose the opening miniature and the first lines of the work, and thus frame the page. Where only two vertical baguettes are employed, the frame is completed by vignettes that extend horizontally at the top and the bottom of the page. The frontispieces in BR 10982 and 10983 are illustrated in Camille Gaspar and Frédéric Lyna, *Les Principaux Manuscrits à peintures de la Bibliothèque Royale de Belgique* (Bruxelles: Bibliothèque Royale, 1984), II, plate CI.
29. For reproductions of miniatures from these four manuscripts see Meiss, *French Painting*, II, plates 1–2 (in color), 12, 14, 19–26, 29–30, and 32–4.
30. There is uncertainty about the circumstances in which the manuscript was made. The inclusion of a number of works dedicated to Louis, Duke of Orleans has led some scholars to argue that the collection was originally intended for him, a plan made impossible by Louis's murder in November 1407. Be that as it may, the collection certainly entered the Duke of Berry's library in 1408 or early in 1409. See Meiss, *French Painting*, I, 37, and Meiss, with S. Off, "The Bookkeeping of Robinet d'Estampes and the Chronology of Jean de Berry's Manuscripts," *Art Bulletin* 53 (1971): 225–35.
31. On the Duke's MS, now in five parts, see Laidlaw, "A Publisher's Progress," 52–9 and 70–2.
32. The studies by Meiss (*French Painting*, II) and Hindman (*Epistre Othéa: Painting and Politics*) include many plates from the Duke's and the Queen's MSS; plates A–D in Hindman are in color. For color plates of the Queen's MS see Altmann, *Love Debate Poems*, plates 2–4. The Egerton Master was also responsible for the miniature at the beginning of the three presentation copies of the *Sept psaumes allegorisés*, completed in 1409–1410.
33. *Christine de Pizan: La Città delle Dame*, ed. Earl Jeffrey Richards, trans. Patrizia Caraffi (Milan, Trento: Luni, 1997), 192.
34. Our understanding of early fifteenth-century manuscripts would be increased by a more systematic study of the work of these undersung marginal masters. For an indication of what might be achieved see Allen S. Farber, "Considering a Marginal Master: The Work of an Early Fifteenth-Century, Parisian Manuscript Decorator," *Gesta* 32/1 (1993), 21–39.
35. See Note 31. For reproductions of selected miniatures see Meiss, *French Painting*, II, plates 35–37, 39–41, 43–44.
36. In BnF, f.fr. 1178 all three miniatures are of double size.
37. In BnF, f.fr. 603 the *Mutacion* is preceded by a copy of the *Fais d'armes et de chevalerie*, which was also illustrated by the *Cité des dames* workshop. See Meiss, *French Painting*, II, plates 11, 13, 15–16, 27–28, and 31.

38. See Note 32.
39. The "*Livre de la Paix*" *of Christine de Pisan*, ed. Charity Cannon Willard (The Hague: Mouton, 1958), 23–5.
40. *Christine de Pizan's "Epistre de la prison de vie humaine*," ed. Angus J. Kennedy (Glasgow: Glasgow University French Department, 1984), 52–3. See also Note 19.
41. *Ditié de Jehanne d'Arc: Christine de Pisan*, ed. Angus J. Kennedy and Kenneth Varty (Oxford: Society for the Study of Mediæval Languages and Literature, 1977), 28 and 41. For the date of the poem see lines 481–84 (40).
42. *Christine de Pisan, Jean Gerson, Jean de Montreuil, Gontier et Pierre Col: Le Débat sur le Roman de la Rose*, ed. Eric Hicks (Paris: Champion, 1977), 49–57.
43. Only two copies of the *Heures de contemplacion* are known: BnF, n.a.fr. 10059, fols. 114r–144r and The Hague, Koninklijke Bibliotheek 73 J 55, fols. 51r–92v. The work is unpublished.
44. *Lavision-Christine*, ed. Sister Mary Louis Towner (Washington, DC: The Catholic University of America Press, 1932; reprinted New York: AMS Press, 1969). Towner did not know of ex-Phillipps MS 128.
45. Towner, *Lavision-Christine*, 69.
46. The standard edition of the poem makes no reference to a second edition. See *Le Livre de la mutacion de Fortune par Christine de Pisan*, ed. Suzanne Solente, 4 vols. (Paris: Picard, 1959–66).
47. Laidlaw, "An Author's Progress," 534–44.
48. Monika Lange, *Christine de Pisan: Livre de la Cité des dames: kritische Textedition auf Grund der sieben überlieferten "manuscrits originaux" des Textes* (unpublished dissertation: University of Hamburg, 1974). Richards, *La Città delle Dame* (1997); Richards, "Editing the *Livre de la cité des dames*: New Insights, Problems and Challenges," *Au Champ des escriptures: IIIe Colloque international sur Christine de Pizan*, ed. Eric Hicks in collaboration with Diego Gonzalez and Philippe Simon (Paris: Champion, 2000), 789–816.
49. Earlier scholars, not realizing the extent to which Christine's texts evolved, tried to determine which of the extant manuscripts stands closest to the author's original copy and therefore provides the best text on which to base a critical edition. They present their conclusions in the form of a stemma or table that takes the author's original as its starting point and shows how the surviving copies derive from it. (For examples see Roy, *Œuvres poétiques*, I, xx, and Solente, *Mutacion de Fortune*, I, cxli.) Such an approach is inappropriate in cases in which more than one original copy is available.
50. *Christine de Pizan: Le livre du duc des vrais amans*, ed. Thelma S. Fenster (Binghamton, NY: Medieval and Renaissance Texts and Studies, 1995); Richards, *La Città delle Dame* (1997); Altmann, *Love Debate Poems* (1998); Parussa, *Epistre Othea* (1999); *Christine de Pizan: Le chemin de longue étude*, ed. Andrea Tarnowski (Paris: Livre de poche, 2000).
51. See above, Note 3. Towner had raised similar questions when she edited the *Advision* in 1932. A close comparison of BnF, f.fr. 1176 and BR 10309 led her to conclude that they were in the same hand and that the same scribe had copied the *Prologue* in the Queen's MS; however, there was insufficient evidence to show

that Christine and the scribe must be the same person. See Towner, *Lavision-Christine*, 55–9.
52. Gilbert Ouy and Christine M. Reno, "Identification des autographes de Christine de Pizan," *Scriptorium* 34 (1980): 221–38 and plates 18–20. They include BnF, f.fr. 580 (*Epistre a la reine*) among the manuscripts copied by scribe X (224–26). See also Reno et Dulac, *Advision*, xl, for a list of those manuscripts.
53. The couplet, intended to follow line 6308 reads "Si croi se Dieu me doint pardons/Qu'en soit de mauvés et de bons"; see Ouy and Reno, "Identification des autographes," 229 and plate 18. The standard edition, which is itself based on Brussels MS 9508, makes no reference to this marginal insertion. See Solente, *Mutacion de Fortune*, II, 70.
54. F. 27r. See also J. C. Laidlaw, "How Long is the *Livre du chemin de long estude*?," *The Editor and the Text*, ed. Philip E. Bennett and Graham A. Runnalls (Edinburgh: University Press, 1990), 83–95 (86).
55. Towner, *Lavision-Christine*.
56. Laidlaw, "An Author's Progress"; Gilbert Ouy, "Une énigme codicologique: les signatures des cahiers dans les manuscrits autographes et originaux de Christine de Pizan," in *Calames et cahiers. Mélanges de codicologie et de paléographie offerts à Léon Gilissen*, ed. Jacques Lemaire and Emile van Balberghe (Bruxelles: Centre d'Etude des Manuscrits, 1985), 119–31; Laidlaw, "A Publisher's Progress."
57. Gilbert Ouy and Christine M. Reno, "Les hésitations de Christine: Etude des variantes de graphies dans trois manuscrits autographes de Christine de Pizan," *Revue des langues romanes* 92 (1988): 265–86.
58. Gabriella Parussa, "Autographes et orthographe: quelques considérations sur l'orthographe de Christine de Pizan," *Romania* 117 (1999): 143–59; Gabriella Parussa and Richard Trachsler with the collaboration of Ildiko Seres, "*Or sus, alons ou champ des escriptures*. Encore sur l'orthographe de Christine de Pizan: l'intérêt des grands corpus," in *Contexts and Continuities: Proceedings of the IVth International Colloquium on Christine de Pizan (Glasgow 21–27 July 2000)*, ed. Angus J. Kennedy in collaboration with Rosalind Brown-Grant, James C. Laidlaw, and Catherine Müller (Glasgow: University Press, 2002), 3 vols., 621–43.
59. Roy, *Œuvres poétiques*, III, 28.
60. Meiss, *French Painting*, I, 8.

# 16

Modern Editions

Makers of the Christinian Corpus

Nadia Margolis

> L'édition des textes est un art qui, comme tous les arts, demande [. . .] avant tout, la faculté de discerner entre le possible, le probable, et le certain.
> Edmond Faral

Although we often think of pre-1970s Christine as an underdog compared to the critical fortunes of other medieval French authors such as Chrétien de Troyes, Marie de France, and such closer contemporaries as Froissart, Villon, and Charles d'Orléans, examination of her reception history invites a revaluation. A survey of her published posterity during the eighteenth through twentieth centuries—well before the "Christine boom" of the past two decades—reveals her to have participated in France's nationalistic rediscovery of its cultural patrimony at least as significantly as the above-named authors. We shall observe the surprising extent to which Enlightenment and nineteenth-century scholars already recognized her merits—certain *fin-de-siècle doctrinaires* such as Gustave Lanson notwithstanding—and how indebted we recent scholars are to their research in shaping our perceptions of her many writings.

In purporting to discuss "editions," I am restricting the focus of this chapter to "critical editions," as distinguished from the early "printed editions"—those first printed texts of Christine done during the fifteenth through sixteenth centuries by what we might label "nonphilological" editors such as Vérard, Le Noir, and Pigouchet.[1] Critical editions—containing linguistic and historical notes, manuscript variants, glossaries, and commentary where necessary, in addition to the primary text—really could not come about until the mid-nineteenth century, with the scientific development of history and philology, as the second part of this chapter will attempt to illustrate.

Somewhere in between early printed editions and the advent of modern critical texts figures a sort of metaphase, arising during the seventeenth through early nineteenth centuries. It parallels the growing awareness of science and its methodologies as applicable to art, literature, and history. This stage is characterized by a rudimentary attempt at philology or codicology, in that Christine is treated as an historical document, a useful refugee from a rival Renaissance humanistic culture (Italy) and from a rival gender, because of her exceptional learning. Methods of evaluating information on her were shaky at best, whether in selecting among her many manuscripts or, by extrapolation, in weighing the relative merits of differing secondary materials. Like the earlier printed phase, this metaphase emphasized prolific textual generation, as a means toward establishing the superiority—by sheer fecundity and diversity—of French culture, over precise authenticity. In other words, it was more important to determine how much written testimony to the glory of France, its history and moral-political institutions, Christine produced than what her exact words were in doing so.

Early editors, working closely with printers, untrammeled by such philological concerns as manuscript authenticity and prioritization, quickly fixed upon her most popular works, such as the *Epistre Othea*, *Cité des dames*, and *Trois vertus*. These would also remain, because of their many manuscript versions, among Christine's most editorially challenging works well into the twentieth century. We shall see how, paradoxically, once nineteenth-century philology and history became more scientific, the profusion of her manuscripts—a professional asset to Christine during her lifetime, ensuring her literary afterlife—would hinder her modern posterity in critical editions by their daunting complexity. The special problems entailed in reading and editing Christine, perhaps more than gender bias, would impede her acceptance within the literary canon.

In certain cases, translations, particularly English, saw print more readily than the original French texts, first in fifteenth-century avatars by Caxton, Scrope, and others, and then in modern translations or editions of these Middle English renderings. Christine's popularity among English readers, together with the relative inertia of French academic publishing toward her for reasons both worthy and irrational, effectively skewed her editorial afterlife. Virtually free of the codicological and ideological constraints impeding Christine editing in French yet without sacrificing its didactic-historical appeal, "Englished Christine" came to surpass the original French among scholars and general readers alike. This new public created a market for critical editions of the English versions of, for example, the *Epistre Othea*, *Fais d'armes et de chevalerie*, and *Corps de policie*, more urgently than French ones. Thus critical editions of these three titles in Middle English were published in 1942 and 1970 (Gordon's edition of Babyngton's *Epistre Othea* and Bühler's edition of Scrope's *Epistre Othea*), 1932 (Byles's *Fayttes of Armes*), and 1977 (Bornstein's *Policie*), whereas their French counterparts did not surface until 1999 for the *Epistre*

Othea and 1967/1998 for *Corps de policie*,[2] with Charity Willard's *Fais d'armes et de chevalerie* still in preparation.

In her evolution from literary-historical curio to real author, her works would await adequate methodology and technology for editing her diverse and abundant output. As a parallel prerequisite, one of the recurrent attributes of Christine scholars, even among supposed establishmentarians, is a certain polymath, maverick quality.[3]

FROM ANTHOLOGY EXTRACT TO AUTHORIAL *OEUVRE:* BOIVIN LE CADET, KÉRALIO, AND THOMASSY

A gratifying abundance of seventeenth- through early nineteenth-century articles not only recounted Christine's life but also cited passages from some of her works (Margolis, 2000, 34–7). Although tending to treat her as a curiosity, and her works as archeological artifacts, such efforts reflect recognition of the historical importance of her writing and thus hastened her acceptance as a serious author documenting her complex times, if not as a serious poet.

Jean Boivin de Villeneuve (1656–1726) signed himself "Boivin le Cadet" to distinguish himself from his more colorful older brother, Louis.[4] But the younger Boivin was no slouch either, as member of the French Academy, keeper of the Paris Royal Library (now Bibliothèque nationale de France [BnF]), who later held the chair of Greek at the Collège Royal (now Collège de France). His posthumously published article on Christine and her father, laced with citations from her various works, is probably the first substantial study of her for a learned public (1736).[5] Aside from inaugurating her relationship with her father as a key topos in current Christine criticism, Boivin also furnishes an early record of the then-known Christinian corpus (order, categories, and titles as set down by Boivin) (714):

Verse works: *Cent balades, Lais, Virelais, Rondeaux, Jeux à vendre, Autrement vente d'amours, Autres balades, L'Epistre au dieu d'Amours, Le Débat des deux amants, Le Livre des trois jugements, Le Livre du dit de Poissy, Le Chemin de lonc estude, Les dits Moraulx ou les enseignements que Christine donne à son fils, Le Roman d'Othea ou l'epistre d'Othea à Hector, Le Livre de la Mutacion de Fortune.*

Prose works: *Histoire du roy Charles le Sage, La Vision de Christine, La Cité des dames, Les Epistres sur le Roman de la Rose, Le livre des faits d'armes & de chevallerie, Instruction des princesses, dames de cour, & autres Lettres à la Reine Isabelle, en M. CCCV, Les Proverbes Moraulx, & le livre de Prudence.*

These lists demonstrate the extensive number of titles of which eighteenth-century scholars were already aware, despite lingering difficulty in sorting them out. For those prescientific times, Boivin's manuscript and other primary sources were fairly reliable because he did apparently manage to find some good manuscripts: for example, Paris, BnF MS fr. 1176 for the *Advision*—containing the poet's literary autobiography—and 1177 for the *Cité des dames*. Only occasionally did he sink to the very popular, useful but derivative historical hodgepodges compiled by Denys Godefroy (1615–1681).[6] Because Boivin documented his quotations with relative care, his work offers a valuable index to what was known of Christine's writing and how it was disseminated.

Godefroy was also the first to cite Christine's *Fais et bonnes meurs du sage roy Charles V*, only to defer quoting from the biography, he explains (1653), because he plans to publish the work in full—a project never realized.[7] Ninety years later, however, in 1743, Abbot Jean Lebeuf (1687–1760), a prolific historian from Auxerre, would publish his deceptively fuller, if flawed, edition, with extensive critical apparatus.[8] Lebeuf's effort nonetheless rendered the *Charles V* the sixth earliest work by Christine to be printed, and arguably the first to have been critically edited in the modern sense.[9]

Another abbot, Claude Sallier (1685–1761), a specialist in Greek tragedy and philosophical texts who held the chair of Hebrew at the Collège Royal, was perhaps the first to approach Christine's works as a "philologue" (philologist). His 1751 article reproduces lengthy quotations from the *Epistre Othea*, based on what are now Paris, BnF MSS fr. 848 and 1644 (515–20) and, to a lesser extent, from the *Debat de deux amans*, from BnF MS fr. 835. In relatively few pages, and despite the preponderance of citation over commentary, Sallier adds insights into the education of Louis d'Orléans as an ideal prince by interweaving passages from Christine's *Charles V* with those from the *Epistre Othea*.[10]

The erudite abbot, who would also "discover" Charles d'Orléans and catalogue the Royal Library, concludes his study of Christine by attempting an apparent reversal of literary-historical fortune in the right direction. That is, based on the allusions to courtly romances in the *Debat de deux amans*, Sallier suggests dating such classics as the *Roman de Tristan* considerably earlier than the fourteenth century, as his contemporaries (even the venerable Du Cange) had evidently believed (525), much to our surprise as moderns taking their twelfth-century dating for granted. This sort of reference to Christine might also reflect her increasing prestige among the French Enlightenment establishment; all of the above-mentioned scholars moved within ranking literary or political circles.

Louise-Félicité Guinement, Mlle de Kéralio (1758–1821), whom Mme Roland described as "une petite femme spirituelle, adroite et fine" (a witty, skilful, clever little woman),[11] composed some fourteen volumes of her unfinished *Collection des meilleurs ouvrages françois, composés par des femmes, dédiée aux femmes françaises*, out of which volumes 2 and 3 (1787) reprint selections from several of Christine's works, plus Boivin's and Sallier's articles mentioned above.[12] As both the first known woman critic of Christine and also her first major anthologist, Kéralio obviously self-identified with the poet, not only in shared gender, but also via a similarly learned father who took charge of her education. Kéralio's patrilineal intellectual gift was also heralded by her name, the feminized version of the father's, Louis-Félix Guinement de Kéralio, military officer and noted *littérateur*—not as lofty as Christine's onomastic self-linkage with Christ in medieval terms, but weighty enough by the more worldly standards of eighteenth-century *salon* society. In another divergence in social values, Kéralio later married one M. Robert, future Convention deputy, who voted for Louis XVI's execution: nothing like the young Christine's husband, Etienne de Castel, in his fealty to Charles VI, despite the latter's madness.

Kéralio's presentation of Christine's works embodies both the feminist and encyclopedic tendencies of her time. Her approach is certainly not philological; she relies on early printed texts—even the 1549 prose edition of the *Chemin de long estude*, rather than on good original manuscripts, for her substantial citations from several of them. But Kéralio was more concerned to make those texts uncovered by her philological brethren (like Sallier and Boivin) accessible to women, to enable the latter to realize their stake in France's cultural heritage: a "patrimony" also indebted to some literary mothers. The polemicists about to foment the French Revolution promised equality to women, a responsibility as well as a right, for which authors such as Kéralio sought to ready them. Her formulation, including extracts from (in order of their appearance) the *Charles V*, *Chemin de long estude*, *Trois vertus*, *Advision*, *Cité des dames*, *Cent balades*, *Rondeaux*, *Jeux a vendre*, *Epistre au dieu d'Amours*, epistles from the Debate on the *Rose*, *Proverbes moraux*, *Fais d'armes et de chevalerie*, and *Mutacion*, recontextualizes Christine as a model for making women into citizens of the new era to be ushered in by the Revolution.[13]

As much as he achieved by way of reforms, Napoleon did not honor the promise of women's equality in France, mainly because, like the later Bismarck in Germany, he did not view such emancipation as reformist. Nevertheless, the historical school inspired by his ethos, and finally inaugurated in 1821 as the Ecole royale des Chartes, trained several scholars instrumental in fostering Christine's reputation. The first two such *chartistes* were Antoine-Jean-Victor Le Roux de Lincy (1806–1869) and Raimond Thomassy (1810–1863), both omnivorous in their historical pursuits as esteemed archivists, although each from a contrasting perspective.[14] Neither author condescends to her gender; both treat her as a serious political commentator.

Of the two, Le Roux de Lincy, although described as an "archéologue" (archeologist), was the more conversant with *belles lettres*, having edited literary journals and several medieval French texts before publishing his 1839 article encompassing some of Christine's political poems,[15] after which he also contributed catalogues and historical manuals.[16] His literary-archeological side comes out when he examines four of her *chansons*, fully reproduced (from what is now Paris, Bibliothèque de l'Arsenal MS 3295) and annotated in his article, revealing the documentary importance of her verses to equal that of the other historical poems by three male poets, one Provençal and the others French. In fact, although Le Roux accords each of the male poets only one example—on topics ranging from Richard I to Philip Augustus and Saint Louis, respectively—he allows Christine four: one on Charles VI and three on the same French–English conflict from 1402.

However, Le Roux de Lincy's potential elevation of her unwittingly undermines her authorial integrity by eviscerating her poems from their original ballade sequences without warning. His innocent plundering of what we have since come to admire as the poet's delicate, yet deliberate, arrangement of her various shorter lyrics indicates the misunderstood status of Christine's *oeuvre* as a structural whole. Most readers would therefore have to wait fifty years for Maurice Roy's edition in order to identify the "Complainte sur la folie de Charles VI" (Complainte on the madness of Charles VI) and three ballades on the combat of seven Frenchmen against seven Englishmen as *Cent balades* 95, *Autres balades* 29, 31, and 30, noting the proper order of the last two (cf. Roy ed. 1: 241–46). Another rough patch in Le Roux's information on Christine's works lies in his confusion of *Trois vertus* with *Prudence/Prod'hommie*.[17]

Raimond Thomassy, early in his career, managed to tear himself away from such subjects as archaeology, geography, salt mining, and hydrology to compose his *Essai sur les écrits politiques de Christine de Pisan* in 1838: the first known monograph entirely devoted to Christine, and also the first book-length critical anthology of her works.[18] Thomassy's *Essai* was also quite daring in that he, an upstart, publicly professes his dismay at the godlike Prosper de Barante's omission of Christine in his multivolume *Histoire des ducs de Bourgogne* (iv).[19] Christine too deserved the status of monument, Thomassy asserts as his book's *raison d'être* (ii–iii), using a lapidary lexicon not unlike Christine's famous masonry metaphor in her *Charles V* (I.191). An enthusiastic but logical extension of Boivin's and Sallier's work, also recalling and fulfilling Gabriel Naudé's even earlier aspiration of 1667 (ii–iii, n.), Thomassy's densely packed *Essai* exposed the following works, albeit in fragments, to the literate public: *Ditié de Jehanne d'Arc*, *Epistre Othea*, *Enseignemens moraux*, *Epistre a la reine*, *Lamentacion*, *Oraison Nostre Dame*, *Livre de la paix*, and *Livre des trois vertus*. Several titles were seeing print for the first time, excluding early printed editions. Thomassy alludes to many others in passing, along with comparable works by her contemporaries.

Because philology and codicology were still only fledgling disciplines, even for the elite *chartistes*, Thomassy's sources were of uneven validity. For example, Achille Jubinal generously shared with him his prepublication text of the *Ditié de Jehanne d'Arc*—intended as the first complete edition but amounting to an inaccurate transcription of the Berne manuscript (Kennedy, nos. 288, 289)—as the basis for the *Essai's* selected *huitains* (xlii–xlix). To his credit, Thomassy ventured into manuscript transcription himself, with the aid of Bibliothèque Royale curator Paulin Paris, to produce his brief selections of the *Epistre Othea* based on what are now BnF MSS fr. 848 and 1185,[20] modestly heralding Campbell's,

Mombello's, and Parussa's researches of 100 years later through fifty manuscripts of this same work.

Some of Thomassy's texts retained their authority into the 1980s, as evidenced by Josette Wisman's editions of the *Epistre a la reine* and *Lamentacion*, which were based on Thomassy's texts, and thus had to be redone.[21] Other twentieth-century editors justly opted to work directly from the manuscripts to complete works abridged by Thomassy, such as Charity Willard's *Livre de la paix* (1958) and her *Trois vertus* with Eric Hicks (1989); Hicks also authoritatively edited the *Rose* Debate epistles in full (1977).[22] All such recent editors have benefited from the "market" created by Thomassy's galvanizing volume.

Like Le Roux de Lincy, Thomassy was also capable of tacitly uprooting Christine's lyric poems from their "native" sequences with the noblest of intentions, comparing her *Rondeaux* 1 to Charles d'Orléans's (106) and remarking upon the refreshingly promarriage thematics of *Autres balades* 26 (107) well before Varty and Deyermond.[23]

Even this early, Thomassy signaled the existence of London, British Library MS Harley 4431, if only by a footnote citing the illustrious Francisque Michel (107).[24] This is now recognized as Christine's "command performance" of her works up until circa 1410 for presentation to Queen Isabeau of France, and thus known as the "Queen's manuscript."[25] For some reason, even later French scholars would be loath to accept its authority for her pre-1410 *oeuvre*,[26] with the same bizarre reluctance as with "Pizan" instead of "Pisan."

Despite these failings and the ineluctable romantic subjectivity of his critical voice, Thomassy's "monument" succeeds in demonstrating Christine's unique political voice as part of modern France's national-self-conscious awakening. His more scientific projects took him eventually around Louisiana, then to Havana, where he died at fifty-three.

OF CREDOS AND CANONS: ROY, CAMPBELL, AND SOLENTE

By the latter half of the nineteenth century, Christine's literary worth had reached the attention of such major philologists as Gaston Paris (1839–1903) at the Collège de France and Ecole des Hautes Etudes, and Paul Meyer (1840–1917) of the Ecole des Chartes.[27] The two scholars, as generals in France's new culture wars with Germany—serving also toward avenging France's military defeat in the Franco-Prussian War of 1870–1871—planned to include editions of her works as part of her adopted country's literary arsenal. Gaston Paris, son of the same Paulin who had advised Thomassy on Christine manuscripts, acted as ideologue and architect of the program, whereas Paul Meyer, with his boundless administrative energy, would implement it. After founding the journal *Romania* in 1872, they then (1875) launched the Société des Anciens Textes Français (SATF), a "phalanx" dedicated to publishing classics of French medieval literature for bibliophiles and the general public alike, to remind them to preserve and take pride in their national heritage during difficult times.[28]

As dryly recondite as it seems to us today, in the late 1800s philology ruled as the *engagé*, politically relevant discipline, often combined with historiography.[29] At this point, it is essential to recognize that this cultural "rivalry" did not so much pit French medieval literature against German medieval *literature*—with scant exception, the Germans rightly yielded that point to the French—but rather, the competition focused on French versus German *philological proficiency* in French or Romance texts.[30] An example of this nationalistic polarizing of philology and historiography had occurred in the "contest" between Quicherat and Goerres to edit Joan of Arc's trial manuscripts, with France's Quicherat the victor in 1841.[31] Now forty years later, rights to Christine in her adoptive country were similarly threatened by Robert Püschel's edition of the *Chemin de long estude* in 1881, boasting consultation of seven manuscripts in three countries—the first complete critical edition of any of her major works.[32] This event, coupled with Gaston Paris's approbation of her, probably hastened her inclusion in the SATF program.

As in other previous competitions, French guardians of culture were often torn between admiration for their adversaries' strong points and nationalistic loyalty. Just as Jean de Montreuil had risked Clamanges's ire by celebrating Petrarch's talents in Christine's time, Gaston Paris openly preferred Karl Lachmann's method of manuscript editing (taking all manuscripts into account) over the principle later associated with Paris's successor, Joseph Bédier (one best manuscript as base), despite both French scholars' joint mission to "exterminate" German influence.[33]

By 1910, to maintain momentum within the SATF enterprise amidst such questions, the ever-practical Meyer simplified matters for his editors in a concise, detailed manual whose credo cautioned against "the affectation of exactitude" and extolled common sense.[34] This manual benefited from Meyer's now long experience as general series editor, including the Christine volumes (229), in addition to his own editing endeavors, which dodged the Lachmann versus Bédier question by limiting themselves to texts contained in only one or two manuscripts.

The contract to edit Christine's poetry in this series was awarded to a young legal-financial historian named Maurice Roy (1856–1932) in 1884. Meyer, no stranger to Christine himself,[35] would act as his mentor—at times, his tormentor—throughout the ensuing hands-on tutorial (scansion, punctuation, collation and variants, and critical preface) resulting in the three-volume *Oeuvres poétiques* (1886–1896).[36] For although Roy held distinguished credentials at the time of his selection, these better suited his concomitant career at the Cour des Comptes (Court of Accounts)—overseeing the nation's finances as public auditor (*conseiller référendaire*)—than as an editor of medieval literature or art historian, his major research interest.[37] Nevertheless, the well-connected, highly cultivated gentleman scholar obtained approval to undertake the largest scale Christine editing project thus far.

Lack of philological and literary training was not Roy's only disadvantage. The eager neophyte had almost no Middle-French editions to look to for models; certainly none dealing with the multifamily manuscript stemmata yielding Christine's poetry, not to mention the special linguistic problems inherent in Middle French. Meyer and Roy rightly settled on a sort of hybrid part-Lachmann, part-Bédier method for dealing with the manuscripts, but unfortunately, misled by certain assumptions, they reversed the now-accepted chronology of the two families, erroneously judging "A" older than "B." This mistake, plus undervaluing the Harley 4431 despite all evidence acceded to in the prefaces by Roy and Meyer (1: xvii, xxv–xxxvii; 3: xxi–xxiv), perhaps for nationalistic reasons (Margolis 2000, 8–9), prompted selection of the wrong "best manuscript"—BnF MS fr. 835 instead of Harley 4431—thus also failing at the Bédier principle, except in the cases of one *Complainte amoureuse*, the *Encore aultres balades*, and the *Cent balades d'amant et de dame*, for which the Harley is the unique manuscript and thus unavoidable. Yet Roy did at least collate the Harley, listing its variants throughout his edition, and reproduces its splendid offertory miniature as the frontispiece to Volume 3.

As for Roy's preface and other commentary, although jejune by current standards, these profited from Meyer's epistolary flogging and his own diligence in incorporating bits of advice from other specialists such as Petit de Julleville,[38] Lucy Toulmin Smith, librarians such as Léopold Delisle, and one possible dogsbody (a certain London-based Lemoine or Lemoing) preserved in his archives.[39] Roy's notes, in their relative lack of literary-critical content and preference for historical information, also reflect a counter-Romantic emphasis on hard facts over editorial subjectivity.

Roy's papers prove that practical considerations governed his edition's scope and structure as much as the manuscripts' ordering, and that he had planned to include more. One can compare the tables of contents in the final, printed version to the tenth *cahier* of MS 4106 at the Bibliothèque de l'Institut, which contains the following original, more ambitious plan for the three volumes:

Vol. 1: 328 pp.

Cent Ballades — 100 pp.

Ballades d'estrange façon — 3

53 *Ballades de divers propos* — 50

16 *Virelais* — 17

Lai de 264 vv. — 10

Autre *Lai* de 244 vv. — 9

69 *Rondeaux* — 50

70 *Jeux a vendre* — 18

3 *Oraisons* — 20 [crossed out by Roy]

Complainte amoureuse — 9

Epistre au dieu d'amours — 30

Dit de la Rose — 24

The most salient difference, aside from volume length and ordering, is the missing *Complainte amoureuse* found only in Harley 4431, which Roy did finally include (1:289–95), placing it *after* the Paris mss. one, mysteriously omitting the rubric marking it as the first.[40]

Volume 2's layout reads this way:

Débat de deux amans — 70 pp.

Dit de Poissy — 72

Duc des vrais amans — 180 = 322 pp.

Comparison of this to the final version shows this middle volume to have caught the ambitious spillover from projected Volume 1 and also most material first destined for Volume 3, obviously prior to discovery of the Harley MS's *Cent balades d'amant et de dame*, to be joined by the *Duc des vrais amans* preceding it in final Volume 3.

By contrast, a glance at proto-Volume 3's layout reveals quite a different selection:

Dit de la pastoure — 77 pp.

Trois jugemens — 52

Dits moraux [=*Enseignemens*] — 16

Trois oraisons [*Nostre Dame, XV Joyes, Nostre seigneur*] — 20

Proverbes moraulx — 7

Epistre a Eustace Mourel — "212 vers" [no pp. given]

Epistre Othea — 158

[no total pagination given].

Another, possibly later, sketch is similar, but replaces *Pastoure, Trois jugemens,* and *Eustace Mourel* with the *Duc des vrais amans*. It still holds out for the *Epistre Othea* as well for a total of 358 pages.

Even without the *Epistre Othea*, the moral tone of final Volume 3 was retained, sealed, in fact, by the "Lay mortel" at the end. Indeed each of the other two of Roy's volumes also possesses a distinctive flavor: Volume 1 shows Christine at her most poetically self-conscious and lyrical, whereas Volume 2 is predominantly discursive, more concerned with exposition and less with stylistic flair. In view of the editorial-logistical problems just observed, the discernible tonal progression over the three volumes is dictated only partially by Christine's chronology.

A fourth projected volume was to contain not only final Volume 3's *Cent balades d'amant et de dame*, planned at 150 pages, but also, preceding it, no less than the *Mutacion de Fortune*, somewhat underestimated at 195 pp. (Laidlaw 2000, 248), and concluding with the "Poème de la Pucelle" (*Ditié de Jehanne d'Arc*). Toward realization of this volume, Roy's papers contain a transcription of the *Mutacion* from BnF MS fr. 603 (MS 4106, *cahiers* 1–9); for the *Epistre Othea*, the prologue and first three chapters (MS 4106, *cahier* 4, verso) before succumbing to what may well have been a "reality check," given that work's sobering codicological exigencies; but nothing for the *Ditié*, whose inclusion would have necessitated venturing beyond the Paris libraries—to those in exotic Berne, Carpentras, and Grenoble (Kennedy 1984, item 288)—to improve upon Quicherat's text. On the other hand, Léopold Delisle, archivist at the BnF, offered him, in a letter from 1896, a newly acquired manuscript (BnF nouv. acq. fr. 4792) of the then unknown *Sept psaumes allegorisés* (Laidlaw 2000, 247), which Roy left no evidence of having pursued.

Although he would publish no more on Christine, having turned instead to the art-historical research guaranteeing his real claim to fame, Roy was still actively on her trail as of 1912 (MS 4106: 10, item 10; Laidlaw 2000, 248). He would later serve twice as president of the SATF during the 1920s–early 1930s. His scholarly achievement would gain him entry into the Académie des Inscriptions, erstwhile foyer of Boivin, Sallier, and others, in 1929.

One should not underestimate the breadth and lasting value of Roy's *Oeuvres poétiques*, not only for his time, but also for ours. The Paris manuscripts favored by him and Meyer (BnF MSS fr. 835, 606, 836, 605, and 12779) are a very close second, or even equal, to the Harley except for the three works listed above. This judicious selection from the numerous Christine manuscripts rendered an immense service to Christine scholars, especially when compared to Le Roux de Lincy's reliance, despite equal access to BnF manuscripts, on what turns out to be an eighteenth-century copy of BnF MS fr. 12779 (Le Roux, 361; Roy, 1: xix), and the haphazard nature of Sallier's and Thomassy's choices.

Roy's triumph of deforestation, along with reconstruction, also affected the content of the corpus. These volumes both define and organize her "poetical works" (i.e., short lyrics, *dits*, and sententiae, as opposed to longer narrative poems and prose), while furnishing the first critical texts of these many thematically diverse, chronologically disparate poems. Because of Roy, the *fin-de-siècle* reader could examine a ballade or rondeau within its parent sequence or grouping, as Christine wished it, rather than as an isolated remnant, artificially anthologized according to theme as in Boivin or Thomassy.[41] Likewise the prospective editor could now see more clearly what remained to be done. Roy's main heroic flaw— beyond lesser errors from inexperience—was, of course, his undervaluing of Harley 4431, the base or one of the base manuscripts for updated editions of his texts, along with Varty's 1965 anthology: Barbara Altmann's *Debat de deux amans, Livre des trois jugemens* and *Dit de Poissy* (1998); Thelma Fenster's *Duc des vrais amans* (1995), and *Epistre au dieu d'Amours* and *Dit de la rose* (1990); and Jacqueline Cerquiglini's 1982 *Cent balades d'amant et de dame*, which, although Roy had consulted the Harley MS, warranted a new reading, with complete introduction, glossary, and notes. Revisions of other parts of Roy's edition are those by Mary V. Reese (*Dit de la pastoure*, 1992) and Jean-François Kosta-Théfaine (*Epistre à Eustace Morel*, 1996).[42]

Returning to the eschatology of Roy's never-realized Volume 4, this study examines Percy Campbell's researches on the *Epistre Othea* and Suzanne Solente's *Mutacion* below. As for Roy's "Poème de la Pucelle," Angus Kennedy and Kenneth Varty published their definitive annotated text and translation of the *Ditié de Jehanne d'Arc* (1977). Perhaps Roy may have wished to include in this volume the *Sept psaumes* of which Delisle had informed him. In any case, Ruth Ringland Rains, a student of Charles Knudson, working from Delisle's groundbreaking notices, accomplished this in 1965.[43]

Soon after Roy's Volume 2 appeared, the king of literary canons for the Third Republic, Gustave Lanson, condemned Christine as a bluestocking and a bore in an infamous passage in 1895.[44] This pronouncement would alienate her from French literary academe, leaving her fate to the rigid mercies of the *chartistes* within France and more diversely talented admirers from other countries unfettered by such proscription.

Percy Gerald Cadogan Campbell (1878–1960), a top Oxford graduate in Classics (Balliol 1902) whose bilingual background enabled him immediately to assume the professorship in French at Queen's University in Canada, intended to publish a critical edition of the *Epistre Othea* circa 1928.[45] His exacting Sorbonne thesis on Christine's sources for the *Epistre Othea* is still useful today, shedding light on another corpus: that of Christine's precise sources, while also attempting to establish the *Epistre Othea*'s manuscript tradition (Campbell 1924, 9–18) far beyond Roy's suppositions, which he refutes, correcting another Roy rubric error along the way (Campbell 1924, 18–20). Similarly, Campbell's two densely packed articles on Christine in England meticulously trace details of her dissemination across the Channel.[46] He was working under the tutelage of the renowned Alfred Jeanroy, who not only advised Roy on *Epistre Othea* manuscripts but who also authored a seminal study on the sources of the *Cité des dames*.[47]

Given the extraordinary promise of his published research it is a pity that Campbell never completed this edition. Even this superman—in athletics and *fais d'armes* (leader of the only battalion raised from a university in World War I, the Queen's Highland), as much as in *estude*; who built up his French department fivefold, then completed his *Etude des sources* in 18 months while on special leave in Paris—seems to have been thwarted in realizing his greatest project, probably the victim of his own excellence as administrator and teacher, which prevented further travels to Paris. We know he was still keenly aware of Christine as of 1933 in his *Fais d'armes* notes, in which he wryly qualifies himself as "one who has been interested in Christine for more years than he cares to remember (217)," but would publish no more during his remaining, otherwise vigorous, 27 years.[48]

The *Epistre Othea* would claim another gifted, productive aspirant, Gianni Mombello, by the 1970s. But his richly informative prolegomena would vastly supplement and organize Campbell's researches on the *Epistre Othea*'s extensive manuscript tradition and historical context: a solid foundation for Mombello's pupil, Parussa, its final editor.[49]

Less colorful but more prolific, Suzanne Solente (1895–1978) edited the *Charles V* and *Mutacion de Fortune* in the grand tradition of the Ecole des Chartes. It was here that she trained (1917–1920), at the top of her class every year (the Ecole was coeducational even back then), to attain the title of *archiviste paléographe* in 1921, her thesis having been the very thorough historical preface to her upcoming *Charles V*. As new librarian at the BnF, she uncovered the *Heures de Contemplacion* and especially the *Epistre de prison de vie humaine*, of which she did a partial edition (1924), later redone in full by Angus Kennedy in 1984.[50] Her two-volume edition of the *Charles V* (1936–1940) would win the coveted Prix Bordin,[51] the same prize offered three times by the Académie des Inscriptions to entice high-quality critical studies of Christine fifty years earlier— in vain (Laigle, 45).

Her debt to Maurice Roy is more direct than the rest of posterity's because he had generously shared a partial transcription of BnF MS fr. 603 and photocopy of the entire Brussels BR MS 9508 (Bib. Inst. MS 4105–4106: 1–9). This allowed her to work through the library-research obstacles wrought by World War II (Solente 1959, 1:vii; Laidlaw, 249–50) and thereby complete her magisterial four-volume edition of the *Mutacion de Fortune* in timely fashion (1959–1966).

Solente then set about updating Püschel's edition of the *Chemin de long estude*, almost finished at her death in 1978. Although Püschel had based his text on Brussels BR MS 10982, Solente selected BnF MS fr. 1188, shunning the Harley 4431—embarrassingly unknown to Püschel—which Tarnowski would favor in her 2000 edition.[52] Despite her achievements as student and scholar, Solente's passing received only the briefest notice in the *Bibliothèque de l'Ecole des Chartes*—perhaps the victim of longevity rather than gender or topical bias.[53]

All three of the above-named pivotal figures in Christine editing worked with great energy and lived a long time, but still not long enough. A few contemporaneous lone wolves, deprived of the same access to quality expertise and training, nonetheless deserve mention. Sr. Mary Louis Towner, fulfilling the hopes of Earle Babcock from circa 1910, courageously published a serviceable annotated text of the *Advision* in 1932, without following editorial conventions of spelling, capitalization, or punctuation. Christine Reno and Liliane Dulac finally replaced this in 2001.[54] Robert Lucas, with equal bravery and more success than most critics concede, published a critical edition of the *Corps de policie* in 1967, later replaced by Angus Kennedy's in 1998.[55]

The *Cité des dames* is another major prose work whose editing history attains epic dimensions. To summarize simply, Maureen Curnow edited it as an impressive Ph.D. thesis in 1977, then, like Campbell, became engulfed by institutional concerns before revising it for publication. Quasisimultaneously, Monika Lange also undertook revision of her own thesis edition, which reveals three different redactions of the *Cité*, but without finishing. Both of these were incorporated into and further revised by E. J. Richards in his 1997 edition.[56] Richards had already published a fine annotated translation of it in 1982, based on Curnow, both responding to and encouraging the tremendous anglophone-feminist popularity of this work beginning in the 1970s.

What remains to be done? Two as yet unedited major titles would be the *Prudence/Prod'hommie*, on which Simone Pagot and Liliane Dulac have been working, and the *Fais d'armes et de chevalerie* promised by Charity Willard. James Laidlaw's findings substantiate a need for a complete reediting of all *formes fixes* lyric poetry, such as the *Cent balades*, *Rondeaux*, and *Virelais*. The *Epistre Othea*'s program of illustrations, which had troubled Jeanroy and Campbell (BSATF 1927, 62), might well be inserted into Parussa's text, some forward-thinking publisher willing, to reconstruct adequately this text's uniquely multimedia didactic stratagem and impact.

CONCLUSION: THE HECUBA OF THE HYPERTEXT: THE IMPACT OF COMPUTERS ON CHRISTINE EDITING

In light of the exceptional demands upon the editor(s) of Christine's major works, the post-1960s decline in rigorous humanities curricula at the secondary-school and college levels, plus university administrators' frequent incomprehension have dimmed prospects for the training of future philologists. In other words, given the present state of education, despite many positive points, it is difficult to imagine any English department nurturing a Byles or Bühler; any French department a Paris, Meyer, or Campbell; nor would they receive tenure anyway.

But all is not lost. The same period that has weakened classical humanistic education has also nurtured its potential ally: information technology that if properly programmed and exploited can compensate for the above shortcomings. Scholars have come to relish how computers can free them from more menial aspects—such as establishing the text, numbering lines, etc.—to permit focusing on literary discussions beyond the old-fashioned *analyse*. Certain software also facilitates composing the historical, codicological, and linguistic information for the *apparatus criticus*. It is perhaps in such prefatory literary-critical discussions that recent editions surpass the old *chartiste*-style introductions. Best of all, as Eric Hicks has observed, computer word processing minimizes the inevitable intermediary of human error plaguing even the most painstakingly executed texts: "Qui dit copie dit faute" (To copy is to make a mistake).[57] In all, the machine portends great things for documenting what philologists love to call *mouvance*: the textual variations occurring from copy to copy among manuscripts of a given work as caused by unwitting error or underlying agenda. Christine was distinctly expert at manipulating *mouvance* to suit her different patrons.

Two principal camps appear to have emerged: those—the majority—using computers mainly to apply text to page, and to generate bibliography, glossary, and concordances; and those deploying the computer for more sophisticated editing or editing-related tasks as well, such as databases and *éditions génétiques*—one controlling and representing all variants chronologically in context. The conservative majority has already contributed much to establishing Christine's texts. In the second category, two very different scholars, James Laidlaw and Eric Hicks, have shown themselves to be true visionaries.[58]

Contemplation of these developments and the personalities behind them cause us to reconsider that "polymath, maverick quality" noted at the outset of this study. Is it a prerequisite condition or occupational hazard for the aspiring Christine editor?

NOTES

1. However, the appearance of editorial nonintervention in these early printed editions of Christine, as in the supposed mere "translations" of her works by Caxton et al., is deceptive. For their role in promoting Christine's literary image, see Cynthia J. Brown, "The Reconstruction of an Author in Print: Christine de Pizan in the Fifteenth andسixteenth Centuries," in *Christine de Pizan and the Categories of Difference*, ed. Marilynn Desmond (Minneapolis: University of Minnesota Press, 1998), 215–35; and Martha W. Driver, "Christine de Pisan and Robert Wyer: The *C. Hystoryes of Troye*, or *L'Epistre d'Othea* Englished," *Gutenberg-Jahrbuch 1997* 72 (1997): 125–39.
2. For these editions of Middle English reworkings, see Angus J. Kennedy, *Christine de Pizan: A Bibliographical Guide* (London: Grant & Cutler, 1984), items 421, 336, 335, and 471, respectively. For original Middle-French editions: Gabriella Parussa, ed., *Epistre Othea*, Textes Littéraires Français [TLF], 517 (Geneva:

Droz, 1999) and Angus J. Kennedy, ed., *Le Livre du corps de policie*, "Etudes christiniennes," 1 (Paris: Honoré Champion, 1998).

3. See N. Margolis, "Christine at 600: The State of Christine de Pizan Studies for the Second Millennium," in *Christine de Pizan 2000: Studies on Christine de Pizan in Honour of Angus J. Kennedy*, ed. John Campbell and Nadia Margolis (Amsterdam and Atlanta: Rodopi, 2000), 31–45.

4. On the Boivins see Joseph F. Michaud, *Biographie universelle* (Paris: Desplaces, 1854; reprinted Graz, Austria: Akademische Druck, 1968), 4: 609–10.

5. "Vie de Christine de Pisan, et de Thomas de Pisan son pere," *Mémoires de littérature tirez des registres de l'Académie des Inscriptions et belles-lettres* 2 (1736): 704–14.

6. Both Théodore and Denys Godefroy, father and son, official French national historiographers, were prodigious catalogueurs and editor-printers, often providing the earliest printed texts of many historical documents, including chronicles and what we now appreciate as literary texts. Boivin's marginal citation from Godefroy (712) would read, in modern terms: Jean Juvenal des Ursins, *Histoire de Charles VI, roy de France, et des choses memorables. . . .* Ed. Denys Godefroy (Paris: Imprimerie Royale, 1653), 79. Suzanne Solente, "Christine de Pisan," *Histoire littéraire de la France*, 40 (Paris: Imprimerie nationale/Klincksieck, 1969), 346, n. 16, cites this passage (on Charles VI's payment to Christine) more completely, giving Godefroy's source, Paris, BnF coll. Dupuy, vol. 755, f. 97v.

7. Juvenal des Ursins (Godefroy), *Histoire de Charles VI*, 799; cited in Suzanne Solente, "Introduction," in *Le Livre des fais et bonnes meurs du sage roy Charles V* (Paris: Honoré Champion, 1936), 1: xcviii–ix.

8. "Vie de Charles V, dit le Sage, roy de France, écrite par Christine de Pisan, Dame qui vivoit de son tems," in *Dissertations sur l'histoire ecclésiastique et civile de Paris . . .* (Paris: Durand, 1743), 83–484. For a complete critical discussion of Lebeuf as Solente's most worthy precursor, and other early editors of the *Charles V*, see Solente 1936, 1: xcviii–cii.

9. After the first French printed editions of the *Epistre au dieu d'Amours* (as *Le contre Rommant de la Rose*, n.d., but pre-1510) (see Roy, 2, ix); the *Othea* (1499–1500); *Fais d'armes et de chevalerie* (1488); *Trois vertus* (1497); and a prose version of the *Chemin de long estude* (1549) (Kennedy 1984, nos. 315, 328, 417, 446, and 461, respectively).

10. "Notice sur deux ouvrages manuscrits de Christine de Pisan," *Mémoires de littérature tirés des registres de l'Académie royale des Inscriptions et belles-lettres* 17 (1751): 515–25. For Sallier's label as "philologue" and other details, see under "Sallier" in the *Nouvelle Biographie générale*, ed. Joseph F. C. Hoefer (Paris: Firmin Didot, 1864), Vol. 43: cols. 188–89; also J.-F. Michaud, *Biographie universelle*, 37: 518.

11. Marie-Jeanne Philipon, Mme Roland (1754–1793), pro-Girondist *salonnière*, and the journalist Jean-Pierre Brissot, both guillotined during the French Revolution, praised Kéralio. See under "Kéralio," in Michaud, *Biographie universelle*, 21: 535–36.

12. Paris: Lagrange, 1787, 2: 109–467; 3: 1–132.

13. See, e.g., Joan B. Landes, *Women and the Public Sphere in the Age of the French Revolution* (Ithaca, NY and London: Cornell University Press, 1988).

14. Matriculation rosters for the Ecole des Chartes (1833, 1835) in *Bibliothèque de l'Ecole des Chartes* [*BEC*] 1 (1839–40): 46–47, listing Le Roux de Lincy, Thomassy, and another classmate rendering scholarly service to Christine, Jules Quicherat, who published a complete, if imperfect, text (see Kennedy 1984, 291) of her *Ditié de Jehanne d'Arc* in his widely read *Procès de condamnation et de réhabilitation de Jeanne d'Arc dite la Pucelle* (Paris: Jules Renouard, 1849), 5: 3–21.

15. "Chansons historiques des XIIIe, XIVe et XVe siècles," *BEC* 1 (1839–40): 359–88, especially 360–61, 374–88.

16. See the *Nouvelle Biographie générale*, ed. Hoefer (1859) 30: 884–5 and the Harvard online catalogue (Hollis) for "Le Roux de Lincy."

17. In Le Roux de Lincy and L. M. Tisserand, *Paris et ses historiens* (Paris: Imprimerie Impériale, 1867), 418. For more Le Roux on Christine, see Kennedy 1984, items 208, 247, and 364.

18. Paris: Debécourt, 1838, 199 pp. Thomassy, apparently moved by the synergy between Christine and Gerson as "esprits fermes et modérés" in tumultuous times (i, xvii), promised an "essai" on Gerson as a sequel. This was published in 1844, per his obituary, "Chronique," *BEC* 25 (1864): 387–88.

19. Paris: L'Advocat, 1824, with several editions thereafter, some lavishly illustrated; one of the most influential histories of Christine's time for the nineteenth and early twentieth centuries.

20. Paris had guided Thomassy well: 848 is one of the main manuscripts for Parussa, 102.

21. Josette Wisman, ed. and trans., *The Epistle of the Prison of Human Life With An Epistle to the Queen of France and Lament on the Evils of the Civil War*, Garland Library of Medieval Literature, series A (New York: Garland, 1984), 70–83, 84–95—mainly useful to readers requiring English translation; for authoritative texts, based on the original manuscripts, see Angus Kennedy's editions of *Lamentacion*, in *Mélanges Charles Foulon* (Rennes: Institut de français, 1980), 1: 177–85, and *Epistre a la reine* in *Revue des langues romanes* [special issue: *Christine de Pizan*, ed. Liliane Dulac and Jean Dufournet] 92: 2 (1988): 253–64.

22. Charity Cannon Willard, ed., *The Livre de la paix of Christine de Pisan* (The Hague: Mouton, 1958); Willard and Hicks, eds., *Le Livre des Trois Vertus*, Bibliothèque du XVe siècle, 50 (Paris: Honoré Champion, 1989); Hicks, ed., *Le Débat sur le Roman de la Rose*, Bibliothèque du XVe siècle, 43 (Paris: Honoré Champion, 1977).

23. For both poems, see Kenneth Varty, ed., *Christine de Pisan, Ballades, Rondeaux, and Virelais* (Leicester: Leicester University Press, 1965), 3, 8, 128–29, 132; for *Autres balades* 26, see Alan D. Deyermond, "Sexual Initiation in the Woman's-Voice Court Lyric," in *Courtly Literature: Culture and Context*, ed. Keith Busby and Eric Kooper (Amsterdam and Philadelphia: John Benjamins, 1990), 124–58, especially 149–53.

24. Michel (1809–1887), a chief proponent of the "Empirical School" of textual editing and mainly known for his Oxford *Roland*, published Christine's *Rondeaux* 1, based on Harley 4431, with commentary, in Louisa Stuart Costello's *Specimens of the Early Poetry of France* (London: Pickering, 1835), 97—according to Thomassy's note.

25. On her manuscripts, see James Laidlaw's chapter in this volume; also his "Christine de Pizan—An Author's Progress," *Modern Language Review* 78 (1983): 532–50 and "Christine de Pizan—A Publisher's Progress," *MLR* 82 (1987): 35–75.
26. Gallic grudging persists, although attenuated in, e.g., Pierre-Yves Badel, review of Gabriella Parussa's edition of the *Epistre Othea, Romania* 118 (2000): 560–61: "non qu'il [Harley ms.] soit sensiblement supérieur à [BnF MS fr. 606], mais parce que l'éditrice a pris le parti légitime d'éditer la dernière version 'approuvée par l'auteur' " (506).
27. Gaston Paris, "Histoire de la littérature française du Moyen âge," *Journal des Savants* (October–December 1901): 779–88; reprinted in Mario Roques, ed., *Gaston Paris. Mélanges* (Paris: Honoré Champion, 1912), especially 61–62; praising her lyric poetry in his *Esquisse de la littérature française depuis les origines jusqu'à la fin du XVe siècle* (Paris: Armand Colin, 1907), 200, 220–27 passim, 252; originally published as *Mediaeval French Literature* (London: Temple Primers, 1903). For Christine's reception by Meyer et al., see Mathilde Laigle, *Le Livre des Trois Vertus de Christine de Pisan et son milieu historique et littéraire* (Paris: Honoré Champion, 1912), 45–8.
28. See Maurice Roy's presidential speech before the SATF in 1928, *Bulletin de la SATF [BSATF]* 53–55 (1930): 88.
29. On the role of *fin-de-siècle* philologists in national affairs, see, e.g., Ursula Bähler, *Gaston Paris Dreyfusard: Le Savant dans la cité* (Paris: CNRS, 1999).
30. See Mary Speer, "Old French Literature," in *Scholarly Editing: A Guide to Research*, ed. D. C. Greetham (New York: Modern Language Association, 1995), 382–416; see also Gerard J. Brault, "Gaston Paris (1839–1903)," and William W. Kibler, "Joseph Bédier (1864–1938)," in *Medieval Scholarship: Biographical Studies on the Formation of a Discipline*, 2: *Literature and Philology*, ed. Helen Damico (New York: Garland, 1996), 151–65, 253–66, respectively. Bédier was Laigle's thesis director.
31. See N. Margolis, "Trial by Passion: Philology, Film and Ideology in the Portrayal of Joan of Arc," *Journal of Medieval and Early Modern Studies* 27: 3 (1997): 445–92, especially 449.
32. *Le Livre du Chemin de long estude par Cristine de Pizan* (Berlin: Dahmköhler; Paris: Le Soudier, 1881; new edition, Berlin: Hettler, 1887; reprinted Geneva: Slatkine, 1974).
33. Per Nykrog's terminology, "A Warrior Scholar at the Collège de France," in *Medievalism and the Modernist Temper*, ed. R. Howard Bloch and Stephen G. Nichols (Baltimore and London: The Johns Hopkins University Press, 1996), 287. See also articles in this volume by Nichols, Ganim, Graham, and Corbellari; and Alain Corbellari, *Joseph Bédier: Ecrivain et philologue* (Geneva: Droz, 1997).
34. Paul Meyer, "Instruction pour la publication des anciens textes français," *BEC* 71 (1910): 224–33, cit. 230.
35. See Kennedy 1984, items 320 and 425.
36. 3 vols., SATF, 24 (Paris: Firmin Didot, 1886, 1891, 1896; reprinted New York: Johnson, 1965). For Meyer and Roy, see correspondence transcribed in James C. Laidlaw, "Maurice Roy (1856–1932)," passim, in *Christine de Pizan 2000: Studies on Christine de Pizan in Honour of Angus J. Kennedy*, ed. John Campbell and N. Margolis, "Faux titre," 196 (Amsterdam and Atlanta: Rodopi, 2000), 233–50.

37. See Laidlaw, 2000, and Nadia Margolis, "Maurice Roy, Maverick Editor, and the Making of the Christinian Corpus," in *"Riens ne m'est seur que la chose incertaine"*: *Etudes sur l'art d'écrire au Moyen Age offertes à Eric Hicks par ses anciens élèves et ses amis*, ed. Jean-Claude Mühlethaler and Denis Billotte (Geneva: Slatkine, 2001), 217–27.
38. See Louis Petit de Julleville's own positive assessment in *Histoire de la langue et littérature française* (Paris: Armand Colin, 1896), 2: 357–66, urging more editions of her works (366).
39. Roy's papers are housed in Paris at the Bibliothèque de l'Institut de France, MSS 4102–4107; MS 4105 (2 vols.) is a photocopy of Brussels BR MS 9508 (*Mutacion de Fortune*) (the Institut catalogue misnumbers this as part of 4106); MS 4106, *cahiers* 1–9 contain Roy's transcription of Paris BnF MS fr. 603, also of the *Mutacion*. Most interesting is 4106, *cahier* 10, containing notes and correspondence. Because Laidlaw, 2000, reproduces almost all correspondence and paraphrases notes pertaining to Roy's *OEuvres poétiques*, "Laidlaw, 2000" is here cited by pages as their primary source. The only material in MS 4106 *not* transcribed in Laidlaw is cited here by ms., *cahier*, and, where necessary, item numbers in the Institut archives. My thanks to the Institut library staff for their generous help.
40. This grave omission may either have been purely accidental—as Roy seemed to find rubrics tedious (e.g., MS 4106: 5 passim)—or due to nationalistic tampering. See Margolis, "Clerkliness and Courtliness in the Complaintes of Christine de Pizan," in *Christine de Pizan and Medieval French Lyric*, ed. E. J. Richards (Gainesville: University Press of Florida, 1998), 135–54, especially 145–46.
41. Varty's anthology, based on the Harley, also anthologizes by theme, but this is an annotated student manual, in which he faithfully gives each selection's provenance.
42. Altmann, ed., *The Love Debate Poems of Christine de Pizan* (Gainesville: University Press of Florida, 1998); Fenster, ed., *Le Livre du duc des vrais amans* (Binghamton, NY: Medieval & Renaissance Texts & Studies, 1995); Reese, ed., "A Critical Edition of Christine de Pizan's *Dit de la Pastoure*" (Ph.D. dissertation, University of Alabama, 1992); Kosta-Théfaine, ed., "Les *Proverbes moraux* de Christine de Pizan," and "L'*Epistre a Eustace Morel* de Christine de Pisan," *Le Moyen Français* 38 (1996): 61–77 and 79–91, respectively.
43. Angus J. Kennedy and Kenneth Varty, eds., *Ditié de Jehanne d'Arc: Christine de Pisan* (Oxford: Society for the Study of Mediaeval Languages and Literature, 1977); *Les Sept Psaumes allégorisés of Christine de Pisan: A Critical Edition from the Brussels and Paris Manuscripts* (Washington, DC: Catholic University of America, 1965). See especially Léopold Delisle, "Notice sur les *Sept Psaumes allégorisés* de Christine de Pisan," *Notices et extraits des manuscrits de la Bibliothèque nationale* 35: 2 (1896), 5–13.
44. *Histoire de la littérature française* (Paris: Hachette, 1895), 167.
45. See P. G. C. Campbell, *L'*Epître d'Othéa: *Etude sur les sources de Christine de Pisan* (Paris: Edouard Champion, 1924), 18 and Alfred Jeanroy's announcement in *BSATF* 51–52 (1927): 62.
46. "Christine de Pisan en Angleterre," *Revue de Littérature comparée* 5 (1925): 659–70 and "Notes on *The Book of Fayttes of Armes and of Chyvalrye*," *Medium AEvum* 2 (1933): 217–18. See Kennedy, 1984, item 147 for corrections to the first; Campbell's second suggests several important corrections and additions to

Byles's 1932 edition, only partially included, without acknowledging Campbell, in the 1937 revised edition.
47. "Boccace et Christine de Pisan: le *De claris mulieribus* principale source du *Livre de la cité des dames*," *Romania* 48 (1922): 93–105.
48. For his many accomplishments, see "P. G. C. Campbell," in *Queen's Profiles*, ed. David G. Dewar (Kingston, Ontario: Queen's University, 1951); 28–36; and the *Balliol College Register* for 1914, 1934, 1953, 1969. My thanks to Alice, reference librarian at Stauffer Library, Queen's University, and Dr. John Jones, Dean and Archivist, Balliol College, Oxford, for their indispensable help in obtaining these materials.
49. See "Per un'edizione critica dell' *Epistre Othea* di Christine de Pizan: I-II," *Studi francesi* 8 (1964): 401–17; pt. III, *Studi francesi* 9 (1965): 1–12; *La Tradizione manoscritta dell'*Epistre Othea *di Christine de Pizan: Prolegomeni all'edizione del testo* (Torino: Accademia delle Scienze, 1967); see Parussa, ed., 87–101.
50. "Un traité inédit de Christine de Pisan: *L'Epistre de la prison de vie humaine*," *BEC* 84 (1924): 263–301; Kennedy, *Christine de Pizan's Epistre de la prison de vie humaine* (Glasgow: University of Glasgow French Department, 1984).
51. *BEC* 103 (1942): 385.
52. Andrea Tarnowski, ed., *Le Chemin de longue étude*, "Lettres gothiques" (Paris: Livre de Poche, 2000); for manuscripts and Solente, see 59–62.
53. For Solente's career, see the "Chronique" in each *BEC* number: 77–81 (1917–1920); also 82 (1921): 230, 235; 84 (1923); 103 (1942): 385, and 137 (1979): 363.
54. Towner, *Lavision-Christine: Introduction and Text* (Washington, DC: Catholic University of America, 1932). On Babcock's announced edition, see Towner, vii, and Laigle, xii, and 47 n. 4. Babcock, of the University of Chicago, contacted Roy and Meyer (Bib. Inst. MS 4106: 10, items 15–16) in 1910; Christine Reno and Liliane Dulac, eds., *Le livre de l'advision Cristine*, "Etudes christiniennes," 4 (Paris: Honoré Champion, 2000).
55. Lucas, *Le Livre du corps de policie*, TLF, 145 (Geneva: Droz/Paris: Minard, 1967); Kennedy, 1998.
56. For Lange and Curnow, see Kennedy 1984, items 387 and 388; Richards, *La Città delle dame*, Biblioteca medievale, 2 (Milan: Luni, 1997; rev. ed. 1998); Richards, "Editing the *Livre de la cité des dames*: New Insights, Problems and Challenges," in *Au Champ des escriptures: IIIe Colloque international sur Christine de Pizan*, ed. Eric Hicks with the collaboration of Diego Gonzalez and Philippe Simon (Paris: Champion, 2000), 789–816.
57. Hicks, "Eloge de la machine: transcription, édition, génération de textes," *Romania* 103 (1982): 88–107, cit. 94.
58. Laidlaw, "Christine de Pizan: From Scriptorium to Database and Back Again," *Journal of the Institute of Romance Studies* 1 (1992): 59–67, and databank website: http://www.arts.ed.ac.uk./french/christine/cpstart.htm; Hicks, "Eloge," and "Pour une édition génétique de l'*Epistre Othea*," in *Pratiques de la culture écrite en France au XVe siècle*, ed. Monique Ornato and Nicole Pons, Textes et études du Moyen âge, 2 (Louvain: Louvain-la-neuve, 1995), 151–60.

Bibliography

PRIMARY SOURCES

Altmann, Barbara K., ed. *The Love Debate Poems of Christine de Pizan: "Le Livre du debat de deux amans"; "Le Livre des Trois jugemens"; "Le Livre du Dit de Poissy."* Gainesville, FL: University Press of Florida, 1998.

Baird, Joseph L., and John R. Kane. *La Querelle de la Rose: Letters and Documents.* Chapel Hill, NC: North Carolina Studies in the Romance Languages and Literatures, no. 199, 1978.

Brown-Grant, Rosalind, trans. *The Book of the City of Ladies.* Harmondsworth: Penguin, 1999.

Cerquiglini, Jacqueline, ed. Christine de Pizan. *Cent ballades d'amant et de dame.* Paris: Union Générale d'Edition, 1982.

Cosman, Madeleine Pelner, trans. *A Medieval Woman's Mirror of Honor: The Treasury of the City of Ladies.* New York: Bard Hall Press and Persea Books, 1989.

Fenster, Thelma S., and Mary Carpenter Erler, eds. *Poems of Cupid, God of Love: Christine de Pizan's "Epistre au dieu d'Amours" and "Dit de la Rose," Thomas Hoccleve's "The Letter of Cupid," with George Sewell's "The Proclamation of Cupid."* Leiden/New York: E.J. Brill, 1990.

———, ed. *Christine de Pizan: Le livre du duc des vrais amans.* Binghamton, NY: Medieval and Renaissance Texts and Studies, 1995.

Forhan, Kate Langdon, trans. *The Book of the Body Politic.* Cambridge: Cambridge University Press, 1994.

Hicks, Eric, ed. and trans. *Le Début sur le "Roman de la Rose."* Paris: Champion, 1977.

Hicks, Eric, and Thérèse Moreau, trans. *Le Livre des faits et bonnes moeurs du roi Charles V le Sage.* Série Moyen Age. Paris: Stock, 1997.

Kennedy, Angus J., ed. *"La Lamentacion sur les maux de la France."* In *Mélanges de langue et littérature françaises du Moyen Age et de la Renaissance offerts à Charles Foulon,* 177–85. Rennes: Institut de Français, Université de Haute-Bretagne, I, 1980.

———, ed. *Christine de Pizan's "Epistre de la prison de vie humaine."* Glasgow: Glasgow University French Department, 1984.

———, ed. *"L'Epistre a la reine."* Revue des langues romanes [special issue: *Christine de Pizan*, edited by Liliane Dulac and Jean Dufournet] 92: 2 (1988): 253–64.

———, ed. *Le Livre du corps de policie.* Paris: Champion, 1998.

Kennedy, Angus J., and Kenneth Varty, eds. and trans. *Christine de Pisan. Ditié de Jehanne d'Arc.* Medium Aevum Monographs, 9. Oxford: Society for Mediaeval Languages and Literatures, 1977.

Kosta-Théfaine, Jean-François. "Les *Proverbes moraux* de Christine de Pizan," "L'*Epistre a Eustace Morel* de Christine de Pisan." *Le Moyen Français* 38 (1996): 61–77, 79–91.

Lawson, Sarah, trans. *The Treasure of the City of Ladies.* New York: Penguin, 1985.

Lucas, Robert H., ed. *Le Livre du corps de policie,* Geneva: Droz, 1967.

McLeod, Glenda, trans. *Christine's Vision.* New York: Garland, 1993.

Parussa, Gabriella, ed. *Epistre Othea.* Geneva: Droz, 1999.

Rains, Ruth Ringland, ed. *Les sept psaumes allégorisés of Christine de Pisan.* Washington, DC: Catholic University of America Press, 1965.

Reno, Christine M., and Liliane Dulac, eds. *Le Livre de l'advision Cristine.* Etudes christiniennes, 4. Paris: Honoré Champion, 2000.

Richards, Earl Jeffrey. *The Book of the City of Ladies.* New York: Persea, 1982.

Richards, Earl Jeffrey, and Patrizia Caraffi, eds. and trans. *La Città delle Dame,* 2nd ed. Milan, Trento: Luni Editrice, 1998.

Roy, Maurice, ed. *Oeuvres poétiques de Christine de Pisan.* 3 vols. SATF, 24. Paris: Firmin Didot, 1886, 1891, 1896. Reprinted New York: Johnson, 1965.

Solente, Suzanne, ed. "Un traité inédit de Christine de Pisan: *L'Epistre de la prison de vie humaine.*" *Bibliothèque de l'Ecole des Chartes* 84 (1924): 263–301.

———, ed. *Le Livre des fais et bonnes meurs du sage roy Charles V.* 2 vols. Société de l'Histoire de France, 437 and 444, Paris: Honoré Champion, 1936–1940.

———, ed. *Le Livre de la Mutacion de Fortune.* 4 vols. SATF. Paris: A. & J. Picard, 1959–1966.

Tarnowski, Andrea, ed. and trans. *Le Chemin de longue étude.* Paris: Livre de poche, 2000.

Varty, Kenneth, ed. *Christine de Pisan, Ballades, Rondeaux, and Virelais.* Leicester: Leicester University Press, 1965.

Willard, Charity Cannon, ed. *The "Livre de la paix" of Christine de Pisan: A Critical Edition with Introduction and Notes.* The Hague: Mouton, 1958.

Willard, Charity Cannon, and Eric Hicks, eds. *Christine de Pizan. Le Livre des trois vertus. Edition critique.* Bibliothèque du XVe siècle, 50. Paris: Champion, 1989.

———, ed. *The Writings of Christine de Pizan.* New York: Persea, 1994.

Willard, Charity Cannon, and Sumner Willard, eds. and trans. *The Book of Arms and Deeds of Chivalry.* University Park, PA: Pennsylvania State University Press, 1999.

Wisman, Josette A., ed. and trans. *Christine de Pizan. The Epistle of the Prison of Human Life, with An Epistle to the Queen of France and Lament on the Evils of the Civil War.* Garland Library of Medieval Literature, 21A. New York and London: Garland, 1984.

SECONDARY SOURCES

Adams, Tracy. "Deceptive Lovers: Christine de Pizan and the Problem of Interpretation." In *Au champ des escriptures: IIIe Colloque international sur Christine de Pizan, Lausanne, 18–22 juillet 1998*, edited by Eric Hicks, Diego Gonzalez, and Philippe Simon, 413–24. Etudes christiniennes, 6. Paris: Champion, 2000.

Altman, Leslie. "Christine de Pizan: First Professional Woman of Letters (1364–1430?)." In *Female Scholars: A Tradition of Learned Women before 1800*, edited by Jeanie R. Brink, 7–23. Montreal: Eden Women's Publications, 1980.

Altmann, Barbara K. "L'Art de l'autoportrait littéraire dans les *Cent ballades* de Christine de Pizan." In *Une femme de lettres au Moyen Age. Etudes autour de Christine de Pizan*, edited by Liliane Dulac and Bernard Ribémont, 327–36. Etudes christiniennes. Orléans: Paradigme, 1995.

———. "Last Words: Reflections on a 'Lay Mortel' and the Poetics of Lyric Sequences." In *Christine de Pizan and Medieval French Lyric*, edited by Earl Jeffrey Richards, 83–102. Gainesville, FL: University of Florida Press, 1998.

———. "Trop peu en sçay: The Reluctant Narrator in Christine de Pizan's Works on Love." In *The Poetry/Poetics of Self and Tradition*, edited by R. Barton Palmer, 217–49. New York: AMS Press, 1999.

———. "Through the Byways of Lyric and Narrative: The *Voiage d'oultremer* in the Ballade Cycles of Christine de Pizan." In *Christine de Pizan 2000. Studies on Christine de Pizan in Honour of Angus J. Kennedy*, edited by John Campbell and Nadia Margolis, 49–64. Amsterdam: Rodopi, 2000.

Angeli, Giovanna. "Charité et pauvreté chez Christine de Pizan." In *Au champ des escriptures: IIIe Colloque international sur Christine de Pizan, Lausanne, 18–22 juillet 1998*, edited by Eric Hicks, Diego Gonzalez, and Philippe Simon, 425–39. Etudes christiniennes, 6. Paris: Champion, 2000.

Autrand, Françoise, "Christine de Pisan et les dames à la Cour." In *Autour de Marguerite d'Ecosse: Reines, princesses et dames au XVe siècle, actes du colloque de Thouars [23 et 24 mai 1997]*, edited by Geneviève Contamine and Philippe Contamine, 19–31. Paris: Honoré Champion, 1999.

Beaulieu, Jean-Philippe. "*Lavision Christine* ou la tentation autobiographique." *Littératures* 18 (1998): 15–30.

Bell, Susan Groag. "Christine de Pizan (1364–1430): Humanism and the Problem of a Studious Woman." *Feminist Studies* 3 (1976): 173–84.

Blanchard, Joël. "Christine de Pizan: les raisons de l'histoire." *Le Moyen Age* 42, 3/4 (1986): 417–36.

———. " 'Vox poetica, vox politica': l'entrée du poète dans le champ politique au XVe siècle." In *Actes du Ve colloque international sur le Moyen Français, Milan 6–8 mai 1985*, 39–51. Milan: Vita e Pensiero, 1986.

———. "Compilation and Legitimation in the Fifteenth Century: *Le Livre de la cité des dames*." In *Reinterpreting Christine de Pizan*, edited by Earl Jeffrey Richards et al., 228–49. Athens and London: University of Georgia Press, 1992.

Blanchard, Joël, and Michel Quereuil. *Lexique de Christine de Pizan*. Paris: Klincksieck, 1999.

Blumenfeld-Kosinski, Renate. "Christine de Pizan and the Misogynistic Tradition." *Romanic Review* 81 (1990): 279–92. Reprinted in *The Selected Writings of Christine de Pizan*, edited by Renate Blumenfeld-Kosinski and translated by Renate Blumenfeld-Kosinski and Kevin Brownlee, 297–311. Norton Critical Edition. New York: W.W. Norton, 1997.

———. " 'Femme de corps et femme par les sens': Christine de Pizan's Saintly Women." *Romanic Review* 87 (1996): 157–75.

———. *Reading Myth: Classical Mythology and Its Interpretations in Medieval French Literature*. Stanford: Stanford University Press, 1997.

———. " 'Enemies Within/Enemies Without': Threats to the Body Politic in Christine de Pizan." *Medievalia et Humanistica* 26 (1999): 1–15.

———. "Two Responses to Agincourt: Alain Chartier's *Livre des quatre dames* and Christine de Pizan's *Epistre de la prison de vie humaine*." In *Contexts and Continuities: Proceedings of the IVth International Colloquium on Christine de Pizan*, edited by Angus J. Kennedy, in collaboration with Rosalind Brown-Grant, James C. Laidlaw, and Catherine Müller, 75–86. Glasgow: Glasgow University Press, 2002.

Boulton, Maureen. "La Passion pour la passion: les textes en moyen français." *Le Moyen Français* 44–45 (2000): 45–62.

———. "Christine's *Heures de la contemplacion de la Passion* in the Context of Late Medieval Passion Devotion." In *Contexts and Continuities: Proceedings of the IVth International Colloquium on Christine de Pizan*, edited by Angus J. Kennedy, in collaboration with Rosalind Brown-Grant, James C. Laidlaw, and Catherine Müller, 99–114. Glasgow: Glasgow University Press, 2002.

Brook, Leslie C. "Christine de Pisan, Heloise, and Abelard's Holy Women." *Zeitschrift für Romanische Philologie* 109, 5/6 (1993): 556–63.

Brown, Meg Lota. "Reputation as Rectitude in *The Book of the Three Virtues*." In *Au champ des escriptures: IIIe Colloque international sur Christine de Pizan, Lausanne, 18–22 juillet 1998*, edited by Eric Hicks, Diego Gonzalez, and Philippe Simon, 295–306. Etudes christiniennes, 6. Paris: Champion, 2000.

Brown-Grant, Rosalind. "Décadence ou progrès? Christine de Pizan, Boccace, et la question de l' 'âge d'or.' " *Revue des Langues Romanes* 92, 2 (1988): 297–306.

———. "*L'Avision-Christine*: Autobiographical Narrative or Mirror for the Prince?" In *Politics, Gender, and Genre: The Political Thought of Christine de Pizan*, edited by Margaret Brabant, 95–111. Boulder, Co/Oxford: Westview Press, 1992.

———. "Les exilées du pouvoir? Christine de Pizan et la femme devant la crise du Moyen Age finissant." In *Apogée et déclin en Europe, 1200–1500*, edited by Claude Thomasset and Michel Zink, 211–23. Paris: Université de Paris-Sorbonne, 1993.

———. "Miroir du prince, miroir d'amour: *L'Epistre Othéa* and John Gower's *Confessio Amantis*." In *Sur le chemin de longue étude . . . Actes du colloque d'Orléans juillet 1995*, edited by Bernard Ribémont, 25–45. Etudes christiniennes, 3. Paris: Champion, 1998.

———. *Christine de Pizan and the Moral Defence of Women: Reading beyond Gender*. Cambridge: Cambridge University Press, 1999.

———. "Christine de Pizan: A Feminist Linguist *avant la lettre*?" In *Christine de Pizan 2000. Studies on Christine de Pizan in Honour of Angus J. Kennedy*, edited by John Campbell and Nadia Margolis, 65–76. Amsterdam: Rodopi, 2000.

———. "Writing beyond Gender; Christine de Pizan's Linguistic Strategies in the Defence of Women." In *Contexts and Continuities: Proceedings of the IVth International Colloquium on Christine de Pizan*, edited by Angus J. Kennedy, in collaboration with Rosalind Brown-Grant, James C. Laidlaw, and Catherine Müller, 155–70. Glasgow: Glasgow University Press, 2002.

Brownlee, Kevin. "Discourses of the Self: Christine de Pizan and the *Rose*." *Romantic Review* 59 (1988): 199–221.

———. "The Image of History in Christine de Pizan's *Livre de la Mutacion de Fortune*." In *Contexts: Style and Values in Medieval Art and Literature*, edited by Daniel Poirion and Nancy Freeman Regalado, 44–56. A special issue of *Yale French Studies*. New Haven, CT: Yale University Press, 1991.

———. "Martyrdom and the Female Voice: Saint Christine in the *Cité des dames*." In *Images of Sainthood*, edited by Renate Blumenfeld-Kosinski and Timia Szell, 115–35. Ithaca, NY: Cornell University Press, 1991.

———. "Widowhood, Sexuality and Gender in Christine de Pizan." *Romanic Review* 86 (1995): 339–53.

———. "Structures of Authority in Christine de Pizan's *Ditié de Jehanne d'Arc*." In *The Selected Writings of Christine de Pizan*, edited and translated by Renate Blumenfeld-Kosinski and Kevin Brownlee, 371–90. New York: W. W. Norton, 1997.

Campbell, P[ercy] G. C. *L'Epitre d'Othéa: Etude sur les sources de Christine de Pisan*. Paris: Edouard Champion, 1924.

———. "Christine de Pisan en Angleterre." *Revue de Littérature comparée* 5 (1925): 659–70.

———. "Notes on *The Book of Fayttes of Armes and of Chyvalrye*." *Medium Aevum* 2 (1933): 217–18.

Caraffi, Patrizia. "Medea sapiente e amorosa: Da Euripide a Christine de Pizan." In *Au champ des escriptures: IIIe Colloque international sur Christine de Pizan, Lausanne, 18–22 juillet 1998*, edited by Eric Hicks, Diego Gonzalez, and Philippe Simon, 133–48. Etudes christiniennes, 6. Paris: Champion, 2000.

Carroll, Berenice A. "Christine de Pizan and the Origins of Peace Theory." In *Women Writers and the Early Modern British Political Tradition*, edited by Hilda L. Smith, 22–39. Cambridge: Cambridge University Press, 1998.

Case, Mary Anne C. "Christine de Pizan and the Authority of Experience." In *Christine de Pizan and the Categories of Difference*, edited by Marilynn Desmond, 71–87. Medieval Cultures, 14. Minneapolis: University of Minnesota Press, 1998.

Curnow, Maureen Cheney. " 'La Pioche d'inquisicion': Legal-Judicial Content and Style in Christine de Pizan's *Livre de la cité des dames*." In *Reinterpreting Christine de Pizan*, edited by Earl Jeffrey Richards et al., 157–72. Athens, GA: University of Georgia Press, 1992.

Delisle, Léopold. "Notice sur les *Sept Psaumes allégorisés* de Christine de Pisan." *Notices et extraits des manuscrits de la Bibliothèque nationale* 35: 2 (1896): 5–13.

Desmond, Marilynn, and Pamela Sheingorn. *Myth, Montage and Visuality in Late Medieval Manuscript Culture: Christine de Pizan's Othea*. Ann Arbor: Michigan University Press, 2001.

Driver, Martha W. "Christine de Pisan and Robert Wyer: The *C. Hystoryes of Troye*, or *L'Epistre d'Othea* Englished." *Gutenberg-Jahrbuch* 72 (1997): 125–39.

Dulac, Liliane. "Un mythe didactique de Christine de Pizan: Sémiramis ou la veuve héroïque." In *Mélanges de philologie romanes offertes à Charles Camproux*, 315–45. Montpellier, 1978.

———. "Inspiration mystique et savoir politique: les conseils aux veuves chez Francesco da Barberino et Christine de Pizan." In *Mélanges à la mémoire de Franco Simone: France et Italie dans la culture européenne, 1: Moyen Age et Renaissance*, 113–41. Bibliothèque Franco Simone, 4. Geneva: Slatkine, 1980.

———. "Dissymétrie et échec de la communication dans les *Cent ballades d'Amant et de Dame* de Christine de Pizan." *Lengas* 22 (1987): 133–46.

———. "Travail allégorique et ruptures du sens chez Christine de Pizan: *L'Epistre Othea*." In *Continuités et ruptures dans l'histoire et la littérature: Colloque Franco-Polonais 9–14 février 1987, Montpellier*, edited by Dominique Triaire, 24–32. Paris: Honoré Champion, 1988.

———. "Authority in the Prose Treatises of Christine de Pizan: The Writer's Discourse and the Prince's Word." In *Politics, Gender, and Genre: The Political Thought of Christine de Pizan*, edited by Margaret Brabant, 129–40. Boulder, CO/Oxford: Westview Press, 1992.

———. "The Representation and Functions of Feminine Speech in Christine de Pizan's *Livre des Trois Vertus*." In *Reinterpreting Christine de Pizan*, edited by Earl Jeffrey Richards et al., 14–22. Athens: University of Georgia Press, 1992.

Dulac, Liliane, and Christine Reno. "L'humanisme vers 1400: essai d'exploration à partir d'un cas marginal: Christine de Pizan, traductrice de Thomas d'Aquin." In *Pratiques de la culture écrite en France au XVe siècle*, edited by Monique Ornato and Nicole Pons, 161–78. Textes et Etudes du Moyen Age, 2. Louvain-la-Neuve: Fédération Internationale des Instituts d'Etudes Médiévales, 1995.

———. "Traduction et adaptation dans *L'Advision-Cristine* de Christine de Pizan." In *Traduction et adaptation à la fin du Moyen Age et à la Renaissance. Actes du Colloque organisé par l'Université de Nancy II, 23–25 mars 1995*, edited by Charles Brucker, 121–31. Colloques, congrès et conférences sur la Renaissance, X. Paris: Champion, 1997.

———. "A propos des représentations du corps souffrant chez Christine de Pizan." In *Mélanges de langue et de littérature françaises du Moyen Age offerts à Pierre Demarolle*, edited by Charles Brucker, 313–24. Paris: Honoré Champion, 1998.

———. "Littérature et dévotion: à propos des *Heures de Contemplacion sur la passion de Nostre Seigneur* de Christine de Pizan." In *Miscellanea Mediaevalia. Mélanges offerts à Philippe Ménard*, edited by Jean-Claude Faucon, vol. I, 475–84. Paris: Champion, 1998.

———. "Thèmes et variations du *Chemin de long estude* à *l'Advision-Christine*: remarques sur un itinéraire." In *Sur le chemin de longue étude . . . Actes du colloque d'Orléans juillet 1995*, edited by Bernard Ribémont, 77–86. Etudes christiniennes, 3. Paris: Honoré Champion, 1998.

———. "La représentation de la France chez Eustache Deschamps et Christine de Pizan." In *Autour d'Eustache Deschamps. Actes du Colloque du Centre d'Etudes Médiévales de l'Université de Picardie-Jules Verne, Amiens, 5–8 novembre 1998*, edited by Danielle Buschinger, 79–92. Amiens: Presses du Centre d'Etudes Médiévales, Université de Picardie-Jules Verne, 1999.

———. "La Gestuelle chez Christine de Pizan: quelques aperçus." In *Au Champ des escriptures*; *IIIe Colloque international sur Christine de Pizan, Lausanne 18–22 juillet 1998*, edited by Eric Hicks, Diego Gonzalez, and Philippe Simon, 609–26. Etudes christiniennes, 6. Paris: Honoré Champion, 2000.

———. "Poétique de l'exemple dans le *Corps de policie*." In *Christine de Pizan 2000. Studies on Christine de Pizan in Honour of Angus J. Kennedy*, edited by John Campbell and Nadia Margolis, 91–104. Amsterdam and Atlanta: Rodopi, 2000.

———. "Sur les fonctions du bestiaire dans quelques oeuvres didactiques de Christine de Pizan." In *"Rien ne m'est seur que la chose incertaine." Etudes sur l'art d'écrire au Moyen Age offertes à Eric Hicks par ses anciens élèves et ses amis*, edited by Jean-Claude Mühlethaler and Denis Billotte, 181–94. Geneva: Slatkine, 2001.

Ehrhart, Margaret J. "Christine de Pizan and the Judgment of Paris: A Court Poet's Use of Mythographic Tradition." In *The Mythographic Art: Classical Fable and the Rise of the Vernacular in Early France and England*, edited by Jane Chance, 125–56. Gainesville, FL: University of Florida Press, 1990.

Fenster, Thelma. "La fama, la femme, et la Dame de la Tour: Christine de Pizan et la médisance." In *Au champ des escriptures: IIIe Colloque international sur Christine de Pizan, Lausanne, 18–22 juillet 1998*, edited by Eric Hicks, Diego Gonzalez, and Philippe Simon, 461–77. Etudes christiniennes, 6. Paris: Champion, 2000.

———. "Possible Odds: Christine de Pizan and the Paradox of Woman." In *Contexts and Continuities: Proceedings of the IVth International Colloquium on Christine de Pizan*, edited by Angus J. Kennedy, in collaboration with Rosalind Brown-Grant, James C. Laidlaw, and Catherine Müller, 355–66. Glasgow: Glasgow University Press, 2002.

Forhan, Kate Langdon. "Polycracy, Obligation, and Revolt: The Body Politic in John of Salisbury and Christine de Pizan." In *Politics, Gender, and Genre: The Political Thought of Christine de Pizan*, edited by Margaret Brabant, 33–52. Boulder, CO/Oxford: Westview Press, 1992.

———. "Reflecting Heroes: Christine de Pizan and the Mirror Tradition." In *The City of Scholars: New Approaches to Christine de Pizan*, edited by Margarete Zimmermann and Dina De Rentiis, 189–96. European Cultures, Studies in Literature and the Arts, 2. Berlin/New York: Walter de Gruyter, 1994.

———. "Reading Backward: Aristotelianism in the Political Thought of Christine de Pizan." In *Au champ des escriptures: IIIe Colloque international sur Christine de Pizan, Lausanne, 18–22 juillet 1998*, edited by Eric Hicks, Diego Gonzalez, and Philippe Simon, 359–82. Etudes christiniennes, 6. Paris: Champion, 2000.

———. *The Political Thought of Christine de Pizan*. Aldershot: Ashgate, 2001.

Gros, Gérard. " 'Mon oroison entens . . . ': Etude sur les trois opuscules pieux de Christine de Pizan." *Bien dire et bien aprandre. Revue de médiévistique* 8 (1990): 99–112.

Guarinos, Marion. "Individualisme et solidarité dans *Le Livre des trois vertus*." In *Sur le chemin de longue étude . . . Actes du colloque d'Orléans Juillet 1995*, edited by Bernard Ribémont, 87–100. Etudes christiniennes, 3. Paris: Champion, 1998.

Hicks, Eric. "Eloge de la machine: transcription, édition, génération de textes." *Romania* 103 (1982): 88–107.

———. "Discours de la toilette, toilette du discours: de l'idéologie du vêtement dans quelques écrits didactiques de Christine de Pizan." *Revue des Langues Romanes* 92,2 (1988): 327–42.

———. "Une femme dans le monde: Christine de Pizan et l'écriture de la politique." In *L'Hostellerie de pensée: études sur l'art littéraire au Moyen Age offertes à Daniel Poirion par ses anciens élèves*, edited by Michel Zink et al., 233–43. Cultures et Civilisations Médiévales. Paris: Presses de l'Université de Paris-Sorbonne, 1995.

———. "Pour une édition génétique de l'*Epistre Othea*." In *Pratiques de la culture écrite en France au XVe siècle*, edited by Monique Ornato and Nicole Pons, 151–59. Textes et études du Moyen âge, 2. Louvain-la-Neuve: Federation Internationale des Instituts d'Etudes Médiévales, 1995.

———. "Situation du débat sur le *Roman de la Rose*." In *Une femme de lettres au Moyen Age. Etudes autour de Christine de Pizan*, edited by Liliane Dulac and Bernard Ribémont, 51–67. Etudes christiniennes. Orleans: Paradigme, 1995.

Hindman, Sandra. "With Ink and Mortar: Christine de Pizan's *Cité des dames* [An Art Essay]." *Feminist Studies* 10 (1984): 457–77.

———. *Christine de Pizan's "Epistre Othéa": Painting and Politics at the Court of Charles VI*. Toronto: Pontifical Institute of Medieval Studies, 1986.

Huot, Sylvia. "Seduction and Sublimation: Christine de Pizan, Jean de Meun, and Dante." *Romance Notes* 25 (1985): 361–73.

Jeanroy, Alfred. "Boccace et Christine de Pisan: le *De claris mulieribus* principale source du *Livre de la cité des dames*." *Romania* 48 (1922): 93–105.

Kellogg, Judith. "*Le Livre de la cité des dames*: Feminist Myth and Community." *Essays in Arts and Sciences* 18 (1989): 1–15.

———. "Transforming Ovid: The Metamorphosis of Female Authority." In *Christine de Pizan and the Categories of Difference*, edited by Marilynn Desmond, 181–94. Minneapolis: University of Minnesota Press, 1998.

Kelly, Allison. "Christine de Pizan and Antoine de la Sale: The Dangers of Love in Theory and Fiction." In *Reinterpreting Christine de Pizan*, edited by Earl Jeffrey Richards et al., 173–86. Athens, GA: University of Georgia Press, 1992.

Kelly, Joan. "Early Feminist Theory and the *Querelle des femmes* 1400–1789." *Signs* 8 (1982): 4–28.

Kennedy, Angus J. *Christine de Pizan: A Bibliographical Guide*. London: Grant & Cutler, 1984.

———. *Christine de Pizan: A Bibliographical Guide—Supplement I*. London: Grant & Cutler, 1994.

Kolve, V. A. "The Annunciation to Christine: Authorial Empowerment in *The Book of the City of Ladies*." In *Iconography at the Crossroads*, edited by Brian Cassidy, 171–96. Princeton: Department of Art and Archaeology, 1993.

Krueger, Roberta L. *Women Readers and the Ideology of Gender*. Cambridge: Cambridge University Press, 1993.

———. "*Chascune selon son estat*: Women's Education and Social Class in the Conduct Books of Christine de Pizan and Anne de France." *Papers on French Seventeenth Century Literature* 24 (1997): 19–34.

———. "Christine's Anxious Lessons: Gender, Morality and the Social Order from the *Enseignemens* to the *Avision*." In *Christine de Pizan and the Categories of Difference*, edited by Marilynn Desmond, 16–40. Minneapolis: University of Minnesota Press, 1998.

Laidlaw, James C. "Christine de Pizan, the Earl of Salisbury and Henry IV." *French Studies* 36 (1982): 129–43.

———. "Christine de Pizan—An Author's Progress." *Modern Language Review* 78 (1983): 532–50.

———. "Christine de Pizan—A Publisher's Progress." *Modern Language Review* 82 (1987): 35–75.

———. "How Long is the *Livre du chemin de long estude*?" In *The Editor and the Text*, edited by Philip E. Bennett and Graham A. Runnalls, 83–95. Edinburgh: University Press, 1990.

———. "Christine de Pizan: From Scriptorium to Database and Back Again." *Journal of the Institute of Romance Studies* 1 (1992): 59–67.

———. "L'unité des 'Cent Balades.' " In *The City of Scholars: New Approaches to Christine de Pizan*, edited by Margarete Zimmermann and Dina De Rentiis, 97–106. Berlin: Walter de Gruyter, 1994.

———. "The *Cent balades*: The Marriage of Content and Form." In *Christine de Pizan and the Medieval French Lyric*, edited by Earl Jeffrey Richards, 53–82. Gainesville: University Press of Florida, 1998.

———. "Maurice Roy (1856–1932)." In *Christine de Pizan 2000: Studies on Christine de Pizan in Honour of Angus J. Kennedy*, edited by John Campbell and Nadia Margolis, 233–50. Amsterdam/Atlanta: Rodopi, 2000.

Lassabatère, Thierry. "La personnification de la France dans la littérature de la fin du Moyen Age. Autour d'Eustache Deschamps et Christine de Pizan." In *Contexts and Continuities: Proceedings of the IVth International Colloquium on Christine de Pizan (Glasgow 21–27 July 2000)*, edited by Angus J. Kennedy in collaboration with Rosalind Brown-Grant, James C. Laidlaw, and Catherine Müller, 483–504. 3 vols. Glasgow: Glasgow University Press, 2002.

Lefèvre, Sylvie. "Christine de Pizan et l'Aristote oresmien." In *Au champ des escriptures: IIIe Colloque international sur Christine de Pizan, Lausanne, 18–22 juillet 1998*, edited by Eric Hicks, Diego Gonzalez, and Philippe Simon, 231–50. Etudes christiniennes, 6. Paris: Champion, 2000.

Leppig, Linda. "The Political Rhetoric of Christine de Pizan: *Lamentacion sur les maux de la guerre civile*." In *Politics, Gender and Genre: The Political Thought of Christine de Pizan*, edited by Margaret Brabant, 141–56. Boulder, Co/Oxford: Westview Press, 1992.

Lorcin, Marie-Thérèse. "Pouvoirs et contre-pouvoirs dans le *Livre des Trois Vertus*." *Revue des Langues Romanes* 92,2 (1988): 359–68.

———. "Le *Livre des Trois Vertus* et le *sermo ad status*." In *Une femme de lettres au Moyen Age. Etudes autour de Christine de Pizan*, edited by Liliane Dulac and Bernard Ribémont, 139–50. Etudes christiniennes. Orléans: Paradigme, 1995.

Margolis, Nadia. "Christine de Pizan: The Poetess as Historian." *Journal of the History of Ideas* 47 (1986): 361–75.

———. "Elegant Closures: The Use of the Diminutive in Christine de Pizan and Jean de Meun." In *Reinterpreting Christine de Pizan*, edited by Earl Jeffrey Richards et al., 111–23. Athens, GA: University of Georgia Press, 1992.

———. "La Progression polémique, spirituelle et personnelle dans les écrits religieux de Christine de Pizan." In *Une femme de lettres au Moyen Age. Etudes autour de Christine de Pizan*, edited by Liliane Dulac and Bernard Ribémont, 297–316. Etudes christiniennes. Orléans: Paradigme, 1995.

———. "Les terminaisons dangereuses: lyrisme, féminisme et humanisme néologiques chez Christine de Pizan." In *Autour de Jacques Monfrin. Néologie et création verbale. Actes du Colloque international, Université McGill, Montréal, 7–8–9 octobre 1996*, edited by Giuseppe Di Stefano and Rose M. Bidler. *Le Moyen Français* 39–40–41 (1996–7): 381–404.

———. "Trial by Passion: Philology, Film and Ideology in the Portrayal of Joan of Arc." *Journal of Medieval and Early Modern Studies* 27, 3 (1997): 445–92.

———. "Clerkliness and Courtliness in the Complaintes of Christine de Pizan." In *Christine de Pizan and Medieval French Lyric*, edited by Earl Jeffrey Richards, 135–54. Gainesville: University Press of Florida, 1998.

———. "Christine at 600: The State of Christine de Pizan Studies for the Second Millennium." In *Christine de Pizan 2000: Studies on Christine de Pizan in Honour of Angus J. Kennedy*, edited by John Campbell and Nadia Margolis, 31–45. Amsterdam and Atlanta: Rodopi, 2000.

———. "Maurice Roy, Maverick Editor, and the Making of the Christinian Corpus." In *"Riens ne m'est seur que la chose incertaine": Etudes sur l'art d'écrire au Moyen Age offertes à Eric Hicks par ses anciens élèves et ses amis*, edited by Jean-Claude Mühlethaler and Denis Billotte, 217–27. Geneva: Slatkine, 2001.

McGrady, Deborah. "What Is a Patron? Benefactors and Authorship in Harley 4431, Christine de Pizan's Collected Works." In *Christine de Pizan and the Categories of Difference*, edited by Marilynn Desmond, 195–214. Minneapolis: University of Minnesota Press, 1998.

———. "Authorship and Audience in the Prologues to Christine de Pizan's Commissioned Poetry." In *Au champ des escriptures: IIIe Colloque international sur Christine de Pizan, Lausanne, 18–22 juillet 1998*, edited by Eric Hicks, Diego Gonzalez, and Philippe Simon, 25–40. Etudes christiniennes, 6. Paris: Champion, 2000.

McKinley, Mary. "The Subversive 'Seulette.'" In *Politics, Gender and Genre: The Political Thought of Christine de Pizan*, edited by Margaret Brabant, 157–71. Boulder, Co: Westview Press, 1992.

McLeod, Glenda, and Katharina Wilson. "A Clerk in Name Only—A Clerk in All but Name: The Misogamous Tradition and *La Cité des dames*." In *The City of Scholars: New Approaches to Christine de Pizan*, edited by Margarete Zimmermann and Dina De Rentiis, 67–78. Berlin/New York: Walter de Gruyter, 1994.

McWebb, Christine. "Lyrical Conventions and the Creation of Female Subjectivity in Christine de Pizan's *Cent ballades d'amant et de dame*." In *Christine de Pizan and Medieval French Lyric*, edited by Earl Jeffrey Richards, 168–83. Gainesville: University Press of Florida, 1998.

———. "The *Roman de la Rose* and the *Livre des trois vertus*." In *Au champ des escriptures: IIIe Colloque international sur Christine de Pizan, Lausanne, 18–22 juillet 1998*, edited by Eric Hicks, Diego Gonzalez, and Philippe Simon, 309–24. Etudes christiniennes, 6. Paris: Champion, 2000.

Meiss, Millard. *French Painting in the Time of Jean de Berry. The Late Fourteenth Century and the Patronage of the Duke.* London: Phaidon, 1967; 2nd ed. 1969.

———. *French Painting in the Time of Jean de Berry: The Limbourgs and their Contemporaries.* 2 vols. London: Thames & Hudson, 1974.

Minnis, A. J. "Theorizing the *Rose*: Commentary Tradition in the *Querelle de la Rose*." In *Poetics: Theory and Practice in Medieval English Literature*, edited by Piero Boitani and Anna Torti, 13–36. Cambridge: D. S. Brewer, 1990.

Mirabella, M. Bella. "Feminist Self-Fashioning: Christine de Pizan and *The Treasure of the City of Ladies*." *European Journal of Women's Studies* 6,1 (1999): 9–20.

Mombello, Gianni. "Per un'edizione critica dell' *Epistre Othea* di Christine de Pizan: I–II." *Studi francesi* 8 (1964): 401–17.

———. "Per un'edizione critica dell' *Epistre Othea* di Christine de Pizan: III." *Studi francesi* 9 (1965): 1–12.

———. *La Tradizione manoscritta dell'Epistre Othea di Christine de Pizan: Prolegomeni all'edizione del testo.* Torino: Accademia delle Scienze, 1967.

———. "J.-M.-L. Coupé e H. Walpole: Gli amori di Christine de Pizan." *Studi francesi* 46 (1972): 5–25.

———. "Christine de Pizan and the House of Savoy," translated and edited by Nadia Margolis. In *Reinterpreting Christine de Pizan*, edited by Earl Jeffrey Richards et al., 187–93. Athens, GA: University of Georgia Press, 1992.

Mühlethaler, Jean-Claude. "Le Poète et le prophète: Littérature et politique au XVe siècle." *Le Moyen Français* 13 (1984): 37–57.

———. "Problèmes de réécriture: amour et mort de la princesse de Salerne dans le *Decameron* (IV, 1) et dans la *Cité des dames* (II, 59)." In *Une femme de lettres au Moyen Age. Etudes autour de Christine de Pizan*, edited by Liliane Dulac and Bernard Ribémont, 209–20. Etudes christiniennes. Orléans: Paradigme, 1995.

Nederman, Cary J. "The Expanding Body Politic: Christine de Pizan and the Medieval Roots of Political Economy." In *Au champ des escriptures: IIIe Colloque international sur Christine de Pizan, Lausanne, 18–22 juillet 1998*, edited by Eric Hicks, Diego Gonzalez, and Philippe Simon, 383–98. Etudes christiniennes, 6. Paris: Champion, 2000.

Nelson, Deborah Hubbard. "Christine de Pizan and Courtly Love." *Fifteenth Century Studies* 17 (1990): 281–89.

Nephew, Julia A. "Gender Reversals and Intellectual Gender in the Works of Christine de Pizan." In *Au champ des escriptures: IIIe Colloque international sur Christine de Pizan, Lausanne, 18–22 juillet 1998*, edited by Eric Hicks, Diego Gonzalez, and Philippe Simon, 517–32. Etudes christiniennes, 6. Paris: Champion, 2000.

Nichols, Stephen. "Prophetic Discourse: St. Augustine to Christine de Pizan." In *The Bible in the Middle Ages: Its Influence on Literature and Art*, edited by Bernard S. Levy, 51–76. Medieval and Renaissance Texts and Studies 89. Binghamton, NY: Medieval and Renaissance Texts and Studies, 1992.

Oexle, Otto Gerhard. "Christine et les pauvres." In *The City of Scholars: New Approaches to Christine de Pizan*, edited by Margarete Zimmermann and Dina De Rentiis, 206–20. Berlin/New York: Walter de Gruyter, 1994.

Ouy, Gilbert. "Une énigme codicologique: les signatures des cahiers dans les manuscrits autographes et originaux de Christine de Pizan." In *Calames et cahiers. Mélanges de codicologie et de paléographie offerts à Léon Gilissen*, edited by Jacques Lemaire and Émile van Balberghe, 119–31. Brussels: Centre d'Etude des Manuscrits, 1985.

Ouy, Gilbert, and Christine M. Reno. "Identification des autographes de Christine de Pizan." *Scriptorium* 34 (1980): 221–38 and plates 18–20.

———. "Les hésitations de Christine: Etude des variantes de graphies dans trois manuscrits autographes de Christine de Pizan." *Revue des langues romanes* 92 (1988): 265–86.

———. "Où mène le *Chemin de long estude*? Christine de Pizan, Ambrogio Migli, et les ambitions impériales de Louis d'Orléans (A propos du ms. BNF fr. 1643)." In *Christine de Pizan 2000. Studies on Christine de Pizan in Honour of Angus J. Kennedy*, edited by John Campbell and Nadia Margolis, 177–95. Amsterdam: Rodopi, 2000.

Parussa, Gabriella. "Instruire les chevaliers et conseiller les princes: *L'Epistre Othéa* de Christine de Pizan." In *Studi di storia della civiltà letteraria francese. Mélanges offerts à Lionello Sozzi par le Centre d'études franco-italiennes, Universités de Savoie et de Turin*, Vol. 1, 129–55. Bibliothèque Franco Simone, XXV. Paris: Champion, 1996.

———. "Autographes et orthographe: quelques considérations sur l'orthographe de Christine de Pizan." *Romania* 117 (1999): 143–59.

Parussa, Gabriella, and Richard Trachsler. "*Or sus, alons ou champ des escriptures.* Encore sur l'orthographe de Christine de Pizan: l'intérêt des grands corpus." In *Contexts and Continuities: Proceedings of the IVth International Colloquium on Christine de Pizan (Glasgow 21–27 July 2000)*, edited by Angus J. Kennedy in collaboration with Rosalind Brown-Grant, James C. Laidlaw, and Catherine Müller, 621–44. 3 vols. Glasgow: Glasgow University Press, 2002.

Paupert, Anne. "Le 'Je' lyrique féminin dans l'oeuvre poétique de Christine de Pizan." In *Et c'est la fin pour quoy sommes ensemble: hommage à Jean Dufournet: littérature, histoire et langue du Moyen Age*, edited by Jean-Claude Aubailly, 1057–71. Nouvelle bibliothèque du Moyen Age, 25. Paris: Honoré Champion, 1993.

———. " 'La Narracion de mes aventures', des premiers poèmes à l'*Advision*: l'élaboration d'une écriture autobiographique dans l'oeuvre de Christine de Pizan." In *Au champ des escriptures: IIIe colloque international sur Christine de Pizan, Lausanne, 18-22 juillet 1998*, edited by Eric Hicks, Diego Gonzalez, and Philippe Simon, 51–72. Paris: Champion, 2000.

———. "Christine et Boèce: de la lecture à l'écriture, de la réécriture à l'écriture du moi." In *Contexts and Continuities: Proceedings of the IVth International Colloquium on Christine de Pizan (Glasgow 21–27 July 2000)*, edited by Angus J. Kennedy in collaboration with Rosalind Brown-Grant, James C. Laidlaw, and Catherine Müller, 645–62. 3 vols. Glasgow: Glasgow University Press, 2002.

Philippy, Patricia A. "Establishing Authority: Boccaccio's *De claris mulieribus* and Christine de Pizan's *Le Livre de la cité des dames*." *Romanic Review* 77 (1987): 167–93.

Picherit, Jean-Louis G. "Les Références pathologiques et thérapeutiques dans l'oeuvre de Christine de Pizan." In *Une femme de lettres au Moyen Age. Etudes autour de Christine de Pizan*, edited by Liliane Dulac and Bernard Ribémont, 233–44. Etudes christiniennes. Orléans: Paradigme, 1995.

Poirion, Daniel. *Le Poète et le prince: L'évolution du lyrisme courtois de Guillaume de Machaut à Charles d'Orléans.* Paris: Presses Universitaires de France, 1965.

Quillet, Jeannine. "Sagesse et pouvoir selon *Le livre des Fais et Bonnes Meurs du sage roi Charles V* de Christine de Pizan." In *D'une cité à l'autre: Problèmes de philosophie politique médiévale*, 305–12. Paris: Champion, 2001.

Quilligan, Maureen. *The Allegory of Female Authority: Christine de Pizan's Cité des dames.* Ithaca/London: Cornell University Press, 1991.

Reno, Christine M. "The Preface to the *Avision-Christine* in ex-Phillipps 128." In *Reinterpreting Christine de Pizan*, edited by Earl Jeffrey Richards et al., 207–27. Athens, GA: University of Georgia Press, 1992.

Richards, Earl Jeffrey. "Christine de Pizan and Dante: A Re-examination." *Archiv für das Studium der Neueren Sprachen und Literaturen* 222 (1985): 100–11.

———. " '*Seulette a part*'—the 'Little Woman on the Sidelines' Takes up her Pen: The Letters of Christine de Pizan." In *Dear Sister: Medieval Women and the Epistolary Genre*, edited by Karen Cherewatuk and Ulrike Wiethaus, 139–70. Philadelphia: University of Pennsylvania Press, 1993.

———. "Christine de Pizan and Sacred History." In *The City of Scholars: New Approaches to Christine de Pizan*, edited by Margarete Zimmermann and Dina De Rentiis, 15–30. Berlin/New York: Walter de Gruyter, 1994.

———. "In Search of a Feminist Patrology: Christine de Pizan and 'les Glorieux Dotteurs.' " In *Une femme de lettres au Moyen Age. Etudes autour de Christine de Pizan*, edited by Liliane Dulac and Bernard Ribémont, 281–96. Etudes christiniennes. Orléans: Paradigme, 1995.

———. "Rejecting Essentialism and Gendered Writing: The Case of Christine de Pizan." In *Gender and Text in the Later Middle Ages*, edited by Jane Chance, 96–131. Gainesville, FL: University Press of Florida, 1996.

———. "*Glossa Aurelianensis est quae destruit textum*: Medieval Rhetoric, Thomism and Humanism in Christine de Pizan's Critique of the *Roman de la Rose*." *Cahiers de Recherches Médiévales* (XIIIe-XVe s.) 5 (1998): 247–63.

———. "Where Are the Men in Christine de Pizan's City of Ladies? Architectural and Allegorical Structures in Christine de Pizan's *Livre de la Cité des dames*." In *Translatio Studii*, edited by Renate Blumenfeld-Kosinski, Kevin Brownlee, Mary B. Speer, and Lori Walters, 221–43. Amsterdam: Rodopi, 1999.

———. "Editing the *Livre de la Cité des dames*: New Insights, Problems and Challenges." In *Au Champ des escriptures: IIIe Colloque international sur Christine de Pizan,* edited by Eric Hick, Diego Gonzalez, and Philippe Simon, 789–816. Etudes christiniennes. Paris: Champion, 2000.

———. "Christine and Medieval Jurisprudence." In *Contexts and Continuities: Proceedings of the IV International Colloquium on Christine de Pizan (Glasgow 21–27 July 2000)*, edited by Angus J. Kennedy in collaboration with Rosalind Brown-Grant, James C. Laidlaw, and Catherine Müller, 747–66. 3 vols. Glasgow: Glasgow University Press, 2002.

Richter, Bodo L. O. "A New Work by Christine de Pizan: "Les Sept Psaumes allégorisés." *Studi francesi*, 34 (1968): 69–73.

Schibanoff, Susan. "Taking the Gold Out of Egypt: The Art of Reading as a Woman." In *Gender and Reading: Essays on Readers, Texts, and Contexts*, edited by Elizabeth A.

Flynn and Patrocino P. Schweikart, 83–106. Baltimore: Johns Hopkins University Press, 1986.

Semple, Benjamin. "The Consolation of a Woman Writer: Christine de Pizan's Use of Boethius in *L'Avision-Christine*." In *Women, the Book and the Worldly. Selected Proceedings of the St. Hilda's Conference, 1993*, edited by Lesley Smith and Jane H. M. Taylor, 39–48. Woodbridge: D. S. Brewer, 1995.

———. "The Critique of Knowledge as Power: The Limits of Philosophy and Theology in Christine de Pizan." In *Christine de Pizan and the Categories of Difference*, edited by Marilynn Desmond, 108–27. Minneapolis: University of Minnesota Press, 1998.

Skemp, Mary L. "Autobiography as Authority in *Lavision-Christine*." *Le Moyen français* 35–6 (1996): 17–31.

Smith, Geri L. "De Marotele au *Lai Mortel*: la subversion discursive dans deux ouvrages de Christine de Pizan." In *Au champ des escriptures: IIIe Colloque international sur Christine de Pizan, Lausanne, 18–22 juillet 1998*, edited by Eric Hicks, Diego Gonzalez, and Philippe Simon, 651–62. Etudes christiniennes, 6. Paris: Champion, 2000.

Solterer, Helen. *The Master and Minerva: Disputing Women in French Medieval Culture*. Berkeley/Los Angeles: University of California Press, 1995.

———. "Fiction vs. Defamation: The Quarrel over the *Romance of the Rose*." *Medieval History Journal* 2 (1999): 111–41.

Strubel, Armand. "Le style allégorique de Christine." In *Une femme de lettres au Moyen Age. Etudes autour de Christine de Pizan*, edited by Liliane Dulac and Bernard Ribémont, 357–72. Etudes christiniennes. Orléans: Paradigme, 1995.

Sullivan, Karen. "At the Limit of Feminist Theory: The Architectonics of the *Querelle de la Rose*." *Exemplaria* 3 (1991): 435–65.

Tarnowski, Andrea. "Le geste prophétique chez Christine de Pizan." In *Apogée et déclin en Europe, 1200–1500*, edited by Claude Thomasset and Michel Zink, 225–36. Paris: Presses de l'Université de Paris-Sorbonne, 1993.

———. "Autobiography and Advice in *Le Livre des trois vertus*." In *Une femme de lettres au Moyen Age. Etudes autour de Christine de Pizan*, edited by Liliane Dulac and Bernard Ribémont, 151–60. Etudes christiniennes. Orléans: Paradigme, 1995.

———. "Perspectives on the *Advision*." In *Christine de Pizan 2000: Studies on Christine de Pizan in Honour of Angus J. Kennedy*, edited by John Campbell and Nadia Margolis, 105–14. Amsterdam/Atlanta, GA: Rodopi, 2000.

Vallet de Viriville, A. "La Bibliothèque d'Isabeau de Bavière, reine de France." *Bulletin du bibliophile*, 14 (1858): 663–87.

Wagner, Barbara. "Tradition or Innovation? Research on the Pictorial Tradition of the Miniatures of the *Livre de la Mutacion de Fortune* de Christine de Pizan: The Miniature 'Le Plus Hault Siège.' " In *Contexts and Continuities: Proceedings of the IVth International Colloquium on Christine de Pizan*, edited by Angus J. Kennedy, in collaboration with Rosalind Brown-Grant, James C. Laidlaw, and Catherine Müller, 855–72. Glasgow: Glasgow University Press, 2002.

Walters, Lori J. "Chivalry and the (En)Gendered Poetic Self: Petrarchan Models in the *Cent Balades*." In *The City of Scholars: New Approaches to Christine de Pizan*, edited by Margarete Zimmermann and Dina De Rentiis, 43–66. Berlin/New York: Walter de Gruyter, 1994.

---. "Metamorphose of the Self: Christine de Pizan, the Saint's Life, and Perpetua." In *Sur le chemin de longue étude . . . Actes du colloque d'Orléans, juillet 1995*, 159–82. Etudes christiniennes, 3. Paris: Honoré Champion, 1998.

---. "*Translatio Studii*: Christine de Pizan's Self-Portrayal in Two Lyric Poems and in the *Livre de la Mutacion de Fortune*." In *Christine de Pizan and Medieval French Lyric*, edited by Earl Jeffrey Richards, 155–67. Gainesville: University Press of Florida, 1998.

---. "Fortune's Double Face: Gender and the Transformations of Christine de Pizan, Augustine, and Perpetua." *Fifteenth-Century Studies* 25 (2000): 97–114.

---. "La ré-écriture de Saint Augustin par Christine de Pizan: De *La Cité de Dieu* à la *Cité des Dames*." In *Au champ des escriptures: IIIe Colloque international sur Christine de Pizan, Lausanne, 18–22 juillet 1998*, edited by Eric Hicks, Diego Gonzalez, and Philippe Simon, 197–215. Etudes christiniennes, 6. Paris: Champion, 2000.

---. " 'Translating' Petrarch: *Cité des dames* II.7.1, Jean Daudin, and Vernacular Authority." In *Christine de Pizan 2000: Studies on Christine de Pizan in Honour of Angus J. Kennedy*, edited by John Campbell and Nadia Margolis, 283–97. Amsterdam: Rodopi, 2000.

---. "Constructing Reputations: *Fama* and Memory in Christine de Pizan's *Charles V* and *L'Advision Cristine*." In *FAMA: The Politics of Talk and Reputation in Medieval Europe*, edited by Daniel L. Smail and Thelma Fenster. Ithaca, NY: Cornell University Press (forthcoming).

---. "The Royal Vernacular: Poet and Patron in *Charles V* and the *Sept Psaumes allégorisées*." In *The Vernacular Spirit*, edited by Renate Blumenfeld-Kosinski, Nancy Warren, and Duncan Robertson (forthcoming).

Willard, Charity Cannon. "An Autograph Manuscript of Christine de Pizan?" *Studi Francesi* 27 (1965): 452–57.

---. "The Manuscript Tradition of the *Livre des trois vertus* and Christine de Pizan's Audience." *Journal of the History of Ideas* 27, 3 (1966): 433–44.

---. "A Fifteenth-Century View of Women's Role in Medieval Society: Christine de Pizan's *Livre des trois vertus*." In *The Role of Women in the Middle Ages*, edited by Rosemarie T. Morewedge, 90–120. Albany: State University of New York Press, 1975.

---. "Christine de Pizan's *Cent ballades d'amant et de dame*: Criticism of Courtly Love." In *Court and Poet. Selected Proceedings of the Third Congress of the International Courtly Literature Society, Liverpool, 1980*, edited by Glyn S. Burgess, 357–64. Liverpool: Francis Cairns, 1981.

---. "Lovers' Dialogues in Christine de Pizan's Lyric Poetry from the *Cent Ballades* to the *Cent ballades d'amant et de dame*." *Fifteenth Century Studies* 4 (1981): 167–80.

---. "A New Look at Christine de Pizan's *Epistre au dieu d'Amours*." In *Seconda Miscellanea di studi e ricerche sul Quattrocento francese*, edited by Jonathan Beck and Gianni Mombello, 71–92. Chambéry/Turin: Centre d'études franco-italien, 1981.

---. *Christine de Pizan. Her Life and Works*. New York: Persea, 1984.

---. "Concepts of Love According to Guillaume de Machaut, Christine de Pizan and Pietro Bembo." In *The Spirit of the Court. Selected Proceedings of the Fourth Congress of the International Courtly Literature Society, Toronto, 1983*, edited by Glyn S. Burgess and Robert A. Taylor, 386–92. Cambridge: D. S. Brewer, 1985.

———. "Women and Marriage around 1400: Three Views." *Fifteenth Century Studies* 17 (1990): 475–84.

———. "Christine de Pizan's Allegorized Psalms." In *Une femme de lettres au Moyen âge. Etudes autour de Christine de Pizan*, edited by Liliane Dulac and Bernard Ribémont, 317–24. Etudes christiniennes. Orléans: Paradigme, 1995.

Wisman, Josette A. "Aspects socio-économiques du *Livre des trois vertus* de Christine de Pizan." *Le Moyen français* 30 (1992), 27–43.

Yenal, Edith. *Christine de Pisan: A Bibliography of Writings By Her and About Her*. London: The Scarecrow Press, 1982.

Zhang, Xiangyun. "Christine de Pizan: la communauté des femmes et l'ordre social." In *Au champ des escriptures: IIIe Colloque international sur Christine de Pizan, Lausanne, 18–22 juillet 1998*, edited by Eric Hicks, Diego Gonzalez, and Philippe Simon, 549–60. Etudes christiniennes, 6. Paris: Champion, 2000.

Zimmermann, Margarete. " 'Sages et prudentes mainagieres' in Christine de Pizan's *Livre des trois vertus*." In *Haushalt und Familie in Mittelalter und früher Neuzeit: Vorträge eines interdisziplinären Symposions vom 6–9 Juni 1990 an der Rheinischen Friedrich Wilhelms-Universität, Bonn*, edited by Trude Ehlert, 193–207. Sigmaringen: Jan Thorbecke Verlag, 1991.

———. "Vox Femina, Vox Politica: The *Lamentacion sur les maux de La France*." In *Politics, Gender and Genre: The Political Thought of Christine de Pizan*, edited by Margaret Brabant, 113–27. Boulder: Westview Press, 1992.

———. "Les *Cent balades d'amant et de dame*: Une Réécriture de *L'Elegia de Madonna Fiammetta* de Boccace?" In *Une femme de lettres au Moyen Age: Etudes autour de Christine de Pizan*, edited by Liliane Dulac and Bernard Ribémont, 337–46. Etudes christiniennes. Orléans: Paradigme, 1995.

———. "Utopie et lieu de la mémoire féminine: la *Cité des dames*." In *Au champ des escriptures: IIIe Colloque international sur Christine de Pizan, Lausanne, 18–22 juillet 1998*, edited by Eric Hicks, Diego Gonzalez, and Philippe Simon, 561–80. Etudes christiniennes. Paris: Champion, 2000.

Contributors

Tracy Adams is Lecturer in French at the University of Auckland, New Zealand, and has also taught at the University of Maryland. In addition to Christine de Pizan, she has published on the medieval French romance and the transformation from manuscript to print. She has recently completed a manuscript on the mind/body dilemma in the Old French verse romance.

Barbara K. Altmann is Associate Professor of French at the University of Oregon. She has published an edition and critical analysis entitled *The Love Debate Poems of Christine de Pizan* (University Press of Florida, 1998). One of her major research interests is the study of Christine's works in the context of the other major authors of late medieval France.

Maureen Boulton, Professor of French at the University of Notre Dame, is particularly interested in religious literature, manuscript studies, and the relation between lyric poetry and narrative. She has edited two fourteenth-century texts, and published a study of lyric insertions in thirteenth- and fourteenth-century romances (*The Song in the Story*, 1993). She collaborated with Ruth J. Dean on *Anglo-Norman Literature. A Guide to Texts and Manuscripts* (1999). She is currently editing a volume of essays on late medieval Passion narratives, and completing *Pious Fictions*, a study of apocryphal lives of Christ in Old and Middle French.

Renate Blumenfeld-Kosinski is Professor of French and Director of the Medieval and Renaissance Studies Program at the University of Pittsburgh. Her books include *Not of Woman Born*: *Representations of Caesarean Birth in*

Medieval and Renaissance Culture (1990), *The Writings of Margaret of Oingt* (1991), and *Reading Myth: Classical Mythology and Its Interpretations in Medieval French Literature* (1997). She also coedited *Images of Sainthood in Medieval Europe* and a number of other volumes. In 1997 she edited and translated (with K. Brownlee) *The Selected Writings of Christine de Pizan, A Norton Critical Edition*. She is currently working on the *imaginaire* of the Great Schism of the Western Church.

Rosalind Brown-Grant, Senior Lecturer in French at the University of Leeds, is the author of *Christine de Pizan and the Moral Defence of Women: Reading beyond Gender* (1999), as well as numerous articles on Christine's feminist and political works. She has recently translated the *Book of the City of Ladies* (1999). She is currently researching a book on constructions of masculinity and femininity in late medieval French romance.

Marilynn Desmond, Professor of English and Comparative Literature at Binghamton University, is the author of *Reading Dido: Gender and Textuality in the Medieval Aeneid* and the editor of *Christine de Pizan and the Categories of Difference*. She and Pamela Sheingorn are coauthors of *Myth, Montage and Visuality in Late Medieval Manuscript Culture: Christine de Pizan's Othea* (2003).

Liliane Dulac, Professor of Medieval French Language and Literature at the University Paul-Valéry in Montpellier (France), has published primarily on Christine de Pizan, Arthurian romance, and the eighteenth century. With Jean Dufournet, she coedited a special issue on Christine de Pizan for *Revue des Langues Romanes* and edited and translated the *Chastelaine de Vergy*; with Bernard Ribémont, she coedited *Christine de Pizan, Une Femme de Lettres au Moyen Age*; with Christine Reno, she coedited a new edition of *Le Livre de l'Advision Cristine* (2001). Dulac has also prepared a French translation of the *Trois Vertus* and is presently working on an edition of the *Heures de contemplacion de la Passion*.

Thelma Fenster, Professor of French at Fordham University, has edited and translated several narrative poems by Christine de Pizan. She has edited *Arthurian Women: A Casebook* (1995) and coedited (with Clare Lees) *Gender in Debate from the Early Middle Ages to the Renaissance* (2002) and (with Daniel Smail) *Fama: The Politics of Talk and Reputation in Medieval Europe* (forthcoming).

Judith L. Kellogg is Associate Professor at the University of Hawaii, where she has been teaching since receiving her Ph.D. in Comparative Literature and

Medieval Studies from the University of California at Berkeley. In addition to her book *Medieval Artistry and Exchange* (1989), she has published on medieval women writers, Arthurian legend, and Chaucer.

Roberta L. Krueger, Professor of French at Hamilton College, is the author of *Women Readers and the Ideology of Gender in Old French Verse Romance* (1993) and editor of *The Cambridge Companion to Medieval Romance*. Her current scholarship focuses on late medieval French books of conduct.

James Laidlaw taught in Belfast and Cambridge, before being appointed Professor of French at Aberdeen in 1975; since 1991 he has been Professor Emeritus. He is at present an Honorary Fellow in the Arts Faculty, University of Edinburgh. His main publications are on Middle French, particularly Christine de Pizan and Alain Chartier. Early retirement in 1991 has given him more time for research on both these authors. He has developed a database (http://www.arts.ed.ac.uk/french/christine) for Christine de Pizan studies, and is collaborating on an anthology of the lyric poetry of Eustache Deschamps.

Nadia Margolis trained at Stanford University and at the Ecole des Hautes Etudes, Paris. Having taught at several institutions around the United States, she has given lectures in Europe and the United Kingdom as well. Her research has produced articles and books primarily on Christine de Pizan, Joan of Arc, and related topics in medieval French and Italian literature, history, and modern medievalism. She has also done several translations of Christine's poetry and of documents pertaining to Joan of Arc.

Deborah L. McGrady, Assistant Professor at Tulane University, is currently the Treasurer of the Christine de Pizan Society. She has published on the shift from manuscript to print, later manuscript versions of the *Roman de la Rose*, and questions of patronage and authorship in Christine de Pizan's works. She is currently completing a book-length study titled *Controlling Readers: The Audience's Role in Late-Medieval French Literature (1350–1450)*.

Christine Reno is Professor of French at Vassar College. She has written numerous articles on Christine de Pizan, and is, with Liliane Dulac, coeditor of the *Livre de l'Advision Cristine,* published in 2001 in the Etudes Christiniennes series, directed by Bernard Ribémont.

Earl Jeffrey Richards received his Ph.D. in 1978 from Princeton University and is currently Chair of French and Italian Literature at the University of Wuppertal. Among his many works on medieval French literature and comparative literature, Richards has published extensively on Christine. He is the editor of two editions of the *Cité des dames* (1982 and 1997), *Reinterpreting Christine de Pizan* (Athens, GA, 1992), and *Christine de Pizan and Medieval French Lyric* (Gainesville, 1999). He is currently completing a book-length study on *National Images in European Literature from the Middle Ages to the Eighteenth Century*.

Andrea Tarnowski teaches medieval French literature at Dartmouth College. Her research focuses on allegory and political writing in the fourteenth and fifteenth centuries, and explores the relationship between the individual and the state. She has published a scholarly edition and modern French translation of Christine de Pizan's *Chemin de long estude*, as well as essays on Christine's use of prophecy, autobiography, and historiography.

Lori J. Walters, Professor of French at Florida State University in Tallahassee, is the author of numerous articles on medieval romance, especially its manuscript transmission. She is also the editor of *Lancelot and Guinevere* (Garland, 1996) and coeditor and contributor to the two-volume study, *The Manuscripts of Chrétien de Troyes* (1993) and *Translatio Studii: Essays in Honor of Karl D. Uitti on his Sixty-fifth Birthday* (1999). Walters has received several awards, including the 1993 FSU Undergraduate Teaching Award, an FSU Developing Scholar Award, and an NEH Fellowship. She is currently serving as the North American President of the International Christine de Pizan Society. This is her fourteenth piece on Christine de Pizan.

Margarete Zimmermann, ex-president of the Christine de Pizan Society, and cofounder and coeditor of "Querelles," is Professor of Romance literatures at Freie Universität Berlin. She has published on medieval and twentieth-century French literature, the "Querelle des Femmes," and gynocentric literary history. She has recently coedited several volumes of scholarship, including *Französische Frauen der Frühen Neuzeit: Dichterinnen, Malerinnen, Mäzeninnen* (1999), *Gender Studies in den romanischen Literaturen* (1999), and *Theater Proben. Romanistische Studien zu Drama und Theater* (2001). With Ingrid Kasten and Gesa Stedman, she is coediting a new volume on *Cultures of Emotions and Gender* (2002) and has completed a monograph on Christine de Pizan (2002).

Index

Advision Cristine
    Autobiography, 32, 58, 59, 84, 123, 159–160, 201–203, 232, 233, 235–236
    Patronage, 199–200
    Political dream, 205
    Political narrative, 12–12, 14, 207–209
    Popularity, 231
    Preface, 45, 205–207
    Sources, 44
    Structure, 200–201
    See also Editors, Towner, Reno and Dulac; Mirror of princes
Advice
    To female aristocracy, 104–107, 119–120
    To the bourgeoise, 107–111
    To the destitute, 111
    To wives, 140–141;
    See also Mirror of princes
Aers, David, 140
Alan de Lille, 189
Album Christine de Pizan, 242–243
Amazons, 67, 139

Anagrams, 29–30
Anastaise, 237–238
Anne de Graville, 200
Aquinas, Thomas
    In Metaphysicorum Aristolelis Exposito, 44, 51–52, 85–86, 207
    On individuation, 47–48
    On women, 48, 85–86;
Aristotle, 133
    Genealogy of Animals, 82
    Metaphysics, 44, 84, 85
    Physics, 44, 82
    See also Oresme
Ars dictaminis, 168–169
Augustine
    City of God, 31, 32, 86, 139, 144n.19
    Confessions, 59–60, 63, 64, 65, 71
    on Aristotle, 44, 49
    on Sibyls, 124n.7
    on women, 81, 83
Authority, 29–30, 181
Autobiography, 11, 12–13, 18, 30, 86–87, 160
    See individual titles
Autres balades, 150, 155–156, 158, 208

Ballade
    Characters, 152, 154–155
    Formal structure, 150
    History, 150–151
    Lyric subjectivity, 149, 151–153
    Readership, 155–156
Barante, Prosper de, 256
Barthes, Roland, 68
Bedford Trend Master, 238
Bédier, Joseph, 258
Biddick, Kathleen, 130
Blamires, Alcuin, 83, 135–136
Blanchard, Joël, 203–204
Boccaccio, *De claris mulieribus*, 67, 71, 91, 116, 118, 125n.7, 192
Body politic, 25, 29, 36, 93–94, 130, 134–135, 139, 141
Boethius, *Consolatio philosophiae*, 118, 154, 187, 189, 201, 203
Books of hours, 216–218
Bouvet, Honoré, 205
Brown-Grant, Rosalind, 101, 204
Brownlee, Kevin, 19
Brunduge, James, 176
Bühler, Curt, xii

Carruthers, Mary, 170
Cent balades, 58, 149, 150, 152–155, 158, 182–183, 238
Cent balades d'amant et de dame, 89, 115, 150, 156–159, 216
Cerquiglini, Jacqueline, 152
    See also Editor, Cerquiglini
Charles V, 9, 10, 13–14, 16, 17, 25, 29–32, 63, 106, 121, 158, 202.
    See also Fais d'armes et de chevalerie
Charles VI, 10, 14, 17, 30, 121, 151, 153, 160, 182, 186, 193–194, 195
Charles VII, 239
Charles the Noble, King of Navarre, 220
Chartier, Alain, 115, 205, 232
Chemin de long estude
    Authority, 28, 30

Allegory, 11
Debate, 189–190, 195
Manuscript tradition, 236, 237
Political advice, 12, 14–15, 193–194, 207–208
Prologue, 181–186
Reading subject, 186–189
Relation to other works, 182–184, 190–192, 194–195
Sibyline guide, 117, 118, 119, 123, 125n.10, 203
See also Mirror for princes
Chicago, Judy, 68
Chrétien de Troyes, 25, 115, 251
Christine de Pizan
    Images of, *70, 72, 73*
    Popularity, 57–58
    Portraits, 68–70
    Translator, 25–26, 32–33
Cicero, 192
Cité des dames
    Advice to women, 88–89, 141, 176
    Allegory, 86, 190–192
    Commemoration, 85, 116
    Marriage, 90
    Miniatures 238
    Misogyny, 92–94, 138–139, 182
    Popularity, 57, 199, 231, 252
    Self-authorization, 33–34, 63–64, 66–68
    Structure, 129–131, 133, 136–138
    See also Editor Curnow
Cité des dames master, 238
Civil War, 10, 17–19
Col, Gontier, 167–168, 169, 170, 232
Col, Pierre, 168, 170, 171, 176
Contemplation sur la passion de Nostre Seigneur, Livre de, 33
Copeland, Rita, 27
Corps de policie, Livre du, 12, 12, 18, 35–36, 62, 69, 92–93, 102, 134–135, 137, 204, 216
Cour amoureuse, 150–151, 170
Courtly love, warnings against, 88–89, 119

Index   *293*

Dante, 21n.8, 44, 46, 47, 71, 122, 123, 184, 203, 213n.29
Debat de deux amans, 234, 235
   See also Manuscripts, Paris, BnF, MS f.fr. 1740, Brussels, BR 11034
Deblé, Colette, 72
Delaisée, L.M. J., xii
Deschamps, Eustache, 150–151, 232
Desmond, Marilynn, 133, 138
Dit de la pastoure, 115, 150, 234–235
   See also Manuscripts, Paris, BnF f.fr. 2184
Dit de la rose, 160, 168, 183–184, 185, 189, 190, 216
Dittié de Jehanne d'Arc, xi, 19, 184, 216, 239–240
Dulac, Liliane, 18, 44, 215
Duke of Berry, *See* Jean de Berry
Duke of Burgundy, *See* Phillip le Hardi; Philippe IV le Bel; Jeans sans Peur
Duke of Orleans, *See* Louis d'Orléans

Earl of Salisbury, 233
Editions
   Critical, definition, 251–252
   Manuscript Sources,, 255, 256, 257, 259, 260, 261, 262, 263
   Printed Sources, 251
   Translations, 252
   See also Editors of Christine's works
Editors of Christine's works
   Altmann, Barbara, xiii, 262
   Boivin de Villeneuve, Jean, 253–254, 255, 256, 261, 262
   Campbell, Percy Gerald Cadogan, xii, 262–263, 264
   Cerquiglini, Jacqueline, xiii, 262
   Curnow, Maureen, 264
   Godefroy, Denys, 254
   Guinement, Louise-Félicité, 254–255
   Hicks, Eric, 257
   Kennedy, Angus, xiii, 264
   Kennedy, Angus and Varty, Kenneth, 262

   Le Roux de Lincy, Antoine-Jean-Victor, 255–256, 257, 261
   Meyer, Paul, 257–259, 261
   Moreau, Thérèse and Eric Hicks, xiii
   Pagot and Dulac, 264
   Paris, Gaston, 252, 257–258
   Paris, Paulin, 256, 257
   Parussa, Gabrielle, 257, 263
   Püschel, Robert, 258, 23
   Reno and Dulac, xiii, 264
   Richards, Earl Jeffrey, xiii, 240, 264
   Roy, Maurice, 256, 258–262
   Sallier, Claude, 254, 255, 256, 261
   SATF, 257–258, 261, 264
   Solente, Suzanne, 263–264
   Tarnowski, Andrea, xiii, 263
   Thomassy, Raimond, 255, 256–257, 261, 262
   Towner, Sister Mary Louis, 240, 264
Enseignemens moraux, 231
Epistre à la reine, 17, 18, 122, 160, 232
Epistre au dieu d'amours, 66, 83, 90, 92, 157, 168, 183, 184
Epistre de la prison de vie humaine, 19, 216, 221–222, 239, 240
Epistre Othea, xii, 10–11, 45, 61, 63, 71, 86, 116, 118, 183, 194, 199, 204, 207, 231, 232, 233, 235, 236, 237, 252
   Illuminations, 233–234, 264
   See also Manuscripts, Paris, BnF f.fr. 848, Duke's manuscript; Editors, Campbell and Parussa; Mirror of princes
Exegesis, 143n.10, 205–206

Fais d'armes et de chevalerie, Livre des, 9, 231
Fais et bonnes meurs du sage roi Charles V, Livre des, 28, 34
   Autobiography, 9
   Authorial identity, 35, 60, 63–66
   Biography, 216
   Genre, 14

History, 15, 16
Leadership, 30–31, 37, 204
Presentation copies, 232
Relation to other works, 194–195
See also Editors, Solente and Willard
Fenster, Thelma, 262
Forhan, Kate, 31, 46
Foucault, Michel, 129, 131
Foulechat, Denis. *See* John of Salisbury
Fourth estate, 92–94
Froissart, Jean, 24n.42, 150, 232
Fumaroli, Marc, 32–33, 34, 35

Gender, 154–155
Gerson, Jean, 17, 22n.26, 215, 216
    Involvement in the *Querelle de la Rose*, 168, 176–177
    Montaigne de Contemplation, 45
Gibbons, Rachel, 121
Gilchrist, Roberta, 129, 140, 141–142
Giles of Rome, 204
Golden Legend, 43
Gravdal, Kathryn, 174–175
Great Schism, 10, 11, 12, 14–17, 188
Gros, Gérard, 215
Grosz, Elizabeth, 127
Guillaume de Tignonville, 168, 170

Hanawalt, Barbara, 137
Heures de la contemplacion sur la Passion, 215, 216, 218, 223–224, 240
Hibernicus, Thomasius, 43–44
Hicks, Eric, 257, 265
Hugh of St. Victor, 90
Hundred Years War, 13, 14, 138, 238, 239

Isabeau de Bavière, 23n.31, 18, 69, 106, 121–123, 127n.32, 155, 160–161, 168, 169, 224, 238

Jean de Berry, 18, 19, 161, 199, 224, 237
Jean de Meun, 168, 170, 171
    translator of Boethius, 27
    (*See also Roman de la Rose*)

Jean de Montreuil, 167, 170, 171, 175
Jeans sans Peur, Duke of Burgundy, 122, 199, 232, 239
Joan of Arc, 19–20, 116
John of Salisbury, Foulechat's translation of *Policraticus*, 28, 36, 46, 134, 135
Julian of Norwich, 201

Kempe, Margery, 201–202
Krynen, Jacques, 204

Lachmann, Karl, 258
Laidlaw, James, 152, 264, 265
Lamentacion sur les maux de la France, 17–18, 19, 161, 216
Lange, Monika, 240, 264
Latini, Brunetto, *Livre dou tresor*, 103, 204
Lebeuf, Jean, 254
Le Goff, Jacques, 66
Literary subjectivity, 140, 182–183
Livre du dit de Poissy, 184
Livre du duc des vrais amans, 89, 115, 118–123, 150
Livre de la paix, xi, 17, 18–19, 57, 204, 231, 238
Livre de Prudence, 120–121, 122
Livre des cent balades, 152
Livre des trois jugemens, xii, 216
Livre des trois vertus, 63, 85, 89, 91
    Finance, 102–103, 105–107, 108–109, 110–111
    Mirror for princesses, 204, 216, 231
    Popularity, 252
    Reputation, 107–108, 109
    Title, 103–105
Livre du chevalier de la Tour Landry pour l'enseignement de ses filles, 101
López de Córdoba, Leonor, 201–202
Louis d'Orléans, 15, 17, 63, 106, 121, 155, 159, 160, 194, 199, 233
Lusignan, Serge, 31

Index

Machaut, Guillaume de, 150, 151, 152, 232, 236
Manuscripts:
  Autograph, 231–245
  British Library, MS Harley 4431, 69, 168, 218, 236, 240, 260
  Brussels, BR 9393, 238
  Brussels, BR 9508, 237
  Brussels, B.R. 10309, 199
  Brussels, BR 11034, 234
  Chantilly, Musée Condé 492–493, 234–235
  Chantilly, 494, 237
  Decoration, 237–238
    See also Anastasie, *cité des dames* master
  Duke's manuscript, 168, 218, 236, 237, 238
    See also Paris, BnF MSS f.fr. 835, 606, 836, 605, 607
  Ex-Phillips 1128, 199
  The Hague, Koninklijke Bibliotheek 78 D 42, 237;
  Livre de Christine, 218, 234–235
    See also Chantilly, Musée Condé 492–493, Paris, BnF, f.fr. 12779
  Material fabrication, 235–236, 239
  Munich, Bayerische Staatbibliothek gall. 11, 238
  Paris, Bibliothèque de l'Arsenal, MS 2681, 69, *image*, 71
  Paris, Bibliothèque de l'Arsenal, MS 3295, 255
  Paris, BnF MS f.fr. 603, 238, 261
  Paris, BnF MS f.fr. 607, 238
  Paris, BnF MS f.fr. 848, 233–234, 254, 256
  Paris, BnF MS f.fr.1176, 199, 253
  Paris, BnF MS f.fr.1177, 253
  Paris, BnF MS f.fr. 1178, 238
  Paris, BnF MS f.fr. 1179, 238
  Paris, BnF MS f.fr. 1185, 256
  Paris, BnF MS f.fr. 1643, 241
  Paris, BnF MS f.fr. 1644, 254
  Paris, BnF MS f.fr. 1740, 234, 235
  Paris, BnF MS f.fr. 12779, 234–235
  Paris, BnF MS f.fr. 2184, 234
  Paris, BnF MS nouv. Acq. Fr. 4792, 261
  Queen's manuscript (*see* British Library, MS Harley 4431)
Marchello-Nizia, Christiane, 205
Margaret of Burgundy, 103
Margaret of Valois, 68
Marguerite de Navarre, 68
Margolis, Nadia, 45, 118, 215
Marie de Berry, 221–222
Martin le Franc, 58
Maximus, Valerius, 192
McGrady, Deborah, 159
McNamara, Jo Ann, 137
Meiss, Millard, xii, 235, 240
Memory
  Authorial, 59, 60–66
  Communal, 59, 66–68
  Cultural, 60
  Faulty, 132–133
  Literary sources, 58–60
  Visual, 68–73
Menagier de Paris, 101, 103, 106, 109
Minnis, A. J., 170
Mirror of princes, 10–11, 14, 20n.6, 36, 86–88, 120, 134, 183, 194, 204–205
Misogyny
  Defense against, 83–94
  Sources, 81–83, 84–86
Mombello, Gianni, xii, 240, 257
Mutacion de Fortune, xii, 11–12, 15, 29, 32, 33, 35, 62, 123, 133, 148–149, 202, 203, 216, 233, 235, 237, 240
  See also Editors, Solente

Naudé, Gabriel, 256
Nederman, Cary J., 102, 134
Neubauer, Hans-Joachim, 119
Nora, Pierre, 65–66

Oexle, Otto Gerhard, 59, 71
Oresme, Nicole, translator of Aristotle, 27, 31, 177
Oroison de Nostre Dame, 33, 215, 216, 218–219, 221, 224
Oroison de Nostre Seigneur, 215, 216, 220
Ouy, Gilbert, 241–242
Ovid, *Ars amatoria*, 172
Ovide moralisé, 44, 49, 117

Parussa, Gabrielle, 45, 242
　See also Editors, Parussa
Patronage, 155, 159–160, 232, 233
　See also individual titles
Patterson, Lee, 140
Paupert, Anne, 123, 201
Petrarch, 71
　De remediis utriusque fortunae, 32
　Rime sparse, 152
Philippe de Mézières, 205, 232
Philippe IV le Bel, Duke of Burgundy, 9
Phillip le Hardi, Duke of Burgundy, 64, 160, 202, 232
Plutarch, 134
Poeta theologus, 46–47
Poirion, Daniel, 157
Primat, *Grandes Chroniques de France*, 27, 28, 32, 36–37, 65, 121
Prod'hommie de l'homme/Livre de Prudence, Livre de 204, 216
　See also Editors, Pagot, Dulac

Querelle de la rose, 84, 119, 202, 216
　Chronology, 167–170
　Defamation, 170–171
　Manuscript history, 168, 169, 232, 240
　Violence, 171–175, 176
　See also Col, Gontier; Col, Pierre; Jean de Montreuil; Gerson, Jean; Guillaume de Tigonville
Querelle des Femmes, 57, 58, 67, 68
XV joyes de Nostre Dame, 216, 218, 219–220

Readership, 182
Reno, Christine, 44, 241–242
　See also Editor
Rhetoric, 181–182
Richards, Jeffrey, 86, 137
　See also Editors, Richards
Roman de la Rose, 26, 66, 88, 167, 172–175, 177, 184
Roman d'Eneas, 117

Saint Christine, 34–35
Semiramis, 47, 138
Seneca, 192, 201
Sept psaumes allégorisés, 17, 32, 215, 218, 220–221, 224
Seulete suy, 149–150, 161–162
Sherman, Claire Richter, 34–35
Sibyl, 116–119, 124n.7, 184–185, 188, 203
Silvestris, Bernardus, 117, 118
Simone, Franco, xii
Solterer, Helen, 171, 177
Sommer, Doris, 177

Theology, 43–55
Tommaso da Pizzano, 31, 49, 59, 66, 202
Trachsler, Richard, 241
Translatio studii et imperii, 26–29
Tuvé, Rosemund, 45

Varty, Kenneth, 262
Virgil, *The Aeneid*, 117, 184
Virgin Mary, 33–34, 36, 216

Walters, Lori, 215
Willard, Charity Cannon, 201, 215, 240–241, 253, 257, 264
　See also Editors, Willard

Zimmermann, Margarete, xiii, 131–132
Zink, Michel, 123, 151